PUNCTUATION

Writer's Handbook

Writer's Handbook

James Flynn
Joseph Glaser

Western Kentucky University

Macmillan Publishing Company
New York

Collier Macmillan Publishers
London

Macmillan Publishing Company
866 Third Avenue, New York, New York 10022

Collier Macmillan Canada, Inc.

Library of Congress Cataloging in Publication Data

Flynn, James.
  Writer's handbook.

  Includes index.
  1. English language—Rhetoric. 2. English language—Grammar—
1950–   . I. Glaser, Joseph. II. Title.
PE1408.F514   808'.042   82–7803
ISBN 0–02–471580–8

Printing: 2 3 4 5 6 7 8   Year: 4 5 6 7 8 9 0

ISBN   0-02-471580-8

Preface

Audience. We intend *Writer's Handbook* to be used alone or with a separate rhetoric text for introductory college-level English courses in writing. Focusing on the prescriptive and technical aspects of student writing, we have tried to include in this one book as much information and practice as possible on the grammar, punctuation, spelling, mechanics, and usage of standard edited English, along with a substantial treatment of the research paper, in-class writing, summaries, book reports, business letters, and résumés.

Theoretical Foundations. Our accounts of grammar, punctuation, usage, and special writing situations are traditional, as are the bulk of the book's exercises. In some sections of the text we include generating activities in addition to, not in place of, analytical exercises.

Objectives. We hope we have provided the technical information a student needs to do well in college composition, and provided it in a way that is both clear and amiable. We wanted to produce a book students might keep throughout their careers as a continuing reference.

Organization. Grammar, mechanics, and usage are the essence of the book and are presented in separate sections. The chapters are short and narrowly focused for the sake of clarity and flexibility. Teachers may start anywhere and assign chapters singly or in combination.

Part Four, The Research Paper, is self-contained and can be assigned whenever convenience or the teacher's objectives dictate.

Content Features. Completeness is the key to our grammar and mechanics sections. The presentation of basic grammar is unusually detailed, and we give separate chapters to many topics, like misplaced modifiers or unnecessary shifts, that are often lumped together with unrelated problems. We feel our discussions of grammatical and mechanical matters are more forthcoming and more complete than those found in competing handbooks.

The research paper also receives an unusual amount of attention, and the chapter on documentation contains forms for citing such nontraditional sources as cassette recordings, performances, and computer programs.

Finally, we have tried to make the contents of the book easy to get at. The numbering system, coded endpapers, index, and synoptic reviews at the ends of chapters provide several keys to just where everything is.

Pedagogical Devices. Points to note concerning the book's usefulness as a teaching device include the following:

—Short and clearly subdivided chapters for ease in assigning and referring to specific material.
—Ample exercises for progress testing, reinforcement, and classroom activity.
—The research project presented in a series of logical steps.
—Documentation based on the 1977 *MLA Handbook for Writers of Research Papers, Theses, and Dissertations*, but including other systems of citation and a bibliography of style sheets in special fields.
—Sentence diagramming to illustrate basic grammatical concepts and to provide analytical practice.
—Short exercises on specific skills as well as longer, more varied review exercises at the ends of chapters.
—"Reference Charts" summarizing each chapter on grammar or mechanics.

Acknowledgments. No undertaking the size of this one could be completed without help from many quarters. We are especially sensible of the debts we owe our families for their patience and support and to our colleagues, superiors, and students here at Western Kentucky University—particularly Edna Laman, J. Walker Rutledge, John Reiss, John Spurlock, Lee Little, Frank Steele, and Janet Lewis. We are also grateful to Terry Tatum for permitting us to use his research paper as an example of such work. In a category by herself for the clerical, organizational, and inspirational help she unstintingly supplied is Pat Nave, without whom half the typescript would never have gotten out of Kentucky.

J. F.
J. G.

Contents

Two
Punctuation

Three

Spelling, Word Punctuation, and Usage

28 Spelling Rules 237

29 Hard Words 246

30 Capitals 251

Four

**The Research Paper and
Special Forms of Writing**

40 | *Sample Research Paper*

41 | *In-Class Themes and Essay Examinations*

42 | *Other Special Forms: Summaries, Book Reports, Business Letters, and Résumés*

CONTENTS

Writer's Handbook

One

Grammar

1 Sentences

Many important decisions you make in your writing will be based on recognizing sentences and sentence patterns. Some exceptional sentence constructions—questions, commands, reversed sentences, context sentences—are discussed at the end of this chapter, but you probably already know quite a bit about standard sentences: those groups of words that express a grammatically complete thought that can stand alone. We say *grammatically* complete because some sentences contain words that refer to things identified elsewhere, and these sentences may not seem complete by themselves:

> *He* told *her* to sit down.
>
> *They* want to know where *we* are.

These are good sentences even though we do not know whom *he, her, they,* or *we* refer to. Such sentences depend on their context to be completely understood, but they still fulfill the basic sentence patterns that we are going to be discussing in this chapter.

There are many ways to construct a sentence, but every standard sentence must have a subject and a predicate:

When you ask what the subject of a lecture or a movie is, you are asking what the lecture or film is about. The subject of a sentence is what the sentence is about. The predicate gives some information concerning this subject. "What about Edgar?" "He writes." "What did they do?" "They stooped." The underlined words here are *verbs.* They are action words that introduce the predicate, which may go on for several more words, detailing the behavior of the subject:

3

Edgar *writes serious but entertaining stories about old people and children.*

The italicized words in this sentence are part of the predicate, part of what Edgar does. But *writes* is still the key. Without this verb there would be no sentence.

1A
Identifying verbs.

Finding the verb is the first step toward seeing how a sentence works, but finding verbs is not always easy. There are three keys to locating them, and at first you may have to try all three. Verbs show themselves through meaning, form, and use.

Verb Meanings.   Often a verb can be identified through its meaning. A verb describes either an action taking place or a state of being. It is the thing *done* in a sentence:

Esther *plays* field hockey.

My cousin *traps* rattlesnakes.

A poet *feels* deeply.

Tennis *is* good exercise.

Verb Forms.   You can often identify verbs by form. Verbs change form in two ways: all of them have a special form ending in *-s* in the present tense to go with singular nouns and third-person-singular subjects, and all of them are capable of indicating various tenses, or times, for the actions they express.

Here is a list of common forms of a number of verbs. Notice the differences between the first two, *am* and *begin*, and the last one, *live*. *Am*, or *to be*, is the most complicated of all the verbs in the way it changes forms. *Begin* is typical of the irregular verbs in that it changes vowels in forming the various tenses. And *live* is typical of the regular verbs (the great majority), all of which behave just as it does:

Present tense

I am, begin, live

You are, begin, live

She *is*, begin*s*, live*s*

We are, begin, live

You are, begin, live

They are, begin, live

Past tense

I was, began, lived

You were, began, lived

She was, began, lived

We were, began, lived

You were, began, lived

They were, began, lived

Future tense

I shall be, begin, live	We shall be, begin, live
You will be, begin, live	You will be, begin, live
She will be, begin, live	They will be, begin, live

Present perfect tense

I have been, begun, lived	We have been, begun, lived
You have been, begun, lived	You have been, begun, lived
She has been, begun, lived	They have been, begun, lived

Past perfect tense

I had been, begun, lived	We had been, begun, lived
You had been, begun, lived	You had been, begun, lived
She had been, begun, lived	They had been, begun, lived

Future perfect tense

I shall have been, begun, lived	We shall have been, begun, lived
You will have been, begun, lived	You will have been, begun, lived
She will have been, begun, lived	They will have been, begun, lived

Present progressive tense

I am being, beginning, living	We are being, beginning, living
You are being, beginning, living	You are being, beginning, living
She is being, beginning, living	They are being, beginning, living

Past progressive tense

I was being, beginning, living	We were being, beginning, living
You were being, beginning, living	You were being, beginning, living
She was being, beginning, living	They were being, beginning, living

There are three features of verb patterns that can be especially helpful. All verbs end in *-s* in the third-person singular of the present tense. All verbs can be combined with the auxiliary verbs *shall, will, have,* and *be* to form various *compound* tenses. And most verbs end in *-ed* in the past tense. Notice also that some verb tenses cannot be formed without auxiliaries; even though they are separate words, auxiliaries are as much a part of the complete verb as is the *-ed* form used to show the past tense.

Verb Use.   The first two tests will help you identify most verbs, but the tests are not infallible. Consider these verbs:

Esther *plays* field hockey.

My cousin *traps* rattlesnakes.

In these sentences, *plays* and *traps* convey action; they say what Esther and my cousin *do*. But the same words could be used in a different setting to name *things* rather than actions:

Coach gave us seven new *plays.*

The *traps* were old and rusty.

The first two tests can establish that a word is *capable* of being a verb, but only the way the word is used confirms whether or not it actually is one in a particular sentence.

Exercise Sentences 1. Circle all the verbs in the following sentences. Watch out for "sometime-verbs" that name things rather than actions, and be sure to include auxiliaries.

1. Mother will understand.
2. Among other things, the transmission whines.
3. Dead microorganisms constantly settle to the sea bed.
4. This blizzard blew down from the north.
5. I removed the works from my father's watch.
6. Her coat was draped gracefully over the back of the chair.
7. Under the trees the haze lingered until noon.
8. I have had a run of good luck.
9. The unpainted garage sloped alarmingly to one side.
10. Stella will run tomorrow.

1B
Identifying subjects.

Once you have identified the verb, find its subject, the person or thing that performs the action expressed by the verb:

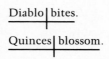

Diablo | bites.

Quinces | blossom.

Bites and *blossom* are the verbs; the subjects are what does the biting or blossoming—*Diablo* and *quinces,* respectively. In diagramming the relationship between subject and verb, separate the two with a vertical line that runs through the base line.

Simple and Complete Elements. Finding subjects and verbs would be child's play if sentences were usually as simple as "Diablo bites." But a more typical sentence is, "My cousin's big, black Diablo bites at the slightest provocation." How do you find your way around in such a jumble of words? Find the verb *bites* (the only word that passes the verb tests) and ask yourself, "Who or what bites?" The answer is "Diablo." Diablo is still the subject.

Diablo and *bites* are the essential elements in this complicated sentence: they are the *simple subject* and the verb. But the writer wants us to know more about his subject. Diablo is big. He is black. He belongs to the writer's cousin. These additional details *modify* or give extra information about the subject. The simple subject plus all its modifiers is called the *complete subject.* Furthermore, the writer also wants to tell us more about Diablo's biting, so he modifies the verb too, creating a predicate that is several words long. Diablo does not merely bite. He bites *at the slightest provocation.* A diagram of the whole sentence would start out with the main elements on the base line, and then the various modifiers would be grouped under the words they modify:

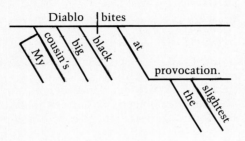

1C
Compound subjects and verbs.

A sentence may have more than one subject and verb:

The *chairs* and *tables trembled* but *stood.*

Neither *Ted* nor *Alice skated, danced,* or *ate.*

The first of these sentences has two subjects and two verbs; the second has two subjects and three verbs. These multiple elements are marked by the coordinating conjunctions *and, but, nor, or,* or *yet,* which link words that are equal. Compound subjects and verbs are diagrammed this way:

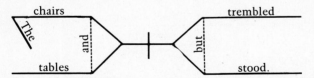

Notice that when such compound elements involve verbs with auxiliaries, many times the auxiliaries are not repeated:

They *had lived, loved,* and *laughed.*

All of the verbs here are in the same tense—"had lived," "had loved," "had laughed"—but the auxiliary is written only once. It is understood to apply to each of the three verbs.

Exercise Sentences 2. Circle the verbs and underline the simple subjects in the following sentences. Be sure to include auxiliaries as well as main verbs and to mark all parts of compound subjects and verbs.

1. Among the flowering plants, geraniums do best indoors.

2. The snow drifted down through the dark leaves of the holly.

3. The mouse finally escaped by dashing under the refrigerator.

4. Oak leaves and pine needles crackled underfoot.

5. In the last game of the tournament all seniors will start.

6. The Appalachian Trail winds for over two thousand miles.

7. Taxis and busses use a special lane.

8. They neither work nor spin.

9. We shall have progressed and matured by then.

10. Alchemists searched for the mythical "philosopher's stone."

Exercise Sentences 3. Write ten sentences on any topic; circle the verbs and underline the subjects. Be sure to include at least two sentences with compound subjects and two with compound verbs.

1D
Basic sentence patterns.

The simplest sentences are those with only a subject and verb. Such sentences are not necessarily short, though; they may have more than one subject or verb, or they may contain modifying words or word-groups:

The faded picture was hanging on the sunlit wall.

This sentence is really no more complicated than "Diablo bites." The subject is *picture* and the verb is *was hanging*. The other words in the sentence modify these main elements:

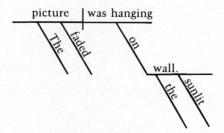

The and *faded* modify *picture*, and *on the sunlit wall* tells us where the hanging took place. These words have no effect on the sentence pattern, the words that are left when the modifiers are stripped away.

Pattern One.   Sentences that reduce to subject and verb are Pattern One sentences and are very common in English. Their distinguishing characteristic is the kind of verb they use: Pattern One sentences always have *intransitive* verbs, or verbs that express an action the subject is doing in and of itself, not an action the subject is doing to something else. If anything comes after the verb in such a sentence, its function, like that of *on the sunlit wall,* is to modify or explain the verb. This verb modifier (a single word or a word group) is not essential to the sentence, but serves to tell how, when, where, or why the action took place. Such modifiers are called *adverbials:*

Subject	*Intransitive Verb*	*[Adverbial]*
Gorillas	snore	horribly.
The corn	grew.	
Diablo	bites	without provocation.

In diagramming Pattern One sentences, place only the subject and verb, the essential sentence elements, on the base line; treat the adverbial, when one is present, like any other modifier:

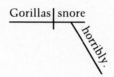

Exercise Sentences 4. Write six Pattern One sentences, three with and three without adverbial elements.

Pattern Two.   Probably the commonest of all sentence patterns is the Pattern Two sentence, in which the subject does something to someone or to something else. The kind of verb that *transmits* an action from the subject to the object is called *transitive:*

Subject	*Transitive Verb*	*Direct Object*
Mike	followed	Juanita.
They	sell	sardines.
My job	pays	the rent.

Notice two things about this basic pattern. Some verbs, such as *followed* or *bites,* can be either transitive or intransitive. "Mike followed." belongs to Pattern One, and "Diablo bites the mailman." belongs to Pattern Two. The second thing to notice is the direct object and how it works. Distinguishing direct objects from adverbials is not difficult. Direct objects answer the question "Whom or what?" as in "Mike followed whom or what?" Adverbials, on the other hand, answer such questions as "How?" "Where?" "When?" or "Why?" about the verb. *Viciously,* for instance, can tell *how* Diablo bites, but never *what* he bites. Diagrams of Pattern Two sentences include the direct object on the base line with the subject and verb:

Mike | followed | Juanita.

The main elements can still be distinguished from those that serve only to explain or modify them:

Old Diablo viciously bit the new mailman.

Diablo | bit | mailman.

Exercise Sentences 5. Write six Pattern Two sentences. Three should be as plain as "Mike followed Juanita," and three should include at least one modifier.

Pattern Three. Pattern Three is restricted to sentences with verbs of calling or naming, or actions through which the subject causes a specific reaction on the part of the direct object:

Subject	Transitive Verb	Direct Object	Objective Complement
They	called	Diablo	vicious.
The paper	proclaimed	Judge Cosby	a crook.
Bad work	makes	her	furious.

These sentences start as Pattern Two sentences do, but then another element is added—the direct object is further identified by the objective complement, which either renames the direct object (*judge = crook*) or tells one of its qualities (*Diablo = vicious*). In diagramming this sort of sentence, use a slanted line to set off the complement from the direct object:

They | called | Diablo \ vicious.

Exercise Sentences 6. Write six Pattern Three sentences. Remember that this pattern works only with verbs of calling or naming—such as *call, name, appoint,* or *elect*—or with verbs like *leave* or *make,* in the sense of producing a certain reaction.

Pattern Four. Pattern Four is another variation on Pattern Two. Only this time the verb must be one of asking, telling, giving, or getting. The direct object is the thing asked, told, given, or gotten, and the indirect object is used to indicate the target of the transaction. It answers the question "To or for whom?" about the rest of the sentence:

Subject	Transitive Verb	Indirect Object	Direct Object
I	got	Mother	roses.
The Bears	will give	us	a good game.
His aunt	provided	him	a job.

This type of sentence can always be turned around so that the direct object comes in its usual place right after the verb. The indirect object will then become part of a phrase with *to* or *for* at the end of the revised sentence. Our last example, for instance, would become "His aunt provided

10

a job *for him.''* In diagramming, the indirect object goes below the base line, almost as if it were a verb modifier:

Exercise Sentences 7. Write six Pattern Four sentences, using verbs of giving, getting, asking, or telling. Then turn each sentence around so that the indirect object comes after *to* or *for*.

Pattern Five.   Pattern Five sentences have a *subject complement* (either a predicate noun or a predicate adjective) rather than a direct or indirect object. This complement renames the subject or identifies one of its characteristics, and that is why the verbs in this pattern are called *linking verbs:* they do not transmit or describe an action; rather, they merely link the subject and its complement together. The commonest linking verb is *to be;* some others are *look, seem, become, taste, feel, sound,* and *remain:*

Subject	*Linking Verb*	*Predicate Noun*
Stalin	was	a tyrant.
Hemingway	remains	my favorite author.
Father	should be	a foreman.

Subject	*Linking Verb*	*Predicate Adjective*
This cup	looks	somewhat dirty.
Your plan	sounds	acceptable.
The girl	was becoming	stronger.

One way to tell the difference between a predicate noun and a predicate adjective is that while the noun renames the subject, the adjective merely describes one of its qualities. *My favorite author* and *Hemingway* are the same thing, but *somewhat dirty* is not the same as *this cup.*
    Pattern Five sentences are diagrammed with a slanted line between the linking verb and the complement:

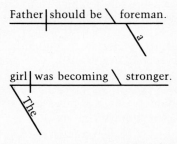

Exercise Sentences 8. Write six Pattern Five sentences, using a variety of linking verbs. The first three should have predicate noun complements and the second three should have predicate adjectives.

1E
Other sentence patterns.

The sentence patterns we have looked at so far are basic to English, but there are some other possibilities—for example, special purpose constructions for asking or answering questions, for giving commands, or for varying normal word order.

Questions.   There are essentially two ways of forming questions in English, and these correspond to the sort of information the questioner wants to receive. Questions that call for a simple "yes" or "no" answer are formed by placing the verb or one of its auxiliaries in front of the subject:

> *Are* you a sophomore?
>
> *Does* he know Mindy?
>
> *Will* they try out for the team?

Another kind of question is introduced by an interrogative word—*who, whom, whose, what, which, when, where, how,* or *why.* These questions generally call for a more detailed answer than "yes" or "no":

> *What* is going on here?
>
> *How* many players will make the trip?
>
> *Whose* foot have I stepped on?

> *Exercise Sentences 9.* Frame six questions, three of the *yes-no* sort, and three using interrogative words.

Commands.   The special pattern for commands starts off with the verb and omits the subject entirely:

> *Get* out of here right now!
>
> *Slow* down.
>
> *Hit* the ball solidly!

These sentences may seem to lack a subject, but the subject is understood to be *you* (meaning whomever the command is addressed to).

> *Exercise Sentences 10.* Write six commands, starting with the basic form of the verb in each case and using *you-understood* as the subject.

Reversed Sentences.   Except for questions and commands, most sentences start with the subject, but sentences can also start with adverbials (words or word groups that modify the verb):

> *Here* is the money for lunch.
>
> *Behind our stove* lived the mice.
>
> *On his left* was the policeman's daughter.

If you ask yourself "Who or what *is, lived,* or *was?"* you will realize that the subjects of these sentences are not *here, stove,* or *left,* but *money, mice,* and *daughter*—all words that come *after* the verbs. Another reversed construction begins with *there,* a word that functions as an *expletive* or slot-filler. It takes over the position ordinarily held by the subject but adds almost nothing to the meaning of the sentence:

> *There* is oil in Venezuela.
>
> *There* are reasons for my decision.

The subjects of these sentences are *oil* and *reasons*.

> *Exercise Sentences 11.* Write six reversed sentences. Start three with *there* and three with adverbial elements.

Context Sentences.   One other sentence type is the context sentence, a construction that depends on the sentences around it for one or more of its essential elements. Context sentences are usually answers to questions:

> Where is Sam? *Out back.*
>
> Are you aware of the time? *Yes.*
>
> How does she plan to arrive? *By car.*

The italicized constructions here depend on the subject or verb (or both) of the question that precedes them: "Where is Sam? [Sam is] out back."

> *Exercise Sentences 12.* Circle all the verbs and underline all the subjects except *you-understood* in the following sentences:
>
> 1. The girls had posted notices within the park boundaries.
> 2. Marla has been president of our club for three semesters.
> 3. Will the meeting adjourn before six?
> 4. Tell the rest of the class the good news.
> 5. There are some postage stamps in that drawer.
> 6. Whales pump milk from their mammary glands with terrific force.
> 7. This winter appears to be the worst ever.
> 8. I will join you before the show.
> 9. Dancing and just listening to music are two of my greatest pleasures.
> 10. Her car, an old Buick, runs as well as ever.
>
> *Exercise Sentences 13.* Diagram the following sentences. Do not worry too much about handling the modifiers, as long as you get them beneath the main sentence elements they explain. Be sure to distinguish between objects and complements in your diagrams:
>
> 1. That small spotted dog is very frisky.

2. Lana and Jim have bought a new car.

3. My old teacher jogged for miles through the park.

4. The army has sent him the notification.

5. The white feather branded him a coward.

Exercise Sentences 14. Identify the basic sentence pattern of each of the following sentences:

1. Glowing with rage, she called him a liar.

2. The picture in question is hanging on her bedroom wall.

3. Henry was the best student in that particular class.

4. Books can be the most expensive thing in your budget.

5. The old tiger severely mauled his keeper last spring.

6. His nurse brought him the latest papers.

7. Many butterflies are born every day throughout the summer.

8. The Smiths have been active in real estate for years.

9. They should award Adam the first prize for fencing.

10. Jennifer has learned all about apostrophes.

2   *Parts of Speech*

Sentence patterns deal only with basic elements. To be able to cope with all the parts of a complicated sentence, you need a more detailed knowledge of grammar. You must recognize and understand phrases, clauses, and parts of speech.

2A
Verbs and verbals.

Modal Auxiliaries.   Much of what you need to know about verbs was covered in the last chapter, but modal auxiliaries require some additional explanation. Some auxiliaries—*shall, will, have,* and *be*—are used as parts of main verbs in forming compound tenses. The *modal auxiliaries* work differently. These verbs—including *should, would, may, might, can, could, ought, must,* and *do*—combine with main verbs to show that they are to be understood in a special sense or mode. For instance, "I *should* exercise regularly" means something very different from "I exercise regularly." The italicized modal auxiliaries change the sense of the main verb in each of these sentences:

> They *may* fire Charley.
>
> I *must* find time for homework every night.
>
> We *could* cause him a lot of trouble.

Because they have a major effect on the meaning of the main verb, modal auxiliaries are considered part of the verb and are included in the verb slot in diagrams:

They | may fire | Charley.

Verbals. Verbals are forms that are derived from verbs but that function as other parts of speech. They include infinitives, gerunds, and participles, all of which are clearly based on regular verbs, but none of which can be used by themselves to make the predicate of a sentence.

Infinitives. Most infinitives consist of *to* plus some form of a main verb: *to be, to sit, to seem,* and *to percolate* are all infinitives. Like other verbals, infinitives are unable to do the work of verbs in making sentences: you cannot say, "He *to sit*"; you must say, "He *sits.*" Since they cannot be main verbs, infinitives have to function some other way in their sentences. They are remarkably adaptable.

Infinitives can work as nouns, adjectives, or adverbs, and to fully identify an infinitive in a sentence, you have to decide what work it is doing at the moment. Most infinitives functioning as nouns are subjects, direct objects, or predicate nouns:

> *To live* is *to feel.* (subject and predicate noun)
>
> He tried *to surrender.* (direct object)

Infinitives functioning as adjectives modify nouns, pronouns, or their equivalents (the kind of words that can be subjects or direct objects), and those that modify anything else (verbs, clauses, or other modifiers) function as adverbs. The dividing line between adjective infinitives and adverb infinitives is often very hazy, but the distinction between both these modifying infinitives and the noun infinitive is sharper. Modifying infinitives are never part of a basic sentence pattern:

> We were reluctant *to leave.* (adverb, modifying *reluctant*)
>
> He is the man *to see.* (adjective, modifying *man*)

Notice that both sentences would be complete without the infinitives. That is a good sign that these infinitives are used as modifiers.

In a diagram, noun infinitives are placed above the sentence slot a noun or pronoun would ordinarily occupy, while modifying infinitives go beneath the base line under the words they modify:

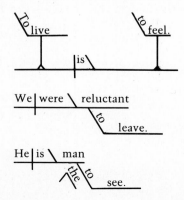

Gerunds. Gerunds are the easiest verbals to deal with. They consist of *-ing* forms of verbs used as nouns. Gerunds can do anything nouns do and are common in all noun functions:

> *Running* builds sound legs. (subject)
>
> He practices his *kicking* every day. (direct object)
>
> Her hobby is modern *dancing*. (predicate noun)
>
> Glenda gave *hiking* its due. (indirect object)
>
> We call such behavior *loafing*. (objective complement)
>
> She gets her way by *crying*. (object of preposition)

Whenever you find an *-ing* verbal in one of these roles, it is a gerund. If you are in doubt, try substituting a real noun for the gerund without changing the meaning of the sentence—for example, "*Exercise* builds sound legs" or "He practices his *skill* every day." In diagrammed sentences, gerunds are always on stilts; other than that, they are treated as if they were nouns:

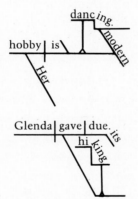

Participles. Participles come in two forms: the present participle, an *-ing* form like the gerund, and the past participle, the form that combines with the auxiliary *have* to make compound tenses. To discover the past participle of a verb, put it in this construction: "I have _____." The form that fits the blank—"I have *eaten*," "I have *been*," "I have *closed*"—is the past participle.

Participles are modifiers. Most modify nouns or pronouns, as adjectives do, but some, especially among the present participles, function as adverbs to modify verbs or whole sentences:

> *Exhausted*, Grandpa put up no resistance. (adjective modifying *Grandpa*)
>
> The *standing* corn was ready to harvest. (adjective modifying *corn*)
>
> *Sliding* into first, Johnny broke his ankle. (adverb telling how the ankle was broken)
>
> Strictly *speaking*, I have no authority. (adverb setting a condition for the whole sentence that follows)

17

Whether they are adjectival or adverbial, though, no participles appear in basic sentence patterns. Diagrammed, they go beneath the main sentence line:

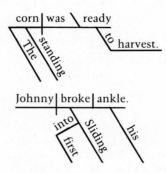

Exercise Parts of Speech 1. Underline the complete verbs in the following sentences. Circle all verbals and identify each as an infinitive, a gerund, or a participle, and analyze its function.

1. They were trying to stop.
2. Though poorly drawn, the portrait had a startling power.
3. Eating should be one of man's lasting pleasures.
4. Knitting furiously, I simply pretended not to hear.
5. May I question him on his grading?
6. May I question him on his grading policies?
7. Her only reason for enrolling is to learn.
8. To succeed often means working beyond one's ordinary ability.
9. Singing or playing certainly beats just listening.
10. Retreating, the cat began to edge toward the fence.

2B
Nouns.

Nouns, like verbs, can be recognized through a combination of meaning, form, and use.

Noun Meanings. A noun is the name of a person, place, or thing. If it names a class of person, place, or thing, it is a *common noun. Farmer, neighborhood,* and *dinner* are all common nouns. If it names a particular person place or thing, it is a *proper noun* and is capitalized. *Robert Redford, Finland,* and *Minnesota Mining and Manufacturing* are all proper nouns.

Noun Forms. Nouns also have some special features, the main one of which is their ability to form plurals. A few nouns, like *deer* or *sheep* do not change form in the plural, but most have separate singular and plural forms. With few exceptions, the noun-forms found in a dictionary are singular, and usually an -s or -es is added to form the plural: *dog, dogs; boot, boots; class, classes.* Some nouns form their plurals in less predictable ways: *man, men; child, children; goose, geese; datum, data.* But in general the ability to form plurals is a hallmark of nouns. If the word you are trying to identify can be made singular and plural, it is likely to be a noun.

Noun Uses. In most sentences, nouns function as subjects, objects, or noun complements:

> *Molly* will not eat. (subject)
>
> They finally accepted *Paul.* (direct object)
>
> She is my favorite *sister.* (predicate noun)
>
> They gave the *dog* nothing. (indirect object)
>
> We called him *uncle.* (objective complement)
>
> Everybody went to *town.* (object of preposition)

But in such a sentence as "My cousin's Diablo, a Doberman pinscher, bites at the slightest provocation," *cousin's* and *Doberman pinscher* are both nouns, but neither is a subject, object, or complement. The apostrophe (') in *cousin's* signals that this word is a *possessive noun,* telling to whom or to what something belongs. And *Doberman pinscher* is an *appositive,* a noun that renames another noun. It is like a modifier, for it gives extra information about Diablo, but it is also like a second name for Diablo. Appositives can rename nouns in any of the noun functions, and their special role in the sentence is indicated in diagramming by putting them in parentheses after the noun they go with:

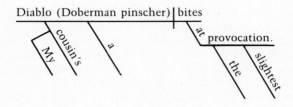

Finally, nouns sometimes modify other words directly, without being possessives or appositives. In such phrases as "peanut farmer," "blood red," or "fish fry," the modifiers *peanut, blood,* and *fish* are all nouns. Modifying nouns, possessive or otherwise, are diagrammed just as any other modifiers would be:

Harvey's sky blue blazer is lost.

2C
Pronouns.

Pronouns are noun-substitutes. Their general role is to take the place of particular nouns (their *antecedents*) in sentences, making it possible to write or talk without using the same nouns over and over. The commonest pronouns are the *personal* ones (*I, me, my, mine, you, your, yours, he, him, his, she, her, hers, it, its, we, us, our, ours, they, them, their,* and *theirs*); the indefinite ones (*each, everyone, some, somebody, either, neither, many, one, none,* and a number of others); and the *demonstrative* ones (*this, that, these,* and *those*). Such words serve the same grammatical functions as nouns and are treated as nouns in diagramming:

You should notify *everyone.*

You | should notify | everyone.

The personal and indefinite pronouns also have possessive forms which are treated like possessive nouns in diagramming.

His feet were in *someone's* way.

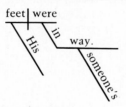

Three other kinds of pronouns have more specialized functions. The relative pronouns *who, which, what,* and *that* (see Chapter 4) not only substitute for their antecedents but also introduce dependent clauses. The interrogative pronouns *who, which,* and *what* form such questions as "*Who* was that lady?" or "*Which* do you like best?" And the intensive/reflexive pronouns, *myself, yourself, himself, themselves,* and so on, are used for emphasis—"We *ourselves* paid the bill"—or for showing that the subject of an action is also its object—"She scolded *herself* for her carelessness."

Exercise Parts of Speech 2. Underline the nouns and pronouns in the following sentences. How does each one function as a subject, object, complement, or modifier? (Some of the nouns and pronouns are objects of prepositions; if you have questions about prepositions, read Section 2F before doing the exercises.)

1. He is my mother's favorite banjo player.

2. The moon was rising over the darkened lake.

3. You know the man I mean; he is the old locksmith.

4. Who has injured himself?

5. The typewriter man will be here soon to fix the machines.

6. Coach Burns himself is working with the children.

7. The circus calls Miami its home base.

8. We gave Meg a new fur stole.

9. It was misty down by the main channel.

10. There were a lot of someone's books on the floor.

2D
Adjectives.

Adjectives modify nouns and noun equivalents such as pronouns and gerunds by answering the questions "Which?" "What kind?" or "How many?" about the words they modify. *Big, bold, brawny, belligerent,* and *brown* are typical adjectives. Such words help provide detail and precision to a sentence.

Adjectives are part of the basic sentence pattern only when they modify the subject through a linking verb or serve as objective complements:

    I | am \ brawny. (predicate adjective)

    They | called | her \ belligerent. (objective complement)

The rest of the time, adjectives supply information in addition to that contained in the basic sentence pattern. They are diagrammed on slanted lines beneath the words they modify:

> The *old* church has seen *some important* changes.

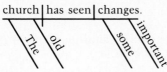

Except when they work as complements, adjectives generally precede the word they modify—"*the tall, dark* house," "*three mean, nasty* individuals."

Special Forms. Most adjectives can be made stronger or weaker by changing their forms or by adding *more, most, less,* or *least.* Typical sequences are *good, better, best; bad, worse, worst; big, bigger, biggest; beautiful, more beautiful, most beautiful;* and *strong, less strong, least strong.* These are called *comparisons.* Any word that can be compared and can also modify a noun or noun-equivalent is an adjective.

A special group of adjectives consists of words known as *articles,* including *a, an,* and *the*. These precede nouns and noun-equivalents: *"the* boy," *"a* lion," *"an* awakening." But articles do not always come immediately before their nouns; sometimes other modifiers come between the two: *"the* rusty bucket," *"a* satisfied customer," *"an* angry, disappointed police chief."

A certain group of words can function as either adjectives or pronouns, depending on whether or not they have anything to modify. For instance, the demonstrative pronouns (*this, that, these,* and *those*) can all be used as adjectives to modify rather than to replace a particular noun. The same is true of such indefinite pronouns as *each, many, some, any, all, both, neither,* or *one.* The way to tell whether these words are used as adjectives or as pronouns in a particular sentence is to see if there is another word in the sentence that they modify. If there is, they are adjectives; if not, they are pronouns:

> *This* is my pride and joy. (pronoun)
>
> *This car* is my pride and joy. (adjective)
>
> *Many* were sold down the river. (pronoun)
>
> *Many slaves* were sold down the river. (adjective)

2E
Adverbs.

Adjectives modify nouns and noun equivalents. Adverbs modify verbs, adjectives, other adverbs, or even whole sentences, answering the questions "How?" "When?" "How often?" "Where?" "In what direction?" or "How much?"

> The collie's tail was *gaily* wagging. (tells *how* about *was wagging*)
>
> *Afterwards,* I had second thoughts. (tells *when* about *had*)
>
> They *occasionally* go to the movies. (tells *how often* about *go*)
>
> *Underneath,* it was pale yellow. (tells *where* about *was*)
>
> The car turned *left.* (tells *in what direction* about *turned*)
>
> His story is *barely* plausible. (tells *how much* about the adjective *plausible*)

Notice that each of these adverbs modifies another element in its sentence. Sentence-modifying adverbs work differently:

> *Frankly,* I am getting tired of this.
>
> *Luckily,* nothing was broken.

In these examples, *frankly* and *luckily* do not modify a specific sentence element; they modify the whole remark that follows.

There are some formal characteristics that help to identify adverbs. Though many words that end in *-ly* are not adverbs, it is true that a large number of adverbs do have this ending. A good rule is that adjectives plus the ending *-ly* make adverbs, as in *quietly, solidly,* or *strongly,* while *-ly* words based on nouns (ones like *manly, lovely,* or *friendly*) are adjectives.

Some adverbs can also be compared as adjectives can, though usually only by adding *more, most, less,* or *least* (*heavily, more heavily, most heavily, less heavily, least heavily*).

On the whole, though, form is not a very reliable clue to adverbs. It is best to find what they modify and what sort of question they answer. If a word modifies anything other than a noun or noun-equivalent, and if it answers one of the adverb questions, then it is an adverb.

Special-Purpose Adverbs.   There is one group of adverbs whose only job is to tell "How much?" about other adverbs and adjectives. Called *intensifiers,* these adverbs include such words as *too, rather, quite,* and *very.* Intensifiers almost always come right before the modifiers they intensify: "*too* good," "*rather* sketchy," "*quite* silently," "*very* fat."

> *Exercise Parts of Speech 3.* In the following sentences, circle all adjectives, underline all adverbs, and identify what each of the words you mark modifies:
>
> 1. One feature of her style is especially noteworthy.
> 2. One can never be sure how to compete most effectively.
> 3. Blue, red, and green streamers fluttered madly in the wind.
> 4. Later the bright lights returned, flaring periodically in the upper windows.
> 5. Sloppily written anonymous articles began to appear daily.
> 6. Goose down has more loft than synthetic insulation.
> 7. Generally his big gas mower failed to start easily.
> 8. Some of them certainly give other people useless advice.
> 9. Briefly, most workers want the best possible wages.
> 10. The big bull sidled up almost silently, nearly catching him unaware.

2F
Prepositions.

A preposition precedes another word or series of words and relates it to the rest of the sentence. Most prepositions, including the following ones, have to do with space or time:

about	beside	out
above	between	over
across	beyond	past
after	by	since
against	down	through
along	during	throughout
among	from	till
around	in	to
at	into	toward
before	near	under
behind	off	until
below	on	up
beneath		

A few prepositions are difficult to analyze in terms of space or time, including very common ones such as *except, for, like, of, plus, with,* and *without.* All prepositions have objects, usually nouns or pronouns. The preposition, its object, and any modifiers that may be attached to the object make up a prepositional phrase. We mention these phrases here simply because many of the words listed as prepositions can also be adverbs, depending on whether or not they have objects. Words like *above, behind, between,* or *near* are prepositions when they have objects; all by themselves they are adverbs:

> *Above* the trees the stone was exposed. (here, with *trees* for its object, *above* is a preposition)

> *Above,* the stone was exposed. (here *above* is an adverb)

Prepositions are diagrammed together with their objects and whatever modifiers the objects may have. Such constructions can get fairly complicated:

The road ran by the old, abandoned farmhouse.

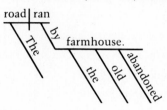

2G
Conjunctions.

Conjunctions are used to connect words, phrases, or clauses. There are two varieties: coordinating and subordinating conjunctions.

The coordinating conjunctions are *and, but, or, nor, for, yet,* and sometimes *so.* These, together with the correlative conjunctions *not only . . . but also, both . . . and, either . . . or,* and *neither . . . nor,* are used to connect words or groups of words of similar grammatical importance and function. For example, coordinating conjunctions can connect compound subjects or verbs, and they can be used between any other similar grammatical units as well. Drawing on the material in this chapter, we can use them to connect two or more verbals, *"slipping* and *sliding"*; nouns, *"not freedom* or *willpower* but *responsibility"*; pronouns, "neither *he* nor *she"*; and so on. Coordinating conjunctions connect equals.

Subordinating conjunctions are used to show that one clause is subordinate to, or dependent on, another. Some common subordinating conjunctions are listed below. Several consist of more than one word and some have optional elements:

after	as far as	as soon as
although	as if	as though
as	as long as	because

before	once	though
considering (that)	provided (that)	till
even if	seeing (that)	unless
except (that)	since	until
if	so that	when
in case	such that	where
in order that	supposing (that)	wherever
in that	than	while
now (that)	that	whether
on condition that		

2H
Interjections.

Any word that does not fit the categories described so far is probably an interjection. Interjections are the little exclamations that delay making a statement—"*Well* . . . it's, *uh*, unusual." Interjections also express emotion—"*Shucks!* I've split open my toe!" "*Wow!* We're going right over the cliff!" Interjections are not grammatically related to their sentences, so they are always set off, by a comma if the emotional charge is not strong, or by an exclamation point if it is.

Exercise Parts of Speech 4. Analyze each word in the following sentences. Identify each part of speech and explain its grammatical function.

1. His tweed jacket is much too large for him.
2. Drag racing is the sport of the future, growing continually.
3. Darn, this old perfume has simply lost its fragrance.
4. Tonight, to be sure, you have shown up very well.
5. Painting is not near the top of my list of favorite jobs.
6. Greg himself has forgotten to read the assignment.
7. This will be the last chance to get good seats for the concert.
8. Not one of them could dance or sing very well.
9. Mike and Kermit should have arrived by now.
10. He was a lefty and mowed the right-handers down.

Exercise Parts of Speech 5. Diagram the following sentences and identify each one according to the five basic sentence patterns:

1. Eddie was running along easily beside the stopping train.
2. The big fruit bats resemble one's idea of Dracula.
3. Bluegills frozen in a pond can often survive for weeks.
4. Gandalf almost called Frodo a traitor.
5. Running has given me a whole new outlook on life.

6. Exhausted, he promptly fainted into Sally's arms.

7. Ty Cobb could have hit that ball much farther.

8. *The Book of Common Prayer* was the masterpiece of the English devotional style.

9. Estelle will have been in Portland for three days tomorrow.

10. He has always enjoyed fishing for tarpon.

3 Phrases

A phrase is a group of related words that lacks a verb and generally a subject as well. Phrases cannot stand by themselves; they function within sentences as single parts of speech—nouns, adjectives, or adverbs. But phrases are often more precise than single words can be, and they lend variety and interest to sentences. The major types of phrases are prepositional, infinitive, participial, and gerund phrases.

3A
Prepositional phrases.

A prepositional phrase consists of a preposition, its object, and whatever words may be attached to the object. Typical examples are *"with* me," *"of* human bondage," *"through* the long, dismal night," and *"by* hook or crook." Such phrases vary in length and may have compound objects, but each is clearly a separate unit, and the preposition always comes first in the phrase.

A prepositional phrase can work as a noun, an adjective, or an adverb. Most prepositional phrases function as adjectives, modifying nouns or noun-equivalents:

> The bells *on the next block* are ringing. (modifies *bells*)
>
> We picked the one *in the window*. (modifies *one*)
>
> The car *on the left* is a lemon. (modifies *car*)

Prepositional phrases functioning as adverbs, modify verbs, adjectives, or adverbs:

> We continued *without a moment's rest*. (modifies *continued*)
>
> Harvey is modest *in thought and deed*. (modifies *modest*)
>
> She played brilliantly *on that hole*. (modifies *brilliantly*)

Prepositional phrases can also function as nouns, but they are not common in this role. When noun prepositional phrases do occur, they usually serve as subjects or predicate nouns:

> *Under the table* is his favorite hiding place. (subject)

> The best route is *by the Merritt Parkway.* (predicate noun)

An interesting thing about phrases is the way they can pile up, producing phrases within phrases within phrases. Prepositional phrases are especially adapted to this sort of multiplication:

> The hands *of the man* AT THE COUNTER were rough and red. (*of the man at the counter* is an adjective modifying *hands; at the counter* is a phrase within a phrase modifying *man*)

> She was emotional *in her summation* FOR THE DEFENSE. (*in her summation for the defense* is an adverb modifying *emotional; for the defense* is an adjective modifying *summation*)

Modifying prepositional phrases are diagrammed under the word they modify:

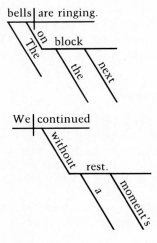

Noun-prepositional phrases are put on stilts above the slot in the diagram that a noun would normally occupy:

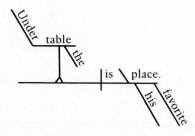

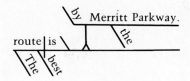

Exercise Phrases 1. Underline all the prepositional phrases in the following sentences. How does each function? What is its grammatical role in the sentence? (Your teacher may want you to diagram some or all of the sentences as well.)

1. Over the Edwards Plateau is the only route with clear markers.

2. Over the Edwards Plateau trudged the settlers with wagons and livestock.

3. He settled for a fifty-dollar raise in the spring.

4. The bill now in the senate is extremely important to good government.

5. Everybody under his supervision is dissatisfied with his methods.

6. She played the piece ponderously, with lots of pedal.

7. I am going with him to the bar on the corner across from the office.

8. They reminded him of the clause in the contract against selling.

9. In the beginning I thought of going with them.

10. By then it was too late for dinner.

3B
Infinitive phrases.

Infinitives can appear in sentences by themselves ("It was time *to go*"), but they can make phrases too. Infinitive phrases are made up of an infinitive plus such other elements as a subject, object, predicate noun, predicate adjective, or modifier. Infinitive phrases can function as nouns, adjectives, or adverbs.

Noun Infinitive Phrases.

To go to France is my ambition. (the whole phrase is the subject of its sentence—*to France* is a prepositional phrase modifying *to go*)

We want *him to leave at once.* (direct object—*him* is the subject of *to leave*, and *at once* is a prepositional phrase modifying the infinitive)

Quincy waited for *them to lift the curfew.* (object of the preposition *for*—*them* is the subject of *to lift*, and *curfew* is its object)

The best way is *to use light yarn on small hooks.* (predicate noun—*yarn* is the object of the infinitive and is modified by *on small hooks*)

Adjective Infinitive Phrases.

It will soon be time *to close the store.* (modifies *time*—*store* is the object of the infinitive)

She appeared *to be feeling ill.* (predicate adjective—*ill* is another predicate adjective that goes with the infinitive *to be feeling*)

Adverb Infinitive Phrases.

To know Spanish, you should live in Spain. (modifies *should live*—*Spanish* is the object of *to know*)

I am anxious *to meet that train.* (modifies *anxious*—*train* is the object of the infinitive)

They left too quickly *to be stopped for questions.* (modifies the adverb *too*—*for questions* modifies the infinitive)

Because infinitive phrases, or any other verbal phrases, are like little sentences, their subjects, objects, complements, and modifiers must be diagrammed in the same way that such elements are diagrammed in whole sentences. Except for ones functioning as predicate adjectives, modifying infinitive phrases go beneath the main sentence line; noun ones are put up on stilts:

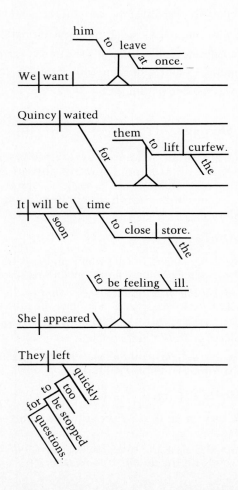

Infinitive phrases can appear more complicated than they are. Just find the infinitive and then treat the whole phrase as a single word. Then analyze the elements within the infinitive phrase, just as you would a basic sentence pattern. One word of warning is needed, however. Most of the time you can identify infinitives easily by the marker *to,* but there are a few that lack this handy signal:

They let *us watch the preparations.*

No one helped *her rope and throw the calf.*

He wants to do nothing but *study French.*

There must be something to do besides *go to sleep.*

The italicized phrases are all infinitive phrases without *to. To* can be dropped from infinitive phrases that are, like the first two examples here, direct objects of verbs such as *let, help, see, make, notice,* or *hear.* It can also be left out when the phrase is the object of *but* used as a preposition, or of such other prepositions as *except* or *besides.* In diagramming these constructions, put the omitted *to* in brackets [ ]; otherwise, the procedure is the same as for any other infinitive phrase.

Exercise Phrases 2. Identify and analyze the function of the infinitive phrases in the following sentences. (Your teacher may ask you to diagram them as well.)

1. They noticed us do all the jobs except make the beds.
2. To be sure of yourself, you must learn to do it blindfolded.
3. To lead a horse to water is not to make him drink.
4. I always wanted to learn needlepoint.
5. Barbara's idea was to surprise him with it.
6. This apartment seems too good to be real.
7. It is very hard to make them to your specifications.
8. Walter called them to find one to buy.
9. The secret of good baked beans is to go easy on the ginger.
10. The lamp he brought to light the steps was too weak to carry through the darkness.

3C
Participial phrases.

Participial phrases consist of a present or past participle (these terms are discussed in Chapter 2A), plus its object, predicate noun, predicate adjective, and/or modifiers, some of which may be phrases themselves. *Slipping through the gate, drinking lemonade under the trees, painted into a corner,* or *untouched by human hands* could all be participial phrases. As participials, such phrases may function as adjectives, but some work more as adverbs do, telling *how, when, how often, where, in what direction,* or *how much* about the main verb:

> *Excited by the news,* Joan danced a jig. (adjective phrase modifying *Joan*)
>
> *Hitting the pothole,* the car broke an axle. (adverb phrase telling *how* the breaking took place)
>
> *Hiding beneath the stands,* John was selling drinks. (adverb phrase telling *where* the sales were made)

To diagram a participial phrase, place it beneath that word in the sentence which it modifies.

Badly winded, Frank gasped the message.

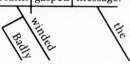

Sid left the room calling Melwood a thief.

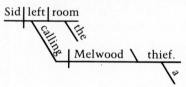

The conductor, looking very pale, had a glass of water.

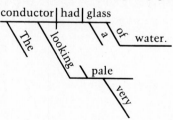

Participial phrases go above the main line only when they are used as predicate adjectives or objective complements:

He seemed shaken by the experience.

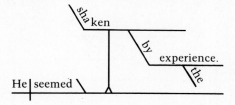

I thought her improved by her failure.

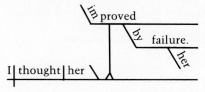

3D
Gerund phrases.

Gerund phrases are all based on *-ing* participles and can include such other elements as subjects of the gerund, objects, predicate nouns or adjectives, and modifiers. The defining characteristic of gerund phrases is how they are used. They always function as nouns:

Having photographs is protection against time. (subject)

He soon mastered *repairing telephones.* (direct object)

My specialty is *poaching fish.* (predicate noun)

Dad gives *watching fireworks* low marks. (indirect object)

She called his habit *spitting into the wind.* (objective complement)

His hobby, *hunting for buried relics,* was costly. (appositive)

They exercise by *running around the golf course.* (object of preposition)

Gerund phrases are diagrammed like other verbal phrases, except that they always go on stilts. Treat objects, predicate nouns and adjectives, and modifiers within gerund phrases just as you would treat them in sentences:

Looking well is the best strategy.

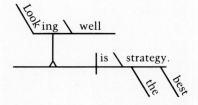

His greatest trick is jumping on the couch.

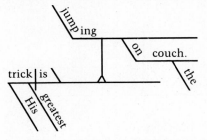

They brought making movies new prestige.

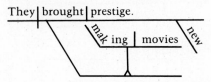

We killed it by holding it under water.

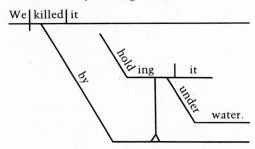

Exercise Phrases 3. Underline all the participial phrases, circle all the gerund phrases, and identify the function of each. Then diagram the sentences:

1. Having settled the debt, he accused Mark of cheating him.
2. Held down by its feet, the bird was unable to escape.
3. Washing cars does not appeal to a thinking woman.
4. House flies, hunted unceasingly, continue to flourish.
5. Seeming fit as ever, Browder took to the field waving his glove.
6. He gave singing in the choir a bad name.
7. Being rather frightened of bears, I do not like teasing them.
8. Judging on style favors the pots made by Zeena.
9. Stricken with remorse, I admitted stealing the refrigerator.
10. They dreaded applying the glazing compound.

Exercise Phrases 4. Identify all the phrases in the following sentences. What type is each? As what part of speech does it function? How does it work in the grammar of its sentence?

1. Under the rug was a pile of dirt testifying to her carelessness.
2. To make gin, you must spend time boiling mash and mashing berries.
3. Passing chemistry would be the high point of my career.
4. By writing her autobiography, she answered the critics of her policies.
5. Joe considers selling brushes an unsuitable job for his mother.
6. I mean to find a place to live for a long time.
7. The figs dried by the sun are used to lure camels into corrals.
8. Shutters were needed to resist the wind in that climate.
9. Oak is useful for making furniture and for selling to townspeople.
10. Digging a big hole is one way to exercise your arms.

Exercise Phrases 5. Diagram the following sentences and identify the basic pattern of each:

1. Splashes of color swept the walls, dazzling our vision.
2. Rodents and reptiles cause me to shiver with fear.
3. Awnings strung from the tops of windows have gone out of style.
4. Of all the books teaching children to read, that is the worst.
5. Cutting hay at midday in June is thirsty work for most people.
6. Ken learned butchering meat from his friend Emge.
7. Her aim was to gather a fine collection of Rackham illustrations.
8. Without food or friends, he still thought begging beneath him.
9. Dinosaurs may have sometimes had feathers to conserve heat.
10. Satisfied with her meal, Fifi went to nap in the living room.

4 Clauses

A clause is a group of related words that includes a subject and a verb. Some clauses are *independent*, or capable of standing alone as separate sentences. Others are *dependent* or *subordinate;* instead of standing by themselves, these function as nouns, adjectives, or adverbs within a larger sentence.

4A
Independent clauses.

Independent clauses express complete thoughts and conform to one of the basic sentence patterns discussed in Chapter 1. All the sentences covered there are also independent clauses. About the only independent clause topic left to consider is *compounding,* the process by which independent clauses may be joined to make one sentence with two or more equal parts.

Compound Sentences. A *compound sentence* works just the way compound subjects, verbs, or modifiers do. A coordinating conjunction (*and, but, or, nor, for, so,* or *yet*) is used to join two or more equal elements. But in this case, the elements consist of whole clauses:

> I went through the woods, *and* I saw the budding trees.
>
> Murphy was angry, *but* she got herself under control.
>
> The coach was satisfied, *for* the team had done its best.

The individual clauses in these examples are equal, just as compound subjects or verbs are equal, but notice the commas in each sentence. These commas signal that the coordinating conjunctions link whole clauses rather than lesser elements. The clauses must be complete for the comma to be justified.

If the sentences are rewritten so that the conjunctions connect predicates rather than clauses, no commas are needed:

I went through the woods *and* saw the budding trees.

Murphy was angry *but* got herself under control.

The coach was satisfied *and* knew her team had done its best.

Compound sentences are diagrammed just like two or more separate sentences, connected only by the conjunction:

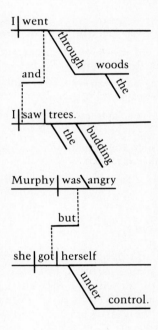

Though most compound sentences have a coordinating conjunction, sometimes this conjunction is left out; in these cases, the comma must be replaced by a semicolon:

Ngaio Marsh is an exciting writer; she has described some bloodcurdling crimes.

The semicolon is also used in compound sentences when the second clause is introduced by one of the conjunctive adverbs (such words as *however, moreover, nevertheless, therefore,* or *then*) instead of by a coordinating conjunction:

They could not pay the bill; therefore, they were not surprised to see the sheriff at the door.

Exercise Clauses 1. Number the independent clauses in the following sentences, and circle the verbs and underline the simple subjects of each one. Explain the punctuation between clauses:

1. His mother had made the pillow; she had worked on it for days and hoped to surprise him with it.

2. They thought that the chair would do; nevertheless, they wanted to see it in the room before committing themselves.

3. Mrs. Quorn, therefore, must be an enemy agent and should be stopped.

4. The pandas were soaking, the giraffe was eating, and the leopard, as usual, was pacing his cage.

5. Stone walls are characteristic of the area; stone was a cheap and abundant material, and labor was plentiful in those days.

6. The bindings on old books are often beautiful, and many collectors are more interested in the cover than the text.

7. Firewood is getting progressively scarcer, but there are some good substitutes, such as newspaper rolls, available.

8. Papa got the axe, and Janie got the churn handle; they were not going to give in without a fight.

9. The jungle plants are tough and long-lived; moreover, the parasites tend to single out weaker specimens.

10. You are wrong; Jesse Stuart wrote books rather than robbed banks.

4B
Dependent clauses.

Dependent clauses do not stand alone. They have subjects and verbs and conform to basic sentence patterns, but they function as nouns, adjectives, or adverbs—parts of sentences rather than as sentences themselves. Most dependent clauses are marked by a subordinating word: *"because* she lied," *"what* they did," *"how* dry I am," *"when* we meet again," *"whether* or not it was a golden retriever."

Noun Clauses. Like noun phrases, noun clauses function as subjects, direct objects, indirect objects, predicate nouns, objects of prepositions, or appositives:

When she left is still uncertain. (subject)

He did not know *what he should charge.* (direct object)

They will give *whoever shows up* the tickets. (indirect object)

This is *how it is done.* (predicate noun)

We blamed it on *whatever caused the delay.* (object of preposition)

He wanted to find one person, *whoever had switched off the light.* (appositive—renames *person*)

Most noun clauses are signaled by one of the relative pronouns—*who, which, what,* and *that* (including variant forms like *whose, whom, whichever,* and so on)—or by such subordinating conjunctions as *when, how, where,* or *why.* When a conjunction is used to introduce a noun clause, the clause is like an ordinary sentence with a separate subordinating word attached: *"when* they left," *"how* it is done," *"where* he had fallen asleep."* But a relative pronoun does more than make its clause dependent. It is also an important element in the structure of the clause. In the second of the sample sentences, for instance, *what* signals subordination, but it is also the direct object of *should charge.*

This dual role of the relative pronouns is one of the interesting facets of English grammar. Generally in English clauses the subject comes first, and other elements follow; in relative clauses, however, the order is often altered: the relative pronoun comes first whether or not it is the subject. Relative clauses often start with a direct object, with a predicate noun, or even with the object of a preposition. All the relative clauses in the following sentences are direct objects of the main verb *asked,* but notice how differently the relative pronouns function within each one:

> I asked *what had happened.* (*what* is the subject of *had happened*)
>
> I asked *whom she had seen.* (*whom* is the direct object of *had seen*)
>
> I asked *who they were.* (*who* is the predicate noun of *were*)
>
> I asked *whom they had given it to.* (*whom* is the object of *to*)
>
> I asked *what they had called him.* (*what* is the objective complement of *him*)

The relative pronoun *that* is especially flexible. Sometimes it functions as a subordinating conjunction introducing a complete clause ("I asked *that they sit down"*). Sometimes it functions as a relative pronoun to introduce a clause and also serves as an element within the clause it introduces ("I want one *that will start"*). And sometimes it is left out entirely ("I hope [*that*] *he is comfortable"*).

As you might expect, diagramming noun clauses produces interesting problems. Because they function as nouns, they go on stilts above the slots in a basic sentence or phrase that a noun would occupy. Noun clauses introduced by subordinating conjunctions or by *that* used as a conjunction present no great difficulty:

They were explaining how we could get into the class.

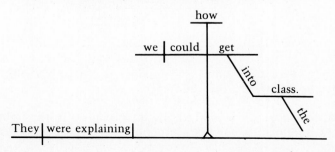

She said that upholstered furniture is difficult to sell.

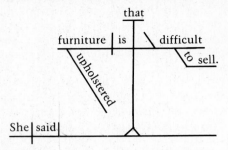

Sentences in which *that* is omitted are handled identically, but *that* is put in brackets.

Noun clauses introduced by relative pronouns which also function within the clause may need rearranging, depending on the role of the pronoun:

I assumed that had happened.

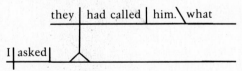

I asked whom he had seen.

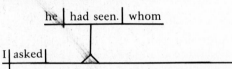

I asked what they had called him.

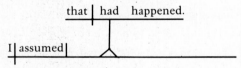

I asked whom they had given it to.

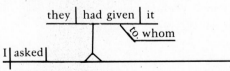

The principle is basically simple. The clause is put up on stilts and then diagrammed as if it were a little sentence.

Exercise Clauses 2. Underline the noun clauses in the following sentences, and identify the noun function (subject, direct object, indirect

8. The castle of Dracula loomed above a valley where wolves prowled.

9. Canaries that sing are outnumbered by those that do not.

10. Where the Encantadas lie is a mystery that was not solved until the twentieth century, when navigation was perfected.

Adverb Clauses.   Adverb clauses modify verbs, adjectives, or other adverbs, and are generally simple in construction. They are made up of subordinating conjunctions followed by straightforward clauses telling *why, how, when, how often, where, in what direction, under what conditions,* or *how much* about the words they modify. *If I were king, although he said so, since she won,* and *unless you give me the microfilm* are typical adverb clauses.

Here are some of the more common subordinating conjunctions used to introduce adverb clauses. Notice that several are more than one word long and some have optional elements:

after	considering (that)	provided (that)	unless
although	even if	seeing (that)	until
as	except (that)	since	when
as far as	if	such that	where
as if	in case	supposing (that)	wherever
as long as	in order that	so that	while
as soon as	in that	than	whether
as though	now (that)	that	
because	on condition that	though	
before	once	till	

The *that* conjunctions on this list are somewhat tricky. *That* is often omitted from *in order that, on condition that, provided that,* and similar constructions; on the other hand, when *that* is used by itself as a subordinating conjunction, it is sometimes short for *in order that:*

I will come on condition [that] they are not invited.

We will strive [in order] that they may be educated.

In general, though, adverb clauses are not complicated. Their structure is familiar, and it is usually easy to see what they modify:

I will eat *when I get hungry.* (tells *when* about *will eat*)

He is so strong *that he can bend steel.* (tells *how much* about the adjective *strong*)

Sally plays more sensitively *than Marshall does.* (tells *how much* about the adverb *more sensitively*)

Adverb clauses are diagrammed under the word they modify with their subordinating conjunctions on a dotted line:

The yacht sank *after the lifeboats were lowered.*

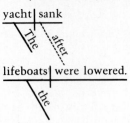

Since Michael is sick, her concern is understandable.

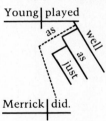

Young played just as well *as Merrick did.*

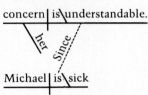

Exercise Clauses 4. Underline the adverb clauses in the following sentences, and explain what each modifies and which questions it answers. (Your teacher might also have you diagram some or all of the sentences.)

1. The well has been a great convenience since it is over a mile to the nearest good spring.

2. Darwin may have been pessimistic about evolution because he belonged to a threatened class himself.

3. When the dogwood blooms, we will take some longer walks.

4. If you are troubled by energy costs, you should consider storm windows, which can cut down on heat loss.

5. He maintained that I was the loser since I had stepped out of bounds before crossing the line.

6. If you agree, I will wait for you where the cab stand used to be.

7. Maria worked nervously, as if there were not enough hours in the day to complete her project.

8. Even if I loaf on the job, I will make enough money so that I can retire comfortably.

9. Where the bridge used to be is hidden because the underbrush has covered the approach.

10. Classical literature is often so topical that it might have been written yesterday.

4C
Clause combination.

Clauses can be combined to make sentences. The least complicated type of sentence, a *simple sentence,* consists of a single independent clause. Next in complexity is the *compound sentence,* composed of two or more independent clauses. A sentence containing one independent clause and any number of dependent ones is called a *complex sentence.* All the sentences in the last three exercises of this chapter are complex. Finally, a sentence with two or more independent clauses and one or more dependent clauses is called a *compound-complex sentence.*

Since we left, Dad has written once, but Mom calls every day.

I want to go if you do, and I will.

Exercise Clauses 5. Which of the following sentences is simple, compound, complex, or compound-complex? Analyze the clause structure of each and explain how the dependent clauses function in each sentence.

1. If she visits the hospital tonight, he will tell her what he told you this afternoon.

2. Mark was digging in the riverbank by the willow that his father had planted when they moved from town.

3. I like to sing, I like to dance, but I do not like to do both at the same time because I get mixed up.

4. The rabbit was bouncing over bushes and furrows, trying to escape from the yapping beagles and still keep an eye on the hunters behind them.

5. Tea is his favorite drink since he came back from the Orient and started importing it from India.

6. You want to be a biologist; therefore, you will have to study anatomy whether it thrills you or not.

7. Before I was in school, my father told me he had admitted he lied to Mother but she would not forgive him.

8. Although she did all she could, I hold her responsible; she did not begin her efforts early enough.

9. We kept coming up against the one indisputable fact—that Val had run away when the police arrived.

10. Unless you close the store and stop the leak, my lawyer will get an injunction that will make you.

5

Agreement between Subjects and Verbs [Agr. s/v]

In English sentences subjects and verbs must agree in number. For the most part, this means watching out for only one special verb form—the one that goes with third-person singular subjects. Consider the verb *take*. It is typical of English verbs in that it has one special form for third-person singular subjects and identical ones for every other kind:

I take	We take
You take	You take
He, she, it *takes*	They take

Furthermore, the characteristic -*s* third-person singular ending occurs only in the present tense:

I took	We took
You took	You took
He, she, it took	They took
I shall take	We shall take
You will take	You will take
He, she, it will take	They will take

The problem of agreement arises again only in some of the compound tenses made with auxiliary verbs that have their own special forms for different kinds of subjects:

I have taken	We have taken
You have taken	You have taken
He, she, it *has* taken	They have taken
I am taking	We are taking
You are taking	You are taking
He, she, it *is* taking	They are taking

The Verb **to be.**   The only verb that does not follow the pattern of *take* is *to be* in its present and past tenses:

I am	We are
You are	You are
He, she, it is	They are
I was	We were
You were	You were
He, she, it was	They were

In all other tenses, though, even *to be* behaves like other verbs.

The problem of subject/verb agreement, then, really involves making sure that you have the right form of the verb to agree with third-person singular subjects. But this kind of subject is extremely common. Not only *he, she,* and *it,* but anything that can be classified as a *he, she,* or *it* can make a third-person singular subject: *mailman, Guernsey, apple, chair, girl, sloop,* and *Mona Lisa* are all third-person singular subjects:

That Guernsey *gives* whipping cream.

The apple *is* polished.

My chair *was* broken.

Subject-verb agreement in English usually presents no great problem. Sometimes, however, things get more complicated. The rest of this chapter is about those special cases in which subject-verb agreement can be difficult.

5A
Make sure your verbs agree with the simple subject, even when other sentence elements come between it and the verb.

Adjectival phrases or clauses can come between the subject and its verb, but subject and verb must agree nonetheless:

The *list* of ancient and medieval remedies *was* very detailed.

Cobbler made with cling peaches *is* my favorite dessert.

Great *books* which change a person's life *are* rare.

Intense *storms* brought on by the jet stream shift *are disrupting* the usual weather pattern.

Exercise S/V Agreement 1. Correct the errors in agreement in the following sentences:

1. That form under the pile of yellow papers are needed for reporting rental income.
2. The chickens shut up in the coop each night is ready to come out by dawn every morning.

3. Thoreau, who was America's greatest naturalist, seem to grow on one.

4. Damascus, the scene of his triumphal entry, were later shelled for two weeks.

5. Furniture, some of which is a necessity for a young couple just starting off in married life, cost more than it did in the old days.

5B
Compound subjects joined by *and* take plural verbs.

King Edward and his court *were hunting* in Kent.

Fred and I *play* pool every night.

This rule gives rise to some special situations. *And* is the only connector that makes plural subjects. Constructions like *as well as, accompanied by,* or *together with* count as prepositions, so the words they introduce are parts of modifying phrases, not of the subject:

Matt, accompanied by Miss Kitty, *was* [not *were*] swilling suds in the Longbranch Saloon.

Copper, together with tapioca, *has* [not *have*] been the biggest export in their economy.

Then too, sometimes a compound subject takes a singular verb even though it is joined by *and*. There are two cases in which this happens. One is if both subjects name the same person or thing:

The long and short of it *is* that he refuses to come.

My friend and protector *was* there to help me.

The second is if a compound subject is modified by a word such as *every* or *each:*

Every cat and dog in town *was* upset for weeks.

Each soldier and sailor *has been hoping* for leave.

Exercise S/V Agreement 2. Correct the errors in agreement in the following sentences:

1. Solly and Mag, the couple closest to us at that time, was arguing in the kitchen.

2. The wolf, along with his cousin the coyote, prey on young domestic animals.

3. Each book and paper were stained with mildew.

4. The outcome and conclusion of your rash action are yet to be seen.

5. Mitchell and his girlfriend Naomi thinks the courses are too hard.

5C
As subjects, *none* or *any* can be singular or plural, depending on the context.

When *none* and *any* refer to *mass nouns* (things that cannot be counted) they are always singular:

None of the salt *has dissolved.*

Is any of the flour unbleached?

When *none* or *any* refer to things that can be counted (pies, candles, marbles, people, and so on), their number depends on what the writer means to say. Make *none* singular when you mean *not one of;* plural when you want it read as *not any of:*

None of my friends *is* coming to my party. (Each friend has decided individually not to come.)

None of the horses *are* visible. (A group of horses that might have been seen are not.)

Any works the same way:

Any of those trees *is* beautiful enough. (Any one of them would do.)

Any of those cars *have* great brakes. (The whole group will stop on a dime.)

5D
Relative pronouns (*who, which,* and *that*) make singular or plural subjects depending on what they refer to.

The relative pronouns have no singular and plural forms. When relative pronouns are used as subjects, the verb must agree with their antecedents.

Those are the machines which *were* supposed to arrive last week. (*Which* refers to *machines,* so its verb is plural.)

He shocked the man who *was listening* at the next table. (*Who* stands for *man,* so it takes a singular verb.)

Our hats and coats, that *have given* such good service, are to be donated to the Salvation Army. (*That* refers to *hats and coats;* its verb must be plural.)

In some constructions, verb agreement with relative pronouns can be tricky:

Mother is the only one of the women who *likes* music. (*Who* refers to *Mother,* the only music lover in the crowd.)

Mother is only one of the women who *like* music. (This time *who* refers to *women;* they all like music, and the verb must be plural.)

Exercise S/V Agreement 3. Correct the errors in agreement in the following sentences.

1. He bought three of the stores which has burned.

2. Some of the men who talks so big are really cowards.

3. Cheese of any kind is one of the foods that leaves me cold.

4. I like a car that start reliably even in cold weather.

5. That record is the only one that seem likely to last long.

5E

Two or more singular subjects joined by *or* or *nor* take a singular verb; if the subjects are plural, they take a plural verb. If the subjects differ in number, make the verb agree with the subject closest to it.

When you say "either an apple or orange," you mean one or the other, but *not both.* When you say "neither fish nor fowl," you mean not either *one.* Both of these constructions join subjects to be considered individually, not together. When all subjects involved are of the same number, simply make the verb agree with any of them:

My mother or my sister *has been* to see him today.

Neither the zone nor the man-to-man *was working.*

Either the firemen or the police *were* on call at all times.

Neither roses, tulips, nor violets *are growing* there.

When the subjects are of different numbers, make the verb agree with the subject closest to it:

The dean or his assistants *were* called in.

Neither the troopers nor their captain *was alerted.*

Exercise S/V Agreement 4. Correct the errors in agreement in the following sentences.

1. There are either a fortune or quick bankruptcy in treasury bonds.

2. Neither the leader nor the members of the band knows "Stardust."

3. Sheila or Freddie were going to open the store this morning.

4. Wire whisks or a good mixer are needed for that recipe.

5. Neither he nor the other one speak Esperanto.

5F

Collective nouns are generally treated as singular. They can be considered plural, though, when individuals within the collective group are acting separately.

Collective nouns include such words as *committee, team, congregation,* or *herd,* which are single names for a group of individuals. American English tends to make such collective names singular:

The *audience was* restless.

We settled ourselves as the *orchestra was warming* up.

His *fraternity is sponsoring* the Easter egg hunt.

Still, collective nouns can be treated as plurals when it is clear that the members of the group are acting individually:

The *committee were* unable to agree on a plan.

The *drill team are packing* their bags at the hotel.

5G
Plural nouns of amount, distance, space, or time are treated as singular when used as single units of measurement.

This rule concerns words like *cent, dollar, acre, yard, mile, day, week,* or *year.* When a number of such units are added together to make a single, specific amount, the sum is treated as singular:

Twenty dollars is a lot to pay for lunch.

Fourteen miles is a long way to pedal.

A thousand acres is an enormous farm for this area.

Such nouns can also be simple plurals when the units they name are separate or are not added up into a specific total:

The *yards were getting* harder and harder to gain.

Ten dollars were lying scattered on the floor.

Six weeks out of the year *were set* aside for "mini-vacations."

Exercise S/V Agreement 5. Correct the errors in agreement in the following sentences:

1. Three years seem too long a period for an apprenticeship.
2. Ninety-five cents are more than that toy is worth.
3. The congregation was at each other's throats.
4. Fifteen inches are long enough for a measuring stick.
5. The whole squad have united as one woman behind Belinda.

5H
Subjects and verbs must agree even when the subject comes after the verb.

In English, the subject usually precedes its verb. But there are two common constructions in which this order is reversed. Many sentences that start off with an adverbial element (often a prepositional phrase) have "delayed" subjects:

Between the two shops *was* an overgrown vacant lot.

Through the gate *were* the house and its famous gardens.

The subject of the first sentence is *lot,* and the subject of the second is *house and gardens,* so the first verb must be singular and the second plural.

Another construction that causes "delayed" subjects begins with an expletive *there:*

There *are* three mice under the refrigerator.

There *is* a man in the attic.

You can tell that *there* is not the subject in sentences like these because if it is left out you still have a sentence, even though it becomes a question: "Are three mice under the refrigerator?"; "Is a man in the attic?"

Exercise S/V Agreement 6. Correct the errors in agreement in the following sentences:

1. There is a pound of Swiss cheese and some mustard in the hamper.
2. Under the steps was a child's wagon and a pile of other toys.
3. There are a team of specialists coming on the chartered plane.
4. Among the reeds were a flock of canvasback ducks.
5. There have been a new flavor featured every month.

5I
Make sure your verbs agree with subjects, not with predicate nouns.

In Pattern Five sentences, a subject may be connected by a linking verb with a *predicate noun:* "Martha was Mary's sister"; "The meat thermometer is a useful device." In such sentences, the first noun or pronoun is the subject, the second is the predicate noun. Agreement is no problem as long as the subject and predicate noun are the same in number, but confusion sometimes results when one is singular and the other plural:

Long hours and exhaustion *are* his daily routine.

My favorite section *is* the songs about her childhood.

It is important to remember that the subject is determined by position. If the examples are turned around, *routine* and *songs* become the subjects, and the number of the verbs will have to be reversed:

His daily routine *is* long hours and exhaustion.

The songs about her childhood *are* my favorite section.

Exercise S/V Agreement 7. Correct the errors in agreement in the following sentences.

1. His favorite vacationing place are the state parks.

2. My friends is the best consolation I could have.

3. Karen's speed and strength is her greatest contribution to the team.

4. Another phase of his life were his political career and his years of teaching.

5. The last part of the report are accounts receivable.

Exercise S/V Agreement 8. Underline the subjects and circle the verbs in the following sentences. Consider all clauses in each sentence, and be prepared to explain how each pair agrees in number.

1. His rash, which was growing worse by the day, had begun to itch, and it now was looking red and inflamed.

2. In a year or two there have been two break-in attempts at his store, and he is getting paranoid about security.

3. I do not think the Seaboard Express that connects those cities is running this week since the storms have done so much damage to the track.

4. While the captain, by this time a nervous wreck, was sulking in his cabin, the crew were arguing about the best way to divide the booty they had taken.

5. Any of my relatives is good enough to meet the governor; after all, his family is not so grand itself.

6. Either Lucy or any one of several of her friends has excellent qualifications: they all have brains and plenty of experience.

7. In our garden at that time were a rustic bench and a marble fountain my sister had brought back from Italy.

8. Neither eggs nor other breakfast food has been ordered; you will have to do without unless one of you brings some of his own.

9. A hundred yards is a tremendous distance when one has played a whole game and is exhausted.

10. Her current dread is that her partner might lose the account and give the firm a bad name.

Exercise S/V Agreement 9. In the following sentences, correct any errors in agreement between subjects and verbs. Be ready to explain your corrections.

1. Young or one of his top aides are supposed to meet the train and welcome the senator.

2. When I checked an hour ago, none of the oxygen were absorbed.

3. Adam, along with his friends, are going on a long tour of the Baja.

4. The best of the many children's books I have read are *The Book of Three*.

5. The saddest part of the proceedings were the valedictory speeches.

6. There was an old, rusty radiator and some brake shoes on the floor of the garage.

7. She is one of those people who is too concerned with what everything costs.

8. The whole union are together behind the decision to strike now.

9. Between Glendale and West Gardiner there are only a distance of five miles.

10. A bonded warehouse for the storage of goods pending payment of taxes have been established in Encino.

Exercise S/V Agreement 10. Following the directions, construct sentences of your own. The context can be anything you like. To help you, each set of directions is keyed to the section of this chapter in which the assigned construction is discussed.

1. Using *has sniffed* as the verb, write a sentence in which the subject is followed by a modifying phrase. Underline the subject and circle the modifier that follows it. (5A.)

2. Using present-tense verbs, write one sentence with "mountain climbing and sky-diving" as the subject and another with the subject "every pot and pan." (5B.)

3. Using present-tense verbs, complete the following sentences:
   Emily is one of those girls who . . .
   GM is the only major car company that . . . (5D.)

4. Write one sentence with a present-tense verb using the subject "Either Ralph or his friends." Write another in which the subject is "Neither his friends nor Ralph." (5E.)

5. Complete the following sentence beginnings in any way you choose. When you have written your sentences, underline the simple subjects.
   There is . . .
   Around his neck were . . .
   In the past there has been . . .
   Here are . . . (5H.)

6. Reverse each of the following Pattern Five sentences, making the predicate noun the subject. Underline the subject and circle the verb in each of your new, turned-around sentences.
   Her current interest is motorcycles.
   Pierced ears are the style.
   Your best bet is the classified ads.
   The streets are the place to find out. (5I.)

Subject/Verb Agreement Reference Chart

> **General rule:**
> **Subjects and verbs must agree in number.**

She *feels* like a million dollars.

Flu shots *are* painful.

Trouble Spots:

5A
Verbs must agree with the simple subject even when other sentence elements come between the two.

The *creatures* in a drop of common pond water *show* great diversity.

5B
Compound subjects joined by *and* take plural verbs.

Watson and Crick *have* very different personalities.

5C
As subjects, *none* or *any* can be singular or plural depending on meaning and reference.

None of the cement *is* hardened. (mass noun)

None of my well-wishers *has* shown up. (not one of)

None of them *were* able to go. (not any of)

5D
Relative pronouns (*who, which,* and *that*) make singular or plural subjects depending on their antecedents.

The cars which *are* left will be sold at a loss.

There is the house which *is* up for auction.

5E
Two or more singular subjects joined by *or* or *nor* take a singular verb; if the subjects are plural, they take a plural verb. If the subjects differ in number, the verb agrees with the subject nearest it.

More money or more time *is* needed if this project is to work.

Neither knives nor spoons *were* provided.

Either psychology or math classes *take* up all her time.

5F
Collectives are generally treated as singular, but they can be considered plural when individuals within the group are acting separately.

The troop *is* easy to handle.

The troop *were working* on their projects.

5G
Plural nouns of amount, distance, space, or time are treated as singular when used as single units of measurement.

Four miles *is* a great distance to carry water.

Six weeks *is* a long time to spend on the road.

5H
Subjects and verbs must agree even when the subject comes after the verb.

Along the side of the road *were* many garish signs.

There *is* something caught in your hair.

There *are* some things you have yet to learn.

5I
Verbs agree with subjects, not with predicate nouns.

Milton's poems *are* a great legacy.

My hobby *is* old cars.

6
Agreement Between Pronouns and Antecedents [*Agr. p/a*]

Only two kinds of pronouns, the demonstrative and personal ones, have special forms for singular and plural use. These must be made to agree in number with their antecedents (the words they stand for), just as verbs must agree with their subjects.

6A
Demonstrative pronouns must agree with their antecedents in number.

The demonstrative pronouns are *this*, indicating an object close at hand, and *that*, which indicates something farther away. The plural forms are *these* and *those*. Choosing between these singular and plural forms in a given context depends on the pronoun's antecedent, which is usually found in a previous sentence or clause:

> Mark drove an old *car*. *This* was his transportation and his hobby.

> You probably saw a big dust *cloud* this morning. *That* was Louise headed for the concert at the Omni.

> Notice the unconventional *tweeters*. *These* are a new piezoelectric design.

> Back then Roberta had *a Porche and a Jeep*, and *those* were two great cars.

Although agreement of demonstrative pronouns occurs almost automatically, there are times, especially when the antecedent is a vague quantity of something, when mistakes are possible:

> I bought several *apples*. *This* was my favorite fruit.

> Feeding with the others was a *kind* of gray bird, and *these* were the rare song sparrows.

The demonstrative pronoun is wrong in both of these examples. In the first case, *apples* is the antecedent, and the pronoun should be *these*, not *this*. In the second example, the antecedent is the word *kind*. The writer probably meant that there were several song sparrows mixed in among the other birds, but grammatically the antecedent is singular and the writer should use the singular form *this* to refer to it.

> *Exercise Pronoun Agreement 1.* Correct the errors in pronoun agreement:
>
> 1. Andy knew a lot of seedy musicians. This was the people he cared most about.
> 2. Mr. Malicious is a master of the cutting remark; these are his main stock in trade.
> 3. I always enjoyed myself when we went to see the parrots. That was my favorite bird.
> 4. Through the glade came several deer. This was the famous palace herd.
> 5. We are justly celebrated for our apple tart. These are the finest to be found anywhere.

6B
Personal pronouns must agree with their antecedents in number.

Personal pronouns show a distinction between the person speaking (first person), the person spoken to (second person), and the person or thing spoken about (third person). No one is likely to be confused about whether the person talking is an *I* or a *we*, and the second person pronouns—*you*, *your*, and *yours*—are the same in both singular and plural forms. Agreement is a problem only in the use of the third-person pronouns. There are no less than twelve of these: the singulars *he, his, him, she, her, hers, it*, and *its;* and the plurals *they, their, theirs,* and *them.* These forms are used constantly in writing and talking:

Mother gave the man *her* address.

When the workers come, tell *them* to start at the back.

The dog was chewing *its* bone when *it* saw Dave and started after *him.*

Some difficult aspects of third-person pronoun agreement are discussed in detail in the following sections.

6C
The indefinite pronouns *anybody, anyone, each, either, everybody, everyone, neither, no one, nobody, some- body, someone,* and *one* are all singular. They take singular personal pronouns.

Most pronoun agreement errors are made in this area. A reference to one of these indefinite pronouns as an antecedent requires a singular pronoun in written English. It is singular even though the sense of the antecedent may be plural and even though using a plural pronoun to refer to it may sound normal in speech. Most people *say* things such as the following:

> *Everybody* got *their* coats and went home.
>
> *Anybody* would worry if the IRS were after *them*.
>
> *Nobody* can be sure how *their* children will behave.

But you are not supposed to *write* sentences like these. In writing, the pronouns that refer back to these indefinite antecedents have to be singular:

> *Everybody* got *his* coat and went home.
>
> *Anybody* would worry if the IRS were after *him*.
>
> *Nobody* can be sure how *his* children will behave.

This rule also applies to such indefinite noun subjects as "a person," "the common man," or "a housewife" when a whole class rather than a specific individual is meant:

> Each girl is responsible for *her* [not *their*] own actions.
>
> A judge loses heart when *his* [not *their*] verdicts are overturned.
>
> A dog will defend *its* [not *their*] territory.

Supplying New Antecedents and Dealing with Uncertain Gender. It is impossible to correct some mistakes in the area of reference to singular indefinite antecedents by simply changing the reference pronoun:

> *Everybody* cried out when *their* seats began to tremble.

Suppose you noticed a sentence like this one in your own writing. *Their* is clearly the wrong form since its antecedent, *everybody*, is singular. But you could not change *their seats* to *his seat* without lapsing into unintentional comedy. You would have to revise the sentence some other way, by changing the subject to *they* or *the audience* or by rewriting it entirely.

Finally, it is conventional to use a masculine pronoun to refer to an antecedent of uncertain gender:

> *Everybody* has got *his* facts mixed up.
>
> *Each* of them said *his* piece.

In sentences like these, the speaker or writer might be referring to men or to women or to a mixture of both. Unless the context clearly establishes that the people referred to are female, though, masculine pronouns are used to refer to the subjects. Some people are bothered by this custom and use *his or her* when gender is uncertain, but *he or she, him or her*, and *his or her* become awkward with repetition. A better solution is to *pluralize* wherever possible. Avoid the problem by using a plural rather than an indefinite antecedent:

> The *students* have *their* facts mixed up.

> The *representatives* got up and said *their* pieces.

Exercise Pronoun Agreement 2. Correct the errors in pronoun agreement in the following sentences:

1. Each of them is aware of their predicament.

2. When someone tells you they are speaking for your own good, look out!

3. I did not know anyone was still in their rooms.

4. When one is down to their last dollar and their friends will not help out, there is no one to turn to.

5. Neither of the two can control their cars on icy roads.

6D
Singular pronouns are used to refer to collectives when the group named by the collective is thought of as a unit. Plural pronouns may be used when the group is acting separately.

The distinction here is the same as that which applies to subject-verb agreement (see 5F). When the group acts in unison, it is treated as a single entity. But when individuals in the group act on their own, the group itself may be treated as a plural:

> The *troop* stopped at nightfall and made *its* camp.

> The entire *squad* scattered and went *their* separate ways.

If you are in doubt which pronoun form to use in referring to a collective noun, the safer choice is always the singular form.

6E
Two or more antecedents joined by *and* are plural. They require a plural reference pronoun. When multiple antecedents are joined by *or* or *nor,* they are singular if the individual antecedents are singular, plural if the individual antecedents are plural. If antecedents joined by *or* or *nor* differ in number, the reference pronoun must agree with the antecedent nearest it.

The rules here are the same as those that apply to compound and correlative subjects (see 5B and 5E). The conditions and exceptions that hold for the choice of singular or plural verbs apply equally to choosing the right form of reference pronouns:

John and Valery paid *their* own way. (compound antecedent)

Each tree and bush was shedding *its* leaves. (compound antecedent made singular by *each* or *every*)

Her lord and master was eating *his* lunch. (compound antecedent naming the same person or thing)

Rex or Tom has lost *his* wallet. (singular antecedents joined by *or*)

Neither the words nor the pictures had *their* full effect. (two plural antecedents joined by *nor*)

Neither the girls nor Mother has finished *her* Wheaties. (one singular and one plural antecedent joined by *nor,* the singular one closer to the reference pronoun)

Exercise Pronoun Agreement 3. Correct the errors in pronoun agreement in the following sentences.

1. Michelangelo and Bernini both brought his special genius to sculpture.
2. Michelangelo and Bernini each brought their special genius to sculpture.
3. Neither Michelangelo nor Bernini is known for their prints.
4. Either Michelangelo or his followers left his mark on that church.
5. Neither his students nor Bernini could have foreseen our interest in their work.

Exercise Pronoun Agreement 4. Circle the reference pronouns in the following sentences. Draw a line connecting each of them to its antecedent. Be prepared to explain why each pair agrees.

1. Neither Barbara nor her four brothers were aware of their father's true occupation.
2. Ed was especially proud of his multitude of Persian carpets. This was the backbone of his Oriental collection.
3. Each of the thousands of birds on the island knows its own nest.
4. My father's family have wrangled among themselves for years about their rights to parts of Grandma's estate.
5. The National Park Administration is concerned about its reputation among the hordes of visitors who use its facilities.
6. Everyone is somewhat touchy about his home and personal property; they are too private to be exposed to the inspection of strangers.
7. Bilbo and the dwarfs continued on their journey, each of them worried about his dwindling food supply.
8. Mike got his boat and trailer, and Charlie got his fishing gear; they had been waiting for good weather since the season opened.
9. *Five Red Herrings* is one of Sayers' weaker books because in it she lets herself get bogged down in technicalities.
10. She fitted one of the corners of her house with a new downspout, hoping it would stop the erosion of her lawn.

Exercise Pronoun Agreement 5. Correct all errors of pronoun agreement in the following sentences. Be ready to explain your corrections.

1. He took delight in preparing unusual dishes. This was the kind of food he preferred to eat himself.

2. The band marched in lock step around the arena, showing their perfect control and excellent training.

3. Not one of the picnickers was aware that their fun was soon to be interrupted by a sudden downpour.

4. Every lamp and electrical appliance took their share of the incoming current.

5. All through the winter we fished through the ice, and every fish we caught battled for their life.

6. Some of us thought the car would hit our camp; everyone did their best to wave it off.

7. Spotted throughout the exhibition were paintings of unusual power; this was the work of Scorpello.

8. Neither a doctor nor a nurse can let their concentration waver when a patient is on the table.

9. When everybody was assembled, we told them how lucky they were to have received invitations in the first place.

10. No one can tell what his fate will be until they have lived their last hour and the time for surprises is over.

Exercise Pronoun Agreement 6.

1. Copy each of the following sentences, and follow it with another sentence of your own about the noun that is underlined. Start each of these additional sentences with a demonstrative pronoun (*this, that, these,* or *those*). Underline the demonstrative pronoun you have chosen. Example: "All she wanted to talk about was *cameras. These* were her passion." 6A.

   His upper lip had just recently sprouted *whiskers.*
   Vanessa has two old MG's in her *garage.*
   Vanessa has two old *MG's* in her garage.
   Following the jacked-up cars was another *kind* that rode just inches above the pavement.

2. Write four sentences that have indefinite pronouns for their subjects and singular personal pronouns to refer back to them. Underline both indefinite and personal pronouns. Example: "Somebody must have lost his wallet." 6C.

3. Write four sentences with *anybody, anyone, everybody,* or *everyone* as their subjects and singular personal pronouns to refer back to these subjects. Example: "*Anybody* could pick that lock if *he* tried."
   Next, *pluralize* each of your sentences: replace the indefinite subjects with plural nouns; replace the singular personal pronouns with plural ones. Example: "*Burglars* could pick that lock if *they* tried." 6C.

4. Write sentences using each of the following phrases as a subject. Refer back to the subject by using an appropriate personal pronoun. Underline both subject and reference pronoun. Example: "Sally and Meg are bringing their skateboards." 6E.

> Either Sally or Meg . . .
> Neither Sally nor the other girls . . .
> Both Sally and Meg . . .
> Neither Sally nor any other girl . . .

Pronoun Agreement Reference Chart

General Rule:
Pronouns with singular and plural forms must agree with their antecedents in number.

Trouble Spots:

6A
Demonstrative pronouns (*this, that, these,* and *those*) must agree with their antecedents in number.

Of all the candies in the jar, my favorites were the *gum drops. These* were the ones I asked for most.

I never lost my love for the spotted *goat. This* was a creature of infinite wisdom and charm.

6B
Personal pronouns (*I, you, he, she, it, we, they,* and all their other forms) must agree with their antecedents.

The *jar* was sitting right there on *its* shelf.

The *fireman* was polishing *his* brass buckle.

When *ducks* land here *they* come in from the south.

6C
Indefinite pronouns (*anybody, anyone, each, either, everybody, everyone, neither, no one, nobody, somebody, someone,* and *one*) are all singular. They take singular personal pronouns.

Anyone would like to have wheels like those on *his* own car.

Everybody picked up *his or her* own litter.

6D
Singular pronouns are used to refer to collectives when the group named by the collective is thought of as a unit. Plural ones may be used when the group is acting separately.

The *gang* was holed up in *its* old hiding place.

The whole *group* had gone off in different directions to eat *their* lunches.

6E
Two or more antecedents joined by *and* are plural. They require plural reference pronouns. When multiple antecedents are linked by *or* or *nor*, they are singular if the individual antecedents are singular, plural if the individual antecedents are plural. If the antecedents joined by *or* or *nor* differ in number, the reference pronoun must agree with the antecedent nearest it.

Bananas and oranges are valuable for *their* vitamin C.

Neither a coat nor a hat is worth *its* weight in this weather.

Ponies or horses are worth what you pay for *them*.

Either John or the other elders will make *their* speeches.

Neither the brothers nor their uncle wants to give up *his* seat tonight.

7

Pronoun Reference [*Ref.*]

Pronouns are useful because they take the place of nouns and other substantives, which otherwise would have to be repeated over and over. But this usefulness does not come free. Not only must many pronouns be made to agree with the words they stand for, but each one must also have a clear and definite antecedent to refer to. Indefinite pronouns—words such as *one, some, any, everyone, many, somebody,* and so on—are exceptions to this rule in that they can be used to refer to unspecified antecedents. But, except for these, all pronouns must be used in such a way as to make their exact reference clear. Problems of faulty reference arise when a pronoun has more than one possible antecedent, when its antecedent is too far away to be easily remembered, or when it has no antecedent at all.

7A
A pronoun must not have two or more possible antecedents.

Ambiguous reference, the problem of having too many possible antecedents, can destroy communication entirely. Consider the sentence: "Marvin told Jim he was getting too old." The writer might know what it means, but the reader does not. *He* is a third-person singular masculine pronoun, and *Marvin* and *Jim* are both third-person singular masculine antecedents. *He* could refer to either of them. Until this reference problem is straightened out, there is no way to be sure what the sentence means.

There are several ways to correct this type of sentence. For example, you can quote Marvin's exact words:

Marvin said to Jim, "Jim, you are getting old."

Marvin said to Jim, "I am getting old."

You can change the wording so that it is clear who is old:

Unable to keep up, Marvin confessed to Jim that he was getting old.

Or you can rewrite the sentence entirely:

Marvin was getting old, and he told Jim so.

Jim was getting old, and Marvin told him as much.

Each revision eliminates the reference problem, and you can probably think of other solutions as well. Correcting ambiguous references is not hard. What is hard is recognizing them in the first place. When a situation you are describing is perfectly clear in your own mind, it can be difficult for you to see how your writing can be confusing to your reader. If you find you often have problems with multiple antecedents, review your writing and check each pronoun for clarity. You will soon learn to avoid unclear constructions automatically.

Exercise Pronoun Reference 1. Find and correct the ambiguous references in the following sentences.

1. When Reagan talked to Bush, he told him he was disappointed with his actions.

2. Those girls all have notebooks with loose leaves which are always lying around.

3. Freda asked Francine whether she looked thinner.

4. Igor presented Frankenstein with a basket of toads, his favorite food.

5. After they talked with the police, they did not know what to think.

7B
The antecedent of a pronoun must be clearly expressed, not just implied.

Having too many antecedents causes trouble, but it is equally bad to have none at all. Missing antecedents are another result of a writer's inability to distinguish what he meant from what he has actually written:

When he went by the dog pound, *they* rushed to the fence and barked at him. (*they* must refer to the dogs, but there are no dogs in the sentence.)

She was impressed with the way her operation had gone; *this* was the vocation for her. (*this* apparently refers to surgery, another unexpressed antecedent.)

In sentences like these, the writer knows what the pronouns should refer to; he simply forgets to include the antecedent. To avoid this error, find the antecedent for each of the pronouns you use. If there does not seem to be an antecedent, drop the pronoun and put in the word you intended it to refer to:

When he went by the dog pound, the *dogs* rushed to the fence and barked at him.

She was impressed with the way her operation had gone; *surgery* was the vocation for her.

Exercise Pronoun Reference 2. Find and correct the unexpressed antecedents in the following sentences.

1. Even though I have never butchered a hog, I suppose it is not too difficult.

2. After we smoke the hive they will come out.

3. I refuse to bake beans because I ate it too much as a child.

4. Julie is a great golfer now because she practiced it when she was young.

5. I went to the gallery expecting great art, but they were all dingy and disappointing.

7C
It, they, and *you* should not be used to refer to indefinite antecedents.

English has a whole string of indefinite pronouns—words like *anyone, some, no one, everybody,* and *one*—to indicate unspecified or unknown antecedents, and it is a mistake to use personal pronouns for this purpose. Consider the following examples:

In the Middle Ages, *you* could not go against the Church.

It says in the paper that the coach may resign.

Throughout Italy *they* think a lot of soccer.

There is nothing in these sentences for *you, it,* or *they* to refer to, not because the writer has forgotten to include an antecedent, but because he uses each pronoun as an indefinite reference, to refer to people or things in general. One way to revise the sentences is to replace the personal pronouns with indefinite ones:

In the Middle Ages, *one* could not go against the Church.

Someone says in the paper that the coach may resign.

Throughout Italy *everybody* thinks a lot of soccer.

Another solution is to eliminate the pronouns entirely:

Medieval people could not go against the Church.

The paper says that the coach may resign.

Italians think a lot of soccer.

Indefinite you. The pronoun *you* is commonly used indefinitely in speech, but it must be used with more precision in writing. *You* should be kept to indicate the person actually addressed or written to. Do not use *you* to refer to some unspecified group, as in "In ancient Rome, *you*

GRAMMAR

had to join the state religion," or "People say *you* cannot avoid death and taxes."

Exercise Pronoun Reference 3. Find and correct the mistaken indefinite references in the following sentences.

1. When I talked to the fire station, they said a truck was on the way.
2. In the pioneer days you had to be a jack-of-all-trades.
3. It says in my textbook that the environment has begun to recover.
4. They say you can't be too careful.
5. In Alaska they grow giant cabbages.

7D
A pronoun must not be too far away from its antecedent.

This rule calls for judgment, for it is not possible to define "too far away" exactly. Sometimes a chain of pronouns all refer to the same antecedent, and the writer can go on and on without repeating the word to which the pronouns refer:

When *Darwin* sailed for South America, *he* fully intended to use *his* findings as a naturalist to justify a literal interpretation of the Old Testament. In particular, *he* hoped to find evidence of a universal flood with which to silence critics of the Bible's historical accuracy. Needless to say, *his* voyage turned out very differently from the way *he* planned.

At other times, though, antecedents can easily be confused:

It was his *opinion* that she had treated him unfairly and that he was justified in leaving her for Marcia. *It* never changed.

In this passage, *it* is intended to refer to *opinion,* but so much distracting material comes between the two words that the reader must look back to the beginning of the sentence to be sure of the reference. The problem can be solved in either of two ways. The noun can be repeated at the end of the passage: "His *opinion* never changed"; or the unbending nature of his opinion can be made clear at the beginning: "It was his unchanging opinion that . . . ." The general principle behind both of these corrections is that the reader should never feel even momentary confusion about the reference of pronouns.

7E
The pronouns *this, that,* and *which* should not be used to refer to general ideas.

In the sentence "I was overjoyed, which he did not suspect," *which* is used as an *idea reference.* It has no specific antecedent; instead, it refers to the whole notion that "I was overjoyed." Idea references are common in the spoken language, but they should be avoided in writing. They generally feature the words *this, that,* or *which:*

> When I got sick, *this* set back my plans.
>
> He learned he had failed; *that* was the last straw.
>
> She has nervous palpitations, *which* she learned from her kindly doctor.

There are two ways to improve such references. You can eliminate the pronoun:

> My getting sick set back my plans.
>
> His failure was the last straw.
>
> She learned of her nervous palpitations from her kindly doctor.

Or you can change the pronoun to a demonstrative adjective by giving it a noun to modify:

> When I got sick, *this inconvenience* set back my plans.
>
> He learned he had failed; *that knowledge* was the last straw.
>
> She has nervous palpitations, *which condition* she learned about from her kindly doctor.

Exercise Pronoun Reference 4. Find and correct all reference problems in the following sentences. Be ready to explain your work.

1. When John and his brother contacted the admissions office, they could not tell them the deadline for his application.
2. Because Martha has not baked a cake in years, she has forgotten how it is done.
3. In science fiction you have to keep on your toes to understand their plots.
4. Even at the minimum wage it will be worth it if it lasts all semester.
5. Over in La Jolla they let government officials squander their money.
6. Once we complete the horse barn, they will have a place to get out of bad weather.
7. When he talked to Sam, he told him his plants were growing over on his property.
8. There are several factors that led to his decision, and this should be taken into account before you reject his ideas.
9. He loves that car, which is why he will not part with it.
10. On TV they claim Potter told Budge that he was getting too greedy.

Exercise Pronoun Reference 5. Find and correct all reference problems in the following sentences. Be ready to explain your work.

1. He ran a junkyard for years and sold it to whoever came in looking for some old part or another.

2. In Mexico, they believe what it says about him in the Bible.

3. Mom told Hilda that the old man they had seen was her father.

4. Karen wants to be an accountant and has made it her major.

5. He married Brenda in a hot air balloon, which shocked everybody.

6. He remembered the vase in the room by the heated swimming pool which he had visited the night before.

7. My friend is one man among many who have journeyed into that mountainous region carrying all they needed in their packs. Each of them has had to call on all his strength to survive. I know he did.

8. After Helen heard that her canary's disease was progressive and could be expected to be fatal, this upset her more and more.

9. Crack the shell as neatly as possible, and eat it right away for the best flavor.

10. Miller told Sam that he was still responsible but could get out of the situation by pretending to be sick, which was his mistake.

Exercise Pronoun Reference 6.

1. Each of the following sentences has a pronoun with more than one possible antecedent. Rewrite each sentence twice, making the pronoun refer clearly to a different antecedent in each version. Example:

> *Carla assured Emily she could clean and jerk one hundred pounds.*
>
> Carla said, "Emily, you can clean and jerk one hundred pounds."
>
> Carla boasted to Emily that she could clean and jerk one hundred pounds. 7A.

When the leopards meet baboon troops, they flee.

Mike announced to his father that his belt was too tight.

Lucy asked her friend whether her moped was still running.

2. Determine who or what is meant by the indefinite references in the following sentences. Rewrite the sentences, using noun subjects. Example:

> *They say, "Youth is wasted on the young."*
>
> Some old people say, "Youth is wasted on the young." 7C.

In college, you have to budget your own time.

It maintains in the paper Jones will win.

Well, I tried the supermarket, but they don't carry pigs feet.

All through the nineteenth century, you had to worry about smallpox.

3. Rewrite each of the following idea references in the two ways explained in the text. 7E.

Next, she became very religious, which surprised everyone.

The room was immaculate; this is what impressed Bob most.

She ran and stole third; that was entirely unexpected.

Pronoun Reference Chart

General Rule:
Pronouns must have clear and definite antecedents.

Trouble Spots:

7A
A pronoun must not have two or more possible antecedents.

Not, *Bill told Ron he had been stupid,* but *Bill said, "Ron, you have been stupid,"* *Ron had been stupid, and Bill told him so,* or *Bill accused Ron of having been stupid.*

7B
The antecedent of a pronoun must be clearly expressed, not just implied.

Not, *Browsing at the furniture outlet, he found it overpriced,* but *Browsing at the furniture outlet, he found* the furniture *overpriced.*

7C
***It, they,* and *you* should not be used to refer to indefinite antecedents.**

Not, *It says in* Dunn and Bradstreet . . . , but Dunn and Bradstreet *says* . . . Not, *In England they drink tea,* but *The English drink tea.* Not *You had to keep on your toes in frontier times,* but *Frontiersmen had to keep on their toes.*

7D
A pronoun must not be too far away from its antecedent.

7E
The pronouns *this, that,* and *which* should not be used to refer to general ideas.

Not, *I went to the circus with Jim; this made Joy jealous,* but *My going to the circus with Jim made Joy jealous,* or *I went to the circus with Jim, and this outing made Joy jealous.*

8 *Misplaced Modifiers* [*mm*]

From a writer's point of view, the main problem with modifying words, phrases, and clauses is how to make it clear what they modify. In general, modifiers are associated with the closest word they could possibly belong to. In a sentence like "The big man shot the bear," for instance, we know that it is the man who is big simply because the words *man* and *big* are close to each other. If it were the bear who was big, the sentence would be "The man shot the big bear." Each of us has gone through life correctly positioning modifiers without a second thought, but problems arise when a modifier slips out of place.

8A
Modifying phrases must be positioned so that they are clearly related to the words they modify.

It is not hard to determine where to put the *big* in the sentence about the man and the bear, but modifying phrases can require more care than one-word adjectives. Most often, it is prepositional phrases that are misused. Since these constructions can function as adjectives or adverbs to modify nearly any part of a sentence, if a prepositional phrase turns up where it is not supposed to be, it can cause considerable confusion:

The Alps attract climbers *with sheer stone faces.*

She laughed as John raged *with delight.*

In these examples, misplaced prepositional phrases cause a grammatical double-take. At first glance it looks as though the climbers have stone faces and John rages with delight. The reader can probably guess that it is really the mountains that have stone faces and that "with delight" should go with *laughed,* but it takes a moment to come to this conclusion. Uncertainty can be avoided altogether if the modifying phrases are repositioned:

The Alps *with sheer stone faces* attract climbers.

She laughed *with delight* as John raged.

As the revised sentences show, prepositional phrases tend to refer to the word that comes immediately before them. The usual way to make the phrases clear is to put them right after the word they modify. The only exception to this rule concerns phrases that modify subjects or whole clauses. These prepositional phrases generally are placed at the very beginning of a clause or sentence:

With luck the dam will hold back the flood.

Under an indictment for fraud, he feared his wife would leave him.

Exercise Misplaced Modifiers 1. Find the modifying phrases that are misplaced in the following sentences. Reposition them so that they clearly modify the words they are supposed to.

1. He found the shapely girl he had been searching for in the green dress.
2. The plane taxied to the runway with a roar and a blast of flame.
3. Henry looked forward to conversing with the President for many days.
4. Sheila snapped at the boy who had been dancing with her in a sudden outburst of irritation.
5. The bomb went off as we sat down to eat under the table with a cloud of smoke.

8B

Modifying clauses must be positioned so that they are clearly related to the words they modify.

This rule applies especially to adjective clauses, which, like modifying phrases, sometimes are placed too far from their target words to be clear:

He returned the lawnmower to a neighbor *that was broken.*

Suzy had a kitten in the house *that ate birds.*

It is, of course, the lawnmower that is broken and the kitten that eats birds, but these ideas are obscured by the fact that each sentence has another noun coming between the adjective clause and the noun that it modifies. The sentences suggest that the neighbor is broken and the house eats birds. Repositioning the words to bring the modifier closer to what it modifies eliminates the confusion:

He returned the lawnmower *that was broken* to a neighbor.

In the house, Suzy had a kitten that ate birds.

In correcting the second sentence, it is necessary to put the prepositional phrase "in the house" at the beginning. The alternative, "Suzy had a kitten that ate birds in the house," corrects the problem of the misplaced adjective clause but makes it sound as though the kitten ate its birds indoors. In repositioning modifiers, moving one element in a sentence often makes it necessary to change other elements as well.

Exercise Misplaced Modifiers 2. Find the misplaced adjective clauses in the following sentences. Reposition the clauses so that they clearly modify the words they are supposed to.

1. He gave June a kiss when he finished his military service which lasted several seconds.

2. Fred took the watch to a repairman that was running slow.

3. Norman wears a wig on his head which looks extremely artificial.

4. The lifeguard winked at the girl who had hair on his chest.

5. Carol was given the grand piano by a friend that had already been restored.

8C
Adverbs must be carefully placed so that they modify what they are intended to.

All adverbs are mobile, but some of them—particularly such common ones as *almost, even, hardly, merely, nearly, only,* and *scarcely*—can be placed almost anywhere in a sentence. The sense they make may not be just what was intended, however. Like other modifiers, adverbs associate with the nearest word they could possibly modify, and misplaced adverbs can make sentences say surprising things:

I strained my voice *almost* singing that high note.

I *nearly* drank two quarts during the afternoon.

In the first of these sentences, *almost* modifies *singing.* The sentence says that the writer strained his voice while almost, but not quite, singing a note too high for him. In the second sentence, *nearly* modifies *drank.* The writer was just about to drink two quarts of something but at the last moment decided against it. In all probability, each of these sentences was intended to say something entirely different:

I *almost* strained my voice singing that high note.

I drank *nearly* two quarts during the afternoon.

Once again, moving a modifier affects the meaning of a whole sentence.

The word *only* must be placed with particular care. *Only* shares qualities with other common adverbs, but it is also frequently used as an adjective. Each time an *only* is moved to modify a different word, there is change in meaning. Consider the following sentence:

I am *only* going to weed the lettuce.

The *only* can be placed in several positions, and in this sentence each placement will have a different impact upon the meaning. Leave the word where it is now or put it after *going,* and the sentence means that my only purpose in going is to weed lettuce. Placed after *to weed* or at the very end of the sentence, the *only* indicates that I plan to let the other vegetables look after themselves while I weed only the lettuce. And there are two other possibilities by which *only* would become an adjective. Before or after *I, only* would make the sentence mean that no one else is going to weed the lettuce. Placed after *the, only* would show that there is just one lettuce plant in the patch. A writer who wishes to express any of these exact shades of meaning has to treat his *only* with care.

Exercise Misplaced Modifiers 3. In the following sentences, consider how many different positions the italicized modifier could occupy. Be prepared to discuss the changes in meaning that would result from each repositioning.

1. The newly-elected mayor spoke here *just* last Thursday.

2. *Only* Mr. Horn knows how to satisfy my special requirements.

3. *Scarcely* anyone was around to see her escape from the wolf pit.

4. *Only* her hairdresser knows whether she dyes her hair.

5. I *merely* wanted to know what plans she had for winning the election.

8D
Squinting modifiers should be avoided.

The problem known as squinting modifiers arises when an adverbial element is placed between two verbs or verbal phrases. In these cases, there is no way to tell which verb the adverbial element is supposed to modify:

The horse he was brushing *conscientiously* bit him.

The fish Dad caught *joyously* expired on the deck.

The adverbs in these sentences could modify either *brushing* or *bit* in the first example, or *caught* or *expired* in the second. The solution to such situations is to move the troublesome adverb in the direction of the verb it is intended to modify:

The horse he was *conscientiously* brushing bit him.

The fish Dad *joyously* caught expired on the deck.

Exercise Misplaced Modifiers 4. Correct the following sentences by repositioning the squinting modifiers. Be prepared to explain why your corrections improve the sentences.

1. The problem he was explaining clearly baffled the others.

2. Suffering a serious illness often can change one's personality.

3. The senator stated after his election he would reconsider the promises he had made.

4. A boa constrictor she was stroking affectionately swallowed her.

5. The car she had maintained lovingly refused to start.

8E
Awkwardly placed modifying elements should be avoided.

Modifying words, phrases, and clauses can pointlessly interrupt other constructions. Such awkward interruptions commonly result when an adverbial modifier comes between subject and verb, separates a verb from its object, or pops up in the middle of a verbal phrase:

Glenda, *with a kleenex in each hand*, treated the runny noses.

We reached, *after a hot, dusty hike*, the falls.

In France she has been *on more than one occasion* honored.

Quincy attempted to *without damaging the eggs* raid the bird's nest.

It is better to stick to a more natural word order:

With a kleenex in each hand, Glenda treated the runny noses.

We reached the falls *after a hot, dusty hike*.

In France she has been honored *on more than one occasion*.

Quincy attempted to raid the bird's nest *without damaging the eggs*.

Exercise Misplaced Modifiers 5. Find the awkwardly placed modifiers in the following sentences, and move them to a more natural position.

1. He held, with fervor and devotion, her hand.

2. I wish to without seeming rude or pushy ask what he is doing here.

3. No one has, at least as far as I know, forgotten you.

4. Tony, following a long interior debate, decided to immediately respond to his friend's letter.

5. She was, wanting the property very much, angered when he declined her offers.

Exercise Misplaced Modifiers 6. Revise the following sentences to eliminate any problems caused by misplaced or awkward modifiers.

1. The judge said after lunch the prisoner would have to serve a ten-year term in the penitentiary.

2. John frightened his little sister who was a brawny brute.

3. Our new gum will delight people with the flavor of wild cherries.

4. I was so hungry I nearly ate the whole steak.

5. Sally is forbidden to no matter how much she wants to date Paul.

6. She faced the crowd which by now was screaming calmly.

7. I got a clock from the discount store that was a real bargain.

8. Charles struck with all his considerable might the constable.

9. The puppy she was feeding tenderly regurgitated the food.

10. We are invited to a meeting in that office by the chancellor.

Exercise Misplaced Modifiers 7. Each of the following sentences is followed by a modifying word, phrase, or clause. Rewrite each sentence, and place the modifier in the position you think it works best. Sometimes more than one solution is possible.

1. The Botanical Gardens were the place to go to see the newest roses. *Only.*

2. My sister studies office management with Professor Skyler. *Who is preparing for a business career.*

3. As long as she returned promptly, she was allowed to use the car. *By eleven.*

4. The shoes she preferred had been sold that morning. *Unfortunately.*

5. He dropped the suit off at the cleaner's. *That was dirty.*

6. He signed each form gladly after a quick trip to the Xerox machine. *In triplicate.*

7. I think the paint was dry before the sun set. *Scarcely.*

8. We had to treat all the rooms with air-freshener. *Which smelled bad.*

9. The ivy cascaded over a rugged boulder. *In the garden.*

10. Her teeth were as white as the snow on the mountains. *Which sparkled with good health.*

Misplaced Modifier Reference Chart

General Rule:
Modifiers must be clearly related to the words they modify.

Trouble Spots:

8A
Modifying phrases must be positioned so that they are clearly related to the words they modify.

Not, *He was searching for a date with desperate intensity,* but *He was searching with desperate intensity for a date.*

8B
Modifying clauses must be positioned so that they are clearly related to the words they modify.

Not, *Louise bought a turntable from her neighbor that squeaked,* but *Louise bought a turntable that squeaked from her neighbor.*

8C
Adverbs must be carefully placed so that they modify what they are intended to.

Not, *He nearly coughed until he choked,* but *He coughed until he nearly choked.*

8D
Squinting modifiers are to be avoided.

Not, *The table he was shaking gently toppled over,* but *The table he was gently shaking toppled over,* or *The table he was shaking toppled over gently.*

8E
Awkwardly placed modifying elements should be avoided.

Not, *Mona read, with grave concentration, the book,* but *Mona read the book with grave concentration.*

9

Dangling Modifiers [dm]

Dangling modifiers are verbal phrases or shortened clauses, often at the beginning of a sentence, that either have nothing to modify or that modify the wrong word in the clauses to which they are attached. Once you become sensitive to the problem of dangling modifiers, it is hard to overlook the unintended and sometimes illogical meanings they create.

9A
Avoid dangling participial modifiers.

It is very common for a sentence to begin with a participial phrase that modifies the subject of the main clause, but problems arise if the subject is a word to which the participial cannot logically apply:

> *Flattened by the impact,* Jane surveyed her wrecked bike.

> *Running down the street,* my nose felt frozen.

In these sentences, the connection between the introductory participials and the subject of the clauses make it seem that *Jane* was flattened and the writer's *nose* was running down the street.

Most dangling modifiers can be corrected by (1) rewriting the modifier as a clause with a subject of its own, or (2) rewriting the main clause so that its subject is what the writer meant to modify. In the sentence about Jane, the first solution works best:

> Jane surveyed her wrecked bike, *which was flattened by the impact.*

The second sentence presents a more complicated problem. The true subject of the participle (*I*) is not expressed at all. To fix the dangling modifier here, *I* must be added to the sentence. Change the main clause so that *I* is the subject:

Running down the street, I felt as though my nose were frozen.

Participial elements at the ends of clauses can also dangle when there is nothing in the clause for them to modify:

A track suit must be worn *running in the stadium.*

Dangling results as well when another noun comes between the participial and the word it is supposed to modify:

The apple was sitting on the dish *half-eaten by the little boy.*

Correcting these situations is just like correcting introductory dangling participles. The participial phrase can be made into a clause with its own subject:

You must wear a track suit *when you are running in the stadium.*

Or the main clause can be changed so that the participial clearly relates to the proper word:

The dish held the apple *half-eaten by the little boy.*

Exercise Dangling Modifiers 1. Find and correct the dangling participial modifiers in the following sentences:

1. Exhausted by the climb to the top, the picnic was entirely forgotten.
2. His father hit the boy angered by his defiant disobedience.
3. Sniffing delicately, the man was inspected by the beagle.
4. The cheese was gradually eaten by my sister, getting riper every day.
5. Kicking and scratching, Miss Pink disciplined the wayward girl.

9B
Avoid dangling gerunds in prepositional phrases.

Gerunds usually cannot dangle, since they do not modify anything, but a special situation develops when a gerund is used as the object of a prepositional phrase. In this case, the whole phrase functions like a participial, and the gerund demands an actor for the action it expresses. If no suitable actor is available, odd sentences can result:

After hiking all day, the mountain seemed no nearer.
Before touching her toes, her muscles were already loose.

These sentences seem to say that the mountain hiked all day and that the woman's muscles touched her toes. Once again, the solution is to introduce a proper actor into the sentences. Either change the modifying phrase into a clause or revise the main clause so that its subject will go with the gerund:

After we hiked all day, the mountain seemed no nearer.

Before touching her toes, she felt her muscles were already loose.

Like participles, gerunds can also dangle at the ends of sentences:

The beans seemed quite tender *before starting to season them*.

The best revision is to make the true actor (*we*) obvious:

The beans seemed quite tender *before we started to season them*.

Exercise Dangling Modifiers 2. Locate and correct the dangling gerunds in the following sentences:

1. After being stuffed, the director was rather proud of the lion.
2. Before getting pickled, we boiled the eggs in their shells.
3. The car was still a mess after washing and waxing.
4. In flying to and from the nest, he discovered the bird covered a lot of ground.
5. While growing five feet a year, Gary thought the tree was unusual.

9C
Avoid dangling infinitive modifiers.

Used as modifiers, infinitives and infinitive phrases demand actors. If no appropriate actor is present, the results can be just as disastrous as in the cases of participles and gerunds:

To be well stewed, you must do it gradually.

To avoid crashing on takeoff, the flaps must be adjusted properly.

The structures of these sentences suggest that it is the person being addressed who wants to be well stewed, and that the flaps are in danger of crashing. Revision would turn the infinitive phrases into clauses or would rewrite the main clauses so that the subjects work logically with the infinitives:

To be well stewed, the prunes must be simmered gradually.

If the plane is not to crash on takeoff, the flaps must be adjusted properly.

Exercise Dangling Modifiers 3. Find and correct the dangling infinitives in the following sentences.

1. To check the oil, a dipstick is essential.
2. At least two filing cabinets are needed to restore order here.
3. To really gush, you have to take the cap entirely off the hydrant.
4. To excel at anything, practice is the first requirement.
5. A steady hand is needed to paint landscapes.

9D
Avoid dangling abbreviated clauses.

In abbreviated or elliptical clauses, the subject or both the subject and the verb are omitted and left to be understood by the reader. Such constructions dangle if their understood subject is not the same as the subject of the main clause. As with other danglers, dangling abbreviated clauses can make sentences say things they are not intended to:

> *When thrown,* the dog will retrieve the ball.

> *While hibernating,* the rangers could not find the bear.

Since abbreviated clauses must share the subjects of their main clauses, these sentences imply that the *dog* must be thrown if it is to retrieve, and that the *rangers* were hibernating. One way to correct dangling abbreviated clauses is to expand the dangler back into a full clause. Another method is to change the subject of the main clause so that it will fit the abbreviated clause as well:

> *When the ball is thrown,* the dog will retrieve it.

> *While hibernating,* the bear was completely hidden from the rangers.

Exercise Dangling Modifiers 4. Find and correct the dangling abbreviated clauses in the following sentences.

1. If spotted, they promised to report the rare orchid.
2. Though perking actively, the men found the diner's coffee weak.
3. The vet, because vicious, could not handle the ocelot.
4. Her toothbrush snapped while scrambling to get ready for the dance.
5. When full of gas, he found the car rode uncomfortably.

Exercise Dangling Modifiers 5. Find and correct the dangling modifiers in the following sentences. Be prepared to classify them as dangling participles, gerunds, infinitives, or abbreviated clauses.

1. Ground down by the advancing waves, he saw that the shore had crumbled by inspecting the beach.
2. In throwing the lifeline, the boat came too near, and John was cut by the propeller drifting in the water.
3. To be sure of passing, the school must be investigated with care before deciding where to go.
4. When greased from top to bottom, the boys had trouble catching the pig though little and not very fast.
5. Rusted and stiff with caked mud, Bruno could not turn the handle of the faucet.
6. When thoroughly burnt, he removed the ashes, cursing fate.

7. Broken in the pan, the girl kept the eggs intact, though inexperienced.

8. To prevent a stink while boiling, the pot should be kept covered.

9. Through popping the clutch in starting out, the car had stripped its gears.

10. Crawling rapidly across the floor, though slick with polish, Grandma captured the escaping snake.

Exercise Dangling Modifiers 6. Write eight sentences of your own, two with dangling participles, two with dangling gerunds, two with dangling infinitives, and two with dangling abbreviated clauses. Try to make them humorous.

When you have finished this first step, rewrite all your sentences to clear up the problems you created.

Reference Chart on Dangling Modifiers

General Rule:
Modifying verbal phrases and abbreviated clauses must clearly apply to the word the writer intends.

Trouble Spots:

9A
Avoid dangling participial modifiers.

Not, *Switched on, Marcia read by the light of the lamp,* but *When the lamp was switched on, Marcia read by its light,* or *Switched on, the lamp gave enough light for Marcia's reading.*

9B
Avoid dangling gerunds in prepositional phrases.

Not, *With training, Bob will have a talking myna,* but *Once his myna is trained, Bob will have a talking bird,* or *With training, Bob's myna will learn to talk.*

9C
Avoid dangling infinitive modifiers.

Not, *To be properly served, you must place them on a bed of rice,* but *To serve black beans properly, you must place them on a bed of rice,* or *To be properly served, black beans must be placed on a bed of rice.*

9D
Avoid dangling abbreviated clauses.

Not, *If sniffed out, he promised to report the skunks,* but *If he sniffed them out, he promised to report the skunks,* or *If sniffed out, the skunks were to be reported.*

10

Adjective and Adverb Problems [a/a]

Incorrect use of adjectives and adverbs is a common problem and one that is hard to guard against. Much of the trouble stems from the wide variety of forms adjectives and adverbs can show. Problems of recognition underlie many specific errors with adjectives and adverbs.

Adjectives modify nouns and other substantives, while adverbs modify everything else—verbs, adjectives, other adverbs, and whole clauses. Adverbs should not be used to modify substantives such as nouns and pronouns, and adjectives should not be used to modify the things adverbs do. In theory, this distinction is quite clear, and it is usually clear in practice. Most adverbs are based on adjectival roots, to which are added the suffix *-ly*. To show a change in function, *beautiful* becomes *beautifully; bad* becomes *badly; cautious, cautiously; clever, cleverly,* and so on. It is not easy to make mistakes with such clear-cut pairs as these. No one would talk about a "cleverly thief" or describe someone as "beautiful built."

But there are cases in which these easy distinctions collapse. Some words that end in *-ly* are adjectives, like *friendly* or *homely,* that have no adverb form. Others, such as *deathly* or *only,* can with no change in spelling be either adjectives or adverbs. Moreover, some adverbs have two forms, one with and one without an *-ly*—among these are *close, closely; high, highly;* and *slow, slowly.* Finally, some common adverbs—words like *far, fast, hard, straight, well,* and many others—have no *-ly* ending at all. Most of these words can also be used as adjectives. But in spite of the complexity of adjectives and adverbs, the mistakes people actually make with these modifiers tend to cluster in a few specific areas.

10A
Use only adverbs to modify verbs.

Most people automatically pick adverb forms to modify most verbs. But in several dialects of American English, there is a strong tendency to use certain adjectives—mainly ones that express qualities such as *good, bad, awful, wonderful, smooth,* or *rough*—to replace adverbs of manner or degree. If the following sentences sound acceptable to you, you will need to be on guard against this mistake:

> I always did *good* in French.
>
> Her cousin limped *awful.*
>
> That engine runs *smooth* now.

In formal English, sentences like these require adverbs to modify their verbs:

> I always did *well* in French.
>
> Her cousin limped *awfully.*
>
> That engine runs *smoothly* now.

Exercise Adjectives and Adverbs 1. In the following sentences, find all the adjectives used as verb modifiers, and replace them with adverbs.

1. That cake was baked by my father; he cooks wonderful.
2. He writes good, but he spells careless.
3. Sheila wants to win bad, so she works out regular.
4. The rain came up sudden and fell steady for an hour.
5. His business sense has improved considerable since he started.

10B
Use only adverbs to modify adjectives and other adverbs.

Another function of adverbs is to modify adjectives and other adverbs. This role is sometimes incorrectly taken over by adjectives, and the result is constructions that may *sound* all right in some dialects but that are not permitted in written English. The worst offenders are adjectives like *awful, considerable, some, real,* or *sure,* which are used erroneously to replace intensifiers or adverbs of degree:

> Beatrice was *awful* mad by then.
>
> He was *considerable* annoyed.
>
> The sergeant returned *real* quickly.

The words used in these sentences to modify the modifiers *mad, annoyed,* and *quickly* should all be adverbs, not adjectives:

> Beatrice was *awfully* mad by then.
>
> He was *considerably* annoyed.
>
> The sergeant returned *very* quickly.

Exercise Adjectives and Adverbs 2. Find all adjectives used incorrectly in the following sentences to modify adjectives or adverbs. Replace them with adverbs.

1. She was terrible upset when he failed to report back to her.

2. The Emir was real happy with his gift camel.

3. Lois is sure angry about losing that medal.

4. I admit I know the swamp awful well.

5. His habits were particular disgusting.

10C
Use adjectives, not adverbs, after linking verbs when the target word (the word modified) is the subject.

People who have problems with this rule have often been warned earlier against using adjectives to modify verbs (10A). As a result, they go to extremes and want to put adverbs everywhere. But there is one construction, the linking-verb sentence that contains a predicate adjective, in which it is not only proper but necessary to use an adjective after the verb. In a sentence such as "I feel bad," *bad* is not a mistake for *badly.* Instead, it is an adjective that works through the linking verb *feel* to modify the subject *I.* An adverb here would be improper.

The most common linking verb is *to be.* Fortunately, this verb is rarely misused. Few people say "He is badly" when they mean "He is bad." But there are other linking verbs that are erroneously followed by adverbs, especially verbs of sense like *feel, look, smell, sound,* and *taste.*

The record sounds *badly* at that volume.

He looks *handsomely* this morning.

Those violets smell very *sweetly.*

In each of these sentences the subject is the target of the italicized modifier. Therefore, a predicate *adjective* is needed:

The record sounds *bad* at that volume.

He looks *handsome* this morning.

Those violets smell very *sweet.*

To determine if the subject is the target word in sentences like these, substitute a form of the verb *to be* for the verb of sense. If the idea is not changed significantly by this substitution, the sentence has a predicate adjective construction. In the first example, you can say "The record *is* bad at that volume" without causing a great change in meaning. This substitution shows that *bad,* not *badly,* is the right choice for the modifier that follows the verb.

Exercise Adjectives and Adverbs 3. Find the adverbs mistakenly used as predicate adjectives to modify subjects in the following sentences, and replace them with adjectival forms.

1. That red wine tastes well with meat dishes.
2. Her voice always sounded shrilly to me.
3. I felt especially badly when the sunburn started to crack.
4. Those eggs smell rottenly and look darkly.
5. Wet feathers smell badly.

10D
Use adverbs, not adjectives, after linking verbs when the target word (the word modified) is the verb itself.

Sometimes modifiers following linking verbs refer not to the subject but to the verbs themselves. In these cases, the modifier must be an adverb, not an adjective. Consider this pair of sentences:

Max looked *weak* at the game.

Max looked *weakly* at the game.

Both of these sentences are correct, but they mean different things. In the first example, Max was seen looking faint and unwell at the game. It was *Max* who was weak. In the second sentence, however, Max squinted and peered at the game because his eyes were giving him trouble. It is Max's *looking* that was weak. Modifiers aimed at subjects must be adjectives; those aimed at verbs must be adverbs.

Exercise Adjectives and Adverbs 4. The adjectives and adverbs in the following sentences are used correctly. Explain the precise difference in meaning between each pair of sentences.

1. a. All hounds smell well.
   b. All hounds smell good.
2. a. After the numbness set in, Jud felt bad.
   b. After the numbness set in, Jud felt badly.
3. a. Having been fed grain, the steer tasted rich.
   b. Having been fed grain, the steer tasted richly.
4. a. Sheila looked childish in her sailor suit.
   b. Sheila looked childishly in her sailor suit.
5. a. The third trumpet sounded weak.
   b. The third trumpet sounded weakly.

10E
Use comparative and superlative forms of adjectives and adverbs correctly.

Most adjectives and adverbs show degrees of intensity by use of positive, comparative, and superlative forms. Care must be used in constructing and employing these forms.

The positive form of an adjective or adverb is the base word all by itself (*long, loosely*). The comparative form (*longer, more loosely*) consists of the base word plus the ending *-er* or the word *more*. This form expresses a greater degree of intensity or makes a comparison between two items:

> My boat is *long,* but his is *longer.*
>
> Judge Hines interprets the law *more loosely* than I do.

The superlative form (*longest, most loosely*) is made by adding the ending *-est* or the word *most* to the base word. It is used to indicate the highest degree in comparisons involving three or more people or things:

> All our boats are *long,* but his is the *longest.*
>
> Of all the judges I have known, Judge Hines interprets the law *most loosely.*

Adjectives and adverbs can be compared negatively too, and these negative comparisons are always made by adding *less* or *least:*

> My boat is *less luxurious* than his.
>
> Of all the officers, Ambrose proceeds *least tactfully.*

Three problems can occur with adjectives and adverbs in comparative and superlative forms. The forms can be misconstructed. They can be based on modifiers that are absolute and so have no comparative or superlative forms. Or they can be used in comparisons involving the wrong number of items.

Misconstructed Comparatives and Superlatives.

Writers sometimes have trouble constructing comparative and superlative modifiers correctly: either they use the endings *-er* and *-est* on modifiers that must be compared with *more* and *most,* or they combine techniques and come up with double comparatives and double superlatives. Most adverbs of any length and all adjectives of three or more syllables are compared by the *more/most* method. It is a mistake in dealing with such words to add the endings *-er* and *-est,* which result in such forms as *beautifuler, beautifulest; surprisinger, surprisingest;* or *quicklier, quickliest.* If you find such forms in your writing, replace the mistaken endings with *more* or *most: more beautiful, most beautiful; more surprising, most surprising; more quickly, most quickly.*

Be equally careful to avoid double forms that combine methods of comparison; it is improper to use such combinations as *more longer, most bluest,* or *more nearer.* Mistakes like these can be corrected by dropping either the ending or the comparative word, whichever is appropriate.

Absolute Modifiers.

Another kind of error results from attempts to compare absolute modifiers—words like *unique, dead, empty,* or *whole.* These words leave no room for degrees of intensity. A person or a substance is either unique, dead, empty, or whole, or it is not; there is no middle ground. In dealing with all–or–nothing qualities, it is logically impossible to make comparisons. Forms such as *most unique, deader,* or *emptiest* are self-contradictory.

Number of Items Compared.   Use the comparative form of modifiers in comparisons involving two objects. Reserve the superlative form for comparisons among three or more objects. In the sentences "He is the *best* of the two boys," and "He is the *better* of the three," comparative and superlative forms are used incorrectly. The sentences should read, "He is the *better* of the two boys," and "He is the *best* of the three."

Exercise Adjectives and Adverbs 5. Find and correct all misused comparative and superlative forms of adjectives and adverbs in the following sentences.

1. Urquart is the most sincerest history teacher I have ever met.
2. His yacht is by far the longer of the six in the harbor.
3. Each act of the play was more unique than the last.
4. The land on that side of the river is fertiler than this field; in fact, it is the most rich soil in the county.
5. Of his emotions at that time, embarrassment was the more apparenter.

Exercise Adjectives and Adverbs 6. Correct all adjective and adverb mistakes in the following sentences. Be prepared to explain your corrections.

1. Whenever she felt badly, Tina became awful irritable.
2. I was real sorry to hear that Michael did so bad.
3. Joan felt under the ledge smoothly; she captured the biggest snake but missed the more little one.
4. My most greatest triumph was scoring good on the verbal test.
5. Patty sure regretted sounding badly in the fight song.
6. The stew tasted badly because it was so terrible salty.
7. Peonies are sure real pretty flowers for a border.
8. Willard acted natural when I saw him, but he was some put out right after the meeting.
9. Connie talks quiet, but she comes straightly to the point.
10. She has always been the prettiest of the Harris twins, just as Bob is the handsomer of the Jones triplets.

Exercise Adjectives and Adverbs 7. Be creative. Write ten original sentences, using each of the adjective/adverb pairs given below correctly. Example: *strong/diligently*

I worked *diligently* to overcome her *strong* objections.

1. more beautiful/immediately.

2. weak/most chauvinistically.

3. silly/barely.

4. plain/unceasingly.

5. good/well.

6. biggest/most quickly.

7. wise/very.

8. less flat/carefully.

9. panicky/hysterically.

10. bad/extremely.

Adjective and Adverb Reference Chart

General Rule:
Adjectives modify nouns and other substantives.
Everything else—verbs, adjectives, adverbs, and whole
clauses—must be modified by adverbs.

Trouble Spots:

10A
Use only adverbs to modify verbs.

Not, *That goal post leans* bad, but *That goal post leans* badly.

10B
Use only adverbs to modify adjectives and other
adverbs.

Not, *His grass turned* real *green* awful *quickly,* but *His grass turned* really *green* awfully *quickly.*

10C
Use adjectives, not adverbs, after linking verbs when
the target word is the subject.

Not, *She looked* beautifully *in her bridal dress,* but *She looked* beautiful *in her bridal dress.*

10D
Use adverbs, not adjectives, after linking verbs when
the target word is the verb itself.

Not, *He looked* angry *in the wallet,* but *He looked* angrily *in the wallet.*

10E
Use comparative and superlative forms of adjectives
and adverbs correctly.

11

Verb Forms [Vb form]

Verbs are the most complicated and demanding parts of speech. To use them correctly and effectively is one of the major challenges that face a writer.

11A
Be sure to use the right tense for your purpose.

Tense indicates when the action expressed by a verb takes place. There are six basic tenses in English, and each of them has both a plain and a progressive form, allowing the time of an action to be indicated with great precision.

PRESENT TENSE (used to show a present or habitual action)

> She *lives* in Italy. She *writes* essays.

PRESENT PROGRESSIVE (used specifically for ongoing actions, but with an implication that the action is temporary)

> She *is living* in Italy. She *is writing* essays.

PAST TENSE (used for an action that took place in the general past)

> She *lived* in Italy. She *wrote* essays.

PAST PROGRESSIVE (used like the past tense, but with a sense that the action was temporary and is now finished)

> She *was living* in Italy. She *was writing* essays.

FUTURE TENSE (used to indicate an action that has not yet happened)

> She *will live* in Italy. She *will write* essays.

FUTURE PROGRESSIVE (used for an ongoing, probably temporary, action belonging to the future)

> She *will be living* in Italy. She *will be writing* essays.

PRESENT PERFECT TENSE (used for a past action that is completed at the present time)

> She *has lived* in Italy. She *has written* essays.

PRESENT PERFECT PROGRESSIVE (used for an ongoing past action extending to—or nearly to—the present. This tense also reports an ongoing past action of most recent date)

> She *has been living* in Italy. She *has been writing* essays.

PAST PERFECT TENSE (used for an action that already had taken place at some definite point in the past)

> She *had lived* in Italy before she went to Spain.
>
> She *had written* essays in high school.

PAST PERFECT PROGRESSIVE (generally used to show that the time of one past action lasted until the beginning of another)

> She *had been living* in Italy before she went to Spain.
>
> She *had been writing* essays when she got an idea for a novel.

FUTURE PERFECT TENSE (used for an action that will be completed at some definite time in the future)

> She *will have lived* in Italy by then.
>
> She *will have written* some essays before the end of the semester.

FUTURE PERFECT PROGRESSIVE (used to show that one future action will extend to the time of another)

> She *will have been living* in Italy a year by this December.
>
> She *will have been writing* essays for months before then.

There are some exceptions to these rules. Two common ones involve specialized uses of the present tense. The present tense is sometimes used in subordinate clauses to express what is really a future action:

> When he *arrives,* we will roll out the red carpet.
>
> By the time I *catch* a cab, it will be snowing.

Verb form mistakes can also result if, in forming the past tense, you try to make regular verbs irregular. The past tense of *drag*, for example, is *dragged*, not *drug*. Other verbs in which this problem occurs are *climb* (past tense *climbed*, not *clumb*), *raise* (past tense *raised*, not *riz* or *ris*), and *use* (which is *used* in the past tense, though some writers tend to keep the same form for all tenses).

Exercise Verb Forms 2. Find and correct all mistaken past tense forms in the following sentences.

1. They catched a cold after they sleeped on the ground on a rainy night.
2. Henry lended me a quarter when he heared my story.
3. Joan leaved the hall before Sengler readed his first poem.
4. Even though we digged deep into his essay, we could never tell what he meaned.
5. The sun setted before the party grinded to a halt.

11C
Do not confuse past tense forms with past participles.

The past tense of a verb is the form used to indicate an action in the general past, as in "The hippo *mangled* its keeper." The past participle, on the other hand, is a form used as a modifier ("the *mangled* keeper"), or with auxiliary verbs to make the perfect tenses or passive voice (the form that indicates its subject is the thing acted upon rather than the actor): "The hippo *has mangled* Max," or "Max *was mangled* by the hippo."

In most verbs, the forms for past tense and past participle are the same. *Mangle* is a good example of a regular verb that works this way, and the irregular verbs listed in section 11B follow suit. These verbs may construct their past tenses in odd ways, but they add no further irregularities in the past participle: the past tense form is used for all past participial functions.

But there are also some irregular verbs that show differences between past tense and past participle. The verb *see* is typical of this class. Its past tense, *saw*, is different from its past participle, *seen*. It is a serious mistake to use *saw* with auxiliaries to make one of the perfect tenses, or to use the past participle *seen* as if it were the simple past:

I have *saw* myself at the bottom of the heap.

They *seen* him before he was halfway there.

In cases where the two forms differ, the past tense is reserved for the simple past, and the past participle is used with auxiliaries to form the passive and the perfect tenses:

I *have seen* myself at the bottom of the heap.

They *saw* him before he was halfway there.

The following is a list of irregular verbs for which the past tense form is different from the past participle. The first word is the base form, the second is the simple past, and the third is the past participle:

arise	arose	arisen
be	was, were	been
bear	bore	borne (withstood or carried)
bear	bore	born (gave birth to)
beat	beat	beaten
become	became	become
begin	began	begun
bite	bit	bitten
blow	blew	blown
break	broke	broken
choose	chose	chosen
come	came	come
do	did	done
draw	drew	drawn
drink	drank	drunk
drive	drove	driven
eat	ate	eaten
fall	fell	fallen
fly	flew	flown
forsake	forsook	forsaken
freeze	froze	frozen
give	gave	given
go	went	gone
grow	grew	grown
hide	hid	hidden
know	knew	known
lie	lay	lain
ride	rode	ridden
ring	rang	rung
rise	rose	risen
run	ran	run
see	saw	seen
shake	shook	shaken
shrink	shrank	shrunk or shrunken
sing	sang	sung
sink	sank	sunk or sunken
speak	spoke	spoken
spring	sprang	sprung
steal	stole	stolen
stride	strode	stridden
swear	swore	sworn
swim	swam	swum
take	took	taken
tear	tore	torn
throw	threw	thrown
wake	waked, woke	waked, woken
wear	wore	worn
write	wrote	written

It is important to remember that in each of these cases the second form is the only one that can be used to express the simple past. The third form—the past participle—is the proper one to use as a modifier or in the passive or in the perfect tenses.

Exercise Verb Forms 3. In the following sentences choose the right form of the verbs in parentheses. Be ready to explain your choices.

1. I have (ate, eaten) a whole pizza and (grew, grown) ill.

2. When I (began, begun) the project, I (bit, bitten) off more than I could chew.

3. I thought I had (beat, beaten) the high cost of clothing before I noticed that the fabric (shrank, shrunk).

4. They (drew, drawn) money from her account and (did, done) her out of it.

5. Sally has (woke, woken) on cold mornings and (arose, arisen) to find the water (froze, frozen) in the basin.

11D
The verbs you use in a sentence must be logically and accurately related in tense.

In sentences that contain more than one verb, mixtures of tenses are often possible and proper:

I often *told* them that I *had gone* to college and *was training* to compete in the Olympics.

I *wonder* what she *has done* that *makes* her feel she *is* unable to face me.

Peter *will be sitting* pretty if it *turns* out that his stocks *continued* to rise while he *was* away.

But illogical and confusing combinations of tenses should be avoided. For example, actions that take place at the same time need to be expressed in the same tense. Sentences that change tense for no reason sound confused and inconsistent:

After we *left* the mountain, we *eat* in the diner in town.

In this sentence, one of the verbs is in the wrong tense, since both actions occurred at approximately the same time:

After we *left* the mountain, we *ate* in the diner in town.

After we *leave* the mountain, we *eat* in the diner in town.

Another kind of illogicality results when tense combinations refuse to add up to a consistent meaning:

Farmers who *had raised* wheat *learn* that they *will be* better off after they *had switched* to corn.

The mix-up here concerns the farmers' current activities. If they have already switched to corn, they should already be better off and should already know about it. If they have not yet switched, there is no reason for the past perfect "had switched." There are many ways to fix this sentence, depending on what the writer really means to say. Notice how the following possibilities all establish different time sequences:

Farmers who *had raised* wheat *learned* that they *were* better off after they *switched* to corn.

Farmers who *have raised* wheat *learn* that they *will be* better off if they *switch* to corn.

Farmers who *have raised* wheat *learn* that they *are* better off after they *switch* to corn.

Do not be afraid to combine tenses to make your meaning clear, but be sure that your tenses add up to a logical sequence.

Exercise Verb Forms 4. Find and correct the unnecessary shifts and illogical combinations of tense in the following sentences.

1. If he gets there, he will know he had unusual ability.
2. The Joneses got up, get in the car, and go to town.
3. He was lucky indeed when he is selected to play Romeo.
4. I had been ready to run if the bull shows any signs that it is considering a charge.
5. When Lisa comes in, the television was on and the shower is running.

11E
Be particularly careful in using verbs that look alike but have different meanings.

A few confusing sets of verbs look alike but are not interchangeable, and choosing the wrong one can destroy an otherwise effective sentence. The most troublesome of these sets are the near-triplets *lie, lay,* and *lie,* three altogether different verbs that often cause uncertainty even among experienced writers. The two *lie*'s are intransitive verbs: they do not take direct objects. One of these verbs—*lie, lay, lain*—is more or less synonomous with *recline* or *rest:*

I often *lie* upon the couch.

When he came in, the body *lay* on the floor.

Judy has *lain* there for hours.

The other *lie* takes the forms of *lie, lied,* and *lied.* This verb means *to speak untruthfully:*

They *lie* about their friends.

Larry *lied* to you.

Historians have *lied* about the Wallachians.

Lay, on the other hand, is a transitive verb meaning to *place* or *put:*

We *lay* the books on the table.

Don *laid* his head on his arms.

I have *laid* your coat across the chair.

If you have trouble with these three verbs, try to remember them in terms of their synonyms.

Other difficult combinations are *sit* and *set,* and *rise* and *raise. Sit, sat, sat* is an intransitive verb used for the act of sitting down, while *set, set, set* usually means *to put down.* This verb takes an object, except when it refers to the sun, hens, concrete, or glue. *Rise* and *raise* work in a similar way. *Rise, rose, risen* are intransitive actions a subject performs on itself, while *raise, raised, raised* are transitive actions performed on an object. Thus the tide, prices, and polite young men *rise,* and audiences or juries *sit;* flags and ransoms are *raised,* and things are *set* down, in motion, or against each other.

Exercise Verb Forms 5. Choose the proper verb from the words in parentheses in the following sentences. Be prepared to explain your choices.

1. I cannot (sit, set) idly by when that scoundrel is (rising, raising) money to take over my business.

2. On the floor (lay, laid) a book of matches, proof that Jastrow had been (sitting, setting) there.

3. After I (rise, raise) in the morning, I like to (sit, set) in the kitchen and read the paper.

4. If she did not (lie, lay), she (lay, laid) the money on the dresser before she went to (lie, lay) down.

5. That hammer has (lain, laid) on the bench for years; I do not even know who (sat, set) it there.

Exercise Verb Forms 6. Choose the right form of the verbs in parentheses in the following sentences. Be ready to defend your choices.

1. I (dealt, dealt) the cards right after he had (set, sat) down and (began, begun) to play.

2. His swing (had been, is) too powerful and the ball (has overshot, overshot) the green.

3. (Rise, Raise) the price; then you will have room to haggle when you (sit, set) down to talk to them.

4. Annie (saw, seen) something was wrong when she noticed the cover was (splitted, split).

5. Walnuts (cost, costed) a lot more last year than pecans (did, done).

6. While the fire was just getting started, Bob (drug, dragged) his own dark-room equipment to safety and (rang, rung) the alarm.

7. Shirley (lay, laid) on the ground under the oak and reflected on the new light (casted, cast) by the latest developments.

8. The balloon (busted, burst) with a pop and sprayed water on the chancellor and the people he had (bringed, brought) with him.

9. His old wound really (hurt, hurted) when the weather was damp and (keeped, kept) him from sleeping.

10. Martha (shaked, shook) the tray to see if the ice cubes were (froze, frozen).

Exercise Verb Forms 7. All of the following sentences are followed by unattached verbs. Rewrite each sentence, substituting an appropriate form of the unattached verb for the one italicized in the original sentence. Example:

Hubie *sprawls* on the couch every evening after work. *Lie.*

Hubie *lies* on the couch every evening after work.

1. The balloon *exploded* one hundred feet in the air. *Burst.*

2. Jennifer *had placed* two speakers in the corners. *Set.*

3. We *have spotted* several Ferraris on the freeway. *See.*

4. Susan *reclined* at the edge of the pool. *Lie.*

5. I *started* to rebuild the sagging shed. *Begin.*

6. Teddy *consumed* every bottle we had. *Drink.*

7. Bill *set* the crosspiece on its supports. *Lay.*

8. Molly *has* always *directed* the chorus. *Lead.*

9. Something in the amplifier *must have blown. Break.*

10. Alice *competed* in the one hundred meter butterfly. *Swim.*

Reference Chart on Verb Forms

General Rule:
The abundance of special forms of verbs makes it necessary that you carefully select the right constructions for your purposes.

Trouble Spots:

11A
Be sure to use the right tense for your purpose.

11B
Be cautious when you form the past tense of irregular verbs.

11C
Do not confuse past tense forms with past participles.

11D
The verbs you use in a sentence must be logically and accurately related in tense.

11E
Be particularly careful in using verbs that look alike but have different meanings.

I (*lie, lay, have lain*) on the floor.

He (*lays, laid, has laid*) his hat on a rock.

Kelly (*sits, sat, has sat*) with the orchestra.

Pam (*set, set, has set*) her radio by the bed.

They (*raise, raised, have raised*) the flag.

We (*rise, rose, have arisen*) early in the summer.

12 *Voice and Mood* [*voice*] [*mood*]

Voice

The voice of a verb shows whether the subject performs the action the verb expresses (active voice) or whether the action is performed *upon* the subject (passive voice). Most verbs are in the active voice, and this is the form we focused on in the last chapter. The table of tenses for the verbs *live* and *write* at the beginning of Chapter 11 shows both verbs in the active voice. Here are corresponding passive forms:

PASSIVE PRESENT TENSE

> The life *is lived.* The essay *is written.*

PASSIVE PRESENT PROGRESSIVE

> The life *is being lived.* The essay *is being written.*

PASSIVE PAST TENSE

> The life *was lived.* The essay *was written.*

PASSIVE PAST PROGRESSIVE

> The life *was being lived.* The essay *was being written.*

PASSIVE FUTURE TENSE

> The life *will be lived.* The essay *will be written.*

PASSIVE PRESENT PERFECT TENSE

The life *has been lived*. The essay *has been written*.

PASSIVE PAST PERFECT TENSE

The life *had been lived*. The essay *had been written*.

PASSIVE FUTURE PERFECT TENSE

The life *will have been lived*. The essay *will have been written*.

All tenses of the passive have some form of the verb *to be* combined with the past participle of the main verb. This construction is a signal that the verb is to be understood in a special sense: it expresses an action done *to* rather than *by* the subject. There are also no progressive forms of the passive future, present perfect, past perfect, and future perfect tenses. It would be possible to construct progressive forms for these tenses, but the results— phrases such as "will have been being lived"—sound awkward and unclear.

Use of the Passive.   The passive voice is a useful tool, but one that is difficult to control. The advantage of passive constructions is that they focus attention on actions and their objects. The passive generally leaves the actor out or gives it only a minor role in the sentence. This characteristic is valuable when a writer wants to emphasize events themselves without giving stress to who or what is responsible for them. For example, "The cake was burned on top," "The car was finally fixed," or "The principle of equality must be upheld" can all be good passives if in the writer's opinion the results are what count and the particular actors are not immediately important.

But while this ability to emphasize actions by down-playing actors makes the passive necessary, it also makes it risky to a writer who wants to communicate effectively. The greatest misuse of the passive occurs when it is used to conceal essential information about the doers of actions. Writers who are unsure of themselves often use passives to hide their own involvement in what they are saying. For example, a student who feels poorly qualified to write about an assigned subject might use passives to make it sound as though no one in particular were responsible for his opinions:

> Gore Vidal *has been said* to be a great contemporary novelist. He *is credited* with a gift for style and characterization. His books *are* widely *read and appreciated*. His *1876*, a historical novel, *has been called* a fine achievement.

These passives are not well used, for they hide the source or sources of the author's points. Are these the opinions of specific critics? Who are the critics, and how typical are their views? Or do the opinions belong to the writer? If so, the writer should make this obvious:

> I think Gore Vidal is one of the best novelists now living. Like many other Vidal fans, I look forward to reading everything he writes. I especially appreciate his gift for style and characterization, which never shows up better than in his historical novel, *1876*.

Exercise Voice and Mood 1. Rewrite the following passages in the active voice. If you wish, you may invent sources for the opinions.

1. Japanese art is highly appreciated for its sophistication and delicacy. The printmakers, painters, and potters of Japan are held in especially high esteem. Their works are marked by purity of line and simplicity of composition. These works are often considered highpoints in the history of world art.

2. An accounting student is put through a real obstacle course on his road to becoming a CPA. He is required to get a degree in accounting from an accredited school. He is expected to pass all the parts of the difficult CPA exam. Then he is forced to work, sometimes for low pay, for two years under the supervision of a CPA before he can himself be certified.

12A
Be especially careful about the construction of sentences containing passives.

Aside from the general vagueness they sometimes cause, passives can lead to serious problems in sentence construction. One of the commonest of these difficulties, sentences that shift from the active to the passive voice, is discussed in detail in Chapter 15. Other problems include awkwardly doubled passives, passives that are later treated as if they were active, and passives that contribute to problems with dangling modifiers.

Doubled Passives. In most cases, sentences should not contain double passive constructions—passive verbs followed by passive infinitives (*to be said, to have been worried*), or passive participles (*being said, having been worried*):

He *was considered to be picked* for the job.

The corn *was eaten having been cooked.*

Neither of these sentences is graceful. Moreover, the first one is quite unclear: it is impossible to tell whether the subject's friends thought he had the job, or whether it was his prospective employers who were doing the considering. Switching at least one verb to the active voice greatly improves each sentence:

His friends *thought* he *had been picked* for the job.

He *was considered* after he *applied* for the job.

We *ate* the corn once it *had been cooked.*

Active Reference to Passives. Awkwardness also occurs in sentences that refer to passive constructions as if they expressed positive actions:

That painting needs *to be reframed,* and if you *do so* it will increase in value.

The "do so" in this sentence needs an active verb to refer to:

You *should reframe* that painting; if you *do so* it will increase in value.

Passives and Dangling Modifiers.   Since passive constructions mini-mize the roles of real actors in sentences, their use can sometimes lead to troubles with dangling modifiers.

> Running up and down the scale with liquid trills, he *was* deeply *moved* by the bird's song.
>
> Gleaming on its stainless hinges, she *was impressed* with the massiveness of the vault door.

The modification problems in these sentences would not occur if the verbs in the main clauses had been active and the true actors clearly indicated:

> Running up and down the scale with liquid trills, the bird's song *moved* him deeply.
>
> Gleaming on its stainless hinges, the vault door *impressed* her with its massive-ness.

Exercise Voice and Mood 2. Correct any errors caused by misused passive constructions in the following sentences.

1. Those brakes badly need to be adjusted, and you should do so without delay.
2. At one time warts were thought to be caused by toads.
3. Her charge was believed to have been uttered in good faith.
4. Yelling and screaming, the mild parson was distressed by the outpourings of the mob.
5. Yardbird was seen to have been overtaken by Determined in the backstretch.

Mood

In addition to *tense,* by which the time of an action can be specified, and *voice,* which tells us whether the action is active or passive, verbs also signal *mood,* or the particular sense in which an action should be understood. There are three moods in English: the indicative, the imperative, and the subjunctive. Of these three, the subjunctive is the only one likely to present problems.

Verbs most often take the indicative mood. They *indicate*—that is, they make straightforward statements or ask questions: *"Is* she quiet?" "Os-car *runs* fast." "The tough *get going."* Imperative verbs, by contrast, make commands such as *"Be* quiet!" *"Get going!"* or *"Run!"* These imperative verbs are distinguished by having only a present tense and by being able to take *you-understood* as their subject. Subjunctive verbs work in yet an-other way. In general, they express things that are merely hypothetical, conceivable, or imaginary.

The effect of the subjunctive may be seen in comparing the following sentences:

> It is vital to his business that the invention *works.*
>
> It is vital to his business that the invention *work.*

The first statement is indicative throughout. In the second sentence, the verb *work* is in the subjunctive, and this mood causes a great difference in meaning. In the first sentence the business is doing well because the invention has proven successful; but the outcome in the second sentence is in doubt because the crucial invention has not yet been tried. The subjunctive *work* in this second sentence tells readers that the invention may or may not turn out well, and the success of the business still hangs in the balance. The first example, as is typical in indicative sentences, states what *is*. Through its use of the subjunctive, the second states what *may* be.

The Construction of Subjunctive Verbs. The most frequent verb in the subjunctive mood is *to be*, and this verb also has the widest range of special subjunctive forms. In the present tense, whenever the indicative form of the verb is *am, is,* or *are*, the corresponding subjunctive form is *be:*

> They requested that I *be* there.
>
> Whatever *be* the case, we will carry on as planned.

Subjunctive constructions are much more common in the past tense. Here, the indicative forms *was* and *were* are replaced by the subjunctive *were*, for all persons and numbers:

> If I *were* President, I would lower taxes.
>
> The deal might go through if she *were* more optimistic.
>
> I wish they *were* here right now.

But *to be* is exceptional. Other English verbs mark the subjunctive only by dropping the *-s* in the present, third-person singular. All other forms remain the same as in the indicative. Only when the subject is a *he, she,* or *it* is the subjunctive mood specially constructed:

> I demand that he *resign.*
>
> It is essential that she *attend* the meeting.
>
> She was worried lest the bill *pass.*

A final subjunctive construction is the split subjunctive, which uses an auxiliary *may, should,* or *had* before the subject to signal a subjunctive situation. This construction is rare in speech and is increasingly uncommon in writing:

> *Had* I only *known,* I might have reacted differently.
>
> *Should* they arrive *later,* housing them may be difficult.
>
> *May* your troubles all *be* little ones.

12B
In formal writing, use the subjunctive mood for suppositions, improbabilities, doubts, wishes, and conditions contrary to fact. Use the subjunctive also in *that* clauses expressing necessity, recommendations, demands, or formal motions.

The subjunctive is a feature of English that is in a state of change. It is therefore impossible to be entirely definite on how and when it must be used. We tend more and more to use auxiliary verbs to replace the subjunctive. In speech, the subjunctive is often ignored altogether.

In general, however, the subjunctive should still be used in clauses pertaining to

Contrary-to-Fact Situations

If I *were* sick [and I am not], I would say so.

He looked as if he *were* about to explode [but he was not].

Suppositions

Assuming she *were* disinherited [who knows otherwise?], who would get the money?

Just pretend he *were* your brother [even though he isn't].

Doubtful or Unlikely Cases

We would have a chance if the team *were* to win five in a row [though it is unlikely they will].

If I *were* chosen [though I probably won't be], I would do my best.

All these examples feature the form *were* combined with a singular subject. This combination dominates general uses of the subjunctive today, as the other possibilities sound increasingly old-fashioned:

If I *be* wrong, on my head *be* it.

If he *resist,* use force.

Most writers avoid such subjunctives. Instead, they either use auxiliaries to make their meaning plain, or they use another form of the verb:

If I *am* wrong, *let* it be on my head.

If he *resists* [or *does resist*], use force.

The Subjunctive in that *Clauses.*   The subjunctive is still used in noun *that* clauses involving necessity, wishes, demands, or formal motions.

It is necessary that he *be* reminded of his position.

I demand that she *relinquish* all claims to my property.

107

He moved that the association *seek* another meeting place.

Etta desired that the matter *be* settled once and for all.

Exercise Voice and Mood 3. Pick the right form of the verbs in parentheses in the following sentences. Be prepared to explain your choices.

1. If that dresser (was, were) as old as it looks, it would be worth a lot of money.
2. I recommend that she (be, is) inducted into our roster of merit.
3. Just suppose that John (was, were) the man you are looking for.
4. The rules require that the former president (step, steps) down.
5. If I (was, were) likely to object, he would hardly want to sponsor the measure.

Exercise Voice and Mood 4. Find all the verbs in the following sentences. Be prepared to state whether each of them is active or passive and identify the mood (indicative, imperative, or subjunctive) it is in. Do not forget that every clause will have at least one verb.

1. "Think!" he said. "Pull yourself together."
2. I was annoyed to find that he was trying to get my job.
3. Should she substantiate your story, you will be released.
4. "Run!" I shouted, and we were swept up in the general scramble.
5. If he were here, he would be required to attend, just as you are.
6. It has been moved and seconded that we recess for lunch.
7. The superintendent asked that the visit be delayed until tomorrow.
8. I have been told that he would come if he were able.
9. Just think what an outcry there would be if the statue were removed.
10. Nijinsky danced that role as if he were divinely inspired.

Exercise Voice and Mood 5. Rewrite the following sentences to eliminate any poor choices of voice or mood in the verbs.

1. If I was you, I would have told him about it long ago.
2. Nelson needs to be trained; if you do so, he will be much easier to live with.
3. Tearing the log to pieces, Mary was startled by the big bear.
4. I respectfully request that the performance is rescheduled.
5. He is carrying on as if he was an unquestioned authority.
6. Ivan was thought to have been passed over for promotion.
7. If he was bursar, the college finances would be even worse off.
8. Wrapped in old electrical tape, Fred was shocked by the lamp cord.

9. Helen was greatly disappointed having been left out.

10. Supposing I was rich, would you still refuse me?

Reference Chart on Voice and Mood

General Rule:
English verbs show distinctions in voice (active and passive) and mood *(indicative, imperative, and subjunctive).*

Trouble Spots:

12A
Be especially careful about the construction of sentences containing passives.

Avoid double passives, "She *was thought to be matured* by the experience"; passives referred to as if they were active, "Parts of Mexico still wait *to be discovered;* you should *do so"*; and passives that lead to dangling modifiers, "Refreshing and tasty, Gail *was cheered* by the meal."

12B
In formal writing, use the subjunctive mood for suppositions, improbabilities, doubts, wishes, and conditions contrary to fact. Use the subjunctive also in *that* clauses expressing necessity, recommendations, demands, or formal motions.

I wish she *were* my sister.

Imagine what would happen if she *were* prettier.

Had Robert *been* there, things would be different now.

I move that the committee *be* commended and dismissed.

The agency recommends that the director *retire.*

13 *Case* [*case*]

The case of a noun or pronoun is determined by how it is used in its clause. As there are only three cases in English—*nominative, objective,* and *possessive*—each serves several different functions. If the noun or pronoun is a subject of a clause, a predicate noun, or is an appositive of one of these, it is in the *nominative* case. If it is a direct or indirect object, an object of a preposition, the subject of an infinitive, or an appositive of any of these, it is in the *objective* case. Finally, if it serves to show possession or is the subject of a gerund, or if it renames a word in one of these grammatical roles, it is in the *possessive* case.

The identification of case, then, is determined by the function of a noun or pronoun in its clause. A writer must make sure nouns and pronouns are in the right form—nominative, objective, or possessive—for their function. This task is enormously simplified by the fact that all nouns and most pronouns are the same in form whether they are nominative or objective (the two most common cases). With these nouns and pronouns, all you have to worry about is getting the possessive right. It is only a small number of personal and relative pronouns that have different forms for the three cases, making the choice of case forms more difficult.

The following chart lists the case forms for these highly inflected pronouns:

Nominative	Objective	Possessive
I	me	my, mine
you	you	your, yours
he	him	his
she	her	her, hers
it	it	its
we	us	our, ours
they	them	their, theirs
who	whom	whose
whoever	whomever	whosever

13A
Use possessive forms to show ownership and for the subjects of gerunds.

Special possessive forms of all nouns and pronouns are available to writers and must be used in the appropriate situations. Troubles in this area fall into two categories: recognizing possessive situations, and constructing possessive forms. The construction of possessives is a complex topic and is explained in Chapter 34, so it is only possessive situations that will be discussed here. The possessive is used to indicate ownership and for the subjects of gerunds.

Except in the case of the pronouns listed above, the sign of the possessive is the apostrophe ('), a mark that makes possessives easy to spot. Most possessive nouns and pronouns are used to show ownership:

Omar's rifle	*whose* raincoat	the *girls'* art
today's work	*anyone's* opinion	*its* reaction

The possessives here work like adjectives, but instead of "Which?" "What kind?" or "How many?" they answer the question "Of whom or what?" about the nouns they modify. "The rifle of whom?" "Omar." "The work of what?" "Today." The "Of whom or what?" formula leads to a good way to test possessives. Any possessive noun or pronoun can be changed into an *of* phrase:

the raincoat *of whom*	the art *of the girls*
the opinion *of anyone*	the reaction *of it*

Any word in a sentence that answers the question "Of whom or what?" and can be changed into an *of* phrase is possessive. It needs to be in the possessive form to show its difference from other nouns and pronouns.

Possessives as Subjects of Gerunds.   The other role of the possessive case is to mark the subjects of gerunds:

John's complaining is getting on my nerves.

Their scoring fell off at the end of the season.

Why do you object to the *army's* recruiting?

Remember, though, that the possessive goes with *gerunds*. The same kind of -*ing* verb forms can also serve as participial modifiers in constructions where possessives are not appropriate. Often the choice of form depends on the writer's meaning. Consider this pair of sentences:

I got enough of *his* going to Frankfort.

I got enough of *him* going to Frankfort.

In the first sentence, *going* is the direct object, and the speaker grew weary of the other person's *traveling* to Frankfort. In the second example, *him* is the direct object, and the speaker became upset with the other *person* during a trip to Frankfort.

| **13B**
Use the nominative forms for pronouns that are subjects or predicate nouns.

With few exceptions, this rule is easy to observe with regard to subjects. A sentence such as *"Him* is my worst enemy" sounds wrong to just about everyone. But the situation is different with predicate nouns: many people see nothing wrong with "My worst enemy is *him,"* though this sentence is just as faulty as the first. Predicate nouns are nouns or pronouns joined to the subject of a sentence or clause by a linking verb:

> Fred is the chief *internist.*
>
> Mona became *one* of their top models.
>
> He seems a nice enough *fellow.*

In sentences like these, the linking verbs establish a kind of identity between subject and predicate noun since both refer to the same person or thing. Because this is so, both should also be in the same case.

Inflected Pronouns as Predicate Nouns.   When a noun or unin-flected pronoun is in the predicate-noun position, there is no problem, for neither of these parts of speech has special forms for nominative and objective functions. Trouble arises when one of the inflected pronouns is put in the predicate noun slot. Many writers erroneously use the objective form in such circumstances:

> It is *me.*
>
> My greatest concern is *them.*
>
> The stranger might have been *her.*

It should be obvious that *me, them,* and *her* are the wrong choices for these sentences. In each example, a predicate noun is being linked to a subject, and the nominative case should be used:

> It is *I.*
>
> My greatest concern is *they.*
>
> The stranger might have been *she.*

If these corrected sentences sound stuffy and over-polite, it is probably a sign that using nominative pronouns in the predicate noun position will not come easily to you. Be on guard for such sentences. Sometimes it is useful to turn around sentences with pronoun predicate nominatives so that the pronoun becomes the subject. The second two example sentences, for instance, sound better and present fewer problems if they are restructured:

They are my greatest concern.

She might have been the stranger.

Exercise Case 1.   Correct the following sentences, making sure the pronouns are in the right case. If the corrected sentences seem strained or awkward to you, rewrite them so that they sound more natural.

1. I told them it was me who had said the new queen should be her.
2. When John made his proposal, the only objectors were them and their opinionated friends.
3. After the excitement died down, I think the first person to realize what happened was him.
4. His aunt later admitted it could have been her who screamed.
5. I have the impression that the man I saw in the back of the room was him.

Exercise Case 2. Write five sentences of your own in which inflected pronouns follow linking verbs in the predicate noun position. Then recast the sentences so that the inflected pronoun becomes the subject.

13C
Use the objective form for pronouns that are direct or indirect objects, objects of prepositions, or subjects of infinitives.

A pronoun should *not* be in the objective case unless it performs one of these functions. Here are examples of objective pronouns used correctly:

DIRECT OBJECTS

Tom saw *them* in the distance. He called *me* a snoop.

INDIRECT OBJECTS

Asparagus gives *her* indigestion. Dad bought *us* tickets.

OBJECTS OF PREPOSITIONS

To *her* it seems different. The man with *us* was Eric.

SUBJECTS OF INFINITIVES

I want *him* to like her. Everyone expected *them* to fold.

Exercise Case 3. Write twelve original sentences illustrating the use of the objective case pronouns *me*, *him*, *her*, *us*, and *them*. There should be three sentences each in which the objective pronoun is a direct object, an indirect object, the object of a preposition, and the subject of an infinitive. (If you need a review, direct and indirect objects are discussed in Chapter 1; prepositional and infinitive phrases are treated in Chapter 3.)

13D
When a pronoun is in apposition to a noun in the same clause, it is in the same case as the noun.

Pronouns refer to other nouns and pronouns, and sometimes they are found in the same clause as the words they rename or identify. Under these circumstances, the pronoun must be in the same case as the word to which it applies:

> *We* Indians reject the twentieth century. (*Indians* is the subject, so *we* must be in the nominative case)

> The twentieth century rejects *us* Indians. (This time *Indians* is the direct object; *us* must be objective)

> Two individuals, *you* and *I*, can make a lot of difference. (*You* and *I* rename *individuals;* each must be nominative)

> They are out to wreck particular people, *you* and *me* for a start. (Here the reference is to the direct object, *people; you* and *me* must be objective)

Exercise Case 4. Correct the following sentences, making sure the pronouns are in the right case. Be prepared to explain your corrections.

1. Us firemen are planning to strike next week.

2. The two nominees, both him and her, will answer any questions.

3. I think you are prejudiced against we girls.

4. The top student, me myself, was chosen to confront the professor.

5. Several of we secretaries organized a scuba club.

13E
When a pronoun is joined to other words by a conjunction, be especially careful to identify its function before deciding its case.

No one would say *"Him* ate" or *"Me* ate," but many people feel comfortable with *"Me* and *him* ate." The rule, however, is that multiplying a sentence element has no effect on its function and should not affect its form. *"He* ate" and *"I* ate" are sentences with one subject each; *"He* and *I* ate" is simply a sentence with two subjects, and each of them should be in the subjective or nominative form. The situation is the same with regard to pronouns that are part of compound objects. You would never say "Killer bit *I"* or "Mike went with *she."* You should also not use *I* or *she* as part of a multiple object. Use objective forms instead: "Killer bit Fred and *me";* "Mike went with Dan, Farrah, and *her."* A good way to decide which case to use in dealing with multiple elements is to consider them one at a time. "They want to talk to either *he* or *I*" might sound correct, but you would not say "They want to talk to *he*" or "They want to talk to *I*." The original sentence should say "They want to talk to either *him* or *me*."

Exercise Case 5. Correct the following sentences, making sure the pronouns in multiple elements are in the right case. If you are in doubt about the right form, consider the elements one at a time.

1. Bobby and me went over to see him and his wife.
2. Neither the foreman nor I could separate he and the hot wire.
3. Between you and I, him and her have had it with we and they.
4. I wanted to interview he or the Pope.
5. Them and Thunderbirds share the same suspension parts.

13F
When a pronoun stands alone after *as* or *than* in a comparison, use the nominative form if it is the subject of an understood verb; if it is the object, or the object of a preposition, use the objective form.

Most sentences to which this rule applies fit a standard pattern. They are sentences such as "Roger is smarter than I," in which the final pronoun is really part of an unexpressed clause: "Roger is smarter than I [am]." *As* is another comparison word that can be used in such constructions. For example, "No one there was as bright as she" really means "No one there was as bright as she [was]." In these sentences, *I* and *she* are the correct pronoun forms because both are subjects, even if the verbs that go with them are omitted. It would be wrong to use *me* and *her* in these places, because these pronouns would give subjects an objective form. Consider how incorrect it sounds to say "Roger is smarter than *me* am" or "No one there was as bright as *her* was."

Most often, nominative pronouns are used in comparisons after *as* or *than*. But there are some times when this is not so. Consider these sentences. Each is correct, but each also has a different meaning:

Godfrey thinks more of football than *I*.

Godfrey thinks more of football than *me*.

The first sentence means that Godfrey thinks more of football than I *do*. But in the second, Godfrey thinks of two things: he thinks more of football than he thinks of me. In this sentence, *me* is the right choice since it is not the subject of an implied clause. Rather, if the implied clause is written out, it is an object of the preposition *of*: "Godfrey thinks more of football than he thinks of me."

Exercise Case 6. Examine the pronouns used in comparison in the following sentences. Correct the ones that are used incorrectly, and be prepared to explain why the others can stand unchanged.

1. The Rams are much stronger than them.

2. You always expect more from him than me.

3. You always expect more from him than I.

4. Not even they are as confused as us.

5. Any girl as experienced as she should have known better.

> **13G**
> **In formal usage, the pronouns *who/whom* and *whoever/ whomever* should be treated the same way as other pronouns with special nominative and objective forms. *Who* and *whoever* should be used as subjects or predicate nouns, and *whom* and *whomever* should be used in objective functions.**

Usage in this area is undergoing changes and is not easy to describe with certainty. *Whom* and *whomever* are still always used as objects of prepositions. It is clearly incorrect to write "after who" or "to whoever" as prepositional phrases, for such phrases require objective pronouns. But here the agreement over this rule ends. Many educated speakers and writers use *who* or *whoever* indifferently as either subjects or objects of clauses. They never write *whom* or *whomever* except after an occasional preposition. Others, however, insist that *who/whoever* be used only as subjects or predicate nouns, and that *whom/whomever* be used whenever the function is objective. You can consult your instructor about his or her preferences. But if you are ever writing formally for someone whose preferences you do not know, it is best to follow the rule.

Choosing the Right Form. *Who* and *whoever* are nominative forms; *whom* and *whomever* are objective. Following the rule, then, is merely a question of knowing the case of a given pronoun. Complications occur, however, with these particular pronouns. They can be used to signal questions or to introduce clauses, and in either of these roles they come at the beginning of their clause, regardless of whether they are subjects, predicate nouns, or objects:

> *Who* is your date tonight? (*Who* is a predicate noun linked to *date*.)
>
> *Whoever* bought that tacky poster? (*Whoever* is the subject.)
>
> *Whom* do you mean? (*Whom* is the direct object of *mean*.)
>
> There is the man *whom* they gave the prize. (*Whom* is the indirect object of *gave*.)
>
> She is a coach *who* gets things done. (*Who* is the subject of *gets*.)
>
> He will take *whomever* he wants. (*Whomever* is the direct object of *wants*.)

In such constructions, it is the pronoun's position that makes it hard to decide on the right form. We expect the first noun or pronoun in a clause to be the subject, so we are drawn to the nominative forms *who* and *whoever,* but these pronouns often upset our expectations. In the clause *"who* gets things done," for example, *who is* the subject; but *whomever* in *"whomever* he wants" is a direct object, and *whom* in *"whom* they gave the prize" is an indirect object (it refers to the person *to whom* the direct object, *prize,* was given).

Teach yourself to disregard position in clauses like these, and base your choice of pronoun form on the pronoun's function in its own clause no matter what its position is. Find the verb, and then analyze the relationship of the pronoun to it. If the pronoun is the doer of the verb, it is the subject. If the verb links it to another noun or pronoun, it is a predicate noun. Both these functions call for the nominative forms *who* or *whoever.* Any other relationship will require the objective forms, *whom* or *whomever.*

One point must be especially emphasized before we leave this issue. It is the pronoun's function *in its own clause* that determines its form: the rest of the sentence, if there is more, does not count. Two special situations make this principle difficult to apply. Be on your guard whenever a *who/whoever* clause comes right after a verb or preposition:

I wondered *who had stolen my shorts.* (*Who* is the subject of its own clause, not the object of *wondered.*)

I will give that book to *whoever wants it.* (*Whoever* is the subject of *wants,* not the object of the preposition *to.*)

Exercise Case 7. Correct the following sentences, making sure the pronouns are in the right case. Be prepared to explain your corrections.

1. Who did she want to take over the accounting office?
2. I never stop thinking of whom attended the meeting.
3. Whomever he is, he has a shock coming to him.
4. Stop telling me who I should trust!
5. We will question whomever comes along this road.

Exercise Case 8. Write five sentences of your own in which all four forms, *who, whom, whoever,* and *whomever,* are used correctly. Be able to defend your choice of form on the basis of the pronoun's function in its own clause.

Exercise Case 9. Find and correct all pronoun case errors in the following sentences. Be prepared to explain your work.

1. Johnny and me are ready for some of that hot apple pie.
2. I have never known a couple as happy as them.
3. I think it was him whom I saw in the bushes that night.
4. They told me and her to welcome whomever came in.
5. Just between you and I, who has the best chance of winning?
6. Us Trojans are going to destroy you Pirates.
7. By who is the payment order authorized?

8. Those puppies are eating Martha and I out of house and home.

9. It would take someone brighter than me to pass this test.

10. Surely they will forgive we free spirits for the damage we did.

Exercise Case 10. Rewrite to correct the case errors in the following sentences. Be prepared to explain your work.

1. Jim spoke to only two salesmen, you and I.

2. He was supposed to bring back whoever he could find.

3. Kelly only wishes she was half as rich as them.

4. Give we boys a chance, and we will show you what we can do.

5. They will get the names of whomever comes to the door.

6. Since I was much quicker than him, I won easily.

7. The stars shone softly down on Arthur and I.

8. It was them, I think, who told her that tale.

9. This zoo is no place for a person who I respect and love.

10. Me and her are learning to play three-dimensional chess.

Case Reference Chart

General Rule:
The case of a pronoun is determined by the way it is used in its own clause.

Trouble Spots:

13A
Use possessive forms to show ownership and for the subjects of gerunds.

13B
Use the nominative forms for pronouns that are subjects or predicate nouns.

Not, "It is *me*," or "It seemed to be *her*," but "It is *I*," and "It seemed to be *she*."

13C
Use the objective form for pronouns that are direct or indirect objects, objects of prepositions, or subjects of infinitives.

13D
When a pronoun is in apposition to a noun in the same clause, it is in the same case as the noun.

Not, *"Us* drivers will be there at noon" or "Harry despises *we* choirboys," but *"We* drivers will be there at noon" and "Harry despises *us* choirboys."

13E
When a pronoun is joined to other words by a conjunction, be especially careful to identify its function before deciding its case.

Not, *"Her* and *me* went shopping" or "This must be decided between Sarah and *I,"* but *"She* and *I* went shopping" and "This must be decided between Sarah and *me."*

13F
When a pronoun stands alone after *as* or *than* in a comparison, use the nominative form if it is the subject of an understood verb; if it is the object, or the object of a preposition, use the objective form.

Not, "I am as fast as *her"* or "No one is more enthusiastic than *them,"* but "I am as fast as *she* [is]" and "No one is more enthusiastic than *they* [are]."

13G
In formal usage, the pronouns *who/whom* and *whoever/ whomever* should be treated in the same way as the other pronouns with special nominative and objective forms. *Who* and *whoever* should be used as subjects or predicate nouns, and *whom* and *whomever* should be used in objective functions.

Not, "I do not know *who* I should turn to" or *"Whomever* will straighten this out?" but "I do not know *whom* I should turn to" and *"Whoever* will straighten this out?"

14 *Parallel Construction* [//]

Suppose you went to the store yesterday and bought three things: a box of matches, a bag of pretzels, and a roll of paper towels. Now imagine that you are telling someone about your trip. You could say, "I went shopping and bought a box of matches. I also got a bag of pretzels. And, oh yes, I picked up a roll of paper towels too." But you would talk at such length only if you were thinking and remembering additional items as you spoke. If your purchases were clear in your mind and you knew from the first what you meant to say, you would never devote a whole sentence to each thing you bought. Instead, you would say something similar to this:

I bought a box of matches, a bag of pretzels, and a roll of paper towels.

or, in diagrammatic fashion:

I bought ||| a box of matches,
            a bag of pretzels,
and ||| a roll of paper towels.

This one sentence that does the work of three is an example of *parallel construction,* a combining technique that allows us to save words by letting some parts of a sentence do multiple duty. In the example sentence, the subject *I* and verb *bought* are mentioned only once and then understood to apply to each of the three direct objects. Parallel construction also helps us to organize thoughts and present them in a coherent fashion.

Using Parallel Construction.   Parallel construction can be used to multiply almost any grammatical element. Here are some random examples of such parallel series:

Tanya	‖	wished for success,
	‖	worked to make it happen,
and	‖	enjoyed it to the full. (three predicates)

	‖	Wishing for success,
	‖	working to make it happen,
and	‖	enjoying it to the full are elements of the good life. (three gerund subjects)

I know	‖	that Tayna wished for success,
	‖	that she worked to make it happen,
and	‖	that she enjoyed it to the full. (three noun clauses)

	‖	Tanya wished for success,
	‖	she worked to make it happen,
and	‖	she enjoyed it to the full. (three independent clauses)

Parallel construction helps writers build economical and clearly focused sentences by combining similar elements, but it also demands that the elements combined *be* similar, that writers not mix apples with oranges, or umbrellas with toaster ovens.

14A
Sentence elements joined by coordinating conjunctions must be grammatically similar.

And, but, and *or* are the three conjunctions used most often to join parallel constructions. The words and groups of words they combine in a sentence must be the same kind of things—they must all be nouns, verbs, participial phrases, adjectives, gerunds, adjective clauses, and so on. In the following sentence, the conjunction *and* tries unsuccessfully to connect two nouns and an adjective clause:

He is a man of action, decision, and who is very bright.

He is a man of	‖	action,
	‖	decision,
and	‖	who is very bright.

This sentence illustrates the kind of situation you should avoid. The mismatch can be corrected in several ways, but the easiest method is to choose one of the two competing kinds of elements and make it the basis for the parallel construction. The combination could include all nouns or all adjective clauses:

He is a man of	‖	action,
	‖	decision,
and	‖	intelligence. (all nouns)

He is a man	‖	who acts,
	‖	who is decisive,
and	‖	who is very bright. (all adjective clauses)

Problem Sentences.   Here are other examples that illustrate *faulty* parallel construction:

My dog is ⎜⎜⎜ mean,
　　　　　⎜⎜⎜ with scars on his face,
　　and　 ⎜⎜⎜ angry with the world.　　(an adjective, a prepositional phrase,
　　　　　　　　　　and another adjective with a modifier)

　　　　⎜⎜⎜ To jump,
　　　　⎜⎜⎜ to run,
　or　 ⎜⎜⎜ just swinging can be all the exercise a child needs.　　(two infinitives
　　　　　　linked to a gerund)

The garage was ⎜⎜⎜ yellow
　　　　　　　 ⎜⎜⎜ with double doors,
　　　　　　　 ⎜⎜⎜ a large window,
　　and　　　 ⎜⎜⎜ had cedar shingles on the roof.　　(an adjective, a prepo-
　　　　　　　　　　sitional phrase, a noun, and a predicate)

Each of these sentences can be corrected if the parallel elements are standard-ized:

My dog is ⎜⎜ mean,
　　　　　⎜⎜ scarred,
　　and　 ⎜⎜ angry with the world.　　(all adjectives)

　　　⎜⎜ Jumping,
　　　⎜⎜ running,
　or　⎜⎜ just swinging can be all the exercise a child needs.　　(all gerunds)

The garage had ⎜⎜ yellow paint,
　　　　　　　⎜⎜ double doors,
　　　　　　　⎜⎜ a large window,
　　and　　　 ⎜⎜ cedar shingles.　　(all noun direct objects)

Note that the nature of a sentence element is not changed just because a modifier is attached to it. In the first sentence, for instance, "angry with the world" is parallel with "mean" because *angry* and *mean* are both predi-cate adjectives linked to *dog.* This is so even though *angry* has its own modifier, the prepositional phrase "with the world." Note as well that paral-lel construction is not the only way or always the best way of placing compli-cated material in a sentence. Sometimes other techniques work more success-fully. The last example, in particular, would be improved if it were given a more varied structure such as "Beneath its cedar shingles, the yellow garage had double doors and a large window."

Exercise Parallel Construction 1. Correct errors in parallel construction in the following sentences. Be prepared to explain any changes you make.

1. The story was about how an oddly mixed group of people were shipwrecked, the island they inhabited, and the events leading up to their rescue.

2. I do not know which I enjoy more, to play basketball or fishing.

3. Oven cleaners are messy, hard to use, and they are dangerous.

4. The company is looking for a woman with a good education, outstanding ability, and who will work for peanuts.

5. To be or not being, that is the question.

14B
Sentence elements joined by correlatives must be grammatically similar.

Correlatives are pairs of conjunctions used in teams to link sentence elements. They include the combinations *either . . . or . . . ; neither . . . nor . . . ; both . . . and . . . ;* and *not only . . . but also. . . .* The elements that go into the positions after these conjunctions must be parallel, as is the case with elements linked by ordinary coordinating conjunctions.

But with correlatives, parallelism must be even more precise, because the correlative conjunctions mark the exact boundaries of the elements linked together. Ordinary parallel constructions give writers greater leeway, especially when only two elements are involved. Consider this beginning of a sentence:

I went to the bank and . . .

The sentence could be correctly completed in at least four ways. The *and* could pick up *bank* and introduce another noun, "I went to the *bank* and the *bakery.*" Or it could link "to the bank" with another prepositional phrase, "I went *to the bank* and *to the bakery.*" The other possibilities are two predicates or two whole clauses: "I *went to the bank* and *stopped at the bakery,*" or "*I went to the bank,* and *I stopped by the bakery.*" Now think of a sentence that begins this way:

I went *both* to the bank *and* . . .

In this sentence, the correlative marks the exact beginning of the first parallel element, "to the bank." The only correct way to finish is with another prepositional phrase, "to the bakery." Imagine two gaps in correlative constructions, one between the correlatives and one right after the second one. The elements that go into these gaps must be precisely parallel. Here are some sentences in which parallelism is *faulty*:

Not only *was she courageous* but also *smart.* (a clause and an adjective)

John was either *lying* or *I am going crazy.* (a participle and a clause)

I said neither *that he was guilty* nor *anything else.* (a clause and a pronoun)

To correct these sentences, you must restructure them so that parallelism is observed:

She was not only *courageous* but also *smart.* (two adjectives)

Either *John was lying* or *I am going crazy.* (two clauses)

I said neither *that* nor *anything else.* (two pronouns)

Exercise Parallel Construction 2. Correct errors in parallel construction in the following sentences. Be prepared to explain your work.

1. I am not only hired but also to begin work tomorrow.
2. He is either demented or he is putting us all on.
3. Neither her name nor where she had come from has yet been discovered.
4. I enjoy both woodworking and to cook big dinners for company.
5. I plan either to stop by the bank or the bakery.

14C
Sentence elements compared with *than* or *as* should be grammatically similar.

Comparisons using *than* or *as* are another linking device that demands parallel construction. Consider this example of a grammatically mismatched comparison:

Buying a puppy is less expensive *than* to look after it properly.

In this sentence, *than* links two things, "buying a puppy" and "to look after it properly." The first of these is a gerund phrase and the second an infinitive one, so the parallelism is clearly faulty. The sentence can be corrected in two ways:

Buying a puppy is less expensive than *looking* after it properly.

or

To buy a puppy is less expensive than *to look* after it properly.

As comparisons work in the same way. In the following example, elements compared are not grammatically equal.

That he could write at all was as much of a surprise *as* his subject matter. (a clause compared to a noun)

Corrections:

That he could write at all was as much a surprise as *that he chose Girl Scouting for a subject.* (two clauses)

His writing ability was as surprising as *his subject matter.* (two nouns)

Exercise Parallel Construction 3. Correct errors in parallel construction in the following sentences. Be prepared to explain your work.

1. For some people progress is more important than what goal it achieves.
2. Finding a good apartment is as difficult as to pay the rent.
3. Having a date in the first place meant as much to him as who went with him.
4. That it be a good story is more of a consideration than the author.
5. She would just as soon go rather than to see him make a fool of himself.

14D
Sometimes a word or words must be repeated to make the meaning of a parallel construction clear.

Occasionally a parallel construction is grammatically correct but ends up not saying what it was meant to. Consider this sentence:

My mother shows her love by cooking and serving her family.

The grammar here could hardly be better; the *and* links two gerunds, *cooking* and *serving.* But the mother has an unusual way of demonstrating affection: by cooking her family and serving them up! The writer meant, of course, to say that the mother shows her love *by* her cooking and *by* the way she serves the family. One way to make the sentence express this meaning without completely rewriting it is to repeat the preposition:

My mother shows her love *by* cooking and *by* serving her family.

A similar situation can arise in sentences that contain adjective clauses:

These trainers must work with animals that are often quite savage and hold advanced degrees.

Repeating a key word, *must,* is enough to straighten out the meaning of the sentence:

These trainers *must* work with animals that are often quite savage and *must* hold advanced degrees.

Exercise Parallel Construction 4. By repeating the necessary word or words, correct any of the following sentences in which the meaning is unclear.

1. Jed uses the same knife for skinning and picking his teeth.
2. The cadets escorted all the girls who entered the pageant but kept in the background.
3. We taught our retriever to fetch and open the door.
4. He picked the patrolman who looked kindest but still blushed with uncertainty as he approached.
5. Sonia can now write and read any book.

14E
Sometimes a word or words must be repeated to keep a parallel construction from distorting normal English usage.

This rule is rather like the last one; only this time the issue is style rather than meaning. Here is a sentence in which parallel construction makes the writer say something extremely awkward:

I once could and often have pitched a knuckleball.

Here the *and* connects two auxiliary verb constructions, *once could* and *often have*, but when we rewrite the separate sentences upon which this combination is based, serious trouble results:

I once could pitched a knuckleball.

I often have pitched a knuckleball.

Once could and *often have* are grammatically similar, but they are not similar from the point of view of usage. Each expression demands a different form of the main verb: "once could *pitch*" and "often have *pitched.*" This difference has to be taken into account by repeating the main verb in making a parallel construction:

I once could *pitch* and often have *pitched* a knuckleball.

Usage demands special choices of forms in the following sentences as well:

She was amused, but her friends horrified. (The second verb must be "*were* horrified.")

This office needs an ashtray and wastebasket. (The second element must be "*a* wastebasket.")

I was devoted and fascinated by his unfolding career. ("devoted *to* and fascinated *by*")

Exercise Parallel Construction 5. By repeating or supplying words necessary for ordinary usage, correct any of the following sentences in which parallel construction forces an awkward combination.

1. Odette has great understanding and experience in the problems of underwater salvage.

2. I have and always did love the way she plays.

3. Penny has no aptitude or commitment to teaching.

4. He quickly produced an orange and carrot from his sack.

5. I know they cheat and have for a long time.

Exercise Parallel Construction 6. Correct any errors in parallel construction in the following sentences. Be prepared to explain your work.

1. That man is dishonest, materialistic, and all the uncomplimentary character defects I can think of.

2. He was thankful for the chance to shave and walk his dog.

3. My pictures are neither beautiful nor do they sell well.

4. Mother said she had and always would welcome our advice.

5. Printing is seldom as fast as to write in cursive.

126

6. A student has a choice of cooking his or her own meals, eating in the cafeteria, or a combination of the two.

7. She is quite grown up now: she has a boyfriend who takes her out and wears lipstick and pantyhose.

8. Beth does not like training as much as to win races.

9. I think you are kind, a good friend, and one who would never go behind my back.

10. Sports are not only enjoyable but also can help you stay fit.

Exercise Parallel Construction 7. Make up an element that fits the empty slot in each of the following sentences that contain parallel constructions. Write down the sentences as you complete them.

1. Dennis told her _____ and to wait until he called.

2. She enjoys going downtown, taking in a movie, and _____.

3. Neither _____ nor the fact that he had put up some of his own money could convince her to invest in his scheme.

4. She wants that contract, knows whom to talk to, and _____.

5. Alice was accustomed and _____ to working those hours.

6. It seems to me that the important things are changing the oil, maintaining the tire pressure, and _____.

7. Tabitha can bowl, ski, play tennis, and _____.

8. _____ is more important than seeming more mature than I really am.

9. Both his real name and _____ came out in the trial.

10. Blue and white pennants, big banners, patriotic music, and _____ enlivened each stage of the rally.

Parallel Construction Reference Chart

General Rule:
Sentence elements joined by parallel construction must be grammatically similar.

Trouble Spots:

14A
Sentence elements joined by coordinating conjunctions must be grammatically similar.

Not, "He likes to hunt and camping," but "He likes hunting and camping" or "He likes to hunt and camp."

14B
Sentence elements joined by correlatives must be grammatically similar.

Not, "I am both dissatisfied and I am disgusted," but "I am dissatisfied and I am disgusted" or "I am both dissatisfied and disgusted."

14C
Sentence elements compared with *as* or *than* should be grammatically similar.

Not, "Becoming a success is less important than to enjoy life," but "Becoming a success is less important than enjoying life" or "To become a success is less important than to enjoy life."

14D
Sometimes a word or words must be repeated to make the meaning of a parallel construction clear.

Not, "Glenda lets off steam by cooking and washing her hair," but "Glenda lets off steam by cooking and by washing her hair."

14E
Sometimes a word or words must be repeated to keep a parallel construction from distorting normal English usage.

Not, "He has and continues to seem conceited," but "He has seemed and continues to seem conceited."

3. Sometimes a person gets depressed, and then a brisk jog always cheers me up.

4. One can never tell when your time is nigh.

5. If you are hungry, one may find some snacks in the refrigerator.

15B
Avoid unnecessary shifts in tense.

It would be hard to talk or write at any length and not change tense from time to time. Some events happen after others, some are happening now, and some have not happened yet:

I have always thought he would be famous, and though he is not famous yet, someday he will be.

But a writer must be sure that changes in tense are based on real changes in time; otherwise, the result is needless confusion:

The photographer *was changing* film when the building *shudders* and *collapses.*

I *was* extremely sorry you *are* injured.

In these sentences, there is no reason for the tense to change. The changing of the photographer's film and the collapse of the building happened together, and the speaker in the second sentence should still be sorry since the person he is talking to is still injured:

The photographer *was changing* film when the building *shuddered* and *collapsed.*

I *am* extremely sorry you *are* injured.

Needless tense shifts are caused by inattention rather than by theoretical mistakes on the writer's part. Keep an eye open for them, especially if they become a recurring problem.

Exercise Unnecessary Shifts 2. Correct any needless shifts in tense in the following sentences:

1. The siren sounded and suddenly the air is filled with smoke and flying metal.

2. Whenever I eat pizza, it disagreed with my stomach.

3. Consuela was keeping her balance but finally falls.

4. The lightning flashes, the great oak splits like a parting curtain, and the two halves fall to either side.

5. Ghosts do not bother me; I knew perfectly well they are figments of the imagination.

15C
Avoid unnecessary shifts in subject and voice.

A writer should never shift subjects in closely related clauses without good reason. Here is a sentence in which the subject changes unnecessarily:

Mike cannot keep orchids alive, but *geraniums* are easy for him to grow.

In this sentence, both clauses are really about how good a gardener Mike is, but the reader may not see this at once. The subject shift implies that the second clause is going to be about something else. The sentence should say

Mike cannot keep orchids alive, but *he* finds it easy to grow geraniums.

Sticking to the same grammatical subject when possible will improve the clarity and focus of your sentences. The same is true of avoiding needless shifts in voice:

Shirley *won* the first prize, while her brother *was awarded* the second.

There is nothing truly wrong with this sentence, but the shift from the active verb *won* to the passive *was awarded* is unnecessary. Most people would prefer two active verbs:

Shirley *won* the first prize, while her brother *got* the second.

However, needless shifts in subject and voice go beyond merely being inefficient and become downright awkward and objectionable when both kinds of shift happen at the same time:

Roger crossed the goal line, and the winning *touchdown was scored.*

Readers of this sentence are forced to make *two* adjustments, first to a new subject and then to a new kind of verb, only to find that neither was necessary and that the writer simply means

Roger crossed the goal line and *scored* the winning goal.

Exercise Unnecessary Shifts 3. Correct any needless or undesirable shifts in subject or voice in the following sentences:

1. I searched the closet, but the missing racquet could not be found.
2. Ivan was standing up in the canoe when it toppled him into the water.
3. When the girl came up for the third time she was seen to be already turning purple.
4. The lion sprang upon its quarry, and the antelope was killed.
5. Whenever he saw a pine forest it reminded him of the night he spent on the mountain.

15D
Avoid unnecessary shifts in mood or speaker.

This problem is most likely to arise when writers report a question or a command uttered by someone else. In such circumstances, they may forget that they are only reporting what happened and reproduce the *imperative* or *interrogative* verb of the original utterance:

Mandy told Tom get out of here.

Ida asked the artist could she watch him at work.

In the first of these sentences, "Get out of here!" is what Mandy told Tom, but the writer should not use that command form unless quoting Mandy's exact words:

Mandy said to Tom, "Get out of here!"

Otherwise, the sentence should merely describe the encounter:

Mandy told Tom to get out of there.

Mandy told Tom that he should get out of there.

The sentence about Ida and the artist presents the same problem. Ida apparently asked "Could I watch you at work?" But the only way the writer can keep this question form is to quote her directly:

Ida asked the artist, "Could I watch you at work?"

To avoid direct quoting, the writer must recount the event by taking the subject out of the middle of the verb.

Ida asked whether she could watch the artist at work.

Ida wanted to watch the artist at work and asked him whether she could.

Exercise Unnecessary Shifts 4. Correct any needless shifts in mood in the following sentences.

1. I was shocked when Greg told me get lost.

2. The firm wanted to know would she consider their offer.

3. He always wondered did he have the determination to succeed.

4. The library told him bring back the books or pay up.

5. How many stars are like our sun is what they were trying to discover.

15E
Avoid unnecessary shifts in number.

Pointless shifts in number are another burden that no one should place on his readers. Consider this sentence:

If state parks become too commercialized, they will no longer be a place to escape the pressures of city life.

Parks and *they* are both plural, but *place* takes the same concept and suddenly makes it singular. Here is another example:

In high school we worked more as a group than as an individual.

We and *group* refer to many students, but these people are abruptly squeezed into one with the term *individual.*

The solution to the problem of illogical changes in number is to reread critically what you have written.

Exercise Unnecessary Shifts 5. Correct any needless shifts in number you find in the following sentences.

1. Above all else, we loved his paintings of flowering roses, a work of genius.

2. Bud makes extremely good upside down cake; his are food for a king.

3. She has never written a bad book because they are all touched by her special talent.

4. Henry had a twinkling eye that peeped out from beneath a pair of bristling white eyebrows.

5. Fox terriers, a dog of remarkable courage, sometimes get badly mauled in fights with larger dogs.

15F
Avoid mixed sentence construction.

Only one kind of shift in sentence structure gives many students trouble, the problem of misplaced subjects. This situation arises when a sentence starts off with an introductory clause or phrase and the writer mistakes it for the subject of the main clause:

In putting the shot requires both muscle and timing.

Since he was coming was the reason for our excitement.

Both of these sentences make the same error. In the first, the writer began to write a prepositional phrase followed by a complete main clause:

In putting the shot, one uses both muscle and timing.

But he got confused after *shot,* forgot about the preposition, and finished the sentence as if it said:

Putting the shot requires both muscle and timing.

He probably had both of these correct sentences in mind as he wrote, but the result is that he failed to do justice to either of them.

The second mixed-up sentence works in the same way, except that

Not, "They wanted to know could they sleep there," but "They wanted to know if they could sleep there," or "They asked, 'Could we sleep there?' " And not, "Will advised us forget it," but "Will advised us to forget it," or "Will advised us, 'Forget it!' "

15E
Avoid unnecessary shifts in number.

Not, "He prefers Burgundy, red wines of powerful character," but "He prefers Burgundy, a red wine of powerful character," or "He prefers Burgundies, red wines of powerful character."

15F
Avoid mixed sentence construction.

Not, "In dancing was her greatest pleasure," but "Dancing was her greatest pleasure" or "In dancing she found her greatest pleasure." And not, "After I graduated created problems for us," but "My graduation created problems for us," or "After I graduated we had problems."

16 *Incomplete Constructions* [*inc.*]

Complete and logically-constructed sentences enable your readers to understand your meaning without an unnecessary struggle.

16A
Catch careless omissions.

If you write more than one draft of your work, you need to guard against carelessly omitting words, phrases, or even whole thoughts when you copy things over:

> They passed the ordinance burning leaves without considering how else people could dispose of them.

> They passed the ordinance against burning leaves how else could people dispose of them.

> They passed the ordinance against burning leaves without considering how else.

All of these sentences look silly when they are isolated, but if one of them were hidden in the middle of a paragraph, catching the omission would be more difficult. It would be harder still if you had written the sentence yourself and knew what it was *supposed* to say. You might read the sentence several times, mentally supplying the missing element, but never noticing that you had left out details.

Being aware of the problem of omissions is one step toward solving it. This awareness is all that many writers require. Others, though, may need such techniques as having a friend read over their final drafts, using a finger or blank piece of paper to isolate the word or line they are copying, or carefully comparing rough and final drafts on a word-for-word basis.

16B
Avoid incomplete comparisons.

There are two basic kinds of incomplete comparisons, the open-ended comparison and the incomplete *than* clause. Of the two, open-ended comparisons occur far more frequently.

Advertising writers use open-ended comparisons so commonly that many people no longer see anything wrong with them. Consider these claims:

White Sow Scotch is better!

Feltz foods are finer foods!

Plutocrat will do more for the common man!

Each of these sentences is literally nonsense: none of them means a thing until the thought is completed. "Better than what?" "Finer than what?" "More than who?" White Sow might be somewhat better than ditch-water and still not be very good. Feltz foods might be finer than dog food, but who wants to eat dog food? And Plutocrat's slogan might merely mean that he will do more for the common man than the little or nothing he has done already.

Open-ended comparisons serve a purpose in advertisements: by not saying anything, they avoid offending people. At the same time, they give uncritical consumers the idea that they are getting a good thing. But this lack of meaning is precisely what should be avoided in writing that is intended to communicate. Remember that whenever you use an adjective in the comparative degree—one with an *-er* ending or one modified by *more* or by *less*—you will not communicate a significant idea unless you go on to make the basis of the comparison clear. Do not say "He is smarter," "She is more dependable," or "The party was less lively"; but "He is smarter than Charley the Chimp," "She is more dependable than a unicycle," or "The party was less lively than Ogden, Utah, on a Sunday morning."

Incomplete **than** *clauses.*   Although this type of incomplete comparison comes up less frequently than the open-ended sort, it can be just as baffling. Look closely at this example:

I loved you more than Aunt Hazel.

There are two ways to interpret this sentence, and there is no way to tell which one is correct. The writer could mean, "I love you more than I love Aunt Hazel," or he could be saying, "I love you more than Aunt Hazel loves you." Be cautious with comparisons in which *than* is followed by a noun: they may require that the noun be expanded into a whole clause to make the meaning clear.

Exercise Incomplete Constructions 1. Find and correct the incomplete comparisons in the following sentences.

1. I have always thought skiing was much more thrilling.

2. Hockey is one of the sports that require more courage.

3. I said I had more respect for him than his wife.

4. Burpobrew is a full thirty per cent less filling.

5. He assured me he was much more clever.

16C
Avoid omitting necessary words from suspended comparisons.

In a suspended comparison, a normal construction is interrupted by an afterthought:

Diablo was as vicious as, if not more vicious than, old Bouncer.

Helen was one of the most beautiful women, if not the most beautiful woman, in the ancient world.

Such constructions are not very efficient, and writers often create additional problems in shortening them:

Diablo was as vicious, if not more vicious, than old Bouncer.

Helen was a beautiful, if not the most beautiful, woman in the ancient world.

Neither of these shortened sentences makes structural sense. In the sentence about Diablo, the commas tell us that *if not more vicious* is parenthetical, that it can be dropped without harming the original clause. But this would leave us with "Diablo was as vicious than old Boucer." It would not be correct, either, to put the second comma after *than*, because the original clause would then be "Diablo was as vicious old Bouncer." Look back at the first, correct, version of the sentence. That second *as* after the first *vicious* may look odd, but it is necessary if the suspended comparison is to work at all.

The sentence about Helen does not work in the same way, but its shortened version is also full of problems. Grammatically, we would have no trouble removing the parenthetical *if not the most beautiful*, leaving the perfectly good sentence "Helen was a beautiful woman in the ancient world." But logically we lose the opposition between "one of the most" and "the most." It is quite possible that Helen could have been beautiful and the most beautiful at the same time, so the afterthought now seems entirely pointless. Here again, every word in the first, correct, sentence is necessary for the suspended comparison to work.

It is probably best never to construct suspended comparisons in the first place. It is generally better to write your way around them:

Diablo was at least as vicious as old Bouncer.

Helen might have been the most beautiful woman in the ancient world.

Exercise Incomplete Constructions 2. Correct the faulty suspended comparisons in the following sentences. First supply the omitted word or words, and then rewrite the sentence without the suspended comparison.

1. Emmy is a very pretty, if not the prettiest, girl in the first grade.

2. Hyman was every bit as generous, if not more generous, than his brother.

3. Mike was as accurate, if not more accurate than, I was.

4. Celia was a good, if not the best, outdoor cook in the group.

5. His apple was as red, if not redder than, mine.

16D
Avoid illogical comparisons.

There are two particular kinds of illogical comparisons to look out for. Neither form is really based on logical confusion, but each seems to be because it makes the writer say something never intended. Consider the following sentence:

Secretariat was faster than any horse who has ever run.

The writer has left out one word, *other,* and this omission causes him to say something he does not mean. Without *other* in front of *horse,* the sentence makes sense only if Secretariat is *not* a horse who has ever run himself. Otherwise, Secretariat would be part of the group *any horse who has ever run,* and the statement would imply that he was faster than himself. The sentence has to be

Secretariat was faster than any *other* horse who has ever run.

The other kind of illogical comparison is also based on an omission—this time of the thing being compared:

The cheerleaders here are better than Notre Dame.

The two things being compared seem to be *cheerleaders* and *Notre Dame,* a group of lively people on the one hand and a Catholic university on the other. The writer meant, of course, to compare the cheerleaders where he is with the *cheerleaders* at Notre Dame, but he has neglected to mention this second group of cheerleaders in his sentence. He should have said:

The cheerleaders here are better than the cheerleaders at Notre Dame.

Or, since a possessive noun can take the place of the thing it modifies:

The cheerleaders here are better than *Notre Dame's.*

Exercise Incomplete Constructions 3. Correct any illogical comparisons in the following sentences by supplying the missing element.

1. The teachers here are certainly more helpful than high school.

2. My father works much harder than any man in his office.

3. Tennis players seem somewhat brighter than football.

4. The streets of Dallas are really no safer than New York.

5. My uncle's sense of humor is greater than that of any person I have ever met.

16E
Avoid incomplete constructions after *so* when it is used as an adverb.

So is not the same as *very* or *extremely* in constructions where it modifies other modifiers. It is correct to simply add a *very* or an *extremely* to an adjective or adverb:

The house was *very* cold.

The storm came up *extremely* fast.

But *so* works differently under these circumstances. Used as an intensifier to modify another modifier, *so* demands a *that* clause to complete the idea. Not:

The house was *so* cold.

The storm came up *so* fast.

but:

The house was *so* cold *that* there was ice in the sink.

The storm came up *so* fast *that* we could not find shelter before it was on us.

This rule affects only the way *so* is used to modify other modifiers. It has no force when the word is used in one of its many other functions.

Exercise Incomplete Constructions 4. Make up a *that* clause to complete each of the unfinished *so* constructions in the following sentences.

1. Daryll looked so handsome and so strong!

2. After working until five, I always find that I am so tired.

3. On the telephone Joan sounded so hopeful.

4. The first thing he mentioned was that her dress was so colorful.

5. Freddie! Your manners are so refined!

Exercise Incomplete Constructions 5. Correct any incomplete constructions in the following sentences. Be ready to explain your corrections.

1. The mail is as convenient, if not more convenient than, the telegraph.

2. Oak lumber has more tensile strength than any other tree.

3. I'll bet my dog is more obedient.

4. I often thought that John was less entertaining.

5. Miss Smythe recounted her adventure so graphically!

6. French art is a great, if not the greatest, tradition in world culture.

7. The academic advisor helped Jim more than his friends.

8. My roommate is sloppier than anyone in our dorm.

9. Any piano's tone is more powerful than a guitar.

10. Karen told policeman not to ticket car.

Exercise Incomplete Constructions 6. Finish the following sentence beginnings in a way that completes the constructions they introduce. The content of the part you supply is up to you.

1. The President of the United States is more influential . . .

2. Walter claims her parents are more stubborn than . . .

3. These peanuts are so salty . . .

4. Judy talks to me more often than . . .

5. Jersey City is somewhat less sophisticated . . .

6. The Vikings are as dangerous as, if not more . . .

7. I think Sarah is more disciplined . . .

8. Tommy owes his parents more than . . .

9. Don't worry, my hide is thicker than . . .

10. Fires on that block are so frequent . . .

Incomplete Constructions Reference Chart

General Rule:
Be sure your sentences are completely and logically developed.

Trouble Spots:

16A
Catch careless omissions.

16B
Avoid incomplete comparisons.

Not, "Henry is more sensitive," but "Henry is more sensitive than Butch." And not, "She confided in Becky more than Leroy," but "She confided in Becky more than *in Leroy*," or "She confided in Becky more than *Leroy did.*"

16C
Avoid omitting necessary words from suspended comparisons.

Not, "Nancy is as brave, if not braver than, Tim," but Nancy is as as brave *as*, if not braver than, Tim." And not "She is a fine, if not the finest, woman I know," but "She is *one of the finest women*, if not the finest woman, I know."

16D
Avoid illogical comparisons.

Not, "Professor Smith is more compassionate than any teacher," but "Professor Smith is more compassionate than any *other* teacher." And not, "The styling of the Chevrolet is better than the new Ford," but "The styling of the Chevrolet is better than *that of* the new Ford," or "The styling of the Chevrolet is better than the new *Ford's*."

16E
Avoid incomplete constructions after *so* when it is used as an adverb.

Not, "Diablo is so vicious," but "Diablo is so vicious *that even the fleas leave him alone*."

Two

Punctuation

17 *Fragments* [*frag*]

A grammatical definition of a sentence maintains that it is a string of words that contains a subject and a verb and is not grammatically dependent on anything outside itself. Another definition focuses on meaning: a sentence is a complete thought that can stand alone; it is an idea that means something all by itself. These definitions are related, and each of them is useful in identifying and eliminating fragments. Sentences are complete thoughts *because* they have subjects and verbs (both a doer and a thing done) and *because* they require no other elements to complete their meaning. A *fragment*, however, is nothing more than a part of a sentence punctuated with a capital letter at the beginning and a full stop (period, exclamation point, or question mark) at the end. A fragment looks as if it were a complete sentence, but in fact it is nothing of the sort:

> Running through the low meadows by the sliding river.
>
> Although he had never seen a more beautiful sports car.
>
> The man who had been standing by the door when she arrived.

The first of these fragments has no subject or verb (*running* and *sliding* are only participles). The second and third have subjects and verbs, but they leave the reader hanging: more has to be said to make their meaning complete. The punctuation in each case proclaims, "Here is a sentence," but the proclamation is not true. Not one of the three contains a whole thought; each leaves the reader looking for more.

If you have trouble with fragments in your writing, work through this chapter carefully. Refer also to Chapters 1–4, which contain more detailed discussions of the grammar of sentences.

17A
Avoid writing fragments without verbs.

Fragments often contain verb-like participles or infinitives which cause the writer to think a verb has been included:

Roger and Lester piling on at the goal line.

A woman to be respected and even feared.

Both of these fragments have words that could serve as subjects, but neither has a main verb to go with them. In the first example, *piling* is a participle rather than a main verb (as Chapter 2 explains, *-ing* forms can never be main verbs without help from auxiliaries). And the second fragment has an infinitive, *to be*, where there should be a main verb (infinitives can never be main verbs either). There are generally two ways to correct fragments without verbs. The fragment can be rewritten so that it includes a main verb:

Roger and Lester *were piling* on at the goal line.

She *is* respected and even feared.

or another subject and verb can be supplied so that the fragment becomes part of a larger sentence:

The umpire spotted a foul, Roger and Lester piling on at the goal line.

She is a woman to be respected and even feared.

Another kind of fragment that lacks a verb looks like this:

The girl who had told him about the concert.

There *is* a verb in this fragment (*had told*) but its subject is *who*, not *girl*. The whole construction amounts to a subject, *girl*, modified by an adjective clause, *who had told him about the concert*. The fragment is then left hanging, with no verb of its own. The solution to this situation is to provide a verb for *girl:*

The girl who had told him about the concert *was gone.*

Exercise Fragments 1. Correct the following fragments in the way that seems most appropriate:

1. The leaves turning every shade of red, with gold, brown, and lingering green for contrast.

2. That boat which has just come back from winning its heat.

3. Diane, who thought she had been given permission to use her book on the test.

4. Jeff to ask about rates during the off season in an attempt to save the group as much money as possible.

5. The railroad bringing settlers, new money, and access to new markets to the territory.

17B
Avoid writing fragments without subjects.

Only one common fragment pattern has a verb but no subject. It comes about when a writer closes a sentence but then thinks of another detail to explain what he has just said:

He is an independent devil. Thinks for himself.

Trees are important on a building site. Break the wind.

There are two standard ways to correct this type of fragment. The loose verb can be tied to the original sentence:

He is an independent devil and thinks for himself.

Trees are important on a building site for breaking the wind.

Or it can be given a subject of its own:

He is an independent devil. *He* thinks for himself.

Trees are important on building sites. *They* break the wind.

Exercise Fragments 2. Correct the following fragments in two ways, first by making them part of the original sentences, and then by giving them subjects of their own.

1. His gelding is quite a horse. Runs like the wind.

2. Brenda puts a lot of pressure on her husband. Wants him to work all the time.

3. This is the most reliable lawnmower I have ever seen. Starts every time.

4. Marine biology is a good major. Stirs my interest.

5. We owe a lot to vitamin C. Wards off colds and flu.

17C
Avoid writing fragments without subjects or verbs.

The fragments in this category are very diverse, including different types of modifying words or phrases and appositives which people sometimes mistakenly punctuate as separate sentences. But these fragments also have a useful feature in common: since they all modify or rename something in a nearby sentence, correcting them is usually just a matter of fitting them back into the constructions they should have been part of all along. Here are some typical examples, each one accompanied by the sentence to which it should belong:

He sank slowly down. *Exhausted.* (participle).

Determined to succeed. Jon tried hard. (participial phrase)

To be loved. One must love. (infinitive)

He found them where he least expected. *On his head.* (prepositional phrase)

Around the corner. There was a drug store. (prepositional phrase)

He was dedicated to his school. *An institution of higher learning.* (appositive)

These fragments can be joined to their sentences in several ways. Here are some good possibilities:

He sank slowly down, exhausted.

Determined to succeed, Jon tried hard.

To be loved, one must love.

He found them where he least expected—on his head.

Around the corner there was a drug store.

He was dedicated to his school, an institution of higher learning.

Exercise Fragments 3. Correct the following fragments by joining them to the sentences to which they belong.

1. His was a strange obsession. Stopping the exploitation of chickens.

2. Encouraged by his luck. He returned to the gaming tables.

3. At that spot on the track. A blown engine had created a dangerous oil slick.

4. She finally attained the recognition she deserved. For her years of patient research.

5. Now Rex had come face to face with his opponent. A dark man with a red beard.

17D
Avoid punctuating dependent clauses as sentences.

Dependent clauses are discussed in detail in Chapter 4. Essentially, they are ordinary independent clauses that are introduced by a subordinating conjunction or a relative pronoun. Adding a subordinating word to a clause transforms it from a complete, self-contained thought to one that functions as a noun, adjective, or adverb in some other clause. A clause that has undergone this transformation is no longer independent and can no longer be punctuated as a sentence. For example, the clause "I was hungry" is a perfectly good sentence, but once we add a subordinating conjunction to it, *"when* I was hungry," it is changed. It is no longer just a statement of an independent fact; instead, it demands another clause to complete the meaning. It could be an adverbial, setting the time for another clause:

When I was hungry, I went down to the snack bar.

or it could be an adjective clause, modifying a noun like *time:*

He came at a time *when I was hungry.*

or it could be a noun—for instance, the direct object of *knew:*

Mother knew *when I was hungry.*

What *"when I was hungry" cannot* be is a sentence by itself, and the same is true of all other clauses introduced by subordinating words. Here is list of some common subordinating conjunctions. All of them turn clauses into fragments.

after	on condition that
although	provided that
as	since
as if	so that
as though	than
because	though
before	unless
even if	while
if	in order that

Another group of subordinating words can also make clauses dependent, but these must be approached with caution because of their ability to introduce questions that are not fragments:

how	whichever
what	who
when	whoever
whenever	whom
where	whomever
wherever	why
which	

In a class by itself is the troublesome word *that. That* can be an adjective "*that* boy," "*that* pencil," "*that* banana." It can be a pronoun: "*That* is my car," "*That* will be the day," "*That* is the last straw." But it can also be a subordinating conjunction introducing a dependent clause: I am glad *that* he came," "It appears *that* you have done your homework," "I believe *that* I can do it." In its role as a subordinating conjunction, *that* is yet another word that makes independent clauses ("I can do it") into fragments ("*that* I can do it").

Dependent clause fragments are like the modifiers and appositives discussed in 17C. They are always found near the sentence of which they should be a part, and correcting them almost always involves getting rid of the period and capital letter and joining the fragments to the sentence to which they belong.

Exercise Fragments 4. Correct the following fragments by joining them to the sentence to which they belong.

1. She sent me a print of a painting by Klee. Who is my favorite painter.

2. Because it had sat out for two weeks. The car refused to start.

3. If he had come from another school. We might have been friends.

4. Benny says he is a sophomore. Although he is not.

5. He told me a secret. That he had bought her a ring.

17E
Some fragments are occasionally permissible.

People often talk in fragments: "Nice guy. Comes in here a lot. Always orders the same thing. Good tipper." It is correct to reproduce these conversational fragments when you are reporting what someone said. It is also permissible to punctuate interjections or exclamations as if they were sentences, even if they are not:

Shucks!

Three cheers for the new treasurer!

Ugh!

It is equally true that good authors use fragments for special purposes, such as for describing a scene naturalistically:

Gray. Gray sky and water. Gray salt marshes flat on either side. Cold gray wind.

or to give a sentence a humorous or shocking turnaround:

His groping hand found the object that had turned beneath his foot in the darkness. A severed finger!

But the use of this kind of writing is often debatable even in the best of hands. There is usually a way to achieve the same effect without the fragments.

Exercise Fragments 5. Correct the following fragments in the way that seems most appropriate.

1. Pigeons were fluttering overhead. And feeding on the bench beside him.

2. Wash the car carefully. Being sure not to scratch the new finish.

3. This is a good watch. Keeps perfect time.

4. The ripples swelling and becoming more widely separated as they spread from the center to the shores of the pond.

5. Hardware stores are especially intriguing. Because of the tools and other gear they contain.

6. Tell me what is missing. Unless that is classified information.

7. The exact quantity to blow a building like P.S. 37 all over Detroit.

8. Walker may possibly be amused. Reading this.

9. Elizabeth has a definite goal in mind. To possess true independence of means and spirit.

10. The sky darkening almost imperceptibly until by noon it was as black as ink.

Exercise Fragments 6. Rewrite the following sentences to eliminate the fragments.

1. You always say things you regret. When you come to your senses.

2. How can I forgive him for what he said? While he goes on saying it.

3. The gale picking up froth and a smoke of vapor from the peak of each heaving wave.

4. This correction tape really works. Blots out mistakes entirely.

5. Through that little door in the garden side of the building. Is his usual working room.

6. Heck! I've thrown another stitch. In this blanket.

7. A resort to relieve you of the pressures of a busy life.

8. The prisoner's lips are sealed, and he refuses to divulge. What he did with the money.

9. Her true nature was hidden in another part of her mind. A room we could never enter.

10. We promising to repay him as soon as we could, the exact date to depend on when we could sell the moped.

Fragment Reference Chart

General Rule:
A sentence must have a subject and a verb and not be grammatically dependent on anything outside itself.

Trouble Spots:

17A
Avoid writing fragments without verbs.

Not, "Wendy playing and rolling in the leaves," or "A river to be treated with respect," but "Wendy *was* playing and rolling in the leaves," and "*It was* a river to be treated with respect."

17B
Avoid writing fragments without subjects.

Not, "Olga is awfully sick. Can't come to work," but "Olga is awfully sick and can't come to work," or "Olga is awfully sick. She can't come to work."

17C
Avoid writing fragments without subjects or verbs.

Not, "Excited by the music. Killer began to bark," or "She is just my kind. A warm, friendly girl," but "Excited by the music, Killer began to bark," and "She is just my kind, a warm, friendly girl."

17D
Avoid punctuating dependent clauses as sentences.

Not, "Donna asked me. If I liked to water ski," but "Donna asked me if I liked to water ski."

17E
Some fragments are occasionally permissible.

18

End Punctuation [end punc.]

Only three punctuation marks in English are used to signal the end of a sentence—the period(.), the question mark(?), and the exclamation point (!). Although these marks do not usually give writers much trouble, each has some secondary functions that you may not know about.

18A
Use a period after a statement of fact or an unemphatic command.

Statements of fact include all ordinary sentences that are neither direct questions nor exclamations:

I scored seventeen points.

July can be torrid in Minneapolis.

The halls have been quiet until now.

But a lot depends on the writer's intentions. A statement of fact can be changed into a question or an exclamation by simply changing the end punctuation:

I scored seventeen points?   (I can hardly believe it myself.)

I scored seventeen points!   (Hurray for me!)

Unemphatic commands range from routine orders to polite requests such as "Pass the salt." Periods, rather than exclamation points, are appropriate for these sentences whenever their emotional force is not particularly strong:

Remember to get margarine at the store.

Allow me.

Please be seated.

18B
Use a question mark after a direct question.

Some questions like "I scored seventeen points?" are outwardly identical to statements of fact. They are questions not because of their structure but because the writer wants them to be. But most questions have a special construction of their own. Many of them are signaled by one of the interrogative pronouns, *who, which* and *what:*

Who was that masked man?

Which of these chairs do you prefer?

What can I say?

Another hallmark of question constructions is inverted word order. The verb or one of its auxiliaries comes before the subject:

Should we *ask* him in?

Was Vanessa ill last week?

Did the bishop *join* in the singing?

While statements of fact can be turned into questions, the reverse is not true. Any sentence that is specifically constructed as a question must be followed by a question mark.

Exercise End Punctuation 1. Write a statement of fact and a question about each of the following situations. Underline the complete verbs (the main verb plus any auxiliaries) in each of your sentences. Notice the difference in verb position between the statements and the questions. Example:

My mother has *dyed* her hair orange.

Does anyone else's mother *behave* that way?

1. Your mother has begun to dye her hair, and you do not like the idea.
2. A friend has just been skinned up riding a skateboard.
3. You are thinking about converting to Buddhism and wonder if it will mean becoming a vegetarian.
4. You are tired of the way you look and thinking about shaving off your eyebrows.
5. There is a terrible smell in your car, and you have not seen your cat for over a week.

18C
Do not use a question mark after an indirect question.

A direct question is the question itself. An indirect question is a remark about the question itself. Consider the following direct and indirect versions of the same question:

Are there antelopes in South America?

He asked whether there are antelopes in South America.

The question mark is appropriate in the first example, because the sentence consists of the actual words of the question combined in question form. But a question mark would not work for the second sentence (unless the writer wanted to express surprise that the question was asked at all) because this sentence is just a statement of fact *about* the question; it is not a question itself. The only legitimate way to combine the actual question with a statement about it is to *quote* what was asked:

He asked, "Are there antelopes in South America?"

The justification for the question mark here is that the actual wording of the question is reproduced.

> *Exercise End Punctuation 2.* Decide whether each of the following is a direct or an indirect question, and punctuate accordingly. Then write an indirect version of each direct question and a direct question corresponding to each of the indirect ones.
>
> **1.** I wanted to know if she was serious
>
> **2.** How long has Mr. Erhardt been with the firm
>
> **3.** When does the next train for Houston come through
>
> **4.** Gilda wondered why she had been chosen for the part
>
> **5.** Does that house have air conditioning

18D
Use exclamation points after ejaculations or strong commands.

Exclamation points indicate emotional force. They go well with interjections:

Ouch!

Darn!

Phooey!

with spontaneous outcries:

Hurray for the team!

Down with tyrants!

Long live the king!

and with emphatic commands:

Get out of here!

Run for it!

Look out!

Exclamation points can also be used to indicate strong emotion, usually surprise, over something that has happened:

She got four thousand dollars for that old junker!

I'm going to be queen of the Harvest Festival!

His hair style is really unusual!

In sentences like these last ones, it is the writer's intention that counts. If the person wants the idea to convey a sense of shock or amazement, the exclamation point is called for. Otherwise, if the sentence is just a matter-of-fact statement, a period is appropriate.

18E
Do not overuse exclamation points.

Exclamation points are like hot peppers: too many is much worse than none at all. If you have any question at all about whether one is needed, use a period instead. Sentences that contain exclamation points ask to be read with excitement. The reader feels pressured to share the writer's sense of wonder or urgency over an unusually vivid piece of information. Exclamation points can produce a real letdown when the material fails to live up to the punctuation.

I got a bicycle three years ago! It was a used one, so I saved money on it! At first I found pedaling quite hard because I was not in good shape. But now I ride my bike everywhere! It has become my constant companion!

Exercise End Punctuation 3. Supply the appropriate end punctuation to the sentences in the following passage. Be prepared to explain your decisions.

"I've been named Man of the Year " Father could not believe it All his life he had been worthy of recognition, but it never came And now that it was his, he could not take it in "Why me What have I done lately that I didn't do before Do you suppose it's a mistake " He even wondered if he should accept the award But his doubts faded as the ceremony drew near On the day of the presentation he accepted his plaque with a delighted "All right "

Exercise End Punctuation 4. Supply the appropriate end punctuation to the sentences in the following passage. Be prepared to explain your decisions.

"Simply incredible " We had been watching a film on the language ability of gorillas and were stunned by what we saw The female gorilla in the movie had been taught over six hundred signs for different words, and she could use most of them without hesitation We saw her ask how the trainer was And then she launched into a long series of signs: "Is this good to eat " "How long is it before lunch " "Where is my cup " The narrator of the film translated these questions for the audience and said that the gorilla was capable of long and involved conversations She asked if this ability to use language was not a sign of real intelligence Based on what we saw, we could answer only with an enthusiastic "Yes "

End Punctuation Reference Chart

General Rule:
End punctuation should be chosen according to the nature of the sentence.

Trouble Spots:

18A
Use a period after a statement of fact or an unemphatic command.

18B
Use a question mark after a direct question.

18C
Do not use a question mark after an indirect question.

Not, "He asked if she was going to the game?" but "He asked if she was going to the game." or "He asked, 'Are you going to the game?' "

18D
Use exclamation points after ejaculations or strong commands.

18E
Do not overuse exclamation points.

19 Comma Faults and Fused Sentences [CF., FS.]

Comma faults (or comma splices) and fused (or run-together) sentences are considered by most teachers and readers to be second only to fragments as serious punctuation errors. You should do everything you can to learn to recognize and avoid them.

19A
Recognize and correct comma faults.

Comma faults are like fragments in reverse. A fragment is a group of words incorrectly punctuated as a sentence. A comma fault is *two* sentences separated by only a comma. The problem with fragments is an absence of sentences; the problem with comma faults is having too many sentences insufficiently set off from one another. Consider this typical example:

He bought his first car last winter, it never ran well.

There are two clauses here, "He bought his first car" and "it never ran well." There are no subordinating conjunctions, so each of the clauses is *independent*, which means that each of them would make a good sentence by itself. A lone comma is insufficient to mark the division between such clauses.

Solving Comma Faults.   Three standard solutions to comma faults will work in every case. Since both clauses can be sentences, the first solution is to *make* them sentences by replacing the comma with a period and supplying a capital letter:

He bought his first car last winter. It never ran well.

The second solution is to replace the comma with a semicolon(;), a punctuation mark with the grammatical force of a period but without the following capital letter:

> He bought his first car last winter; it never ran well.

And the third solution is to keep the comma, but to give it some help from one of the coordinating conjunctions (*and, but, or, nor, for, so,* and *yet*):

> He bought his first car last winter, but it never ran well.

While any of these solutions will correct the comma fault, however, they are not all the same in their effect on the reader. The *period* makes each clause a sentence by itself, and emphasizes the separateness of the ideas. The *semicolon* draws both clauses into the same sentence, and implies that the ideas are more closely related. And the *comma-plus-conjunction* technique makes for an even closer connection, as it shows a definite logical relationship between the clauses.

> *Exercise Comma Faults 1.* Correct each of the following comma faults in all of the three standard ways: once with a period and a capital letter, once with a semicolon, and once with a comma-plus-conjunction (think about which conjunction works best). Be prepared to discuss the relative effectiveness of each correction.
>
> **1.** Sonny's moped is in the shop, he will be driving his car today.
>
> **2.** She is very tall, she is also unusually graceful.
>
> **3.** The Yankees play the Royals this afternoon, they defeated Boston yesterday.
>
> **4.** I have been coughing all week, the weather is changing now.
>
> **5.** Martha looked in at her pumpkin pies, they were burned black around the edges.

Other Solutions.   All comma faults can be fixed in one of the three standard ways (period, semicolon, or comma-plus-conjunction), but sometimes other corrections are also possible and may be more effective. Many comma faults, for instance, result when one clause *explains* the other. In these circumstances a colon (:) may offer the best way of punctuating the sentence:

Comma Faults

I think she cheats, she keeps shuffling behind her back.

He has a strange notion of work, it is something one never does if he can get out of it.

Revisions

I think she cheats: she keeps shuffling behind her back.

He has a strange notion of work: it is something one never does if he can get out of it.

The colons in these revised sentences accomplish more than most punctuation marks do. They divide the clauses, but they also *mean* something. In the first revision the colon means *because;* in the second the meaning is *that is* or *in other words.*

Another way to correct certain comma faults is to attack the problem at its root. Comma faults occur because two independent clauses are insufficiently set off from each other. It is often possible to change one of the clauses to a *dependent* one:

Comma Faults

Sid is not running, he broke his leg.

Charlotte is late, I am not worried.

Dinner was ready, I sat down to eat.

Revisions

Sid is not running *because* he broke his leg.

Although Charlotte is late, I am not worried.

When dinner was ready, I sat down to eat.

The revisions here serve two useful purposes: by eliminating one of the independent clauses, they correct the comma fault, and by specifying a logical relationship, they make the connection between the clauses clear.

Exercise Comma Faults 2. Correct the following comma faults. Replace the comma with a colon if the relationship between the clauses is *because, that is,* or *in other words.* If the relationship is not one of these, attach an appropriate subordinating conjunction to one of the clauses.

1. He is quite a man, he is eighty years old and still wrestles alligators.
2. The starter had stopped even trying to turn the engine over, they knew they would have to push the car to get it going.
3. He says he will be there with Sue, I am not going to go.
4. Desmond explained his motto, no one should ever stop trying.
5. She typed the footnotes to his paper, the project was finished.

19B
Be especially alert for comma faults involving compound-complex sentences or conjunctive adverbs.

Compound-Complex Sentences. Compound-complex sentences have two or more independent clauses and at least one dependent one. They sometimes lead to comma faults simply because their structure is hard to grasp:

> The new mall construction project is going ahead, although the paper has crusaded against it, no one has listened.

The problem here stems from the *although* clause. At first glance, this subordinate construction seems to modify the independent clause about the construction project, and the comma between the two seems justified. But the writer has put another comma between the *although* clause and "no one has listened," suggesting that *these* two parts make up a unit (a suggestion that makes even better sense). Meanwhile, the confusion over what modifies what leads the writer to make a comma fault. He overlooks the fact that there are really two separate sentences here:

> The new mall construction project is going ahead. Although the paper has crusaded against it, no one has listened.

Conjunctive Adverbs. Although conjunctive adverbs are discussed in detail in the next chapter (20C), they are also relevant in a section on comma faults. These words—adverbs such as *however, moreover, therefore, consequently, nevertheless,* and the especially troublesome *then*—look like conjunctions and do the work of conjunctions, but are *not* conjunctions. When they come between independent clauses, conjunctive adverbs demand the full period, semicolon, or comma-plus-conjunction treatment:

Comma Fault

It looked dangerous, therefore, we did not try.

Revisions

It looked dangerous. Therefore, we did not try.

It looked dangerous; therefore, we did not try.

It looked dangerous, and therefore we did not try.

Exercise Comma Faults 3. Correct the following comma faults in the way that seems most appropriate.

1. We were ready to buy the house, moreover, we had sold our old one.
2. Cathy piled some fresh logs on the fire, then she sat down to enjoy the solitude.
3. He did not make the team, although I know he trained hard, the competition was overwhelming.
4. The ecology movement has become quite a fad, while there is a great need for conservation, some of its proponents have gone overboard.
5. We were looking for a female puppy, nevertheless, that male is so attractive we have changed our minds.

| **19C**
Avoid fused sentences.

Fused sentences are nothing more than comma faults without the commas. Instead of consisting of two independent clauses joined by a comma, a fused sentence is composed of two or more independent clauses joined by nothing at all:

> Young men like blue jeans they wear them all the time.

> Since the last major fish kill there has been a terrible smell around the lake all the summer residents are complaining about it.

The standard solution for fused sentence problems is to decide where the clauses join. Then insert a period, semicolon, or comma-plus-conjunction:

> Young men like blue jeans. They wear them all the time.

> Young men like blue jeans; they wear them all the time.

> Young men like blue jeans, and they wear them all the time.

The rules for comma faults apply to fused sentences as well. If you can handle comma faults, fused sentences should be no problem.

Exercise Comma Faults 4. Correct each of the following fused sentences in all of the three standard ways: once with a period and capital letter, once with a semicolon, and once with a comma-plus-conjunction. Be prepared to discuss the relative effectiveness of each correction.

1. His upper-body strength is outstanding lack of distance work has left his legs weak.
2. The downed wires were crackling with electricity a policeman directed passing motorists around them.
3. Young couples want houses that can expand to fit their needs cost is a factor also.
4. Trees were slowly growing visible in the early-morning gloom Charley was beginning the camp's breakfast.
5. Framing pictures calls for some artistic judgment not all color combinations set off prints effectively.

Exercise Comma Faults 5. Correct the comma faults and fused sentences in the way that seems most suitable. Be prepared to explain your choice of method.

1. I am a professional bartender, Mary is listening to the record player.
2. Igor lived in the cellar, since he was lame, the stairs were too much for him.
3. Bridget squealed her tires, then she roared off through the park.
4. Fire is partly burning gasses these are driven off from heated material.

5. The agents were called undercover men, they worked without revealing their identity to anyone.

6. Don't sit there that chair is broken and will collapse.

7. His sister is angry with us, in fact, she never wants to see either of us again.

8. I thought I had passed with flying colors, however, they said my feet were too flat for marching.

9. Biltmore is an impressive estate, I do not think anyone should have had the money it took to build and maintain it.

10. Look here it is apparent that you are talking out of turn.

Exercise Comma Faults 6. Correct the comma faults and fused sentences in the way that seems most suitable. Be prepared to explain your choice of method.

1. Put the chair in the corner by the television no one ever sits in it anyway.

2. Uganda is a dangerous place to be, therefore, I wish you would agree to stay home.

3. The Arctic fired men's imaginations for centuries, it was not conquered until comparatively recent times.

4. I was halfway down the stairs, when the gong rang, I turned and started back up in a hurry.

5. First wash the car thoroughly, then start applying the wax.

6. Where is my hat and coat I am already late for my appointment.

7. That store sells shoelaces, Henry will be in the bank this afternoon.

8. Day lilies are his favorite flowers, they are beautiful and easy to care for.

9. Denise said her raise was "acceptable" it more than doubled her take-home pay.

10. We took a hike, while the dinners were heating up by the fire, something came along and ate them.

Comma Fault Reference Chart

General Rule:
A break between two independent clauses must be punctuated by a period and capital letter, a semicolon, or a comma helped by a coordinating conjunction.

Trouble Spots:

19A
Recognize and correct comma faults.

Not, "The room was cold, the heat had been off for hours." but "The room was cold. The heat had been off for hours." "The room was cold; the heat had been off for hours." or "The room was cold, for the heat had been off for hours."

19B
Be especially alert for comma faults involving compound-complex sentences or conjunctive adverbs.

Not, "The barns were separated by water, because the flood had spread across the valley, the area was evacuated." but "The barns were separated by water. Because the flood had spread across the valley, the area was evacuated." And not, "I wanted to go on the trip, however, I couldn't fit it in." but "I wanted to go on the trip; however, I couldn't fit it in."

19C
Avoid fused sentences.

Not, "The pot was boiling over John raced to take it off the stove." but "The pot was boiling over. John raced to take it off the stove." or "The pot was boiling over; John raced to take it off the stove." or "The pot was boiling over, *so* John raced to take if off the stove.

20 Punctuation Between Independent Clauses [*punc. between*]

An independent clause can make a sentence by itself, but closely related clauses often sound better and communicate better when combined. Sentences that consist of two or more independent clauses (known as *compound* sentences) are common in good writing. Compound sentences express not only the ideas of their separate clauses but also the relationship between them. Knowing the combining techniques that make this possible will enable you to communicate these relationships with precision.

20A
Independent clauses may be combined through the comma-plus-conjunction method.

One of the major functions of the coordinating conjunctions—*and, but, or, nor, for, so,* and *yet*—is that with commas they can link independent clauses:

> Scientists claim they have heard an echo of the "Big Bang" of creation, *but* the evidence does not seem conclusive.
>
> I am not surprised to hear of his arrest, *for* he has been headed for trouble all along.
>
> The *Odyssey* seems to be based on the real geography of the Mediterranean, *and* scholars enjoy debating which islands and coasts Odysseus visited.

Comma-plus-conjunction linking is the most common method for combining independent clauses.

When To Use a Comma. A comma precedes a coordinating conjunction between two independent clauses. As a rule, however, a comma is *not* used when the conjunction comes between two subordinate clauses or two grammatical units that are not clauses at all:

He cut down the trees around the cabin, *and* he cleared the stumps.

He cut down the trees around the cabin *and* cleared the stumps.

Although these sentences are very much alike, the comma-plus-conjunction is called for in the first example because the *and* separates two whole clauses, each with its own subject and verb. No comma is necessary with the *and* in the second sentence because this time there is only one clause: a subject (*he*) with a double predicate (*cut down* and *cleared*).

Special Cases.   Other features of comma-plus-conjunction linking concern very short clauses and sentences that contain *three* or more independent clauses. When combining short clauses of seven words or less, many writers feel that it is excessive to add a comma to the conjunction, so they leave it out.

Harvey held the dog *and* his wife snipped its nails.

It would not be wrong to put a comma after *dog* in this sentence, and a cautious writer probably would do so. Once the decision is made, though, be consistent. It is best not to use one system of punctuation sometimes and then switch for no particular reason to the other.

Compound sentences that have three or more independent clauses need commas, but they can sometimes drop one or more of their conjunctions:

Peace is a classic yellow rose, First Prize is pink, *and* Oklahoma is dark red.

It may appear at first that there is a comma fault here after *rose*, but the *and* really applies there as well as between the last two clauses, so the comma is justified.

Exercise Independent Clauses 1. Write a compound sentence joined by the comma-plus-conjunction method for each of the seven coordinating conjuctions (before you start, read the comments on *so* in Chapter 35, "Problems in Usage"). Next, write three compound sentences with clauses short enough to make a comma unnecessary. Finally, write three compound sentences of three or more clauses each. Be prepared to show your sentences in class and discuss their punctuation.

Exercise Independent Clauses 2. Decide what punctuation, if any, should go in the slots marked by parentheses in the following sentences. Be prepared to explain your decisions.

1. Lavon has an advanced degree in journalism ( ) yet he has never learned to spell or punctuate properly.
2. The hurricane is moving this way ( ) and the town will be evacuated.
3. Catherine studied music at some of the best conservatories in the world ( ) but never attained the concert career she had hoped for.
4. My eyes are blue ( ) my hair is auburn ( ) and my dress is vivid green.

5. When the third quarter started, the Cougars were down by only three points ( ) but they had fallen further behind by the end of the game.

20B
Independent clauses may be combined by semicolons without conjunctions.

Semicolons (;) work like periods, except that they do not mark the end of a sentence. The capital letter after a period announces the beginning of a new sentence. There is no capital letter after a semicolon, and the sentence goes on:

> His wife is fascinated by violent movies; he is horrified by them.

> Wine was the drink of the upper classes; beer and ale were the beverages of the workingmen.

In these examples, the clauses linked by the semicolons are related to each other in meaning and form. The first sentence, for instance, compares the wife's reaction to violent movies to that of her husband, and each of the clauses is a Pattern Five construction as well. Semicolon linking works best with clauses like these—ones that have a lot in common—and most writers use semicolons sparingly because such balanced clauses do not come up too often. It would be an error in punctuation to use semicolons as you would periods, between any two clauses that happen to be independent. Readers expect some special relationship between clauses linked by semicolons, and they will feel misled if no such relationship is there.

Special Cases. A minor exception to the semicolon rule concerns very short clauses, which may be linked with commas instead of semicolons, even when there are no conjunctions present:

> I came, I saw, I conquered.

> John is twenty-one, Sheila is a teenager, Fred is just starting school.

Another exception concerns long and complicated sentences in which large numbers of commas mark minor divisions. Under these circumstances, many writers use semicolons *with* coordinating conjunctions just to give prominence to the important break between clauses:

> It was an old, battered guitar without strings, tuning pegs, and half its frets; *but* she cherished it because it had belonged to her father, a man she remembered only dimly.

Exercise Independent Clauses 3. Decide whether a comma, a semicolon, or no punctuation at all should go in the slots marked by parentheses in the following sentences. Be prepared to explain your decisions.

1. I was wrong ( ) you were right ( ) I'm sorry.

2. Many people felt Ali really *was* the greatest ( ) and they hated to see him trying to stretch his career beyond his prime.

3. He likes those restaurants where there is elaborate service ( ) I prefer the deli, where the customers look after themselves.

4. The Grand Prix season with all its glamor, suspense, and danger was on ( ) and no one could tell whether the new teams, whose cars and drivers were untested, stood any chance at all.

5. The river continued its rise inch by inch ( ) by morning all the moveable items in our garage had been washed away.

20C
Semicolons may be used with conjunctive adverbs and introductory phrases to link independent clauses.

Conjunctive adverbs and introductory phrases can lead to confusion because they look like conjunctions. Conjunctive adverbs are especially difficult. They resemble conjunctions, and they often mean the same thing as conjunctions, but yet they demand semicolons when they come between independent clauses. The following is a list of the ones you are most likely to use:

accordingly	likewise	otherwise
also	indeed	similarly
besides	instead	still
consequently	moreover	then
furthermore	namely	therefore
hence	nevertheless	thus
however	nonetheless	

When one of these words comes between independent clauses, the sentence should be punctuated almost as if there were no connecting word at all. The only difference is that the longer conjunctive adverbs are set off by a comma from the clause they introduce:

I thought I had been elected; *consequently,* I was shocked to hear Joan introduced as president.

I have one very important objection; *namely,* she has done nothing for the organization in the past.

One way to tell conjunctive adverbs from conjunctions is by their mobility: unlike conjunctions, conjunctive adverbs do not always appear at the beginning of their clauses. For instance, *consequently* in the first example above could occupy several positions in its clause. Although the semicolon would still be needed, it stays where it is; it does not travel with the conjunctive adverb:

I thought I had been elected; I *consequently* was shocked to hear Joan introduced as president.

I thought I had been elected; I was *consequently* shocked to hear Joan introduced as president.

I thought I had been elected; I was shocked, *consequently,* to hear Joan introduced as president.

The Conjunctive Adverb Then.   *Then* probably causes more difficulties than all other conjunctive adverbs together. It looks more like the subordinating conjunction *when* than like the other conjunctive adverbs, and it is rarely followed by a comma at the beginning of a clause. Nevertheless, *then* is a conjunctive adverb too, and it demands a semicolon when it appears between two independent clauses:

> I reached for my wallet; *then* the lights went out.

> Ollie will be coming for an extended visit next fall; *then* we will have some real parties again.

Note, though, that *then* requires a semicolon only between *independent* clauses. When one clause is dependent, as is the *if* clause in the example below, a semicolon would be out of place:

> If she sells her car, *then* she will have to walk to school.

Other Introducers.   Introductory words and phrases such as *for instance, for example, in short, in conclusion, first, second, finally, that is,* or *in other words* work like conjunctive adverbs. They do not have the force of conjunctions, so they take semicolons when they come between independent clauses in compound sentences:

> He has been behaving oddly; *for instance,* he always sits with his back to the table.

> *Exercise Independent Clauses 4.* Decide whether a comma, a semicolon, or no punctuation at all should go in the slots marked by parentheses in the following sentences. Be prepared to explain your decisions.
>
> 1. I imagine that you will sell the property ( ) then ( ) you can do some of that traveling you have talked about.
> 2. It is her intention ( ) furthermore ( ) to attend the meeting.
> 3. The rain showed no signs of letting up ( ) besides ( ) the day was steadily growing colder.
> 4. That was ( ) nevertheless ( ) an excellent rug ( ) that is ( ) it was well designed, beautifully made, and signed by the weaver.
> 5. She could never abide the thought of eating chicken ( ) thus ( ) she got very little enjoyment from the meal.

20D
Colons (:) may be used to separate independent clauses when the second clause explains or amplifies the first.

When they are used between independent clauses, colons have a special meaning: they are equivalent to such connecting words and phrases as *because, in other words,* or *that is.* Whenever the second clause of a compound sentence gives the reason for or restates some part of the first clause, colons can be used both to separate the two and to indicate the relationship between them:

> Shadburn was very irritated with his wife: she had refused to vote Democratic. (the second clause explains the first)

> He noted a very curious optical illusion: the truck seemed to be floating on thin air. (a *that is* relationship in which the second clause explains *illusion*)

The colons in these sentences are not strictly necessary. They could be replaced by periods, by semicolons, or by some other linking technique. But periods and semicolons can go between any pair of independent clauses. Colons do the job more precisely when the second clause explains or amplifies the first.

Exercise Independent Clauses 5. Decide whether a comma, a semicolon, a colon, or no punctuation at all would be the best choice for the positions marked by parentheses in the following sentences. Be prepared to explain your decisions.

1. She certainly was well-educated ( ) she had multiple degrees from some of the best universities in Europe.
2. The state should increase its spending for elementary and secondary education ( ) then we would have reason to believe in its determination to support learning.
3. The computer department was plagued by "down time" ( ) there were whole stretches in which the machines refused to work properly.
4. First, wash the walls thoroughly with detergent and water ( ) second ( ) apply the paint with a roller.
5. I *deserve* that new opening ( ) I have given my all for this firm ( ) and I have brought in more new business than any of the partners.

Exercise Independent Clauses 6. Decide whether a comma, a semicolon, a colon, or no punctuation at all would be the best choice for the positions marked by parentheses in the following sentences. Be prepared to explain your decisions.

1. *To* is a preposition or an infinitive marker ( ) *two* is a number ( ) and *too* is an intensifier or an adverb meaning "also."
2. Patrick has known her family for years ( ) but met her husband and child only recently.
3. Many cobras can spit their venom with great force and accuracy ( ) in fact ( ) people have been blinded by spitting cobras.
4. Please run this battery over to Holmender's garage for me ( ) it has almost completely lost its charge.
5. It seems that the news is presented with more urgency every year ( ) yet most of it is clearly trivial and insignificant.

6. We can afford to downplay Halloween this year ( ) then ( ) we will be able to concentrate our resources on the Thanksgiving party.

7. He is tall ( ) he is dark ( ) he is handsome.

8. Patagonia ( ) indeed ( ) is one of the last frontiers ( ) however ( ) even there progress makes itself felt.

9. Television is often influenced by the movies ( ) a successful movie ( ) for instance ( ) can inspire a whole series of television shows.

10. Doctor Temple has been feeling unwell herself ( ) consequently ( ) her appointments for today have been canceled.

Exercise Independent Clauses 7. Change the wording in the following sentences as directed, and correct the punctuation as needed. Be prepared to discuss your corrections.

1. Omit *although*
   Although he had always liked a good cigar, he found he also enjoyed smoking a pipe.

2. Change *in fact* to *thus*
   She has a talent, almost a genius, for mountain climbing; in fact, she was the only one of her party to make the new traverse.

3. Omit *she*
   Wanda had said her teacher was against her from the first, yet she changed her mind when he provided her bail.

4. Change *since* to *therefore*
   I know he was the only one in the room since the window was not opened after he left.

5. Change *then* to *when*
   We were in the process of changing lanes; then the motor died and the power steering failed.

6. Omit *in other words*
   Hamlet is full of dramatic irony; in other words, Shakespeare intended for us to take the characters quite differently than they take themselves.

7. Omit *and*
   Kermit cursed violently when he lost his balance, and he was even angrier when we laughed at his tumble.

8. Omit *if*
   If you go all the way to the end of the street, then you should see the cathedral half a block down to your left.

9. Change *though* to *however*
   I always expect to win though I never have won so far.

10. Change *besides* to *for*
    Each of his patents was returning a steady income and there were more inventions to look forward to; besides, he was paid well for his research and could afford to wait out the occasional dry spell.

Punctuation Between Independent Clauses Reference Chart

20A
Independent clauses may be combined through the comma-plus-conjunction method.

She was careful about changing the oil regularly, *and* her car ran well for years.

Ken scrabbled desperately for hold, *but* nothing he could do would stop his slow slide toward the edge of the rock.

20B
Independent clauses may be combined by semicolons without conjunctions.

Lawyers see that their clients' wishes are carried out; they also keep their clients from being victimized by other people's plans.

20C
Semicolons may be used with conjunctive adverbs and introductory phrases to link independent clauses.

I will get to work on it next week; *then* you will see some real progress.

Paula must have gone the long way; *otherwise,* she would be there by now.

He has a lot of expensive toys; *for example,* his sound system alone is worth more than a thousand dollars.

20D
Colons (:) may be used to separate independent clauses when the second clause explains or amplifies the first.

Ben Jonson led an adventurous life: he fought duels and was thrown into prison more than once.

Mitochondria are really free-living symbionts: they have their own genetic material and trace their ancestry to independent life forms.

21

Punctuation Before Independent Clauses [*punc. before*]

To separate independent clauses from subordinate elements of different kinds, you must master the distinction between places where punctuation is demanded and the places in which it is merely optional. For each situation in which punctuation is up to the writer, you must also determine what your usual practice will be. This way you can stop uncertainties before they develop and ensure that your punctuation will be as consistent as possible.

21A
Use a comma to set off introductory words and phrases that modify the whole clause that follows.

Many introductory words and phrases modify particular parts of a main clause, but there are others such as *first, second, last, finally, in fact, on the other hand, in other words, that is, by contrast, for instance*, or *in the first place* that modify the whole clause that follows, usually by showing its relationship to the sentences around it. Most of the conjunctive adverbs listed in 20C also fit into this category since they, too, provide transitions between whole clauses. They modify the clause they introduce by tying it to the ones that have gone before. Sentence modifiers of any of these types should be set off with commas from the clauses they introduce:

By the way, have you seen his latest book yet?

Consequently, she has sued the paper for libel.

All things considered, the job has worked out well.

Exercise Before Independent Clauses 1. Write ten sentences of your own, using an introductory sentence modifier set off with a comma from the main clause. Try to use modifiers not included in the examples given so far.

21B
Use a comma to set off introductory words or phrases when their relationship to the rest of the sentence would be unclear without punctuation.

There would ordinarily be no need to set off short introducers like *above, with Ada,* or *under the tree,* but observe the confusion that results when such words and phrases are combined with clauses whose subjects could also work as part of an introductory phrase:

Above the tall sails swelled majestically.

With Ada Henderson has had some memorable moments.

Under the tree frogs were croaking despondently.

In each of these sentences, the introducer threatens to swallow up the subject of the main clause, and a comma is needed to prevent a momentary misunderstanding:

Above, the tall sails swelled majestically.

With Ada, Henderson has had some memorable moments.

Under the tree, frogs were croaking despondently.

Exercise Before Independent Clauses 2. Put a comma in each of the following sentences to prevent the subject of the main clause from mistakenly being read with the introductory element. Be prepared to explain why the comma is necessary.

1. Underneath the boat was painted a creamy yellow.
2. Besides John Henry was the only participant from Michigan.
3. Around the corner grocery stores lined the street for half a block.
4. For example number one teams are rarely beaten by unranked ones.
5. All around the dog house flies buzzed lazily in the heat.

21C
Use a comma to set off long introductory phrases unless they cause a reversal of word order in the main clause that follows.

Long is a vague word, but because the practice of good writers varies widely there is no way to be much more specific about this rule. In general, introductory phrases of more than seven words should be set off:

Under the looming bulk of the seaward cliffs, the sails of the little boats looked threatened and vulnerable.

Across the top of the table by the front door, a selection of magazines was fanned out like a card hand.

Shorter phrases—unless they are sentence modifiers, verbal phrases (see 21D), or sources of potential confusion—need not be set off. It is not wrong to put commas after short introductory phrases, but some writers feel that doing so makes sentences appear too complicated. These writers regularly place no punctuation between short introductory elements and their main clauses:

> *After lunch* he always liked to have a nap.

> *Through there* you will find a place to sit down.

The one time it is definitely wrong to set off an introductory phrase, no matter how long or short it is, is when the phrase causes a reversal of word order in the main clause that follows:

> *Beside the stone barn and cast into shade by its overhanging roof* was an incredible find, a 1919 Ford in mint condition.

> *In France* live some of the most knowledgeable bibliophiles in the world.

In both of these sentences, the word order of the main clause is turned around, with the verb coming *before* the subject. When this happens, the introductory element is not set off, even if it is twelve words long as is the case in the example about the stone barn.

> *Exercise Before Independent Clauses 3.* Decide whether or not you would put a comma in the slots marked by parentheses in the following sentences. Be prepared to explain your reasoning.

> **1.** Beside the stone barn and cast into shade by its overhanging roof ( ) the old Ford sat rusting on sagging axles.

> **2.** In French ( ) words for kinds of food are especially numerous.

> **3.** Over the ridge between our farm and the broad valley of the Red River ( ) was spread a silent forest of tall pine trees.

> **4.** In my closet ( ) I have clothes for all occasions.

> **5.** After our lunch of sausages, brown bread, cheese, and beer ( ) we felt less inclined than ever to walk the next ten kilometers.

21D
Use a comma to set off introductory modifiers based on verbals.

Two kinds of introductory elements come under this rule: verbal modifiers themselves, and introductory prepositional phrases that have gerunds as their objects. Verbal modifiers consist of introductory infinitives or participles, appearing alone or as parts of phrases. These are always set off from the main clause that follows:

> *To love,* one must first understand. (infinitive)

> *Satisfied,* she leaned back against the wall. (participle)

To ward off a cold, one must practice preventive medicine. (infinitive phrase)

Sighing with boredom, Max toyed with his buttons. (participial phrase)

Introductory prepositional phrases with gerund objects must be set off the same way:

In dreaming, one often confronts his deepest fears.

By being ready on time, Ken gave us a chance to stop for a late breakfast.

Watching Out for Subjects.   One special note of caution is necessary here. Gerunds and infinitives can both serve as *subjects* of clauses, and when they do they are not set off from the rest of the clause:

Being ready on time will help us a great deal.

To love is to have the courage to risk getting hurt.

To tell the difference between a verbal that is part of a modifier and one that is a subject, see how the sentence would sound without the word or phrase in question. If you could safely omit the verbal and whatever words go with it, you are dealing with a modifier and it should be set off. If dropping the verbal or verbal phrase would leave the sentence incomplete, it is the subject and should not be set off. In a sentence like "To love, one must first understand," *to love* can be omitted. It is a modifier and should be set off. In "To love is to have the courage to risk getting hurt," *to love* is the subject. It cannot be omitted and should not be set off.

Exercise Before Independent Clauses 4. Decide whether or not you would put a comma in the slots marked by parentheses in the following sentences. Be prepared to explain your decisions.

1. By bellowing at the top of her lungs ( ) she was finally able to make herself understood.

2. To be up in the airplane by yourself at last ( ) comes as a relief after your instructor's critical scrutiny.

3. Dripping with sweat ( ) Lanny began to feel the chill.

4. Driving in that kind of rain ( ) will take years off your life.

5. To mend that leak ( ) you will need tar paper and roofing nails.

21E
Use a comma to set off long introductory clauses or ones whose relation to the rest of the sentence would be unclear without punctuation.

It is best to develop the habit of setting off all introductory clauses.

When I arrived, the house had already been sold.

Because she had seen the new comet first and had called general attention to it, it was given her name.

The comma in the first sentence is not strictly necessary, but it is still a good idea to use it. The writer who punctuates all introductory clauses does not have to worry about how long each one is, and there is another thing he does not have to worry about as well. Sometimes introductory clauses, like introductory phrases, can cause misreadings by seeming at first glance to include words that are really part of the main clause following them:

> *Though the dogs smell* the air freshener covers the odor.

> *When he swears* often he is just seeking attention.

Neither of these introductory clauses needs to be punctuated on grounds of length, but both of them should be set off for clarity:

> *Though the dogs smell,* the air freshener covers the odor.

> *When he swears,* often he is just seeking attention.

The writer who punctuates all introductory clauses handles problem constructions like these automatically.

Exercise Before Independent Clauses 5. Mark with a comma the end of each introductory clause in the following sentences. Be prepared to say whether each comma is necessary or optional and why.

1. Unless I am entirely mistaken about the nature and seriousness of his illness he should be back before next week.
2. After she came down the path I saw she had dropped a glove.
3. Wherever he led the three little ducks followed him.
4. Since we have graduated from the university and help support it with our contributions we feel we are entitled to tickets.
5. Before he returned the package was waiting for him.

Exercise Before Independent Clauses 6. Decide whether or not a comma should go in the slots marked by parentheses in the following sentences. Be prepared to explain your decisions.

1. Beneath the button ( ) holes had worn through the fabric.
2. In the first place ( ) there is no reason to suppose she is coming.
3. All around the desk ( ) were pages that had been crumpled and rejected.
4. Because the tight bands were cutting in ( ) his flesh lost all feeling.
5. Hearing the bells peal ( ) Helga realized she was late already.
6. Beyond the fence but still in plain view of everyone on the porch ( ) the tom turkey strutted defiantly back and forth.
7. To be sure of a good reception ( ) it is best to bring a gift for each of the children.

8. Tearing down the alley on his skateboard ( ) calmed his nerves but irritated his mother's.

9. While she was still in Turkestan and recovering from her accident ( ) she began to gain an appreciation of Near Eastern history.

10. At the moment the nurse squeezed ( ) the hypodermic burst in her fingers.

Exercise Before Independent Clauses 7. Decide whether or not a comma should go in the slots marked by parentheses in the following sentences. Be prepared to explain your decisions.

1. If Willy asks me ( ) I will tell him everything I know about it.

2. By tightening the set screw ( ) Vernon was able to fix the spindle firmly in its slot.

3. To be absolutely sure of what happened ( ) is impossible after all this time.

4. At the dead end of the street that ran by our house ( ) was the enormous field where we spent most of each summer day.

5. Farther down ( ) the river divides, and only one branch feeds the new reservoir.

6. Although Karen has never met him to the best of my knowledge ( ) she has read all his books and speaks of him with reverence.

7. Cooking over an open fire ( ) is a good way to burn your cuffs.

8. When we were touring ( ) Europe was not as expensive as it is now.

9. Looking down the shaft ( ) she could see the bend in the club.

10. After playing softly for several measures ( ) the orchestra blared a single chord with all its power.

Punctuation Before Independent Clauses Reference Chart

21A
Use a comma to set off introductory words and phrases that modify the whole clause that follows.

In other words, he is crooked as a corkscrew.

Incidentally, I did very well in that class.

21B
Use a comma to set off introductory words or phrases when their relationship to the rest of the sentence would be unclear without punctuation.

Not, "*Throughout* the season went from bad to worse," but "*Throughout,* the season went from bad to worse."

21C
Use a comma to set off long introductory phrases unless they cause a reversal of word order in the main clause that follows.

Between the brick houses on either side of the street, the residents had planted tiny gardens.
but
Between the brick houses on either side of the street were narrow passages.

21D
Use a comma to set off introductory modifiers based on verbals.

Weakening visibly, he staggered toward the finish line.

To do well, you must try hard.

Through cutting corners, they were able to save a good amount.

21E
Use a comma to set off long introductory clauses or ones whose relation to the rest of the sentence would be unclear without punctuation.

After Pam came in from the all-night disco party, she slept until four in the afternoon.

As Freddie turned, the screwdriver dropped to the floor.

22

Punctuation After Clauses [punc. after]

In the position after a clause, almost anything can crop up, and knowing how to handle particular problems can be difficult. But many writers develop a fondness for punctuating elements that follow clauses. It presents some interesting challenges.

| **22A**
Use a comma to set off nonessential subordinate clauses that come after other clauses.

If there is a no-man's land in punctuation, this is it. Some very good writers cannot easily explain why they have or have not punctuated a specific modifying clause following another clause—the circumstances are sometimes that uncertain. But one general principle is worth honoring: when you are unsure about an *introductory* clause, the best plan is to set it off; but when you have doubts about a subordinate clause that *follows* another clause, you should take the opposite approach—do *not* punctuate:

When he comes back from the movies, we will ask him.

We will ask him *when he comes back from the movies.*

Whether or not a subordinate clause coming after another clause should be set off is determined not by length but by *function.* When the subordinate element presents information that is vital to a proper understanding of the sentence as a whole, it is part of the sentence and should *not* be set off. But when the trailing subordinate clause simply adds another thought to an idea that was already clear and complete without it, it should be set off, just to show that it is not essential:

I will cooperate *if you will.*

John was satisfied, *though no one else was.*

Without its subordinate clause the first of these sentences would not express the writer's intention. The speaker plans to cooperate *only if* the other person goes along. But in the second sentence, John is satisfied no matter what. It is interesting to know that no one else felt the same way, but that does not change what the first clause says.

In actual writing, sentences that clearly reflect this difference between essential and nonessential information can seem rare. One way to resolve doubtful cases is to read the sentence aloud. Most people can *hear* where the comma, if there ought to be one, should go. Try saying these sentences to yourself:

> He swiped your lunch because he was hungry.
>
> Now he will be unwelcome even if he does come.

In the second sentence, there should be a pause in your reading right after the word *unwelcome.* This pause tells you that there should be a comma at that point, that *even if he does come* is nonessential information.

If the voice method does not work for you at first, try considering the nature of the conjunction at the head of your subordinate clause. Some subordinating conjunctions—such as *because, before, if, since, so that,* and *when*—commonly introduce essential ideas, and their clauses are unlikely to be set off. Another group of conjunctions—ones like *although, as if, as though, even if, even though, though,* and *whether or not*—lend themselves to introducing concessions or other nonessential information, and their clauses are set off more often.

Finally, remember the general principle: when in doubt *do not* punctuate a subordinate clause that follows another clause.

> *Exercise After Clauses 1.* Decide whether or not a comma should go in the slots marked by parentheses in the following sentences. Be prepared to explain your decisions.
>
> **1.** Thomas is a handsome man ( ) even if he does have dandruff.
>
> **2.** The foreman asked her ( ) if she could run a lathe.
>
> **3.** Although we have long been the best of friends, she is a rabid Dodgers fan ( ) while I always pull for the Yankees.
>
> **4.** There will be time to get the shopping done ( ) after this game is over.
>
> **5.** He thought I could help him with all his subjects ( ) just because I had been accepted to medical school.

22B
Use a comma to set off sentence modifiers, questions, and contrasts that follow a clause.

Of the many modifying words and phrases that can come at the end of a clause, the only ones that need to be set off are those that amplify, question, or explain the whole thought that has gone before:

He has been a great success, *especially in plastics.*

We are interested in quantity, *not quality.*

You have my telephone number, *haven't you?*

Alice sulked, *slamming the dishes around in the sink.*

I plan to be there tomorrow, *as a matter of fact.*

The modifying phrases in these sentences resemble the nonessential clauses discussed in 22A: each of them adds extra information to an idea that would be complete without it, and each would be preceded by a pause if its sentence were spoken aloud. The commas are needed to signal these pauses. By contrast, each of the modifiers marked in the next group of examples goes with a particular word that is part of the main clause. All of these are closely tied to their clauses, and none should be set off:

We searched *for my adventurous aunt.* (modifies *searched*)

Charles saw a man *changing a tire.* (modifies *man*)

I am sorry *to say so.* (modifies *sorry*)

Exercise After Clauses 2. Decide whether or not a comma should go in the slots marked by parentheses in the following sentences. Be prepared to explain your decisions.

1. Sylvester greeted the diplomats ( ) entering the air terminal.

2. They steered for the shore ( ) sailing close to the wind.

3. We are playing bridge tonight ( ) not canasta.

4. On her plate was a mountain ( ) of mashed potatoes.

5. I am excited about the new baby ( ) to be sure.

22C
Use a comma or a dash to set off a short appositive or summary at the end of a clause.

An appositive renames or redescribes an element that has gone before, and a summary ties a sprawling or undefined idea into a neat, concise package. Words or phrases that serve either of these functions should be set off from the body of the clause by a comma or a dash when you are writing informally or when the element to be set off is short and clear:

He did not invent much—*just the ballpoint pen.*

Myra has one important virtue—*determination.*

There was my oldest friend, *Howard Zermatt.*

It was a good apple, *tart and crisp.*

No very definite rule exists about when to choose commas and when to use dashes to set off such phrases. You have to decide for yourself how you want the sentence to sound. A dash is like a spotlight. It indicates a strong pause and makes the words that follow stand out dramatically. Dashes are good choices for appositives or summaries that are amusing, surprising, or particularly important. Punctuating with a comma, on the other hand, causes the final element to blend smoothly with its clause, and this produces the effect you want if there is nothing especially dramatic about your final element. Say the sentence to yourself and notice how long your voice pauses at the end of the clause. A strong pause will require a dash, a weaker one a comma.

22D
Use a colon (:) to set off a long or formal appositive, summary, or list at the end of a clause.

Section 20D discusses the use of a colon to connect two independent clauses when the second explains or amplifies the first. An extension of that rule is that a colon may be used to set off not just an independent clause but any long or formal explanatory element at the end of another clause.

Vote for Prokbroom: *a man of vision, sensitivity, courage, and tenacity.*

She is an impressive woman: *intelligent, determined, and effective.*

Butch was a big, strong pointer: *an imposing animal with the stamina to hunt all day.*

Colons also frequently introduce lists, especially long and formal ones:

His classes this semester include the following: *Biology 101, Ancient Civilization, Modern Algebra, and Psychology 100.*

There are several important steps in serving: *1) get the proper grip, 2) make a high, consistent ball toss, and 3) follow through.*

Be careful to use colons only to set off *additional* information following clauses that are already complete. It is always a mistake to put a colon before a list that is an essential part of a larger clause or phrase:

Henry is: *young, lively, handsome, and available.* (the colon is unjustified because the words in the list are predicate adjectives, parts of the basic clause)

I prefer: *rare steaks, well-done potatoes, and cold beer.* (unjustified colon setting off three direct objects)

You've always been attracted to: *Monet, Ryder, and Klee.* (unjustified colon setting off three objects of the preposition *to*)

Exercise After Clauses 3. Decide whether a comma, a dash, a colon, or no punctuation at all should go in each of the slots marked by parentheses in the following sentences. Be prepared to explain your decisions.

1. He has one all-consuming passion in his life ( ) rock music.

2. I admit I felt ( ) useless, rejected, and washed-up.

3. The contents of his basket were as follows ( ) a bag of corn chips, a carton of soft drinks, a package of Almond Joys, a box of crackers, and fourteen cans of deviled ham.

4. There is one especially lovely tree in their yard ( ) a Norway Maple.

5. I set a record for the whole real estate business ( ) getting fired after my first eighteen minutes on the job.

Exercise After Clauses 4. Decide whether a comma, a dash, a colon, or no punctuation at all should go in each of the slots marked by parentheses in the following sentences. Be prepared to explain your decisions.

1. It was a great injustice ( ) because she had already paid off most of the note.

2. You do want part of my Snickers bar ( ) don't you?

3. Mel said he was concerned about her safety ( ) though he had never cared what happened to her before.

4. David has always had a soft spot for ( ) puppies, kittens, ducklings, and baby chicks.

5. I am sure the man said to turn left ( ) not right.

6. We will not be sure of our diagnosis ( ) until the results of the latest tests come in.

7. This was a man who was all things to all people ( ) a farmer among farmers, a businessman in the town, an academic when he came on campus, and a friend to everyone he met.

8. Quinn asked me to be his sponsor ( ) in short.

9. She had only one dedicated and formidible enemy ( ) her brother.

10. I plan to see that movie tonight ( ) whether you like it or not.

Exercise After Clauses 5. Decide whether a comma, a dash, a colon, or no punctuation at all should go in each of the slots marked by parentheses in the following sentences. Be prepared to explain your decisions.

1. His greed overcame his scruples in the end ( ) apparently.

2. That clerk has been expecting the worst ( ) since he told Kathy he would not accept her check.

3. When I went to the store, I bought ( ) bananas, bread, baked beans, and braunschweiger.

4. He heard something moving in the darkness ( ) his cat in all probability.

5. Ammonia will do just as good a job ( ) provided that the grime is not too thick.

6. Jean was a woman who cared for her family, worked hard, and took an interest in the affairs of her town ( ) an all around good citizen.

7. Bobby has had a number of hobbies ( ) butterflies, bird watching, stamp collecting, shortwave radio, and gourmet cooking.

8. He is the same man who was here earlier ( ) isn't he?

9. I have always wanted to watch Dr. Kennedy ( ) when she operates.

10. That axe was gnawed by a porcupine ( ) not a beaver.

Punctuation After Clauses Reference Chart

22A
Use a comma to set off nonessential subordinate clauses that come after other clauses.

Make him come to you, *even if he seems reluctant at first.*

22B
Use a comma to set off sentence modifiers, questions, and contrasts that follow a clause.

He made all-conference at defensive end, *for example.*

Tom has been notified, *hasn't he?*

She was elected senator, *not representative.*

22C
Use a comma or a dash to set off a short appositive or summary at the end of a clause.

It was a sizeable gash—*122 stitches!*

The first printing was small, *only four hundred copies.*

22D
Use a colon (:) to set off a long or formal appositive, summary, or list at the end of a clause.

I am impressed with your many good traits: *courtesy, honesty, vitality, compassion, and insight.*

It was quite a car: *an old sedan with rusted-out fenders and four different kinds of paint.*

23 *Restrictive and Nonrestrictive Modifiers [res. mod., nonres. mod]*

As with the use of a colon between independent clauses or a question mark at the end of an otherwise ordinary statement, punctuation for restrictive and nonrestrictive modifiers has real impact on meaning. In writing, the difference between restrictive and nonrestrictive modifiers is communicated entirely by punctuation.

A *restrictive* modifier is an adjective clause or phrase that *restricts* or limits the noun it modifies:

> All students *who do their work* should pass easily.

The italicized clause in this sentence is restrictive: it limits the subject to *only* those students who do their work. Taking the clause out would make the sentence mean something else, that all students of any kind will pass easily. The modifying clause, in other words, is essential to the full meaning of the sentence.

A *nonrestrictive* modifier works differently. It too is an adjective clause or phrase, but it functions to provide *additional* or nonessential information about its noun:

> My roommates, *who do their work,* should pass easily.

In this sentence, *roommates* is not limited by the adjective clause; instead, the clause merely presents some additional information about the subject. Two things are true about these roommates: they will pass easily, and they do their work. Taking the modifier away would not destroy the writer's meaning. It would only leave us knowing a little less about his hardworking roommates.

Punctuating Restrictive and Nonrestrictive Modifiers. *Restrictive* modifiers are essential to their sentences. The subject of the first example sentence is not just *students*, but *students-who-do-their-work*. Because restrictive modifiers are essential, they are not set off by commas. *Nonrestrictive* modifiers, on the other hand, are not essential. Their sentences can do without them. And because they present only additional information, they are set off from the rest of the sentence to show that they could be left out without harming the basic idea.

The difference between restrictive and nonrestrictive modifiers sometimes depends on exactly what the writer wants to say:

> My cousin *who had a broken leg* was at the picnic.
>
> My cousin, *who had a broken leg*, was at the picnic.

In the first sentence, the writer singles out the cousin he has in mind from all his other cousins by mentioning the broken leg as an identifying characteristic. The writer of the second sentence assumes we already know which cousin he means (maybe he has only one). In this second sentence, "who had a broken leg" is presented as additional information. The difference between these situations is established entirely through punctuation.

23A
Use commas or dashes to set off nonrestrictive modifying clauses.

Most of the clauses that come under this rule and the next start with one of the relative pronouns—*that, what, whatever, which, whichever, who, whom, whose, whoever,* and *whomever*. These clauses come after the noun they modify, and each one requires that the writer decide whether it is restrictive or nonrestrictive. Nonrestrictive modifying clauses are always set off from the rest of their sentence:

> My mother, *who had always believed Bobby*, was upset.
>
> Jim Howe, *whom I favor for magistrate*, is Catholic.
>
> Chicago, *which was settled about the same time*, monopolized shipping.
>
> Her answer, *whatever it was*, went unrecorded.

In each of these sentences, the main clause can be read *without* the italicized modifier and still adequately express the writer's basic idea. The modifiers do not restrict or define the subjects, and they are therefore set off.

Special Cases. Some special situations arise in punctuation of nonrestrictive modifying clauses. Most of these clauses are like the ones in the example sentences above: they are set off with *two* commas, one before and one after the modifying element. But sometimes a nonrestrictive clause comes at the end of a sentence, and it is then set off by *one* comma. The period at the end of the sentence marks the close of the sentence and the close of the modifier at the same time:

> They consulted Father Murphy, *who was an expert on insects*.
>
> We shop at Buellers, *which is the best store in town*.

On other occasions, nonrestrictive modifying clauses may have internal punctuation of their own. In these cases, *dashes* are the best choice for setting them off. The advantage of dashes under these circumstances is that they make the nonrestrictive element stand out clearly, whereas the usual commas might merely get lost amid the other punctuation:

> Our postman—*who is a man of generosity, tolerance, and great physical courage*—has become resigned to facing Diablo each morning.

> They raised thousands to protect the Charter Oak—*which had stood for over a hundred years as a symbol of democracy, a monument to political commitment, and a tourist attraction*—but their effort was unsuccessful.

Exercise Restrictive and Nonrestrictive 1. Supply the correct punctuation to set off the nonrestrictive clauses in the following sentences.

1. Aunt Eudora who has taken an interest in poker gambled away Cousin Jeff's tuition.

2. The doctor told Vera her problem was an ingrown toenail which is rarely fatal.

3. My motorcycle which is an old, broken-down Harley runs well enough to get me to work most days.

4. She found she was supposed to return a call from her pastor who was handling the bake sale himself.

5. Juanita's kitten whatever breed it may be is attractive and friendly.

23B
Do not set off restrictive modifying clauses.

Restrictive clauses look just like nonrestrictive ones, but they are more closely tied to the basic meaning of their sentences. Instead of providing interesting additional information, restrictive clauses present vital identifying characteristics, information without which the meaning of the sentence would be incomplete or inaccurate:

> All students *who have school spirit* will attend the rally.

> He met a World War II veteran *who had known his father.*

> The John Jones *I knew* was an outstanding biochemist.

In each of these sentences, the italicized clause is an essential part of what the writer is trying to communicate. The sentences do not concern just any students, veteran, or John Jones, but students-who-have-school-spirit, a veteran-who-had-known-his-father, and the John Jones-I-knew. When a modifying clause is restrictive—when, as in these example, it singles out one particular individual or group from all the individuals or groups that might otherwise be meant and the sentence would be incomplete or inaccurate without it—the clause is necessary to the sentence as a whole and *should not* be set off.

Exercise Restrictive and Nonrestrictive 2. Decide whether each of the italicized clauses in the following sentences is restrictive or nonrestrictive, and punctuate accordingly.

1. Will the individual *who found the handkerchief* please turn it in at the box office?

2. Standing like a beacon in the middle of that vast plain was Salisbury Cathedral *which had been a landmark since the Middle Ages.*

3. I will give this stuffed panda to the one *who can come closest to guessing his own weight.*

4. Bishop Ridlet *who was no stranger to hard, grinding labor* was especially appreciated by the working families of the diocese.

5. The only barn *that I could see* was a red one beneath the crest of the ridge.

23C
Use commas or dashes to set off nonrestrictive modifying phrases.

Like adjective clauses, phrases that modify nouns or pronouns can be either restrictive or nonrestrictive. Nonrestrictive phrases present extra information about their target words and should be set off from the rest of their clause:

> The red buck, *young and powerful,* steadily wore his older opponent down.

> My coach, *excited by the play,* bit through his cigar.

> Mother, *with her fighting spirit aroused,* went after the salesman with her broom.

The italicized modifiers in these sentences include a pair of adjectives, a participial phrase, and a prepositional phrase, but each of them functions like the nonrestrictive clauses discussed in 23A. Each one brings additional information about its noun into a sentence that would be complete and accurate without it, and each one should be set off to show its nonessential nature.

Most nonrestrictive modifying phrases are set off with commas, but dashes can be used when the element to be set off includes some internal punctuation of its own:

> Their latest album—*light, entertaining, and slickly packaged*—seems likely to be a great success.

23D
Do not set off restrictive modifying phrases.

Any nonrestrictive modifying phrase can also be restrictive: the difference is a matter of meaning rather than form. A restrictive modifying phrase presents information essential to its sentence:

The doctors *most affected by the rate increase* will be those *most often involved in malpractice suits.*

We need a person *with experience* to run the machine shop.

The last man *to see her* was Xavier.

None of these sentences can express the writer's full intention without the italicized modifying phrases. Each phrase is necessary, or restrictive, and none should be set off.

Exercise Restrictive and Nonrestrictive 3. Decide whether each of the italicized modifying phrases in the following sentences is restrictive or nonrestrictive, and punctuate accordingly.

1. The man *at the back of the line* was getting impatient.

2. My father *at the back of the line* was getting impatient.

3. His figure *short and dumpy* was not his strongest point as a model.

4. The corn *producing the greatest yield per acre* will be exported.

5. The slumping figure they had seen was Dean Mounce *exhausted by the strain of defending the arts against the unimaginative, hostile comments of the committee.*

23E
Use commas or dashes to set off nonrestrictive appositives.

Appositives are words or groups of words that rename nouns or pronouns. Because appositives add information to a clause, they can be restrictive or nonrestrictive, depending on whether the information they present is essential or not. As with other nonrestrictive elements, nonrestrictive appositives bring additional, nonessential material into their sentences and should be set off:

Howard's druggist, *a man of the world*, endorses Brut aftershave lotion.

The orange tree, *an unusually efficient plant*, often has fruit and flowers at the same time.

When nonrestrictive appositives are long and complicated, dashes set them off clearly. Use dashes especially when appositives contain their own punctuation:

Billy was a local hero—*a hobo with nothing but a harmonica, a pet mongrel, and the clothes he stood up in, but a man who had resisted all the pressure the county government could exert on him to become "rehabilitated."*

23F
Do not set off restrictive appositives.

A restrictive appositive is important to the full meaning of its sentence because it limits or defines the word it renames. Restrictive appositives are not frequently used, and they tend to conform to a pattern. Usually the renamed noun refers to a class of individuals, and the appositive itself gives the proper name of the particular individual meant:

> The pianist *Serkin* is noted for the clarity of his phrasing.
>
> My cousin *Ted* opens cans with his teeth.

In this area as in others, the writer's precise meaning is critical. Notice the difference in implication between these two sentences:

> My brother *Bob* spends money as fast as he gets it.
>
> My brother, *Bob*, spends money as fast as he get it.

In the first sentence, *Bob* is not set off. The implication is that the writer has more than one brother and has included the name to make it clear which one he means. In the second sentence, *Bob* is treated as a nonrestrictive appositive. The implication this time is that the reader knows to whom *My brother* refers and that the name is included just as an additional reminder.

Exercise Restrictive and Nonrestrictive 4. Decide whether each of the italicized appositives in the following sentences is restrictive or nonrestrictive, and punctuate accordingly.

1. The egg *a miracle of nature* is one of the most efficient containers the world has yet seen.
2. They were altogether enchanted with my uncle *an old man with a lively, interesting mind and a charming manner.*
3. The scientists *Watson and Crick* are credited with the unraveling of the DNA molecule.
4. Three underclassmen *Thompson, Fredricks, and Ware* were present.
5. The horse *a lean animal with a wicked, cunning glint in its eye* sized me up immediately.

Exercise Restrictive and Nonrestrictive 5. Decide what punctuation, if any, should go in the slots marked by parentheses in the following sentences. Be prepared to explain your decisions.

1. All students ( ) who are either male or female ( ) can tell you about sex discrimination in the schools.
2. My history teacher ( ) a man of great dignity ( ) was upset when he stuck his foot in the wastebasket.
3. Anyone ( ) who knows what is really important in life ( ) is unlikely to work himself to death.
4. The latest stray ( ) foot-sore, matted, and painfully thin ( ) was already at home in her kitchen.
5. The astronaut ( ) Gregarniev ( ) was arrested for driving without a license.

6. Timmy Fox ( ) one of the best baseball, basketball, and football players ever to live on our block ( ) is now selling shoes.

7. She plans to have a career ( ) with as much excitement as possible.

8. She is looking forward to taking over this office ( ) which has become known as a refuge for oddballs, goof-offs, and rebels.

9. Is this the face ( ) that launched a thousand ships?

10. The President ( ) besieged by critics ( ) finally resigned.

Exercise Restrictive and Nonrestrictive 6. Decide what punctuation, if any, should go in the slots marked by parentheses in the following sentences. Be prepared to explain your decisions.

1. The gentleman ( ) with the top hat and cane ( ) is her escort.

2. We were concerned about the Third Division ( ) which had been shelled continuously since dawn.

3. The poet ( ) Longfellow ( ) is no longer so highly regarded as he was in the first half of the century.

4. They were selling Arkansas Toothpicks ( ) long, heavy fighting knives with wicked-looking blades.

5. The prairie dogs ( ) which had grown accustomed to her by now ( ) crowded around.

6. The prairie dogs ( ) which she studied ( ) were inside the city limits of Amarillo.

7. Cherry pie ( ) my all-time favorite ( ) is especially good when warm from the oven.

8. The clerk ( ) found responsible for this shortage ( ) will be in deep trouble with the bank.

9. Chamber works ( ) usually intimate in scale ( ) allow all the instruments to be clearly heard.

10. Beware of Greeks ( ) bearing gifts.

Restrictive and Nonrestrictive Modifiers Reference Chart

General Rule:
Nonrestrictive modifiers should be set off from their clauses. Restrictive ones should not be.

Trouble Spots:

23A
Use commas or dashes to set off nonrestrictive modifying clauses.

His dentist, *who had served in Vietnam,* was also an interesting storyteller.

My house—*which has tall ceilings, big windows, and lots of gables*—is somewhat different from the ranch houses of the suburbs.

23B
Do not set off restrictive modifying clauses.

The person *whom he blames for the failure* is not here.

23C
Use commas or dashes to set off nonrestrictive modifying phrases.

The old mastiff, *too feeble to eat,* had to be fed by hand.

My little sister—*joyful, enthusiastic, and creative*—would be a great help to the decorations committee.

23D
Do not set off restrictive modifying phrases.

The man *with his hand on his hip* has been watching us.

23E
Use commas or dashes to set off nonrestrictive appositives.

The racoon, *an unusually engaging animal,* makes a fine pet.

Three authors—*Thoreau, Melville, and Twain*—were covered in the seminar.

23F
Do not set off restrictive appositives.

The philosopher *Kant* thought best while walking.

24 *Parenthetical Elements* [*parenth.*]

A parenthetical element is an interruption that needs to be set off from the clause in which it appears. Parenthetical elements (as is the case with the nonrestrictive modifiers discussed in Chapter 23) are always *extra*. They are never part of the basic structure of the clauses they interrupt. To omit them never harms the essential meaning of the sentence.

24A
Use commas to set off words in direct address.

Direct address is, as its name implies, an utterance aimed directly at specific listeners or readers:

Yes, *Virginia*, there is a Santa Claus.

My dear, I believe that you are mistaken.

Attention, *troop*, this is not the Cub Scout way!

Each of these sentences would be complete and accurate without the name of the person or group addressed. It is because these names are not really necessary to their clauses that they must be set off.

Exercise Parenthetical Elements 1. Decide what punctuation, if any, should go in the slots marked by parentheses in the following sentences. Be prepared to explain your decisions.

1. Pardon me ( ) sweetheart ( ) but you are standing on my toe.
2. Kenny ( ) you are the worst liar on the Eastern Seaboard.
3. He told ( ) Thelma ( ) she would have to stay where she was.
4. Well ( ) gang ( ) what's next?
5. See here; I plan to collect what you owe me ( ) Schindler!

24B
Use commas to set off mild or unemphatic interjections.

Interjections are exclamatory words *interjected,* or slipped into, other constructions. If the emotional force of the interjection is not strong, the words should be set off with a comma or commas:

Darn, here he comes again.

I know, *alas,* there are no pretzels left.

Now we will hear again about his tournament, *ho hum.*

The basic meanings of these sentences would not be changed if the italicized interjections were removed. Interjections are set off because they are not really parts of their sentences; they only establish the writer or speaker's emotional reaction to what he is saying.

24C
Use commas to set off conjunctive adverbs and other transitional devices.

Conjunctive adverbs are words such as *moreover, however, consequently, therefore,* or *otherwise.* These words serve as transitions between their clauses and the material that precedes them. Other transitional devices include phrases such as *for example, that is, in other words,* or *on the other hand.* Also in this category are single words such as *first, second, next,* or *finally.* Such conjunctive adverbs and transitional devices often are placed at the head of their clauses and set off with one comma:

For example, the change in leaf color is triggered by changes in light rather than by temperature.

However, the menu for the dinner party is not set.

Third, the peel must be carefully removed.

In other cases, they occur in the middle or at the end of clauses and must be punctuated accordingly:

Her career in health care is finished, *in other words.*

My goal, *moreover,* is to retire at thirty.

Special rules govern the punctuation of the shorter conjunctive adverbs. *Then* is usually not set off when it has to do with time, but it is punctuated when it means *therefore* and comes in the middle or at the end of its clause:

Then I came home and walked the dog.

My conclusion, *then,* is that the study should continue.

Also is set off at the head of a clause but not in the middle or at the end:

> *Also,* peanut butter has been known to contain rodent hairs.
>
> They *also* serve who only stand and wait.

Words such as *thus, hence,* and *thence* are usually not set off at all.

> *Exercise Parenthetical Elements 2.* In the following sentences, supply as many commas as are needed to set off parenthetical elements. Be prepared to explain your corrections.
>
> **1.** He was glad to get that letter by gosh.
>
> **2.** We have therefore registered your complaint and will consequently strive to give you satisfaction.
>
> **3.** Also we are enclosing the wool mittens ordered earlier; your shipment then is now complete.
>
> **4.** It seems however that she alas does not return my affection.
>
> **5.** Her motion in other words killed the proposition before it came to a vote.

24D
Use commas to set off mild interruptions—explanations, contrasts, concessions, or afterthoughts closely related to the thoughts they interrupt.

A range of constructions from single words to whole subordinate clauses fits into the category of mild interruptions. They all attempt, however, to clarify material in the main clause, and all of them could be left out without harming the basic grammar or content of the sentence:

> We have, *it seems,* failed in our duties.
>
> Dan felt, *by then,* thoroughly confused.
>
> This, *I think,* is a totally new concept.
>
> You are, *of course,* free to disagree.

Each of these interruptions attempts to aid the reader, to make sure that he sees exactly what is meant. The main clause is not changed but is made more precise by the interruption, and it is this helpful spirit, combined with the shortness of the elements set off, that calls for commas rather than stronger punctuation.

> *Exercise Parenthetical Elements 3.* In the following sentences, supply as many commas as are needed to set off parenthetical elements. Be prepared to explain your corrections.
>
> **1.** It is the smaller cars not the big ones that are dangerous.
>
> **2.** After that incident it is your best course to resign we feel.

3. It was although a mature specimen not very strong or active.

4. She seems to judge by appearances uninterested in the class.

5. The main thing it seems to me is to keep calm.

24E
Use dashes or parentheses to set off abrupt interruptions.

Abrupt interruptions do not serve just to clarify material: they also change meanings, often dramatically:

> His aunt—*the only person in the world who called him Chuckie*—was sitting in the back seat.

> John's mind—*if he can be said to have one*—is elsewhere.

Strong punctuation is needed here because the parenthetical elements change the meaning radically. The first parenthetical remark shows that the writer is more concerned with characterizing the aunt than with the bland content of the main clause. The second changes a neutral statement into a snide remark.

Choosing Dashes or Parentheses. In setting off abrupt interruptions, the difference between dashes and parentheses is a matter of emphasis. If you want the interruption to stand out boldly, use dashes; use parentheses if you want the interruption to be less forceful:

> Nestor said—*though no one believed him*—he was sorry.

> Nestor said (*though no one believed him*) he was sorry.

There are also differences between the ways parentheses and dashes are handled in punctuating some sentences. Parentheses are *always* used in pairs, even at the ends of sentences, while only one dash is used to set off a final parenthetical element:

> Nestor said he was sorry—*though no one believed him.*

> Nestor said he was sorry (*though no one believed him*).

Moreover, while dashes replace other punctuation marks, parentheses do not. If a sentence would need punctuation without a parentheses, punctuation is still necessary even with the parentheses in place. It is just delayed until the parentheses are closed:

> When I got home that night—*tired out by my efforts at work*—I had to cook supper for the children.

> When I got home that night (*tired out by my efforts at work*), I had to cook supper for the children.

> The tires squealed—*the engine revving at 6,000 rpm*—black smoke billowed behind the car.

199

The tires squealed (*the engine revving at 6,000 rpm*); black smoke billowed behind the car.

Exercise Parenthetical Elements 4. Punctuate the abrupt interruptions in the following sentences twice, once with dashes and once with parentheses.

1. Jem presented when he could be heard his defense.

2. When my mind is finally made up and you'll be the first to know I will act immediately.

3. She had never liked his looks a flat nose and fleshy lips.

4. My school first in basketball three years running has a long tradition of athletic excellence.

5. The ceremony because it was rainy and cold that day had to be moved indoors.

24F
Use dashes or parentheses also to set off long interruptions, those that are complete independent clauses, and those that contain internal punctuation.

Strong punctuation helps to clarify long parenthetical expressions:

The man—*wearing cherry red trousers set off with a bright green vest and a yellow shirt for additional impact*—was hard to overlook.

Use dashes or parentheses also to set off parenthetical elements that are independent clauses themselves:

The old seamstress (*she had plied her needle in the same shop for forty-five years*) washed her black dress each night, dried it on the radiator, and wore it the next day.

or parenthetical elements that contain internal punctuation:

Some countries—*France, Italy, and Spain, for instance*—consume more wine than milk.

Exercise Parenthetical Elements 5. Choose commas, dashes, or parentheses to set off the unpunctuated parenthetical elements in the following sentences. Be prepared to explain your choices.

1. He thought moreover that your comment was unjustified.

2. It would appear my little chickadee that we are headed for an argument.

3. Watson elected by only thirty votes now claims he has a mandate to enforce the city's blue laws.

4. It seems to me you bumbling idiot that your calculations are slightly off.

5. The air conditioner is working now, and oh it has made a difference.

6. The paper it had been in operation continuously since its establishment in 1855 folded just last month.

7. You see Kevin most people would not enjoy catchup on tapioca.

8. My aunt as a matter of fact was the Miss Vermont of 1953.

9. High clouds they reminded her of childhood summers stood on the horizon.

10. His eyes small, watery, and constantly blinking were not his most attractive feature.

Exercise Parenthetical Elements 6.

1. Write and punctuate three sentences in which dashes or parentheses set off abrupt interruptions. 24E.

2. Write and punctuate three sentences in which commas are used to set off interjections. 24B.

3. Write and punctuate three sentences that contain words in direct address. 24A.

4. Write and punctuate three sentences that contain conjunctive adverbs or other transitional devices. In two of your sentences, put the conjunctive adverb or transitional device between sentence elements. In the other, place it at the beginning or at the end of its clause. 24C.

5. Write and punctuate a sentence with a long, complicated interruption; one with an interruption that is a complete independent clause; and one with an interruption that contains its own internal punctuation. 24F.

6. Write three sentences in which commas set off mild interruptions. 24D.

Parenthetical Elements Reference Chart

24A
Use commas to set off words in direct address.

Your manners, *Hermione,* are atrocious.

Come on, *team,* rip them apart!

24B
Use commas to set off mild or unemphatic interjections.

Heck, I've seen this show before.

In my opinion, *by golly,* you would be better off single.

24C
Use commas to set off conjunctive adverbs and other transitional devices.

My ankle feels much better now, *however.*

His blood pressure, *for one thing,* is quite normal.

24D
Use commas to set off mild interruptions— explanations, contrasts, concessions, or afterthoughts closely related to the thoughts they interrupt.

Her plan, *I guess,* is to graduate in May.

Oaks, *not poplars,* were used for shipbuilding.

His confidence, *at that time,* was ebbing.

24E
Use dashes or parentheses to set off abrupt interruptions.

The mouse—*the place had been exterminated just the week before*—regarded him serenely from beneath the chair.

He gave tongue to his opinion of required courses (*all this overheard by his teacher in the hall*) and then slipped on his friendly, interested expression for the beginning of the lecture.

24F
Use dashes or parentheses to set off long interruptions, those that are complete independent clauses, and those that contain internal punctuation.

Candice was so absorbed—*reading the very last chapter of her current thriller and chewing her nails*—that she did not hear the door open.

The appeal of this cereal (*millions start their day with it*) is well established by its sales record.

My friend—*finding the dark, forbidding house deserted*—was not in the least tempted by the open door.

25

Items in Series, Coordinate Adjectives, Dates, and Addresses [*series, date, address*]

While most of this chapter will simply review things you already know, some of the niceties of punctuating dates, series, and addresses may have escaped you, and now would be a good time to learn them. Bear down especially hard on such things as coordinate adjectives, the final comma in dates and addresses, and the use of semicolons between items with internal punctuation.

> ### 25A
> **Use commas to separate three or more words, phrases, or clauses in a series.**

Three or more parallel items in a series must be separated by commas:

He is *tall, slim, clever, and unscrupulous.* (four predicate adjectives)

Mother *boxed the gift, wrapped it in foil, and left it on their doorstep.* (three predicates)

Michael, Jason, Fred, Pete—all of them were there. (four proper nouns in apposition to the subject *all*)

The only area of uncertainty about this rule concerns the final comma. Some writers omit the last separating comma in a series (the one before the *and*) if the items are short and the situation informal:

The audience *laughed, cried and cringed in horror.*

But unless you are very experienced in writing, it is simpler and safer to use all of the commas all of the time. Standardizing on the full number of commas gives you one less choice to make in writing, and it will keep you out of trouble in those sentences where—because the items in a series are long, because there is a possibility of confusion, or because there is no conjunction—the final comma is required.

Exercise Items in Series 1. Use commas to separate the items in series in the following sentences.

1. Her bodyguard was short stocky and solid as a fireplug.

2. Thinking of others setting a good example living according to principle and generally striving to do good—these are the traits we try to inspire in our students.

3. I found I could no longer visualize her hair the shape of her face or the set of her head and shoulders.

4. He wrote of love and death time and change and feeling and ceremony.

5. Custom is capable of making the unknown familiar making the exception the rule and making the innovation a hallmark of the new status quo.

25B
Use semicolons to separate three or more items in a series that already contains internal punctuation.

Establishing different levels of punctuation for different purposes can be a great help to your readers. Consider the following sentence:

> When he got to the store, he found the shelves were bare, having been stripped by the bargain hunters, the manager was nowhere to be seen, and the clerk, who was new on the job, did not know what to do.

The problem in this example is that the same punctuation marks—commas—are called upon both to signal the divisions *within* the items in series and to separate the items in the series itself. Confusion can be easily avoided if commas are kept for the minor divisions but semicolons are used to mark the major ones:

> When he got to the store, he found the shelves were bare, having been stripped by the bargain hunters; the manager was nowhere to be seen; and the clerk, who was new on the job, did not know what to do.

Semicolons guide the reader through the series. They head off possible ambiguity by making it clear that it was the shelves, not the manager, that the bargain hunters stripped.

The following sentence illustrates another aspect of punctuating series with semicolons:

> Waiting for me were Kenny; Don; Mike, the office boy; and Maureen.

The semicolons here are needed, for without them it would sound as though there were five people, not just four, waiting for the speaker. And even though only one item in the series (*Mike, the office boy*) contains internal punctuation, *all* of the semicolons are necessary. Items in any parallel series are equal and must be punctuated equally. If you decide to use semicolons for one part of the series, you must use them throughout.

Exercise Items in Series 2. Choose either commas or semicolons to separate the items in series in the following sentences. Be prepared to explain your choice.

1. Four dogs—Merlin Bowser a coon hound Princess and Molly—went to the picnic with their owners.

2. I was angry with the university I was hurt by my professors' indifference and I was determined to go elsewhere.

3. She said the job consisted of typing long, complicated reports answering the telephone and, of course, making coffee.

4. Victor, who was at that time my best friend, convinced me to sell my books clothes and stereo to withdraw from all my classes and to move out of my comfortable, paid-up apartment.

5. Oranges are full of nutrition refreshing cheap readily available and easy to store.

25C
Use commas to separate coordinate adjectives.

Coordinate adjectives work together to modify the same noun and should be separated from each other by commas:

her *nervous, frightened* son   a *plump, tender* turkey
some *dirty, faded* pictures   the *long, slow* curve

The commas indicate that the adjectives are separate, and that each applies individually and equally to the noun modified. But not all adjective series are coordinate. Consider the following group of *noncoordinate* adjectives:

his *final spring* vacation   a *fancy dress* ball
my *new knit* skirt   a *costly color* TV

The adjectives in these phrases do not work independently, but act in combination (as in *fancy dress*) or cumulatively (as in the first example, where *final* does not modify just *vacation* but the entire notion of a *spring-vacation*).

Tests for Coordinate Adjectives.   Coordinate adjectives are punctuated; noncoordinate ones are not. Luckily there is a very simple way to make the distinction. Only coordinate adjectives (the kind that must be punctuated) can be freely rearranged or separated by conjunctions. Suppose you had to know whether or not to punctuate the phrase "a *big burly* tackle." Could you just as easily say "a *burly* big tackle," or "a *big* and *burly* tackle"? If such changes are possible, the adjectives are coordinate and should be separated by commas—"a *big, burly* tackle." Noncoordinate adjectives cannot change positions. You could not say "my *knit new* skirt"

205

or "my *new* and *knit* skirt." This inflexibility indicates that these adjectives cannot be separated by a comma.

Note also that when commas are used they separate the adjectives from each other only: you should *not* put a comma between the final adjective and the noun.

Exercise Items in Series 3. Decide whether or not commas should go in the slots marked with parentheses in the following sentences. Be prepared to explain your decisions.

1. He reached out a big ( ) calloused ( ) work-scarred hand toward the frightened ( ) special deputy.

2. Her rusty ( ) trail bike sat in the corner of the dusty ( ) overheated ( ) front room.

3. The booming ( ) downtown stores were full of anxious ( ) determined ( ) scurrying shoppers.

4. The massive ( ) metallic transformer fell with an ear-splitting ( ) terrifying crash.

5. "It was a dull ( ) muffled thud," he said. "It was like the sound of a big ( ) soft ( ) grapefruit struck by a heavy ( ) baseball bat."

25D
Use one comma for each major unit in a specific address, date, or geographical name.

A specific address includes at least a street number, street name, and name of a town, though it may go on to include more. A specific date contains the name of the month, day, and year. A specific geographical name includes the local name and the name of the state, province, or country:

They were married on *June 2, 1969,* by her minister.

I live at *235 Macadamia Avenue, Orlando, Florida, The United States, North America, Western Hemisphere, Earth, Our Solar System, Milky Way Galaxy, The Universe.*

He moved from *West Grove, Pennsylvania,* to *Beaverton, Oregon.*

Notice that with dates and addresses, it is necessary to put a comma *after* the last item in the series. This last comma can be dispensed with only when another punctuation mark (such as the periods in the last two examples above) replaces it:

I am going to *Tempe, Arizona,* in the fall.

December 14, 1876, was the date of her last performance.

There are some other kinds of dates that need not be punctuated, and some in which punctuation is positively wrong. You have a choice with dates that provide only the month and year. You can put in or omit a comma:

They bought that car in *May, 1981.*

I haven't had a check-up since *February 1979.*

But you should *not* use commas for military dates, in which the day comes before the month:

The form was dated *7 March 1953.*

Commas are also *not* used for dates, addresses, and place names in which prepositions come between the items:

Ruth lives at *36 Steelhead in Seattle.*

The offensive came on *April 16 in 1919.*

Exercise Items in Series 4. Correctly punctuate the dates, addresses, and place names in the following sentences.

1. I bought a house at 5110 Capitol in Alexandria Virginia.
2. November 15 1818 was his birth date, and he died in May 1869.
3. Fresno California Midland Texas and White Plains New York all applied for the federal grant.
4. During the autumn of 1980 she was ill, and she checked into the hospital at Rock Hill South Carolina on 6 October 1980.
5. Your letter of August 19 1978 is still in our files, and I find we replied to you on September 3 of the same year.

Exercise Items in Series 5. Punctuate the items in series, coordinate adjectives, dates, addresses, and geographical names in the following sentences. Be ready to explain your work.

1. His head was bald shiny and round; and he protected it with a blue stretch cap.
2. The tobacco shop used to be at 6 South Union Saint Paul but now it is located in Minneapolis Minnesota.
3. The equipment must arrive before July 27, 1986 because that is when the building should be ready for occupancy.
4. Judd Bobby Lamont William the tuba player and Jeff were all ready to board the bus.
5. My tour took me through Quito Ecuador Santiago Chile and La Paz Bolivia during December 1972.
6. One dirty dented bucket the broken harness the faded patched silks— these were not what I expected to find in a successful racing stable.
7. You remember the fun we had climbing trees and camping by the river hiking along the rim of the canyon and telling stories by the fire.
8. Omaha Nebraska is one center of the beef trade; Kansas City Missouri is another.
9. The ship *Little Gidding,* a pleasure craft out of Miami Florida was last sighted October 28 1979.

10. We have studied in Gainesville Florida Chapel Hill North Carolina Ann Arbor Michigan and Baltimore Maryland.

Exercise Items in Series 6.

1. Write three sentences that have coordinate adjectives separated from one another by commas. 25C.

2. Write three sentences with specific dates including month, day, and year, in that order. To practice use of the final comma, place at least one date in the middle of its sentence. 25D.

3. Write three sentences that include three or more items in series separated by commas. 25A.

4. Write three sentences that contain specific addresses, including street numbers and names, cities, and states (you may invent the addresses if none come to mind). To practice use of the final comma, place at least one address in the middle of its sentence. 25D.

5. Write three sentences that have three or more items in series. In at least one of the sentences, arrange for the items in series to have internal punctuation. Separate these items from each other with semicolons. 25B.

Items in Series Reference Chart

25A
Use commas to separate three or more words, phrases, or clauses in series.

He hated her *because she laughed at him, because she was friendly with the inspector, and because she knew too much.*

Nancy's favorite sports are *eating, drinking, and sleeping late.*

25B
Use semicolons to separate three or more items in a series that already contains internal punctuation.

Before the party they *washed the windows; beat the dusty, old carpets; put the casserole, vegetables, and rolls in the oven to warm; and lit a fire in the dining room grate.*

25C
Use commas to separate coordinate adjectives.

Jon's *large, expensive* apartment was the scene of their *cozy, intimate* graduation party.

25D
Use one comma for each major unit in a specific address, date, or geographical name.

His home is *988 Maple Street, Fall River, Massachusetts,* in the summers.

Monday, June 7, 1760, the work finally went to press.

Is *Billings, Montana,* farther than *Ogden, Utah?*

26 Unnecessary Punctuation [*unnecess. punc.*]

This chapter is about where you should *not* punctuate, a topic every bit as important as where you should. Illogical, unnecessary punctuation chokes a sentence and prevents its meaning from coming through: the reader is snagged by needless punctuation marks and starts paying attention to how badly the sentence is punctuated rather than to what it says:

> His plan, was, now, to steal the diamonds, and escape from the watchful eyes, of the customs agents.

You are a rare reader if this sentence does not make you feel confused and irritated. Punctuation is supposed to mean something, but the commas here serve only to clutter up a construction that should flow easily:

> His plan was now to steal the diamonds and escape from the watchful eyes of the customs agents.

The key to good punctuation is to have a clear reason for every mark you use. Think about punctuation in the same way that a businessman thinks about expenses: be willing to spend as much as you have to, but never waste a mark. If you are genuinely undecided about the need for additional punctuation, leave it out. And be especially careful to avoid the specific errors discussed below.

26A
Do not use a comma with a coordinating conjunction between two words or phrases.

The comma-plus-conjunction construction should be saved for linking two independent clauses or the last two items in a series. There is seldom any need to add punctuation to a conjunction that connects two words or phrases, or even two subordinate clauses:

It was promised for today *but* did not arrive.

She was sitting on the porch *and* thinking of Fred.

Since he has said nothing *and* the time has passed, I suppose we are in the clear.

The only times when this rule does not apply are when a parenthetical element comes before a conjunction or when extra punctuation genuinely helps to make a sentence clear:

He was her date, you see, *and* had to put up with her.

Henry is tall and handsome, *but* not very bright.

The first sentence is not really an exception to the rule. Its commas serve to set off the parenthetical *you see,* and the conjunction just happens to follow. In the second sentence, the comma before the *but* seems to break the rule, but its use is justified because it comes about as the result of an intelligent attempt to make things clear. The writer has not just thrown in this extra comma: he has used it to help mark the shift from Henry's positive characteristics to his negative one.

Exercise Unnecessary Punctuation 1. In the following sentences, decide whether or not a comma should go in each of the slots marked by parentheses. Be prepared to explain your decisions.

1. The old man was proud ( ) and had lived independently for years ( ) but his illness had brought him low.

2. Although you are my older sister ( ) and I ought to listen to your advice, I doubt that you know how I feel ( ) and do not plan to do as you say.

3. Ned asked his father, an old hand at shortwave radio ( ) and listened attentively to his reply.

4. We expect democracy to be responsive ( ) and to give equal consideration to everyone ( ) but it sometimes disappoints us.

5. Does anyone believe that she is impartial ( ) or that she will not rule according to her emotions ( ) and preconceptions?

26B
Do not put a comma between a subject and its verb unless there is a parenthetical element between the two.

Subjects can be complicated. They range from nouns plus modifiers to gerund phrases or whole clauses used as nouns. But not even complicated subjects should be set off from their verbs. Punctuation should come between a subject and its verb only when the subject is followed by an interrupting element that needs to be set off for its own sake. No punctuation should come between subject and verb in sentences such as the following:

Cooking which demands a lot of ingredients and special equipment is not always justified by its results.

That he has a record, a violent temper, and shady associates is entirely irrelevant here.

In these sentences, every element that occurs before the verb is part of the complete subject. This situation does not change unless a nonrestrictive modifier, appositive, or some other parenthetical element is inserted between subject and verb. In these cases, *two* commas are needed:

Cooking which demands a lot of ingredients and special equipment, *he argued,* is not always justified by its results.

That he has a record, a violent temper, and shady associates, *in other words,* is entirely irrelevant here.

26C
Do not put a comma between a verb and its complement unless there is a parenthetical element between the two.

A complement of a verb is its direct or indirect object or its predicate noun or adjective. Not all verbs have complements, but those that do should not be set off from them, even if the complement is a clause or a long and complex phrase rather than a single word. In the following sentences, the italicized complements should *not* be set off:

After much soul-searching I finally decided *that she was entitled to my apologies.* (direct object)

The jury awarded *the man who had complained about the unfair commercial* one hundred thousand dollars. (indirect object)

He had been *the principal actor in the company's two productions that season.* (predicate noun)

Susan had grown *weary of the demands Roger made on her time and attention.* (predicate adjective)

As with subjects, a complement should be separated from its verb by punctuation only when the two are separated by a parenthetical element which must be set off for its own sake:

After much soul-searching I finally decided, *taking all that had happened into consideration,* that she was entitled to my apologies.

Exercise Unnecessary Punctuation 2. Revise the punctuation of the following sentences to remove unnecessary commas between subjects and verbs or between verbs and their complements. Be prepared to explain your work.

1. Father, a strict Baptist, agreed, that the stores should be closed on Sundays.
2. Whoever says I have not tried my hardest, is misleading you and has, I feel, some ulterior motive for doing so.
3. The team that scores the most points, often has, the weakest defense.

4. The tribe we visited—progressive, sophisticated, and well-educated—was not, what I had expected to find.

5. When we see the flames beginning to catch, our usual practice, is, to fan the fire and give it, a good start.

26D
Do not put a comma between a single adjective or the final adjective of a group and the word it modifies.

In section 25C we discussed the need to separate coordinate adjectives from *each other*. But adjectives, whether alone or in groups, should not be separated from the words they modify:

You are a *dirty, rotten, lying, cheating faker!*

The commas here break up the string of adjectives, giving each one full weight as an independent modifier. There is, however, no comma after *cheating*. Punctuation at that point would separate the whole series of adjectives from *faker*, the noun they all modify. In punctuating coordinate adjectives, follow this model: put a comma after each adjective in the series except for the last one.

26E
Do not use commas to set off restrictive modifiers.

The distinction between restrictive and nonrestrictive modifiers is considered at length in Chapter 24. Restrictive modifiers limit the words they modify to a certain application or special meaning. Unlike nonrestrictive modifiers, which contain extra information about a subject that is already well-defined, restrictive ones make essential distinctions important to the basic meaning of the sentence. Nonrestrictive modifiers (which contain mere extra information) are set off to show that the sentence could communicate effectively without them. The following two sentences contain nonrestrictive modifiers. Each is set off because the noun it modifies is sufficiently specific without the additional information:

Hector Gomez, *who plays goalie,* was injured last week.

He called their downtown office, *which handles his account.*

And here are the same modifiers, this time used restrictively to define nouns that would be vague or imprecise without them. Used this way, the modifiers are not set off:

The man *who plays goalie* was injured last week.

He called the particular office *which handles his account.*

Exercise Unnecessary Punctuation 3. Revise the punctuation of the following sentences to remove unnecessary commas that separate adjectives and the nouns they modify or that set off restrictive modifiers. Be prepared to explain your work.

1. The dark, glistening, leaves were the perfect background for the round, shining, berries.

2. Idella's fresh, new, crisp, ten-dollar bills were distributed to the children, who needed them most.

3. The teller, who had taken my money, was now lost in the crowd of employees behind the dark walnut, counter.

4. Any car, that can get to sixty in under eight seconds, is too fast for an old man, with no interest in drag racing.

5. Daniel Boone and other figures, from the first period of westward settlement, are now idolized by their safe, civilized, descendents.

26F
Do not use punctuation to set off short introductory elements or closely related modifiers from their clauses.

Some writers are uncomfortable about letting any introductory element go unpunctuated. There is something to be said for their point of view, because so many kinds of introducers require punctuation (see Chapter 21). But introductory punctuation is not always necessary to set off any word or phrase that happens to come before a main clause. In particular, brief opening phrases should not be set off unless they modify the whole clause that follows (21A) or would be unclear without punctuation (21B). In the majority of cases, such phrases should blend smoothly into the clauses they introduce:

On his left he could see a gap in the undergrowth.

Beyond the city limits the road became much rougher.

The same considerations apply to modifying phrases and clauses in other parts of the sentence. Unless these definitely interrupt the flow of the sentence, there is no reason to punctuate them. Study the following sentences. No internal punctuation is required, because the modifying phrases and clauses are so closely related to the main idea:

I thought the light *we saw* was coming *from the window on the left side of the porch.*

The girl *in the box office* wound up protecting the usher *who had come when she called for help.*

People *who know him* say he is the man *to call for good advice about any problem having to do with real estate.*

Exercise Unnecessary Punctuation 4. Remove the unnecessary commas in the following sentences.

1. In August, the man my father had met, in New York, came for a workshop that lasted, three weeks.

2. During wet weather, the stream rises, and the banks that are usually exposed are covered, by the rushing water.

3. Higher up, the tree was still green and flourishing, but its trunk had been splintered, by the lightning.

4. On his mother's side, Harvey is descended from the General Fairfax who fought, on the Parliamentary side, in the English Civil War.

5. Among the Indians, it was an accepted fact, that man had as many responsibilities as rights, in the natural world.

26G
Do not use commas to set off indirect quotations or direct ones that fit naturally into the rest of the sentence.

Some writers, flustered by quotations, or even by near-quotations, nervously punctuate them wherever they occur. But direct and indirect quotations should not be set off without a definite reason.

Indirect quotations (statements *about* what someone said rather than the person's exact words) are unlikely to require punctuation. The typical indirect quotation is a noun clause serving as the direct object of a verb such as *said, testified, charged,* or *claimed:*

Yolanda said *that she was too tired to cook dinner.*

Fisley admitted *that his comment was ill-advised.*

To set off these indirect quotations would violate the rule (26C) against separating verb and complement.

Direct quotations (the original speaker or writer's exact words enclosed in quotation marks) range from single words to whole clauses. Short quotations that function within other clauses and quotations introduced by prepositions or subordinating conjunctions should *not* be set off by commas:

Jones claims he is *"hot"* and *"will win hands down."*

Karen proclaimed that *"the student government has failed to reflect student concerns."*

The poet Herbert described prayer as *"The Christian plummet sounding heav'n and earth."*

Exercise Unnecessary Punctuation 5. Revise the punctuation of the following sentences to remove unnecessary commas that set off direct and indirect quotations.

1. Henry swore, that he would have nothing to do with the play.

2. After their hike the boys were, "famished," and ready to, "eat a horse."

3. Edwina later said, she was coming to understand how the, "corrupt," system worked.

4. His, "intuition," led him to believe, that his luck would change after midnight.

5. Each one of the women said, that she would return, "soon."

Exercise Unnecessary Punctuation 6. Revise the punctuation of the following sentences to eliminate unneeded commas. Be prepared to explain your work.

1. Alongside, the lights of the tugs shone brightly, and gleamed against the sides, of the big ship.

2. Her husband said he was, "disappointed," and he blamed the others, who had gone along on the trip.

3. Noting the time, I reluctantly hailed a taxi, which had been circling the hotel.

4. The square, upright, letters, gave his handwriting a secure, confident, look.

5. Climbing frozen waterfalls, is a winter sport, that will never appeal to everyone.

6. Mother said she doubted, that we would ever amount to anything.

7. By then, the game was out of hand, and the fans had started, to leave the arena.

8. The wires, he said, were, "stripped," and would have to be rewound.

9. Being the only girl, in a family of boys, is no fun.

10. The car, that I buy, must be a large, roomy, powerful sedan.

Exercise Unnecessary Punctuation 7. Revise the punctuation of the following sentences to eliminate unneeded commas. Be prepared to explain your work.

1. Before long, you will regret what you said, and want me back.

2. We discovered long ago, that we could not trust him, to do what he promises.

3. Bambi, everyone's favorite deer, will be returning to the theaters, forever.

4. Justin knew "nothing," and said, that he was as surprised as, "anyone else."

5. The contractor who wins that new rig, will have a reason to celebrate: it is worth a fortune, and will cut his work load dramatically.

6. His notion of a good, "deal," sounds like grand larceny, to me.

7. Building the fishing rod, I found, that getting tight, strong, windings to secure the guides, was the biggest problem.

8. Over there, is the site of the old fort, but you will find the ground is muddy, and too wet to dig.

9. Our coach complained, that we were not trying to improve, and were just, "dogging it."

10. I have never met the woman, you mean, but I would recognize her, from your description.

Unnecessary Punctuation Reference Chart

General Rule:
Have a definite reason for each punctuation mark you use.
Trouble Spots:

26A
Do not use a comma with a coordinating conjunction between two words or phrases.

Not, "He *is my brother, and has said a lot about you,*" but "He *is my brother and has said a lot about you.*"

26B
Do not put a comma between a subject and its verb unless there is a parenthetical element between the two.

Not, "*Whether or not she is coming to the dance,* has not been decided," but "*Whether or not she is coming to the dance* has not been decided."

26C
Do not put a comma between a verb and its complement unless there is a parenthetical element between the two.

Not, "We later learned, *that the bracelet was missing,*" but "We later learned *that the bracelet was missing.*"

26D
Do not put a comma between a single adjective or the final adjective of a group and the word it modifies.

Not, *a warm, friendly, greeting,*" but "*a warm, friendly greeting.*"

26E
Do not use commas to set off restrictive modifiers.

Not, "Any house, *that has air conditioning,* will do," but "Any house *that has air conditioning* will do."

26F
Do not use punctuation to set off short introductory elements or closely related modifiers from their clauses.

Not, "*At that time,* we were inexperienced, *on defense,*" but "*At that time* we were inexperienced *on defense.*"

26G
Do not use commas to set off indirect quotations or direct ones that fit naturally into the rest of the sentence.

Not, "He said, *that his rash was getting better,*" but "He said *that his rash was getting better.*" And not, "Barbara called him, *'an angel,'* " but "Barbara called him *'an angel.'* "

27

Punctuating Quotations [quote]

The handling of quotations in written English can quickly become a tangle. The basic idea is fairly simple, but the special punctuation needs of quotations produce a blizzard of rules for particular circumstances. To help you find the rule you need, we have subdivided this chapter into five sections: the use of quotation marks, punctuation to introduce quotations, punctuation within quotations, punctuation at the end of quotations, and the rules for block quotations.

The Use of Quotation Marks

27A
Use double quotation marks (") to enclose direct, word-for-word quotations from any written or spoken source.

Setting off direct quotations is the basic role of quotation marks. The marks are used in pairs, one set before and one after the quoted material, to indicate two things clearly: that you are switching from your own content to what someone else said and that you are giving your source's *exact* words:

> He said he had given up coffee *"for medical reasons."*

> *"My dedication to the team,"* said she, *"is second to none."*

> Milton's task, as he outlined it himself, was to *"justify the ways of God to men."*

Be sure to distinguish between direct and indirect quotations. Indirect quotations are statements about what someone said. These do not require quotation marks:

> He said he had given up coffee because it was not good for him.

> She claimed her dedication to the team was second to none.

Be sure, too, that when you quote directly you quote *accurately.* Writers have some leeway in quoting spoken sources, because their memory of what was said may not be exact; and in creative writing involving dialogue, the quotations may even be made up. But quotations from written sources must be letter-perfect, with every word and punctuation mark just as it appeared in the original.

27B
Use double quotation marks (") to enclose the titles of poems, songs, short stories, chapters, or articles in books, magazines, newspapers, or other longer works.

Each title in this rule belongs to a short work or one that is part of a longer whole. The names of major works—books, magazines, newspapers, shows, record albums, and the like—are underlined, or italicized; and using quotation marks for individual songs, poems, short stories, chapters, and articles provides a way to distinguish between the part and the whole. A short story may appear in a magazine. Its title is quoted; that of the magazine is italicized. A particular song is part of a record album, and the distinction is handled in the same way:

"Maxwell's Silver Hammer" is my favorite song from the Beatles' *Abbey Road.*

He wrote a feature article called "New Hope for the Blind."

Kilmer's poem "Trees" continues to be popular despite all the criticism it has received.

27C
Use double quotation marks (") to enclose a word or phrase understood in a special sense.

Quotation marks can be used to make a comment on what you are saying, regardless of whether or not you use a direct quotation:

Many "civilized" people are routinely inhumane to animals.

The instructor asked us to "trip" on "dynamic ego affirmation."

In the first sentence, the writer wants us to see that the people under discussion are not really civilized at all. The word in quotation marks means the opposite of what it says. The writer of the second sentence is holding the instructor's jargon up for scorn. The quotation marks show that the writer does not think much of the phrases quoted and assumes that the reader will share this attitude.

Satiric quotation marks can be effective, but only if you use them sparingly. Be on guard against overuse (nothing sours faster than sarcasm) and keep your probable audience in mind. Satirical quotation marks *imply* that there is something wrong with the word or phrase they enclose, but they do not express any specific criticism. They work only if your reader understands and shares your point of view.

Do *not* use quotation marks around nicknames, clichés, or clever expressions unless you want to make fun of them.

Exercise Quotations 1. Write ten sentences about things your roommate or best friend has said. Use direct quotations in five of the sentences and indirect quotations in the other five.

Exercise Quotations 2. Put quotation marks wherever they are needed in the following sentences. Be prepared to explain your work.

1. You know what I mean, he said. I just think she's much more popular than I am.
2. I enjoyed her article Fall Color, and I also liked Manhattan Autumn, the poem printed right after it.
3. It seems to me, Cynthia argued, that it's mostly the rich people who want strict enforcement of drugs laws. She paused and then went on, They get their pills by prescription anyway.
4. You are my sunshine, he bellowed beneath her father's window. You make me happyeee, when skies are ba-looo.
5. Skinny Miller played The Carnival of Venice with his tissue paper and comb. Heck, he blushingly admitted, there's nothing to it.

Punctuation to Introduce Quotations

As section 26G points out, it is often unnecessary to use special punctuation to introduce quotations. When the words quoted are parts (subjects, verbs, or complements) of your own sentence or when they follow a conjunction or a preposition, no special punctuation is needed:

His *"little brunch"* turned out to be a gourmet's delight.

Kenneth often condemned *"the fraternal disorder of police."*

There I read that *"California is the cultural bellwether of the nation."*

But quotations that are not parts of some other construction and ones that are introduced by such conventional tags as "he said," "she cried," or "the author maintains" do need extra punctuation to set them off. These are the subjects of the following sections.

> **27D**
> **Use commas to introduce quotations that are associated with credit tags, especially if the quotation contains an independent clause.**

Special punctuation conventions govern quotations that are associated with *credit tags,* or brief identifications of the source of the words. Typically, the sentence or clause opens with the name of the source, followed by a verb of speaking or writing and then the quotation. The quotation itself is really the direct object of the verb of speaking or writing, but convention calls nevertheless for a comma between the two:

Warren said, *"I don't know what you're talking about."*

The Chief Justice always held, *"A man is only as good as his credit at the bank."*

Commas are also used to set off credit tags that occur in the middle or at the end rather than at the beginning of a quotation:

"Billiards," he pontificated, *"is the only game for a true genius."*

"You are standing on the hem of my gown," she hissed between clenched teeth.

27E
Use a colon (:) to introduce long or formal quotations or ones preceded by independent clauses.

Colons indicate a stronger, more formal pause than commas do, and they work best to introduce long or formal quotations:

Generalizing, perhaps falsely, from his own experience, Wordsworth proclaims: *"Nature never did betray the heart that loved her."*

As Edward Young once said: *"By night an atheist half believes a God."*

Overpopulation has been seen as a problem since the time of Thomas Malthus (1766–1834), who pointed out: *"Population, when unchecked, increases in a geometrical ratio. Subsistence only increases in an arithmetical ratio."*

A colon is also used when a quotation is introduced by a whole independent clause, not just by a credit tag that would seem incomplete without the quotation:

Malory's account of the words on the stone is unforgettable in its simplicity: *"Whoso pulleth out this sword of this stone and anvil is rightwise King born of all England."*

Richard Hooker was something of a cynic when it came to popular political movements: *"He that goeth about to persuade a multitude, that they are not so well governed as they ought to be, shall never want attentive and favourable hearers."*

27F
In capitalizing the first word of your quotations, be guided by your original.

Whenever you quote a whole sentence that starts with a capital letter in a written source, keep the capital in your quotation, even when it occurs in the middle of one of your own sentences. When quoting a spoken source, imagine the words written out like the words in a cartoon balloon. If the quotation is a whole sentence in this imaginary balloon, capitalize the first word just as if you were reproducing a written comment:

She objected, *"You are changing the subject!"*

She accused me of *"changing the subject."*

Exercise Quotations 3. Supply punctuation and capital letters as needed to introduce the quotations in the following sentences.

1. My mother had had enough of this talk and exclaimed "drop the subject!"

2. William Henry Vanderbilt had an eloquent reaction to popular objections to his luxurious trains "the public be damned!"

3. "This plant" he stoutly maintained "is *Trifolium dubium* and no other."

4. Tod introduced his roommate "on my left is the one and only Hendricks."

5. Emerson firmly believed in the importance of individuals "there is properly no history, only biography."

Punctuation Within Quotations

Punctuation within quotations most often should remain exactly as you found it. Getting the punctuation right is part of getting the quotation right. But there are times when you must modify a quotation in some way to suit your special needs. Special punctuation for these situations can indicate just what changes you have made.

27G
Use square brackets [ ] to enclose your own corrections or comments within quoted material.

Brackets show that the material enclosed is your own and that you intend it to replace or explain what was originally written or said:

Dr. Johnson was aware of his subject's faults, but chose to overlook them: "We fix our eyes upon his [Shakespeare's] graces and turn them from his deformities."

"S[hadwell]," wrote Dryden, "never deviates into sense."

The author makes some shocking blunders: "The poet was born in 1796 [1794] and baptised William Collins [Cullen] Bryant."

A special use of brackets is to enclose the Latin word *sic* ("thus it is") as an indication that some obvious error in the quotation is the original writer's mistake, not your own:

He wrote that "the armored unit is probly [*sic*] not well prepared for active combat."

Sic is always italicized or underlined as a foreign term, and it should not be enclosed in quotation marks or followed by an exclamation point, no matter how gross the error. Be sure to save [*sic*] for genuine mistakes on the part of your source; do *not* use the device as the writer of the following example does, as a way of protesting the judgment of the person quoted:

The instructor announced, "Nineteenth century economics were a real source of social change—much more influential [*sic*] than scientific developments such as the theory of evolution."

27H

Use a series of spaced periods (. . .) to show that you have omitted some original material from your quotation.

Sometimes it is useful to pick and choose among an author's words, including ideas that are relevant to your concerns and leaving out the rest. Omissions of this sort are indicated by *ellipses*, or spaced periods:

> The instructor announced, "Nineteenth century economics were . . . more influential than scientific developments such as the theory of evolution."

Three spaced periods show that you have left something out of a single sentence. When your quotation jumps from one sentence to another, however, you need *four* periods (one regular followed by three spaced ones) to show that what you have quoted includes material from more than one sentence in your source. Suppose you wanted to quote selectively the following sentences from a book review:

> Ralph was always attached to his older sister, the beloved "Sis" of his autobiography. He felt he owed her everything and constantly referred to her generosity.

If your ellipsis bridged these two sentences, four periods would allow you to indicate the fact:

> According to the reviewer, "Ralph was always attached to his older sister. . . . and constantly referred to her generosity."

The first period comes immediately after the last letter of the opening of the quotation. The other three periods are spaced. This technique is used whenever omissions from a quotation include one or more periods.

Ellipses make it possible to tailor a quotation to fit your needs, but they also involve a serious obligation. You hold the responsibility of seeing to it that the quotation still accurately reflects the meaning of the source. Never distort your original by leaving out words or phrases essential to the writer's intentions. That would put you in the same league as the copywriters who sometimes distort critics' remarks in composing ads for movies, writing things like "This is a great . . . film" when the critic really said, "This is a great, flabby failure of a film."

27I

Use single quotation marks (') for quotations within quotations.

When quoting someone quoting someone else, use single quotation marks around the quoted quotation:

> "Do you know what your grandmother means by 'a pinch of salt'?" mother asked.

> He stuck to his story: "The doctor told me, 'Drink as much as you like.'"

It rarely happens, but to quote a quotation within a quotation within yet another quotation, alternate between double and single marks to keep the various levels separate:

> He explained, "The librarian read the part in which the hero asks, 'Did I hear you say, "I am yours"'?' "

Notice that any quotation you start must be closed, hence the accumulation of marks at the ends of these example sentences.

Exercise Quotations 4. Write nine sentences that contain quotations you have invented. In the first three quotations, include a pronoun or abbreviation identified in brackets. Include a factual error corrected in brackets in the next three. And include an error in spelling or punctuation followed by [*sic*] in each of the last three.

Exercise Quotations 5. Devise four selective quotations from the following passage. In the first two, quote single sentences with material omitted and replaced by ellipses. In the second two, combine parts of more than one sentence with omitted material between them.

> Up to the age of thirty or beyond it, poets such as Milton, Byron, Wordsworth, etc. gave me great delight. But now for many years I cannot endure to read a line of poetry. I have lost my taste for pictures and music. My mind seems to have become a kind of machine for grinding general laws out of large collections of facts.
>
> Charles Darwin

Exercise Quotations 6. Analyze the bracketed material, ellipses, and quotations within quotations in the following sentences. Be prepared to explain exactly what is going on in each case.

1. "I want to give him [Robert Frost] his . . . due," wrote the critic.

2. She announced, "My child would never trouble me with questions like 'Where did I come from?' "

3. "My eddication [*sic*]," the letter-writer complained, "has been called into dobt [*sic*]."

4. He went on for half a page, but what he had to say boils down to this: "His [the mayor's] unwillingness to compromise. . . . has held up the project from the beginning."

5. Rodger acknowledged that he "had long suspected . . . someone else had yelled, 'Fire!' when the lights were dimmed."

Punctuation at the End of Quotations

If some of the rules for punctuation at the ends of quotations seem illogical, it is probably because they are. Concentrate on one rule at a time, and do not expect to find consistency.

27J
Put commas and periods inside final quotation marks.

This rule is hard and fast. It does not matter how long the quotation is or what the quotation marks signify. If a comma or a period comes at the end of a direct quotation, a quoted title, or a satirical quotation, include it within the quotation marks:

Ronny said he was "into" what he called "the God scene."

"It will be a few minutes," she said.

I have always enjoyed singing "Rock of Ages."

27K
Put colons and semicolons outside final quotation marks.

This rule is dependable too, but it unfortunately contradicts the previous one. Colons and semicolons always go *outside* final quotation marks:

"I will never," she vowed, "drive again": her brakes had gone completely out halfway down the mountain.

Leonard may not have meant it when he said, "You can kick me if you want"; however, I took him at his word.

27L
Put question marks, exclamation points, and dashes inside quotation marks when they punctuate the quotation itself; place them outside when they do not.

If the material quoted is a question or exclamation, or if it ends in a dash, the punctuation goes inside the final quotation marks:

He asked, "Why do you keep following me around?"

Grandpa was beside himself: "Enough of this tomfoolery!"

"The theme of the novel is the same throughout—" the speaker insisted, "freedom."

In these examples, the punctuation is part of the quotation: it would have appeared in the original utterance, so it is included within the quotation marks. Notice that question marks and exclamation points are put inside quotation marks whenever they apply to the quotation, even if they apply to the sentence that contains the quotation as well:

Did he ask, "Why do you keep following me around?"

It makes my blood boil to hear Grandpa snort, "Tomfoolery!"

It follows that question marks, exclamation points, and dashes go outside quotation marks *only* when they apply to the sentence containing the quotation but *not* to the quotation itself:

Did he say, "Charlotte has agreed to be my wife"?

Never let me hear you say, "That's cool," when you mean, "I think I understand"!

Bill says he is devoted to his "old lady"—meaning my cousin Jennifer.

27M
Quotations that contain exclamation points or question marks keep their end punctuation no matter where or how they are used.

Quoted exclamations or questions can appear at the beginning or in the middle of sentences as well as at the end, but they keep their end punctuation even when the sentence goes on around them:

"Get going!" barked the mounted policeman.

"Do I have to?" was his only reaction to her demand.

Lucy shouted, *"Look out!"* and darted for cover.

He admitted that *"Who do you think you are?"* is not the sort of question that leads to a constructive answer.

27N
Quotations that would ordinarily end in periods lose their end punctuation when they are used at the beginning or in the middle of another sentence.

Though quoted sentences keep their initial capitals, they lose their periods when they come at the beginning or in the middle of another sentence:

"It has begun to rain harder," he announced.

Every few minutes Joan would complain, *"I can't make up my mind,"* and go back to biting her nails.

The quotations here were originally complete sentences, but as soon as they become elements in a larger construction, their end punctuation is dropped.

Exercise Quotations 7. Decide where the quotation marks should go in the following sentences. Use special caution in placing final quotation marks. Be prepared to explain your decisions.

1. Have I ever failed to ask, Do you want some?
2. Of course she has read his poem The Second Coming, but she says she prefers A Prayer for My Daughter.
3. Has Fergus approached you yet with his favorite line—I have never met anyone like you?
4. I have one great passion in life—Weaver said, horses.
5. Jonathan threw down his fork, exclaiming, Spinach makes me sick!

Exercise Quotations 8. Some of the final quotation marks in the following sentences are misplaced. Decide which ones they are and how they should be corrected. Be ready to explain your decisions.

1. We had reached what she called the "crisis point—" either my motorcycle went or she did.

2. Tom stood for fifteen minutes before Burne-Jones' painting *The Golden Stairs:* "I have never," he said, "seen anything so absolutely unreal".

3. Why would anyone object to his "little eccentricities?"

4. "Hoist ye lubbers"! the captain called to his men.

5. Martha minced no words: "Your outlandish behavior", she said, "has made me despise you!"

Exercise Quotations 9. Make up sentences of your own to contain each of the following as quotations. Your sentences can be about any subject, but be sure to punctuate the quotations correctly.

Get out of here!	My prints are selling well.
Why should we?	Did you say something?
Step aside!	Please forgive me.
Haven't you heard?	Devil take the hindmost!

Block Quoting

27P
Use block quoting for prose passages of more than four lines or for verse passages of more than three.

Block quoting is a technique for clearly setting off longer quotations. If a prose quotation runs more than four lines or a verse quotation more than three, the quotation marks can get lost. Convention calls for a clear visual break between your text and that of the quotation.

In a typed paper a long prose quotation should be introduced by a colon, preceded by triple-spacing, indented ten spaces from the left margin, and typed double-space. No quotation marks should be used unless they are part of the quotation itself (the indentation takes the place of your own quotation marks). The first line of the quotation should not be indented more than the rest unless you are quoting a full paragraph, in which case it should be indented an additional three spaces. At the end of the quotation, leave another three blank lines, and then pick up your own text where you left off.

In typing a long verse quotation, observe the same conventions. Triple-space after the last line of your text, indent ten spaces (or a little less if the lines will not fit or will look unbalanced after a ten-space indentation), and type the quotation in double-space. There is, however, a complication in quoting verse passages: you should try to make the quotation look like the original, which often means using additional indentations to imitate the poet's plan for placing his lines. At the end of the quotation, triple-space again and carry on with your own text.

If your paper is handwritten, write out the quotation so that it looks approximately the way it would if it were typed.

The following are two examples of block quotations of prose. The first quotation is a whole paragraph, and the second consists of part of a paragraph taken from the original. Each quotation is preceded and followed by a line or two from the quoter's own text. Although the spacing had to be adapted to our page size this general format is appropriate for a college essay:

Lin Carter has written very convincingly about the

historical currents in fantasy literature, pointing out

how writers like E. R. Eddison were influenced by the

previous generation of fantasy writers:

Eddison followed Styrbiorn four years later

with something even closer to the sort of

thing Morris did, a book called Egil's Saga,

published in London in 1930. This was an

actual prose translation of one of the

longer, book-length sagas—one of the ones

Morris never got around to doing. Both in

his preface and in his notes to the Egil,

Eddison mentions William Morris.[1]

As Carter goes on to point out, the relationship between

Eddison's work and that of Morris . . .

Twain has the heroic tone of traditional American bragging

down pat, and there is something self-mocking in its very

exaggeration:

When I'm playful I use the meridians of
longitude and parallels of latitude for a
seine, and drag the Atlantic Ocean for
whales! I scratch my head with the lightning
and purr myself to sleep with the thunder![6]

This kind of unqualified exuberance . . .

The next two examples illustrate methods for quoting verse. The first
quotation begins in the middle of a line. It is preceded by ellipsis marks
and is placed over toward the right margin so that the final word of the
first line is situated about where it would be if the whole line had been
quoted:

Occasionally a famous line shines out of an

undistinguished passage:

                . . . Adam and his wife

        Smile at the claims of long descent.

        Howe'er it be, it seems to me,

            'Tis only noble to be good.

        Kind hearts are more than coronets,

            And simple faith than Norman blood.[14]

""Kind hearts are more than coronets'' has made its mark;

the rest of the passage, though, is as close as Tennyson

ever comes . . .

A lot of Christopher Smart's poetry is inspired nonsense:

Strong is the lion—like a coal

His eye-ball—like a bastion's mole

His chest against his foes:

Strong, the gier-eagle on his sail,

Strong against tide, th' enormous whale

Emerges as he goes.[2]

A kind of faith in nature is implied in such lines, but it is really the near-Biblical rhythm . . .

Exercise Quotations 10. Using any sources you like, write four paragraphs that contain block quotations. Choose two from prose works and two from verse. Remember to make your quotations accurate in every detail, including punctuation, spelling, capitalization, and (in the verse quotations) even spacing.

Exercise Quotations 11. Analyze the quotations in the following sentences. Be prepared to discuss the meaning of such details as bracketed material, ellipses, single quotation marks, capitalization, and the choice and placement of introductory and concluding punctuation.

1. "How did you guess?" she asked. "Where did I slip up?"
2. "Its [the CIA's] role in government has never been precisely defined," he complained in "CIA Impact," an article in the *Kansas City Star.*
3. Television, he argued, is at the root of much social evil: "Televised violence has warped the values of a whole generation!"
4. "Willy has only one interest in life—" explained Theresa, "taxonomy."
5. "Did I hear someone ask, 'Where's Ted?' " Brenda inquired.
6. "Did someone say, 'Soup's on'?" Brenda inquired.
7. It was Donald's opinion that "the old order has been preserved by the failures of the new."

8. Don't tell me, "The masses will eventually rebel": I know better!

9. He wanted blood from his "so-called friends"—me and Nat.

10. On this as on many subjects, Shakespeare has the last word:

> . . . Our basest beggars
> Are in the poorest thing superfluous:
> Allow not nature more than nature needs,
> Man's life is cheap as beast's.[3]

Quotations Reference Chart

27A
Use double quotation marks (") to enclose direct, word-for-word quotations from any written or spoken source.

27B
Use double quotation marks (") to enclose the titles of poems, songs, short stories, chapters, or articles in books, magazines, newspapers, or other longer works.

27C
Use double quotation marks (") to enclose a word or phrase understood in a special sense or a word or phrase you want to satirize.

Punctuation to Introduce Quotations

27D
Use commas to introduce quotations that are associated with credit tags, especially if the quotation contains an independent clause.

Mother gently reminded me, *"You were young once, too."*

27E
Use a colon (:) to introduce long or formal quotations or ones preceded by independent clauses.

In John Dewey's view: *"Every great advance in science has issued from a new audacity of imagination."*

Oscar Wilde was never overburdened by a sense of obligation: *"Duty is what one expects from others."*

27F
In capitalizing the first word of your quotations, be guided by your original.

Punctuation within Quotations

27G
Use square brackets [ ] to enclose your own corrections or comments within quoted material.

27H
Use a series of spaced periods (. . .) to show that you have omitted some original material from your quotation.

27I
Use single quotation marks (') for quotations within quotations.

"What do you think the author means by 'filial duty'?" he asked.

Punctuation at the Ends of Quotations

27J
Put commas and periods inside final quotation marks.

27K
Put colons and semicolons outside final quotation marks.

27L
Put question marks, exclamation points, and dashes inside quotation marks when they punctuate the quotation itself; place them outside when they do not.

He asked, *"When are you going?"*
Did he ask, *"When are you going?"*
Did he say, *"I am going too"*?

27M
Quotations that contain exclamation points or question marks keep their end punctuation no matter where or how they are used.

I heard her snort, *"Nonsense!"* but *"Are you sure?"* was my only reply.

27N

Quotations that would ordinarily end in periods lose their end punctuation when they are used at the beginning or in the middle of another sentence.

"I think my judgment was hasty," she admitted.

Vera spluttered, *"You can't do this to me,"* but we already had.

Block quoting

27P

Use block quoting for prose passages of more than four lines or for verse passages of more than three.

Three

Spelling, Word Punctuation, and Usage

28 *Spelling Rules* [*sp*]

Spelling presents a constant challenge in English. Even the most gifted spellers are driven to their dictionaries more frequently than you might suppose. At the other extreme are writers who must look up every third or fourth word they use. The spelling rules in this chapter and the word lists in the next are designed to help you master some of the principal spelling difficulties. That way you can concentrate your efforts on words that give you particular trouble and ones that fail to observe the rules.

28A
Be especially careful about pronouncing the words you want to spell.

Many people are sloppy about pronunciation, and this carelessness can have a dire effect on spelling. Misspellings such as *probly, usully, excape,* or *athelete* often result from careless pronunication by writers who have never taken the trouble to sound out prob*a*bly, usu*a*lly, e*s*cape, or *athlete*. Special pronunication-spelling problems concern word endings, especially final *s*'s or the *-ed* endings on past tense verbs.

Keep a close eye on the spelling mistakes you make in your writing. If any are caused by sloppy pronunciation, learning to say the word accurately may be all it takes to get the spelling firmly fixed in your mind. Dropped endings are more difficult to deal with, because you not only need to work on pronunciation but you must also learn when the endings are necessary and when they are not. A good drill for this problem is to copy out passages from books, leaving out all the final *s*'s and *-ed*'s. Go back and see if you can put the endings where they belong. Then compare your work with the original.

Exercise Spelling Rules 1. Pick the right spelling of the words in parentheses in the following sentences.

1. I (use, used) to know a lot of (sophmores, sophomores).

2. Our (representative, represenative) will advise you on the right (quanity, quantity) to order.

3. (Warmth, warmpth) is hard to maintain at that (heighth, height).

4. We mink ranchers (support, supported) our own (canidate, candidate) in last month's election.

5. (Does, dose) anyone seem (suprised, surprised)?

28B
Observe the *i* before *e* rule.

Many spelling rules are wildly unreliable, but this one is really useful:

Put *i* before *e*

Except after *c*

Or when sounded as *ay*

As in *neighbor* or *sleigh*.

To decide whether the *i* or the *e* should come first, follow this rule: if a *c* comes immediately before the combination, put the *e* first, as in *receive*. If the two letters are sounded *ay*, put the *e* first, as in *weigh*. In any other circumstances, start off with the *i*, as in *friend, niece,* or *shield*.

NOTE: Even this old grandfather of spelling rules has some exceptions. *Efficiency, either, foreign, height, leisure, neither, scientific, seize,* and *weird* are some of the most common ones.

Exercise Spelling Rules 2. Pick the right spelling of the words in parentheses in the following sentences.

1. This is surely a (piece, peice) of her (veil, viel).

2. His (cheif, chief) concern was the cracked (ceiling, cieling).

3. We (siezed, seized) the (sheild, shield) and ran.

4. (Foriegn, foreign) cars made up that ship's (frieght, freight).

5. Honest people suffer when a (theif, thief) (riegns, reigns).

28C
Nouns and verbs that end in a sound that can be smoothly combined with *s* take the ending -*s* in the plural (for nouns) or in the present third-person singular (for verbs). But if a plain *s* added to the base word would be difficult to pronounce, these forms are made with -*es*.

Some sounds can be smoothly combined with *s*, and some cannot. If the combination works, merely add an *s* to the base word to make a plural or a third-person singular form:

photo + s = photo*s*	hold + s = hold*s*
run + s = run*s*	house + s = house*s*
critic + s = critic*s*	mountain + s = mountain*s*

But there are cases in which the combination would be unpronounceable. Who could enunciate *passs* or *porchs?* To avoid situations like these, add an *e* between the base word and the ending -*s:*

church + s = church*es*	dash + s = dash*es*
ax + s = ax*es*	mass + s = mass*es*
bus + s = bus*es*	box + s = box*es*

There are, however, some exceptions to this rule. The commonest ones are a group of words ending in *o*. These should take a plain -*s* but do not:

buffalo + s = buffalo*es*	potato + s = potato*es*
Negro + s = Negro*es*	tomato + s = tomato*es*
hero + s = hero*es*	zero + s = zero*es*

28D
Words ending in a final *e* lose it when a suffix is added that starts with a vowel (*a, e, i, o, u,* or *y*). The *e* is kept when a suffix that starts with any other letter is added.

This rule holds true most of the time. Here are some cases in which the final *e* is lost:

hide + ing = hiding

prejudice + al = prejudicial

meditate + ion = meditation

retrieve + able = retrievable

precede + ence = precedence

late + er = later

The following words retain their final *e*'s:

lone + some = lonesome	care + ful = careful
time + ly = timely	lime + s = limes
manage + ment = management	love + lorn = lovelorn

There are some exceptions here too, however. Words that end in a soft *c* or *g* followed by a final *e* keep the *e* when adding suffixes that begin with *a* or *o*. There are not many such words, but this exception explains cases like these:

notice + able = noticeable	change + over = changeover
courage + ous = courageous	peace + able = peaceable

And some words unexpectedly drop their final *e*'s before the suffixes *-ful*, *-ly*, and *-ment:*

Awe + ful = awful

true + ly = truly

judge + ment = judgment

acknowledge + ment = acknowledgment

due + ly = duly

abridge + ment = abridgment

Keep your dictionary handy for doubtful cases.

28E
Double final consonants before adding a suffix that starts with a vowel when *1*) the consonant is single and is preceded by a single vowel and *2*) the consonant comes at the end of a one-syllable word or an accented syllable. Do not double the consonant unless both these conditions are met.

This rule is easier to work with than to explain. The following examples illustrate the problem. Here are some one-syllable words ending in a single consonant preceded by a single vowel:

sit	man
rap	pot
stir	sad

If you add a suffix beginning with a vowel to any of these words, you must double the last consonant:

sitting	manned
rapped	potter
stirring	sadden

The same rule holds for similar syllables that are accented at the end of a longer word:

regrét + ed = regretted	contról + er = controller
upsét + ing = upsetting	outfít + er = outfitter
forbíd + en = forbidden	prefér + ed = preferred

These are the only cases in which the final consonants get doubled. Words that have two vowels before the final consonant—for example, *out, soup,* or *need*—do not double; nor do words with no final consonant at all—such as *hoe, time,* or *hope*—or those with more than one—like *ask, stand,* or *fast.*

Problems arise only with words that have more than one syllable. How do you tell whether or not the last syllable is accented? The only way is to listen carefully to how the word is pronounced. Accented syllables are enunciated with more breath and force than unaccented ones. Compare the last syllables of *forbid* and *morbid.* In *forbid,* the *-bid* part gets the stress; that is why the *d* doubles before suffixes that start with vowels. In *morbid,* it is the *mor-* part that is stressed. This word's final consonant does not double.

Exercise Spelling Rules 3. In the following sentences, choose the correct spelling of the words in parentheses. Be prepared to explain your choices.

1. The bus gave some violent (lurchs, lurches) (hopping, hoping) the railroad tracks.

2. My childhood (heroes, heros) were often (careless, carless) about my feelings.

3. When I'm (lonely, lonly) any visitor is (truely, truly) welcome.

4. His (bigotted, bigoted) uncle was (noticably, noticeably) silent during dinner.

5. The (handicaped, handicapped) children were (giving, giveing) a Nativity play.

Exercise Spelling Rules 4. Combine the following base words and suffixes. Be ready to explain your work.

tomato + s	bet + or	bush + s
rash + s	divorce + ing	hid + en
sled + ing	come + ing	lift + ing
slide + ing	defer + ed	arrange + ment
argue + ment	love + ly	lunch + s

28F
Nouns and verbs ending in *y* preceded by a consonant form their plurals or third-person singulars by dropping the *y* and adding *-ies.*

The following examples illustrate this familiar rule:

carry + s = carries	ally + s = allies
mommy + s = mommies	daily + s = dailies
pity + s = pities	rally + s = rallies

About the only exception concerns proper nouns that end in *y.* These are made plural by adding an *s:* "Several Harrys [not *Harries*] have occupied the English throne."

28G

Nouns and verbs ending in _y_ preceded by a vowel (_a, e, i, o,_ or _u_) form their plurals or third-person singulars by adding _s._

This is simply the reverse of the previous rule. When a vowel rather than a consonant comes before the _y,_ keep the original spelling and add an _s_ at the end:

turkey + s = turkeys   boy + s = boys
day + s = days   alloy + s = alloys
enjoy + s = enjoys   corduroy + s = corduroys

Exercise Spelling Rules 5. Combine the following base words and suffixes. Be prepared to explain your work.

toy + s   anchovy + s   decoy + s
secretary + s   buoy + s   artery + s
hostility + s   play + s   monkey + s
obey + s   treasury + s   Danny + s
decay + s   anniversary + s robbery + s

28H

When other suffixes are added, final _y_'s preceded by vowels are usually kept, and ones preceded by consonants are changed to _i._ If the suffix itself begins with _i,_ however, the _y_ is always kept.

Final _y_'s preceded by vowels are generally retained before any suffix:

toy + like = toylike   monkey + shines = monkeyshines
key + stone = keystone play + er = player

Final _y_'s preceded by consonants become _i_'s when you add a suffix to the base word:

necessary + ly = necessarily crazy + ness = craziness
artery + al = arterial   felony + ous = felonious

But when the suffix starts with an _i,_ the _y_ is retained even if it is preceded by a consonant; otherwise, there would be two _i_'s in a row:

fly + ing = flying   cry + ing = crying
boy + ish = boyish   enjoy + ing = enjoying

28I

Words ending in _l_ retain the letter when _-ly_ is added. Those ending with an _n_ keep it when adding _-ness._

People do not tend to put too many _l_'s or _n_'s into words that do not need them; rather, the tendency is to skimp on the ones that do. The rule to remember is that all the letters that were part of the word before the ending was added should still remain once the ending is in place:

vain + ness = vainness
human + ness = humanness
lean + ness = leanness

ideal + ly = ideally
occasional + ly = occasionally
critical + ly = critically

28J
Make up spelling rules of your own.

Jingles and memory-jogging devices can help you deal with problem words. For example, lots of people remember how to spell *piece* by thinking of the *piece* of pie at the beginning of the word, or distinguish *loose* from *lose* by thinking that the one that means "free or slack" must be the one with room for the extra *o*. Try making up little rules and mnemonic (memory-saving) devices like these for the words that give you trouble. It is fun and can be very effective.

Exercise Spelling Rules 6. Choose the correct spelling of the words in parentheses in the following sentences. Be prepared to explain your choices.

1. (Ever, every) time she comes we start (arguing, argueing).

2. (Letting, leting) someone else rule your life is not my idea of being (couragous, courageous).

3. The (crunchs, crunches) we heard were (coming, comming) from the basement.

4. The (scratchyness, scratchiness) of that record makes it almost (unplayable, unplaiable).

5. (Neither, niether) you nor he will (receive, recieve) the ribbon.

6. Her (openess, openness) to the opinions of others is not (necessaryly, necessarily) a good trait.

7. You are (suppose, supposed) to hold a (lein, lien) on her car.

8. Death and (taxes, taxs) (wiegh, weigh) heavily on everyone.

9. (Rais, rays) of sunshine were (dancing, danceing) on the new snow.

10. Glen was (brutaly, brutally) frank about the (unsuitableness, unsuitableness) of my outfit.

Exercise Spelling Rules 7. Combine the following base words and suffixes. Be ready to explain your work.

detonate + ion	Mindy + s	counsel + ed
hunch + s	gullible + ity	yesterday + s
checker + ed	cut + ing	gulch + s
employ + ing	orgy + s	usual + ly
holy + ness	x-ray + ed	holly + s
mean + ness	omit + ing	shut + er
begin + ing	guide + ance	real + ly
excite + ment	loss + s	eye + ing

Spelling Rules Reference Chart

28A

Be especially careful about pronouncing the words you want to spell.

28B

Observe the *i* before *e* rule.

Put *i* before *e*

Except after c

Or when sounded as *ay*

As in *neighbor* or *sleigh*.

28C

Nouns and verbs that end in a sound that can be smoothly combined with *s* take the ending *-s* in the plural (for nouns) or in the present third-person singular (for verbs). But if a plain *s* added to the base word would be difficult to pronounce, these forms are made with *-es*.

fund + s = funds   pouch + s = pouches
banana + s = bananas   dress + s = dresses

28D

Words ending in a final *e* lose it when a suffix is added that starts with a vowel (*a, e, i, o, u,* or *y*). The *e* is kept when a suffix that starts with any other letter is added.

slide + ing = sliding   slide + s = slides
excite + able = excitable   excite + ment = excitement

28E

Double final consonants before adding a suffix that starts with a vowel when 1) the consonant is single and is preceded by a single vowel and 2) the consonant comes at the end of a one-syllable word or an accented syllable. Do not double the consonant unless both these conditions are met.

rip + ing = ripping   reap + ing = reaping
knot + ed = knotted   note + ed = noted
occúr + ing = occurring   láyer + ing = layering

28F
Nouns and verbs ending in *y* preceded by a consonant form their plurals or third-person singulars by dropping the *y* and adding *-ies*.

city + s = cities
story + s = stories

bully + s = bullies
quarry + s = quarries

28G
Nouns and verbs ending in *y* preceded by a vowel (*a, e, i, o,* or *u*) form their plurals or third-person singulars by adding *s*.

annoy + s = annoys
buy + s = buys

medley + s = medleys
destroy + s = destroys

28H
When other suffixes are added, final *y*'s preceded by vowels are usually kept, and ones preceded by consonants are changed to *i*. If the suffix itself begins with *i*, however, the *y* is always kept.

lay + er = layer
deploy + ment = deployment
convoy + ing = convoying

moldy + ness = moldiness
itchy + er = itchier
rally + ing = rallying

28I
Words ending in *l* retain the letter when *-ly* is added. Those ending with an *n* keep it when adding *-ness*.

typical + ly = typically
casual + ly = casually

tan + ness = tanness
plain + ness = plainness

28J
Make up spelling rules of your own.

29   *Hard Words* [sp]

Most of this chapter consists of spelling lists, but no list we can provide will help you as much as one only you can make, a list of your own particular spelling nightmares. Keep such a list handy as you write; the more you use it, the more helpful it will be. Each time you find that you have misspelled a word, add it to your list. When you have accumulated more than twenty or thirty words, do two things. Alphabetize the list (so you can find any particular problem word quickly), and divide it into groups of about ten words each so that you can master the words one segment at a time.

What follows is a general spelling list of some of the most troublesome words in the language. Many of these words may seem easy to you. Fine! Ignore them and concentrate on the others. It may also be that some words that give you trouble will not appear. Discover what these are and get them into your own list. The words that are starred are all especially easy to misspell.

1
absence
achieve
*across
address
*alcohol
*all right
*a lot
arctic
arguing
*argument

2
arithmetic
article
*athlete

*benefit
bachelor
*beginning
believe
biscuit
bulletin
*bureau

3
bureaucratic
*careful
category
ceiling
cemetery
*certain
character

chief
cigarette
cocoa

4

column
coming
commit
controlled
*criticism
*criticize
dealt
deceive
*defense
*definite

5

dependent
descent
despair
*desperate
*destroy
*develop
disappear
disappoint
*divide
divine

6

doctor
dominant
duly
efficient
*eliminate
embarrass
*enemy
envelope (noun)
envelop (verb)
environment

7

*escape
especially
*everybody
excellent
exhaust
*existence
expense
experiment
*explanation
*familiar

8

February
*finally
foreign
forty

friend
fulfill
ghost
goddess
*government
grammar

9

guarantee
guard
guidance
heroes
humor
ignorance
imagery
inasmuch as
incredible
*independent

10

indestructible
indispensable
infinite
insistent
intellectual
intelligence
interference
*interpretation
*interrupt
irrelevant

11

irresistible
judgment
labor
*laboratory
legitimate
leisure
*library
*license
loneliness
lonely

12

maintenance
maneuver
marriage
medieval
merchandise
*miniature
*minute
mischief
misspell
mortgage

13

muscle
*necessary

*ninety
noticeable
*occasion
occurred
omitted
*opportunity
oppose
optimist

14

*paid
parallel
paralysis
paralyze
particular
partner
perceive
perform
*permanent
physical

15

*playwright
pleasant
poison
politician
*possess
*possession
practically
practice
prairie
*precede

16

predominant
*preferred
preference
pretension
prevalent
privilege
*probably
procedure
proceed
professor

17

psychology
*pursue
*realize
*really
recede
*receive
recipe
recognize
recommend
referred

18

regretted
relieve
remembrance
repellent
repentence
repetition
resemblence
resistance
*restaurant
ridiculous

19

roommate
sacrifice
sandwich
schedule
*secretary
seize
*sense
*separate
sergeant
shepherd

20

shriek
siege
*significance
similar
simultaneous
skiing
smooth
*sophomore
*source
specimen

21

sponsor
*strength
strictly
substantial
succeed
superintendent
suppose
suppress
*surprise
syllable

22

symbol
symmetry
sympathize
synonym
technique
temperament
*temperature

tendency
testament
*therefore

23

thorough
*through
tobacco
traffic
tragedy
transcendent
transferring
tries
*truly
turkeys

24

tyranny
unanimous
unmistakable

unnecessary
unwieldy
vacillate
vacuum
valuable
*vegetable
vengeance

25

venomous
victim
villain
warring
*Wednesday
weird
wintry
withhold
woeful
worshiped

Exercise Hard Words 1. Find and correct the misspellings in the following sentences.

1. My roomate was embarassed when everbody saw him supress a yawn.
2. An optamist is one who realy labers to beleive the best.
3. On the prarie Febuary tempatures make the enviament hostile.
4. Artic plants are often minature versions of ones prevelent elsewhere.
5. The docter gave an independant opinion, but not one formed in a vaccum.
6. Finaly the emeny has moved accross to take posession of the mined resterant.
7. Labratory animals should have certan rights similiar to those given other animals.
8. They laid seige to the wintery north face of the mountain, always looking for an opertunity to climb higher.
9. He persued a career in the goverment lisencing buro.
10. I took time to develope a smoothe style of sking.

Exercise Hard Words 2. Find and correct the misspellings in the following sentences.

1. Alot of writers preceeded him as playrights concentrating on caracter.
2. It is probly irrelevent that they were argueing before she dissappeared.
3. Alchahol can poisen a mariage; trajedies of this kind are common.
4. In defence of polititians it should be pointed out that they do not always recieve the best advice.
5. Permenent phisical damage can result when a weekend athelete trys to do too much.

6. I suppose with enough practise one can acheive an efficent technic.

7. Practicaly all my muscels were siezed by a definate cramp.

8. It is no suprise that you have no rememberence of the events at the cematary.

9. Roland wanted to suceed and was willing to sacrafice his best frends to fullfil his ambitions.

10. Familar burocratic tendancies include resistence to change and intelectual paralisis.

30 *Capitals* [*cap.*]

Capitalization was developed to aid readers by marking the beginning of each new sentence with a different, bigger kind of letter. It soon spread to other uses. In the eighteenth century, the heyday of English capitalization, capitals were sprinkled around so liberally that almost any noun was likely to start with a capital letter:

> As we determined when we first sat down to write this History, to flatter no Man, but to guide our Pen throughout by the Directions of Truth, we are obliged to bring our Heroe [*sic*] on the Stage in a much more disadvantageous Manner than we could wish; and to declare honestly, even at his first Appearance, that it was the universal Opinion of all Mr. *Allworthy's* Family, that he was certainly born to be hanged.
>
> Henry Fielding, *Tom Jones*, 1749

Modern writers capitalize much more conservatively, in accordance with a whole system of conventional rules.

30A
Capitalize the first word in a sentence.

This is the original rule about capitalization and should give you little trouble. Special cases requiring capitalization, however, include quotations that consist of whole sentences:

She finally gave up: "I just don't know what to do."

Baley held "Plot is the first necessity of drama."

conversational fragments uttered as sentences:

Is the omelet burned? Afraid so. Tough luck!

Was he there? Where? Your place.

and whole sentences in parentheses between other sentences:

> The light was good that morning. (The trees that usually shade the window were bare.) I saw her quite clearly.

In connection with this last example, though, notice that no capital would be needed if the parenthesis came in the middle of another sentence:

> The light (it was almost painful in its intensity) was especially good that morning.

30B
Capitalize the pronoun *I* and the interjection *O*, but do not capitalize *oh*.

30C
Capitalize proper nouns.

Proper nouns are the names of specific persons, places, and things. The following are some categories to look out for:

Particular people, races, and nationalities:

Bob Meadors	Caucasian	Frenchman
Father Smith	Mongolian	Aussie
Eddie	Aborigine	German

Particular places:

Lakeville	Delaware	Nicaragua
Saint Louis	the Great Plains	Europe
Jefferson County	the Gobi Desert	the Western Hemisphere

Particular geographical features:

the Great Lakes	the Sierra Nevada	Clingman's Dome
Pike's Peak	the Eiger	the Colorado River
the Sinai Peninsula	the Humboldt Current	the Piedmont

Religious denominations and sacred names and concepts:

Hindu	Amon-Ra	the Ten Commandments
Methodism	the Holy Spirit	the Incarnation
the Bible	the Koran	Shinto

Particular units of time:

Monday	Memorial Day	Guy Fawkes' Day
June	Bastille Day	Pentecost
Lent	Easter	Mardi gras

Particular events and movements:

World War I	the Potato Famine	the Children's Crusade
the Boxer Rebellion	the Great Vowel Shift	the United Way
the Exodus	Populism	the Age of Reason

Particular organizations:

Bell Telephone	the U.S. Senate	the Boy Scouts
General Motors	the Marine Corps	the Elks
Georgia Pacific	the Supreme Court	Yale University

Particular programs and courses of study:

Psychology 100	the Junior Olympics
Studies in Marketing	Western Civilization II
Operation Crimecheck	Small Engine Repair

If you are ever in doubt about whether or not to capitalize a particular name, look it up in a college dictionary. If the name is capitalized in the dictionary entry, capitalize it in your writing.

In some cases writers are tempted to capitalize but should not. *Do not* capitalize names that fall into the following categories:

Do not capitalize names of seasons:

spring	winter	fall
summer	autumn	

Do not capitalize *black, red, yellow,* or *white* when using the words to refer to races.

Do not capitalize the names of academic areas if they are not part of the title of a specific course:

psychology	animal husbandry	philosophy
botany	astronomy	data processing
secretarial science	history	design

This last category is especially troublesome. You are supposed to capitalize the names of courses but not the names of disciplines. The following sentence illustrates this difference: "I am majoring in history and taking History 200." The first *history* is just the name of the field; the word does not require capitalization. The second, *History,* is part of the official name of a particular course; this word must be capitalized. An added problem comes from the fact that some academic areas are languages, and the names of languages are always capitalized: "I am majoring in French and taking French 303."

Exercise Capitals 1. Supply as many capitals as are needed in the following sentences.

1. John marley was not about to take it seriously: "o, i'm sure you saw something, but there hasn't been a bear in indiana for years."

2. The islamic observance of ramadan extends from spain to the hindu kush.

3. On trinity sunday we went to salisbury cathedral and attended an anglican service.

4. The mare tranquillitatis or sea of tranquillity was one of the first features on the moon to be named.

5. According to the central intelligence agency, "this fall may see an attempt by the eskimo liberation front to blow up the aswan dam on the nile river.

30D
Capitalize proper adjectives.

Adjectives that are formed from proper nouns generally require capitalization. Most of these proper adjectives are based on the names of people, places, and particular systems of belief:

Jeffersonian	American	Anglican
Lincolnesque	French	Buddhistic
Socratic	Roman	Democratic

The proper adjectives that refer to systems of thought can present special problems. *Democratic* with a capital means "of or pertaining to the Democratic party," one of the two major political parties in America. With a small *d, democratic* simply means "of or pertaining to a democracy." Capitalize this word only if it relates to a particular organization. The same considerations apply to other words, such as *catholic*. With a capital *c*, this word refers to the Roman Catholic Church. With a small *c* it simply means "universal."

Exercise Capitals 2. Supply as many capitals as are needed in the following sentences.

1. He said there was nothing less democratic than the democratic party.

2. The gandhian revolutionary is now as extinct as the pure marxist.

3. In the evenings our caribbean lagoon was a deep prussian blue.

4. My favorites are french vanilla and dutch chocolate.

5. Mencken used to call his fellow-baltimoreans "baltimorons."

30E
Capitalize the titles of books, magazines, newspapers, plays, shows, albums, songs, poems, essays, chapters, short stories, paintings, sculptures, and other creative works.

Titles are often made up of words that ordinarily would not be capitalized, but when these words are made part of the name of a specific work the situation changes. The conventional rule for titles is to capitalize the first and last words and all the words between, *except for* determiners (*a, an, the*), coordinating conjunctions (*and, but, or, nor, for yet,* and *so*), and prepositions that contain fewer than five letters (*in, out, over, with, of,* and so on):

The Songs of Christmas	*Washington Crossing the Delaware*
Catcher in the Rye	*"My Days Among the Indians"*
"A Psalm of Life"	*Life Along the Amazon*
Stereo Review	*As You Like It*
"Break Out!"	*"The Masque of the Red Death"*

Notice that the necessity of capitalizing first and last words overrides the other parts of the rule so that words that would not be capitalized in the middle of a title get capitals anyway when they come at the beginning or the end, as in "A Psalm of Life" or "Break Out!" Notice also that *among* and *along* are capitalized in "My Days Among the Indians" and *Life Along the Amazon.* These words are prepositions, but each of them has five letters and therefore must be capitalized.

> *Exercise Capitals 3.* Supply as many capitals as are needed in the following sentences.
>
> **1.** Have you heard their latest album *Regatta in the sky* with the song "hot air balloon"?
>
> **2.** The *Kansas City star* ran a good review of their production of *kiss me Kate.*
>
> **3.** My poem "Jefferson parkway in winter" appeared last month in *ventures in new verse.*
>
> **4.** The chapter "a Victorian view of revolution" is really the clearest example of what his book has to say about the period.
>
> **5.** No one has ever played "tangerine" the way Desmond did on the album *Jazz goes to junior college.*

30F
Capitalize common nouns when they become essential parts of a proper noun.

Included in this rule are such common nouns as *street, county, clinic, lake, river,* or *building,* when they are used as part of the official name of a particular place or organization:

South Elm Street	Dollar General Store
Missouri River	St. Joseph's Hospital
Bunker Hill	Ford Motor Company

But note that such common nouns are *not* capitalized when they are used in the plural to refer to two or more specific units:

Manioc and East streets	Jackson and Till counties
the Green and Barren rivers	lakes Huron and Erie

30G
Capitalize forms of address that come before a person's name.

Words such as *doctor, professor, general, officer, vice president, nurse,* or *uncle* are not usually capitalized, but when they come before a person's name, they become part of his or her title and should be capitalized:

Doctor Shirley Ores	Judge Landon
Cousin Kenneth	Reverend Mills
Professor Sawyer	Dean Smithers

Notice that this rule applies only to forms of address that are combined with specific names. If the title is separated from the name, it goes back to being a common noun and is not capitalized:

My doctor is Shirley Ores.

Kenneth Pytlac was always her favorite cousin.

Some titles, like *president, pope,* or *chief justice,* are very exclusive, as they are held by one well-known individual at a time. When this is the case, the title alone guarantees that your reader will know whom you mean. An exclusive title of this sort should be capitalized as if it were a name:

The *Prime Minister* arrives tomorrow.

Will the *Archbishop* agree with your decision?

The *Speaker of the House* has wide connections.

Another special provision applies mainly to family relationships. When you use a word such as *father, mother, brother,* or *aunt* in place of a person's name, capitalize the term to show that you are using it as a proper noun:

We saw *Father* in the cafeteria line.

I heard *Auntie* was coming for a visit.

Does *Mother* know you are here?

This rule applies to terms of relationship only when they are used as if they were proper names. The moment you modify them by saying things like "his father," "my older sister," or "your favorite uncle," the modifiers take over the work of identification and no capitals should be used.

Exercise Capitals 4. Supply as many capitals as are needed in the following sentences.

1. Did you see cousin Eleanor walk up to officer Baynam and thumb her nose?

2. My professor, Delphine Lubke, said the pope was wrong about the roots of terrorism.

3. We heard that the president outlined his tax proposal to congressman Sennett.

4. My father's dumb brother has now become senator Ryan, an expert on educational legislation.

5. Tell mother that lawyer English called to say her will was ready.

30H
Capitalize the names of directions only when they indicate a specific geographical area. Do not capitalize them when they merely indicate compass headings.

Although they may not be precisely defined, places such as the Old South, the Midwest, or the Northeast are as real as Tennessee or Idaho: you can point to them on the map. Names such as these should be capitalized, and so should ones like *South Pacific, North Dakota,* or *West Indies* which just happen to contain the names of directions. What should *not* be capitalized are direction names that are used merely to orient a reader. Compare the following sentences:

Grant struck out to the southwest along the ridge.

The Southwest has developed a culture all its own.

The first *southwest* is not capitalized because it is just a direction away from wherever Grant happened to be. When he gets to the end of his ridge, the same area will be to his northeast. In the second sentence, Southwest *is* capitalized, though, because it names a specific region of the United States. This region would still be the Southwest whether the writer were in Boston, Seattle, or Mexico City.

30I
Abbreviations after a name are generally capitalized.

People's names are sometimes followed by abbreviations that give special information about their status. Commander Ray Trissick, U.S.C.G. (Ret.), is a man who held rank in the Coast Guard and has since retired. Father Eustace Barrini, S.J., is a Jesuit priest (a member of the Society of Jesus). Olivia Axe, R.N., is a registered nurse. The abbreviations in these examples are parts of the person's official identity. All of them should be capitalized.

The only identifying abbreviations that are not covered by this rule are the ones for *senior* (*sr.*) and *junior* (*jr.*). Most people capitalize these too, but the uncapitalized form is acceptable as well.

Exercise Capitals 5. Supply as many capitals as are needed in the following sentences. Be ready to explain your work.

1. Professor Susan Meyers, ph.d., did her graduate work at the University of southwest Lousiana.

2. I saw Grover Friedrich, d.v.m., squabbling with Albert K. Joiner, d.d.sc., over the last piece of custard pie.

3. From Key West you have to go north to reach the old south.

4. Leaving India, Sir Alexander Horne-Bunting, o.b.e., sailed west, toward east Africa.

5. The French voyageurs helped open up Canada's northwest Territories.

Exercise Capitals 6. Supply as many capitals as needed in the following sentences. Be ready to explain your work.

1. He looked at me and shouted, "those were the men who won the west!"

2. I told doctor Ross that his address had been listed as 277 south maple street by the article in the *times-leader*.

3. In *the odyssey* the greeks finally overcome Hector, the leader of the trojans.

4. Zeena Crowder, l.p.n., is the name listed in the directory of the medical towers building.

5. Later, officer Smiley announed that the winner, Michael Markle, jr., had been notified. (his prize was still unclaimed.)

6. According to professor Keller, *the voyage of the African queen* was the greatest movie since *the birth of a nation*.

7. "The midnight ride of Paul Revere" was the longest poem ever memorized at stratford memorial high school.

8. For my psychology requirement I plan to take a course called adolescent problems, while invertebrate anatomy will complete my studies in biology.

9. Are anglican bishops selected the way catholic ones are?

10. May day celebrations were underway when the iraqi ambassador announced his country's dissatisfaction with russia.

Exercise Capitals 7. Supply as many capitals as needed in the following sentences. Be ready to explain your work.

1. Wasn't it at lake Louise that the international institute of dental hygienics held its symposium last march?

2. It is odd that the eastern Bloc now includes countries like cuba from the western Hemisphere among its members.

3. Please tell father Watson that the spaniard, don Sebastian Mendosa, is here to discuss the situation in madrid.

4. He likes mexican food, i think, but his tastes might have changed since we were together in new mexico.

5. *The red badge of courage* is one novel almost every student of american literature has read.

6. Captain Lucinda Tilden, u.s.m.c., was listed as the author of the article "the political stability of south yemen."

7. From its first words, "o, say can you see . . . ." the national anthem always moves me deeply.

8. The hittites of ancient syria had a great influence on other cultures, but little is known about the hittites themselves.

9. Can anyone explain the connection between charles martel and the holy roman empire?

10. He was very definite on the subject: "there's no cat like a persian cat!"

Capitals Reference Chart

30A
Capitalize the first word in a sentence.

30B
Capitalize the pronoun *I* and the interjection *O*, but do not capitalize *oh*.

30C
Capitalize proper nouns.

Carmen Jones	the Ural Mountains	the Renaissance
Italian	Christian Science	Xerox
Des Moines	October	Accounting 100

30D
Capitalize proper adjectives.

Brazilian	Early American	Christlike
Newtonian	Methodist	Virginian
Chinese	Serbo-Croatian	Elizabethan

30E
Capitalize the titles of books, magazines, newspapers, plays, shows, albums, songs, poems, essays, chapters, short stories, paintings, sculptures, and other creative works.

Without Feathers	*Swan Lake*
The Last Supper	*The Rape of the Lock*
"Rumplestilskin"	*Time Magazine*

30F
Capitalize common nouns when they become essential parts of a proper noun.

30G
Capitalize forms of address that come before a person's name.

30H

Capitalize names of directions only when they indicate a specific geographical area. Do not capitalize them when they merely indicate compass headings.

30I

Abbreviations after a name are generally capitalized.

31 *Italics* [*ital*]

The typestyle found in most printed books is called roman (it includes the type you are reading right now). Another form already familiar to you is the spindly, slanted *italic* typeface (*these words are set in italic type*). Both typestyles are kept in use because they make possible a visual contrast between particular words, numbers, and letters and the mass of type around them. Italicized words jump out at a reader from a page of roman print.

There are many occasions that require the visual shift from ordinary to italic lettering. But most typewriters are supplied only with roman type, and few writers can switch to italic lettering in handwritten work. When typing or hand-writing your work, you should underline the words that you would put in italics if you could. Underlining is a conventional substitute for italics, and everything that requires italics should be underlined instead in your handwritten or typed work.

31A
Italicize the titles of books, magazines, newspapers, works of art, plays, musicals, movies, television shows, record albums, and other major works of creativity or scholarship that are issued separately.

The key here is "issued separately." Italics (or underlining in written or typed work) combine with capitals to set off the titles of major, independent works or publications:

Moby Dick	*The Thinker*	*All in the Family*
Road & Track	*Damn Yankees!*	*The Mikado*
The Last Supper	*King Kong*	*Bach's Greatest Hits*

Parts of these independent works, when named separately, have their titles set off with capitals and quotation marks (27B). The name of a song from

Damn Yankees! is enclosed in quotation marks; the name of the show itself is italicized. You would put quotation marks around the title of a chapter from *Moby Dick* or an article from *Road & Track,* but you would italicize the names of both the book and the magazine.

Special Cases.   The distinction between the part and the whole is unfortunately not always clear. Sometimes, for example, it is hard to know how to handle the names of poems or short stories of intermediate length. Alexander Pope's *The Rape of the Lock* (a poem of 794 lines) was published separately, but it is not really book-length, and you might know nothing of its publishing history if you came across it in an anthology or poetry textbook. Philip Roth's *Goodbye Columbus* (ninety-seven pages in one edition) falls in length somewhere between a short story and a novel. What do you do with such titles? Most people set their own standards. In general, titles of poems of more than two hundred lines or stories of more than sixty or seventy pages should be italicized regardless of how the works were published originally.

Additional difficulties can arise when the title of a book or other work is the same as the name of one of its parts, characters, or settings. Edith Wharton's novel *Ethan Frome* is largely about a character named Ethan Frome. *South Pacific* is set in the South Pacific. "The Admiral and the Nuns" is a short story in collection of stories by Frank Tuohy called *The Admiral and the Nuns.* In cases like these, be careful to distinguish between references to the whole and references to the part. The title of the work as a whole must be italicized (underlined) when you refer to the whole work; but when you refer only to the part with the same name, you must be guided by the circumstances:

> "Oklahoma" is one of several hit songs from *Oklahoma.*

> The most memorable character in *Huckleberry Finn* is Huckleberry Finn himself.

> "West-Running Brook," one of Frost's best poems, appeared in his fifth collection of poetry, *West-Running Brook.*

There are also some exceptions to the rule about italicizing titles. In particular, the Bible and books of the Bible are not italicized, and neither are the titles of legal or constitutional documents:

> Genesis is the first book of the Bible.

> Where did he stand on the Emancipation Proclamation?

Exercise Italics 1. Supply italics (underlining) wherever needed in the following sentences.

1. Does the character Humphrey Clinker appear in any of Smollet's books besides Humphrey Clinker?

2. I know the painting Mona Lisa, but I don't know anything about Mona Lisa herself.

3. Lord Jim and Nostromo are two of Conrad's best novels.

4. According to Time Magazine, the musical Hair was the most controversial show of the decade.

5. Last week the television show News Views staged a round-table discussion of the Equal Rights Amendment.

31B
Italicize the names of ships, planes, trains, and spacecraft.

The names of particular ships, planes, trains, and spacecraft are always italicized (or underlined):

The Spirit of Saint Louis   *Mariner I*
H. M. S. Bounty   the *Santa Fe Chief*

However, the names that are italicized must be official and public. If you call your Toyota "Fred" or the local freight train "Old Frustration," these are private names; they should not be italicized.

31C
Italicize letters, numbers, and words used for their own sakes.

The distinction to keep in mind here is that between letters, numbers, and words used to indicate something else and letters, numbers, and words used as objects in their own right. If you write that you have 3,043 dollars or live at 929 South Park, for example, you would not italicize the numbers because they are used to name something else, the amount of money in your account or the position of your house on its street. Italics are required only if you wish to call attention to the numbers *as* numbers:

At the top of the page she scrawled a number—*7752.*

Is that a *XVIII* or an *XVII?*

Try to make your *6's* more distinct from your *5's.*

Letters used as letters, rather than as parts of words, should also be italicized (or underlined):

I can't tell whether this is an *i* or an *e.*

He had not crossed a single *t* in the whole essay.

And words need to be italicized as well when you wish to call attention to the word itself and not the thing it names:

I could never pronounce the word *irony.*

Taradiddle is a good term for that kind of foolishness.

The poet makes great use of *love* and *spring* in her description of her affair with him.

Exercise Italics 2. Supply italics (underlining) wherever needed in the following sentences.

1. She recognized her ship, the steamer Haiti Princess, by its blue stacks and the number 3 painted on its side.

2. Air Force 1 had landed before Air Force 2 was cleared for takeoff.

3. How many i's are there in the word Mississippi?

4. The number 566 meant nothing to the crew of the sloop China Shore.

5. In the year that announcer has been with us, he has had 365 chances to learn to pronounce Wilkes-Barre properly.

31D
Italicize foreign words and phrases.

Although this rule seems clear, it is not always easy to decide if a word is foreign. If you want to quote a German article or a French song in the original, or drop a passage of Danish into your writing, you are clearly dealing with a foreign language and ought to italicize the words. But isolated terms and phrases pose greater problems.

Thousands of English words started life in other languages, and we still borrow words and phrases today. It is these comparatively recent borrowings that make it difficult to decide if italics are to be used. Some foreign words—such as *de facto, bourgeois,* or *siesta*—have been familiar long enough to be treated as English words, even though they retain their original form. (They are italicized here not because they are foreign but because they are used as examples—31C.) But other borrowings occasionally used in English have retained their foreign identity. These words—for example, the French *coup de grâce,* Spanish *hombre,* or German *Übermensch*—are still italicized. When in doubt, look up the word in a good dictionary (for instance *Webster's New Collegiate* or *The American Heritage Dictionary*). The words that must be italicized are printed in italics at the head of their alphabetical entries. Words that do not require italics are listed in roman type in the dictionary.

Exercise Italics 3. Look up the following words and phrases in a college dictionary. Underline the ones that need italics:

coup d'état	junta	Weltschmerz
sine qua non	diminuendo	Bolshevik
ciao	tutu	ab ovo
couturier	au revoir	quid pro quo

31E
Italicize scientific names for plants, animals, birds, or insects.

The names meant here are taxonomic ones, formal names that classify a life-form by genus and species. Such names are always italicized (or underlined):

The local coral snake, *Micrurus fulvius,* is exceedingly venomous.

I am fascinated by the ant bear, *Myrmecophaga jubata.*

Juglans nigra, the black walnut, is native to the Western Hemisphere.

31F
Italicize words that carry special stress, but use this technique sparingly.

Since the function of italics (or underlining) is to make certain words stand out from the text around them, italicizing is sometimes useful for spotlighting important ideas:

That Audi has neither four nor six but *five* cylinders!

She'd got it in her head that I was *Russian.*

But be careful to avoid overusing this kind of italics. Save them for situations in which the whole point of a sentence rides on a single word or phrase. Italics for stress promise a reader something out of the ordinary, a surprise or an unusually meaningful insight. A good writer will make sure to deliver on that promise, and will carefully justify each use of stress italics to himself before trying it on a reader.

Exercise Italics 4. Supply italics (underlining) wherever needed in the following sentences. Be prepared to explain your decisions.

1. A typical nuthatch is Sitta carolinensis, with a length of just under six inches.
2. Did Verdi write the opera Don Juan?
3. On the wall over the sideboard there was a print of the Inness painting Peace and Plenty.
4. What do you think of Scrub Brush as a name for a cleanser?
5. Under her arm was a heavy book, The Oxford Anthology of English Literature.
6. There is an article on tape decks in this month's Esquire.
7. That hotel is a real temple of haute cuisine.
8. The state flower of Oregon is a shrub, Mahonia aquifolium.
9. All she would say was ''dolche far niente.''
10. Christopher Morley's Where the Blue Begins was one of the popular novels of the period.

Exercise Italics 5. Supply italics (underlining) wherever needed in the following sentences. Be prepared to explain your decisions.

1. No successful organization can be created ex nihilo.
2. The text begins with a beautifully decorated initial T.

3. His favorite quarry is the brown trout, Salmo trutta fario.

4. Astern, he could see H. M. S. Vengeance, wallowing like the Clivedon herself in the slow swell.

5. She read us several passages from Straight Up, an account of the direct assault on the Eiger.

6. I saw his picture once: he was wearing a striped outfit with the number 35880 stenciled across the front.

7. As Cicero observes, a field "qui cum multos annos quivit uberiores efferre fruges solet."

8. Does anyone here know the correct pronunciation of vagary?

9. Speeches with too many s's in them cause actors difficulty.

10. Did Brando win an Oscar for The Godfather?

Italics Reference Chart

31A
Italicize the titles of books, magazines, newspapers, works of art, plays, musicals, movies, television shows, record albums, and other major works of creativity or scholarship that are issued separately.

31B
Italicize the names of ships, planes, trains, and spacecraft.

31C
Italicize letters, numbers, and words used for their own sakes.

Be sure your *l*'s are taller than your *e*'s.

4709 was the number printed on the label.

The word *continually* is hard to pronounce distinctly.

31D
Italicize foreign words and phrases.

31E
Italicize scientific names for plants, animals, birds, or insects.

31F
Italicize words that carry special stress, but use this technique sparingly.

32

Numbers and Abbreviations [*num.*, *ab.*]

The rules about numbers and abbreviations include many special cases and exceptions. However, there is one general rule to follow: *In writing essays, spell out all numbers that are formed with one or two figures, and avoid all abbreviations except the commonest ones* (Mr., Mrs., Ms., Jr., Sr., M.D., Ph.D., *and a few others*). This general principle will keep you from making mistakes like the following:

The coach signed *16* new players. (should be *sixteen*)

Govt. agents also carry identification. (should be *Government*)

Exceptional situations do occur, however, and you must be aware of them. Go over the following special cases to get a sense of the exceptions to the general rule. You might not be able to remember each of them, but when you meet them in writing your memory will click and you can look up the proper treatment.

32A
In general, spell out numbers of one hundred or less, and use figures only for those over one hundred.

This is the three-digit rule, and it is widely accepted for general writing. A number that can be expressed with one or two figures should be spelled out, while one that requires three or more digits should be set down in numerals:

The professor ordered *seventy-six* trombones.

By the middle of June we had handled *634* complaints.

Even here, though, there is an exception to keep in mind. Round figures that can be indicated in one or two words—*one hundred, five thousand, a billion*—should be spelled out, even though they might run to many digits if numerically expressed.

> *Exercise Numbers and Abbreviations 1.* Write sentences that include each of the following numbers. Use the three-digit rule to decide whether to spell out the numbers or to express them as figures.
>
> | | | |
> |---|---|---|
> | 32 | 19 | 101 |
> | 174 | 345 | 10,978 |
> | 3,902 | 99 | 56 |

32B
Spell out numbers at the beginning of sentences, no matter how large they are.

When a number begins a sentence, it must be spelled out, even if it has more than two digits:

> *One thousand six hundred and thirty-three* hamburgers were consumed before half time.

Alert writers avoid this situation, however, by making sure that their sentences do not start with large numbers:

> By halftime the crowd had consumed *1,633* hamburgers.

32C
Use figures for numbers that contain decimals or fractions.

> My car speakers need *3⅝* inches of clearance from the face of the mounting surface.
>
> In their culture, family groups average *4.654* members.

An exception here is that the fractions ½ and ¼ can be spelled out when used with numbers of less than three digits:

> His largest trout measured *twenty-four and a half* inches.

But do not mix spelled-out fractions with numbers expressed as figures. It is inconsistent to write

> The champ weighs *211 and a quarter* pounds.

32D
Use figures for numbers in dates and addresses.

> Room *32,* The Federal Building; *1609* State; Huntington, West Virginia *25701.*
>
> I met Molly June *4, 1975.*

One note of caution is necessary with respect to dates. In addition to regular, or cardinal, numbers, English has another set, the ordinal system, which can be written *two* ways (*first, second, third, fourth* . . . or *1st, 2nd, 3rd, 4th* . . .). In dates that do not mention the year, ordinal instead of cardinal numbers can be used:

I met her on the *fourth of June.*

I look forward to seeing you on *May 22nd.*

It is wrong, however, to use ordinal numbers in dates that specify the year. Do not write

The contract was signed February *6th,* 1979. (should be *6*)

32E
Use figures for page, chapter, and volume numbers in books and for the numbers of acts, scenes, and lines in drama or poetry.

The exciting passage is in Chapter *2,* which starts on page *30.*

The index to the whole work is at the end of Volume *4.*

With plays, the convention is to cite act numbers in large Roman numerals, scene numbers in small Roman numerals, and line numbers in Arabic:

In Act *III,* Scene *ii,* lines *1–36,* Hamlet gives his advice on acting to the players.

32F
Use figures with A.M. or P.M. and with abbreviations in measurements.

Odd times of the day are usually recorded in figures, followed by A.M. or P.M.: *2:15* A.M., *5:07* P.M. Whole hours are also handled in this way when it is necessary to specify morning or evening: *6* A.M., *7* P.M. But when the part of the day is understood, whole hours are usually written out and followed by *o'clock: six o'clock, seven o'clock.* Remember that figures go with A.M. and P.M., and that written-out numbers go with *o'clock.*

In measurements, abbreviated units call for figures. Spelled-out units require spelled-out numbers:

14 ft. 3 in.	fourteen feet, three inches
5 lb. 11 oz.	five pounds, eleven ounces
34 cc.	thirty-four cubic centimeters

32G
Be consistent in the way you handle numbers that refer to the same thing, especially if they occur close together.

Sometimes it is necessary to use figures for numbers that would ordinarily be spelled out, just to avoid the kind of shift that takes place in the following sentence:

The strength of the local chapter varied between *eighty-one* and *111* members.

Both numbers in this case refer to members of the local chapter, but the relationship is obscured by the jump from written-out to numerical style. It would be much better to write

The strength of the local chapter varied between *81* and *111* members.

Exercise Numbers and Abbreviations 2. In the following sentences, correct any mistakes in the handling of numbers. Be prepared to explain your corrections.

1. By 9 o'clock I had interviewed everyone in the houses around sixty-three State Avenue.

2. 906 applicants for the vacancy must be screened before six forty-five P.M.

3. What is so special about April fourth, 1987?

4. Each unit weighs twenty-five g. and the unit price is fifteen point six eight cents.

5. There were fifty–100 visitors in the hall throughout the day.

32H
Use abbreviations sparingly in general writing.

In general, abbreviations should be confined to situations in which time and space are limited. It is fine to abbreviate words in hasty notes or when addressing an envelope or passing along a recipe, but the same abbreviations look careless and inappropriate in more formal settings.

Wm. is lecturing tonight on *govt.* problems.

Silver *tsps.* are more impressive than stainless *st.* ones.

It is somewhere on Fifth *Ave.* in *N.Y.*

In particular avoid the following kinds of abbreviations:

Days and Months

This year *Xmas* falls on a *Mon.* (*Christmas, Monday*)
Last *Oct.* we saw them in concert. (*October*)

Place Names

He is living in *L.A.* (*Los Angeles*)
Tony spend six weeks in *Md.* (*Maryland*)

Titles Not Followed by Names

The *Dr.* refused to treat her. (*doctor*)
I was waiting to speak to the *Gen.* himself. (general)

Sciences and Academic Disciplines

I really earned that *A* in *Chem.* (*chemistry*)
Some students actually enjoy *P.E.* (*physical education*)

Units of Measurement Not Preceded by a Figure

I came within an *in.* of dying. (*inch*)
Richard had already waited an *hr.* (*hour*)

Ampersands (&)

He & I have never got along. (*and*)
The French marched out & attacked. (*and*)

32I
Abbreviations for titles are acceptable as parts of specific names.

The list of acceptable abbreviations include titles such as *Mr., Mrs., Ms., Dr., Jr., Sr., M.D., Ph.D.,* or *C.P.A.,* when they are used as parts of proper names:

> *Mr.* Jones has become Thaddeus Jones, *D.V.M.*
>
> *Ms.* Katie Brown, *C.P.A.,* turned out to be Mindy's sister.

32J
Abbreviations for institutions, government agencies and programs, or awkward technical terms are acceptable, provided that their meanings are clear.

This rule applies mainly to awkward or complex names which are too cumbersome to bear much repetition. Instead of saying "United States Department of Agriculture," for example, it is acceptable to use the abbreviation *USDA.* (Note that this kind of abbreviation is usually written without periods.) Similar cases are *CIA* for Central Intelligence Agency, *DNA* for deoxyribonucleic acid, *ROTC* for Reserve Officers' Training Corps, and *PLO* for Palestinian Liberation Organization. Be sure, however, that when you use abbreviations in this fashion their meaning will be clear to the audience you have in mind. People in the Navy, for instance, know that an LST is a landing craft (*Landing Ship Tank*), but the abbreviation needs to be identified at least once for most other audiences:

> For amphibious attacks, the Navy created an extraordinary vessel, the landing ship tank (LST). These LST's were perfectly designed for their function . . .

271

32K
Abbreviations for some Latin terms are acceptable in general writing.

A short list of mostly Latin words can be used in abbreviated form everywhere. B.C., A.D., A.M., and P.M. are used with figures to indicate points in time:

517 B.C.   3:10 P.M.
A.D. 62   8 A.M.

(Note that B.C. comes after the number of the year, while A.D. comes before.) Other common Latin abbreviations are *i.e.* (*id est* or "that is"), *e.g.* (*exempli gratia* or "for example"), and *etc.* (*et cetera* or "and others"):

He spoke of his "old pain reliever," *i.e.,* bourbon.

Some colors just don't go with yellow, *e.g.,* purple.

Joan constantly complains about imaginary ailments—aches, shooting pains, hot flashes, *etc.*

The abbreviation *etc.* requires two special notes. It is illogical to write "and etc." The *et* in *et cetera* means "and"; therefore, "and etc." means "and and others."

Nor should you use *etc.* when the "others" will not be clear to your readers. In the sentence about Joan's imaginary ailments, the "others" can be any minor symptoms that come to mind—headaches, a stuffy nose, or chills. But consider this sentence:

The behavior of chickens is fascinating, especially their territoriality, aggression, *etc.*

The reader (in fact, the writer) may have no earthly idea what the *etc.* in this example is supposed to indicate.

Exercise Numbers and Abbreviations 3. In the following sentences, correct any mistakes in the handling of abbreviations.

1. I am sure we will hear from the good prof. by Sept.

2. I have a lot of things to sell: my record player, a tennis outfit, an electric typewriter, and etc.

3. Psych. & ed. majors are planning a jt. picnic.

4. Henry has a lot of fascinating hobbies, i.e., scuba diving.

5. The UCLA students waited hrs. for a plane to Ca.

Exercise Numbers and Abbreviations 4. In the following sentences, correct any mistakes in the handling of numbers or abbreviations. Be prepared to explain your corrections.

1. 205 nurses have applied for training at Methodist General.

2. Thirteen in. separated the window sill from the floor.

3. I usually make do with a hamburger & fries.

4. The first day, seventy-two conventioneers registered; the next day, they were joined by 281 others.

5. Our state pk. system is, according to the article, sec. to none.

6. I told the officer I was doing only forty-five mph.

7. The last piece had to be exactly four thirty-seconds of an inch longer than the first.

8. Humbert looked long and hard for the right house, fifteen twenty-six Hardy Ave.

9. The Chev. Division is worried about being overtaken by the Olds. Div.

10. I saw yr. sarcastic lk. this A.M.

Exercise Numbers and Abbreviations 5. In the following sentences, correct any mistakes you find in the handling of numbers or abbreviations. Be prepared to explain your corrections.

1. Sp. out all nos. of 100 and under.

2. The bookmark was between pages three hundred twelve and three hundred thirteen.

3. The zoo has a great collection of cats: tigers, lions, leopards, cheetahs, civets, & etc.

4. I am a student of the greatest naturalist of all time, e.g., Louis Agassiz.

5. Napol. had an immediate influence on the politics of all Eur.

6. The course for the race measured three point two mi. from start to finish.

7. By six P.M. we were ready to eat, but dinner was not served until after 9 o'clock.

8. "17 ⅝," he called to the man marking the boards.

9. We have already canned seven bu. of swt. peas.

10. The reception began at six P.M., June Thirteenth, 1980.

Numbers and Abbreviations Reference Chart

32A
In general, spell out numbers of one hundred or less, and use figures only for those over one hundred.

The club has *fifty-three* members.

The state owns *3,096* vehicles.

32B
Spell out numbers at the beginning of a sentence, no matter how large they are.

Four hundred thirty-five runners had entered the marathon.

32C
Use figures for numbers that contain decimals or fractions.

The milling process removed only *3/32* of an inch of steel.

Pi can be rounded off to *3.141592.*

32D
Use figures for numbers in dates and addresses.

The meeting was held on October *20, 1979,* at the Hilton Inn, *344* Fairlane, Dearborn, Michigan.

32E
Use figures for page, chapter, and volume numbers in books, and for the numbers of acts, scenes, and lines in drama or poetry.

Chapter *41* starts on page *166* of volume *2.*

Caliban curses Prospero in Act *II,* Scene *ii,* lines *1–14* of *The Tempest.*

32F
Use figures with A.M. or P.M. and with abbreviations in measurements.

We worked from *8:05* A.M. to *6* P.M.

The engine should never exceed *6,000* rpm.

32G
Be consistent in the way you handle numbers that refer to the same thing, especially if they occur close together.

Not, "Its wing beat varied from *forty-two to 164* beats per minute," but, "Its wing beat varied from *42 to 164* beats per minute."

32H
Use abbreviations sparingly in general writing.

32I
Abbreviations for titles are acceptable as parts of specific names.

32J
Abbreviations for institutions, government agencies and programs, or awkward technical terms are acceptable, provided that their meanings are clear.

He told me it had been approved by the *FCC.*

LSD can be unpredictable and dangerous.

32K
Abbreviations for some Latin terms are acceptable in general writing.

33   *Hyphens and Syllabification*

Hyphens are little half-dashes (-) used to link words and syllables. Used between words, hyphens provide one way of combining the meanings of each word into a single concept. Between syllables, they make it possible to divide a single word between two lines of writing or print.

33A
Use hyphens in compound words that are not yet spelled as one word.

This is not a very explicit rule, but it is impossible to be more precise because the spelling of compound words is constantly changing. Combinations often start as two separate words, such as *post card;* move from that state to a hyphenated one, as in *post-free;* and eventually become one word, like *postman.* If you are not sure of how to treat an unfamiliar combination, look the word up in a good dictionary (for example, *Webster's New Collegiate* or *The American Heritage Dictionary of the English Language*). If it should be spelled as two words, there will be a space between the words in the dictionary entry. If it is a hyphenated compound, the dictionary will reproduce the hyphen, as in *long-range* or *all-star.* And if the combination has become one word, the dictionary will print only a raised period (·) between the elements to show that they are all parts of the same word: *band · wag · on, cow · boy.* Even dictionaries differ, though, in their treatment of compound words. The way you handle a given example may depend upon where you look it up.

Exercise Hyphens and Syllabification 1. Look up the following combinations in a good dictionary. Be prepared to tell whether each is one word, two words, or a hyphenated compound.

horse + fly	gilt + edged	brush + off
horse + faced	gift + wrap	free + form
horse + sense	catch + word	good + natured
morning + glory	bar + graph	out + come
more + over	blue + chip	monkey + shines
pocket + money	blue + pencil	monkey + business

33B
Use hyphens for compound words of more than two elements and for words formed with the prefixes *all-*, *ex-*, *self-*, or the suffix *-elect*.

Several long compound words, usually ones including prepositions, are always hyphenated: *sister-in-law, editor-in-chief, good-for-nothing*. Also hyphenated are combinations including the prefixes *all-, ex-* (in the sense of *past*), and *self-* or the suffix *-elect:*

ex-wife	self-conscious	secretary-elect
ex-treasurer	all-conference	president-elect
self-appointed	all-inclusive	

Words that follow other prefixes can be hyphenated too, particularly if the prefix is attached to a capitalized word (*anti-American, pro-French*), a number (*pre-1887*), or a combination that is in itself more than one word long (*pro-labor union*).

33C
Use hyphens to join combination modifiers before a noun.

Included here are such combinations as *fast-approaching* or *well-schooled* when they are used as single adjectives before a noun:

We watched the *fast-approaching* storm.

She projected the words with a *well-schooled* delivery.

Such combinations are *not* hyphenated, however, when the first part of the modifier ends in *-ly:*

The book's *explicitly political* purpose was the issue.

My *apparently unconcerned* aunt glanced in my direction.

Moreover, with one exception combination modifiers of any sort lose their hyphens when the modifiers appear *after* the nouns they modify:

The storm was *fast approaching*.

I thought her delivery was *well schooled*.

The exception is that some combination modifiers have been together so long that they are listed as hyphenated compounds in the dictionary. In these cases, the hyphen is retained no matter how the modifier is used:

Walter is certainly a *well-groomed* young man.

It is rare to meet a young man who is so *well-groomed.*

33D
Use hyphens in writing out the numbers from twenty-one to ninety-nine and to separate numerator from denominator in spelled-out fractions.

Numbers from twenty-one to ninety-nine (except for those that begin new decades—*thirty, forty, fifty*, etc.) are all hyphenated, as are any spelled-out fractions that contain numerators and denominators. This rule applies to cardinal as well as ordinal forms:

three-eighths	sixty-second	seventeen-sixteenths
thirty-three	forty-five	fifty-seventh

33E
Use hyphens to prevent ambiguity.

Consider this sentence:

My cousin married a small appliance salesman.

This writer can mean one of two things. The writer's cousin might have married a man who sells small appliances, or she might have married a small man who sells appliances. In this type of situation, a hyphen can make the correct meaning clear:

My cousin married a *small-appliance* salesman.

My cousin married a small *appliance-salesman.*

See if you can spot the difference in meaning created by the hyphens in the following pair of sentences:

He was looking for a *foreign-car* mechanic.

He was looking for a foreign *car-mechanic.*

Exercise Hyphens and Syllabification 2. Supply hyphens wherever needed in the following sentences. Be prepared to explain your corrections.

1. By the end of the year he was building quite a large animal practice.

2. The walnut table is forty three and one eighth inches across.

3. Unfortunately, the would be commissioner quarreled with the ex mayor.

4. Her anti British policies were condemned by thirty two of the delegates.

5. Aggressive sounding statements won't impress the governor elect.

33F
Use hyphens to divide words between two lines of writing or print. Such words may be divided only at the breaks between syllables.

The technique of dividing words between separate lines of text is called *syllabification.* Sharp writers can usually find a way to word their ideas so that syllabification is kept to a minimum, but sometimes a word simply must be divided. In these cases, the division must take place at a break between the word's syllables. Most often the syllable breaks can be found by sounding a word out carefully, but if sounding-out leaves you uncertain, you will need to look the word up in a dictionary, where the syllables will be distinguished by raised periods (*syl · lab · i · fi · ca · tion*). The hyphen and division must be placed where one of these raised periods is (for example, *syl-labification,* or *syllabi-fication*). It is wrong to divide a word in the middle of one of its syllables (*syll-abification, syllabificat-ion*).

Special Cases. It is never possible to divide a one-syllable word between two lines, even when it is a long word like *twelve, rhythm,* or *through.* Words that contain double consonants usually divide between the doubled letters when these come in the body of the word (*pos-sessive, mammal*) or when the doubling results from an added suffix (*stop-ping, knotted*). But watch out for suffixes that follow double consonants that are part of the root word. In a word like *missing,* for example, the double *s* was part of the root word *miss* before the *-ing* was added. That second *s* is part of the original word; it is not something added along with the suffix. The correct way to break this word is *miss-ing.*

Exercise Hyphens and Syllabification 3. Put slashes (*/*) between the syllables of the following words. Look up the syllabification of any you are not sure about.

length	maple	emancipate
betting	fraternity	kissable
assonance	independence	enlargement
motorcycle	interrogation	leadership
driveway	embarrassment	caught

33G
Do not divide a word in such a way as to leave only one letter at the end of a line or fewer than three at the beginning of the next.

Do not leave one letter stranded at the end of a line (*a-head, e-rupt*), and do not break a word in such a way that you have fewer than three letters to carry over to the start of the next line (*cel-lo, divid-ed*). Encountering such short units can puzzle a reader. There is always room for two more letters at the end of one line or for one or two more at the beginning of the next.

33H
Divide an already-hyphenated word only where it is already hyphenated.

Suppose you want to end a line with a word like *self-conscious,* a word that already contains a hyphen. You find that there is not room for the whole word, so it will have to be divided. The rule is that the only place in which the division can be made is after *self,* where there is a hyphen already. The alternative, to divide after *con,* would give you a confusing duplication of hyphens (*self-con-scious*). This should be avoided. Another method would be to recast the sentence so that the division is not necessary at all, or to think of a synonym, like *embarrassed,* that has several dividing places from which to choose.

33I
Never divide proper nouns, proper adjectives, or initials.

Many proper nouns and adjectives, like *America* or *Italian,* have more than one syllable, but convention does not allow these words to be divided. Also unacceptable is the division of a person's name (*Thom-as, Char-lotte*) or the splitting of a set of initials between two lines. The following division is incorrect:

He had always been attracted to the works and life of *T.*
E. Lawrence.

Both initials can appear on one line, with the last name on the next, but the initials themselves cannot be split.

33J
Do not divide a word between pages or divide the last word of a paragraph.

Both provisions of this rule are meant to keep little orphan parts of words from cropping up in awkward, exposed places. If a word is divided between pages, the reader is faced with something like *-red* or *-iness* at the beginning of the second one. Most people would have to look back at the previous page to be reminded of how the word started. It is better to run a line over at the bottom of the page than to start a new page with the second half of a divided word.

The second part of the rule is based more on appearances than function. People do not have difficulty reading a divided word at the end of a paragraph, but the extra syllable or two will look odd sitting alone at the end of a block of whole lines. It is better to squeeze the word in on the original line or to leave that line short so that you will have a whole word to put on the next line.

Exercise Hyphens and Syllabification 4. Be prepared to explain what is wrong with the divisions of words in the following sentences.

1. We were excited about our most recent production, *Much A-do About Nothing.*

2. He remarked that there was very little optimism in the works of B. F. Skinner.

3. Susan plans to spend the first part of her coming fall vacation in Califor-nia with her aunt.

4. By the end of the next month Ned owed a lot of money to his sis-ter-in-law.

5. There were only two games to go when the champion was decid-ed.

Exercise Hyphens and Syllabification 5. Supply or correct hyphens wherever needed in the following sentences. Be prepared to explain your decisions.

1. He went off to consult with the ruptured tissue specialist.

2. Three eighths of the members, twenty one persons in all, voted for the new bylaws.

3. The slowly-weaving wasp searched for a gap in the screen.

4. Her father was a dyed in the wool conservative.

5. Our ex president is also an all conference linebacker.

6. The new bride was looking forward confidently to many years of blis-sful married life.

7. Sandra's father was only forty five years old.

8. Our mayor explained that she had no special use for self-proclaimed experts on civic government.

9. I think he's saving the well done slice for Sonia.

10. "I've eaten too much," he complained. "I feel absolutely gorg-ed and ready to burst."

Exercise Hyphens and Syllabification 6. Supply or correct hyphens wherever needed in the following sentences. Be prepared to explain your decisions.

1. He is as crooked as a corkscrew—an out and out swindler!

2. More than anything else, they need a complete description of the mis-sing child.

3. She practically lives in the potting shed behind her bright green house.

4. Barbara found her glasses where she hadn't thought to look, among the silverware.

5. She said she had a lot of points to settle with the new president-elect.

6. I think I will enter the *Sculpin* in the big boat race.

7. He planted the seventy two little hemlocks at three foot intervals around his back yard.

8. Across the street was a ramshackle customs station; beyond that was Mexico.

9. It took all the control he had (and that wasn't much) to accept the lesser of the two evils.

10. Her well considered and clearly-articulated remarks entirely won her audience over.

Hyphens and Syllabification Reference Chart

33A
Use hyphens in compound words that are not yet spelled as one word.

33B
Use hyphens for compound words of more than two elements and for words formed with the prefixes *all-*, *ex-*, *self-*, or the suffix *-elect*.

father-in-law	ex-sheriff	all-star
two-by-four	self-educated	treasurer-elect

33C
Use hyphens to join combination modifiers before a noun.

33D
Use hyphens in writing out the numbers from twenty-one to ninety-nine and to separate numerator from denominator in spelled-out fractions.

33E
Use hyphens to prevent ambiguity.

Not "He replaced the *flat sounding board*," but "He replaced the *flat-sounding board*," or "He replaced the *flat sounding-board.*"

33F
Use hyphens to divide words between two lines of writing or print. Such words may be divided only at the breaks between syllables.

33G
Do not divide a word in such a way as to leave only one letter at the end of a line or fewer than three at the beginning of the next.

33H
Divide an already-hyphenated word only where it is already hyphenated.

33I
Never divide proper nouns, proper adjectives, or initials.

33J
Do not divide a word between pages or divide the last word in a paragraph.

34 *Apostrophes* [*apos.*]

Apostrophes (') serve three different purposes in English: they show possession; they signal dropped letters in contractions; and they create certain plural forms. Most writers have little trouble with contractions, and the sorts of plurals that are formed with apostrophes are rare. But the problem of using apostrophes correctly in possessives is complicated, frequently encountered, and important.

34A
Use possessive forms to indicate ownership or grammatical possession.

Recognizing Possessive Situations. One problem with possessives is knowing when to use them. Possessive nouns and pronouns are used as modifiers to identify other nouns and pronouns, usually through ownership, location, or duration:

the *rat's* tail	the *people's* favorite
my *cousin's* broadsword	a *day's* work
Lucy's motorcycle	the *church's* windows

But notice that there is a difference between grammatical possession and possession in the usual sense of "ownership." With reference to the preceding examples, we do not usually think of a *day* as owning *work*, for instance, or of *people* owning something just because it is their *favorite*. If the possessives *everybody's*, *day's*, and *church's* in these examples seem correct to you, you probably have an good instinct for choosing possessives. If not, it might help to think of the possessive in some other ways.

Possessive nouns and pronouns are like adjectives. They answer such questions as "Which?" "Whose?" "What kind?" or "How much?" about the nouns they modify. Consider this example:

The *church's* windows were shattered by the blast.

The sentence is not about the church itself, but about the windows in the church. *Windows* is the subject, and *church's* merely identifies which windows are meant. The same considerations apply to the possessive in the following sentence:

Arnold put in a full *day's* work.

Work is the direct object; *day's* only specifies the amount of work involved.

Another hallmark of possessives is that they can be turned into *of* phrases. Instead of "the people's favorite," it is possible to say "the favorite of the people." The other examples can be transformed in the same way: "the tail *of* the rat," "the broadsword *of* my cousin," "the motorcycle *of* Lucy," "the work *of* a day," and "the windows *of* the church."

Nouns and pronouns that signify possession, that work like adjectives to modify other nouns, and that can be put into *of* phrases following the noun they modify are possessive and need a special construction to show their special function.

Exercise Apostrophes 1. Identify the possessive nouns and pronouns in the following sentences. Be prepared to tell what they modify and to turn them around into *of* phrases.

1. Marcia's running shoes were in the back of Linda's brother's car.

2. Somebody else's watch turned up in the magician's hat.

3. He was then informed of the rebels' landing and the citizens' resistance.

4. We gave the Ferrari's clutch a good workout.

5. A week's wages is too much to bet on a game's outcome.

34B
Use -'s to form the possessive of indefinite pronouns and most nouns.

Indefinite pronouns (*anybody, someone, no one, each, everybody*, and so on) and nouns that do not end with an *s* sound form their possessives by adding an apostrophe and an *s*. Here are some typical examples:

man's	everyone's	pressure's
men's	alumni's	children's
Martha's	bicycle's	Italy's

Some of these words name people, and some do not. Some are plural and some are singular. Some are proper nouns, some common ones, and one (*everyone*) is not a noun at all. But these variations do not matter when it comes to forming possessives. Since none of the base words ends in an *s* sound, each is made possessive in the same way, by adding an apostrophe and an *s*.

34C
Use an apostrophe by itself to form the possessive of plural nouns that end in *s* sounds.

Many plural nouns—words such as *women, media,* or *children*—end in sounds other than *s,* and these plurals form their possessives in the usual way, by adding apostrophe *s* (*'s*). But most plurals *do* end in *s,* and these words add only an apostrophe in the possessive; they do not take on an additional *s.* The following are several plural possessives that demonstrate this construction:

ladies'	Fords'	Navahos'
buildings'	United States'	boys'
boxes'	shoes'	necessities'

In this case, the written language is more precise than speech, for in speech there is no distinction between singular forms like *lady's* or *boy's,* and plural ones like *ladies'* and *boys'.* The distinction, in other words, is one you often cannot hear. Instead, choosing the right form is a matter of being certain of what you mean. Suppose you wish to say something about an injury suffered by a student you know. The word to make possessive is *student,* a singular noun ending in *t.* You would write "the student's injury." Now imagine that there has been a riot and a lot of students are hurt. This time the word that needs to be possessive is *students,* a plural noun ending in *s.* In this case you would write "the students' injuries."

Another way of being sure just what the base word is that you are making possessive is to make transformation to an *of* phrase. The word that follows the *of* is the one that should determine the possessive form. Talking about damage done to a single student, the transformation would be "the injuries of the student," and *student,* once again a singular ending in *t,* would be your base word. To make this word possessive, you would add an apostrophe and an *s.* But if you were thinking of injuries suffered by more than one student, the transformation would be "the injuries of the *students.*" The word *students* already ends in an *s,* so to make it possessive requires only an apostrophe.

Exercise Apostrophes 2. Write sentences of your own in which each of the following base words appears as a possessive. Example: *Everyone's* toes were blistered.

everyone	Knoxville	balloon
babies	two months	balloons
Fred	armies	toads

Exercise Apostrophes 3. Correct any misconstructed possessives you find in the following sentences. Be prepared to explain your work.

1. The girls' tent had collapsed on her during the storm.
2. The girl's tent had collapsed on them during the storm.
3. The dog's heads were down as they tried to pick up the scent.

4. Everybodys' guests wanted to talk about their own relative's connections with the governor.

5. Sarah was reluctant to return her aunts' diary without reading it first.

34D
Use either -'s or an apostrophe by itself to form the possessive of singular nouns ending in s sounds, depending on how many s's you hear when you pronounce the word.

Plural nouns that end in s are made possessive by adding just an apostrophe; nouns ending in any sound other than s are made possessive by adding an apostrophe and an s. With the remaining possibility, singular nouns ending in s sounds, forming the possessive is governed by pronunciation. Say the word to yourself along with the noun it modifies. If you hear an extra s, make the possessive by adding -'s; if not, add only the apostrophe.

Suppose you wanted to say something about the construction of the nucleus of a cell. Would you write "the nucleus' structure" or "the nucleus's structure"? If you are like most people, you will put two s's into the possessive of *nucleus* and know that the second choice is the right one. On the other hand, if you were writing about a car, you might find yourself wanting to say something about the strength of its chassis. Would you write "the chassis' rigidity" or "the chassis's rigidity"? Pronouncing these forms should quickly convince you that the second has too many s's for comfort and that in this case the first choice is the right one.

If the pronunciation test should ever let you down, leaving you genuinely undecided about how to form the possessive of a singular noun ending in an s sound, you can always adopt an *of* phrase: "the structure *of the nucleus*," "the rigidity *of the chassis.*"

Exercise Apostrophes 4. Correct any poorly constructed singular possessives in the following sentences. Be prepared to explain your corrections.

1. Massachusetts's governor was in the thick of the race.

2. Haloran is the middle class' first choice.

3. "I beg your graciousness's pardon," he apologized.

4. Who knows what goes on in an octopus' mind?

5. He had neglected to mark the oasis's location on the map.

34E
Add possessive markers to the last word of common compound constructions.

This rule applies to the possessives of familiar nouns and pronouns that are more than one word long. The possessives of such combinations as *editor-in-chief, sisters-in-law, someone else,* or *president-elect* are formed by adding the possessive marker (almost always -'s) to the last word in the sequence: *editor-in-chief's, sisters-in-law's, someone else's, president-elect's.*

This kind of construction is limited, however, to brief and familiar compounds. It is a mistake to take any noun phrase and add a possessive marker at the end: "a man that I know's brother," "a carton of cigarettes' price." Handle situations like these last two with *of* phrases: "the brother of a man that I know," "the price of a carton of cigarettes."

34F
In cases of joint possession, make only the last noun possessive. To show individual possession, make each noun possessive.

Joint possession occurs when two or more owners share the same property. In individual possession, each owner has property of his own. The distinction between these situations is clearly indicated by the handling of possessive markers. Consider the following possessives:

Jim and Lana's furniture

Jim's and Lana's furniture

In the first example, only the last noun is made possessive; this shows that Jim and Lana own the same furniture together. But in the second sentence both nouns have possessive markers, showing that Jim owns some of the furniture in question and Lana owns the rest.

34G
Use apostrophes to indicate the omission of letters or numbers from contracted forms.

The most common contractions are for negated verbs (*don't, isn't, can't*) or for subject and verb combinations (*he's, we'll, they're*). But there are also others, including words like *o'clock* (for *of the* clock) and dates like *'75* (in which the century number is omitted). In these kinds of contractions, the apostrophe takes the place of the letters or numbers that are left out. To decide where to place the apostrophe in a contraction, spell out the whole construction. The apostrophe belongs wherever letters or numbers were omitted. *Won't* is the only exception to this principle: as a contraction for "will not," it simply does not follow the rules.

34H
In the case of personal and relative pronouns, apostrophes signal contractions only, never possessives.

The following are the possessive forms of the personal pronouns and the relative pronoun *who:*

my, mine	his	their, theirs
your, yours	her, hers	whose
its	our, ours	

Some of these pronouns have two possessive forms. When two forms are given, the first is the regular possessive, used to modify some noun (*my* suit, *their* peanut butter), and the second is the form used by itself in place of the noun (Is *yours* better than *hers.*) The other possessives in the list—*its, his,* and *whose*—have to do double duty, filling either of these grammatical roles (*His* is better than *his* brother's).

None of these possessive forms takes an apostrophe. Possessive nouns and indefinite pronouns (*anyone's, somebody's,* and so on) are formed with apostrophes; possessive personal and relative pronouns are not. Forms such as *your's, our's,* or *their's* are always incorrect. Even more troublesome are the forms *it's* and *who's,* because these have legitimate meanings of their own, but meanings that have nothing to do with possession. *It's* is *always* a contraction for "it is" or "it has," and *who's* is a contraction for "who is" or "who has." The possessives of *it* and *who* are the forms *its* and *whose,* both of which lack apostrophes.

> *Exercise Apostrophes 5.* Correct any misconstructed possessives or contractions you find in the following sentences. Be prepared to explain your corrections.
>
> **1.** Whose going to furnish your's?
> **2.** It's velocity is much greater than our's.
> **3.** Who's umbrella did you mistake for your's?
> **4.** Its a shame it's color has faded.
> **5.** Whose going in who's car?

34I
Use apostrophes in forming the plurals of letters, numbers, and words used for their own sake.

In 31C it was explained that single letters, numbers, and words used as words (as opposed to words used as names for things), should be italicized, or underlined. To make an italicized letter, number, or word plural also calls for special treatment, adding an apostrophe and an *s.* Notice, though, that the *-'s* in such plurals is not included in the italics:

> All the asymmetrical parts were marked with *l*'s or *r*'s.
>
> Your 7's are especially hard to make out.
>
> Lawyers use *whereas*'s the way roofers use nails.

> *Exercise Apostrophes 6.* Correct any apostrophe problems you find in the following sentences. Be prepared to explain your corrections.
>
> **1.** There are too many *and*s in your second sentence.
> **2.** What do Jodys parents say about the companys future?
> **3.** I cannot tell Fred and Sue's records apart.
> **4.** Dont tell me you wont cooperate with the investigation!

5. He wants a weeks work for a days pay.

6. Its not certain who's car we will take.

7. Have you seen the commander's in chief suspenders?

8. We had a chance to see the Indians's new school building.

9. Henry James' novels are sometimes set in Europe.

10. They are out of water and want to borrow some of your's or our's.

Exercise Apostrophes 7. Correct any apostrophe problems you find in the following sentences. Be prepared to explain your corrections.

1. Is it time yet for the childrens' naps?

2. I put in an hours work in the firms library.

3. Everything he owns is monogrammed with *A*/s.

4. Carol's and Nancy's mother has just been elected to the city commission.

5. At least she did not hear her father's-in-law comments.

6. I know my habits get on the boss' nerves.

7. Have you thought hard about the witnesses's reliability?

8. Its a pity it's broken leg has ended it's career.

9. Wasnt he supposed to meet us at four oclock?

10. Stewarts opinions come straight from Dr. Millers lectures.

Apostrophe Reference Chart

34A
Use possessive forms to indicate ownership or grammatical possession.

the *fraternity's* plans   *Tom's* glove
a *year's* accumulation   *someone's* sister

34B
Use -'s to form the possessive of indefinite pronouns and most nouns.

| Molly's | anybody's | Methodism's |
| women's | firemen's | mower's |

34C
Use an apostrophe by itself to form the possessive of plural nouns that end in *s* sounds.

| calamities' | oranges' | Frigidaires' |
| axes' | individuals' | clubs' |

34D

Use either -'s or an apostrophe by itself to form the possessive of singular nouns ending in s sounds, depending on how many s's you hear when you pronounce the word.

Pegasus'   caress's   thesis'
cross's   Moses'   mess's

34E

Add possessive markers to the last word of common compound constructions.

mother-in-law's   second in command's
someone else's   theater-in-the-round's

34F

In cases of joint possession, make only the last noun possessive. To show individual possession, make each noun possessive.

Bob and Mary's accounts (they share accounts)

Bob's and Mary's accounts (each has separate ones)

34G

Use apostrophes to indicate the omission of letters or numbers from contracted forms.

I'll   '69   I'm
you're   we've   she's

34H

In the case of personal and relative pronouns, apostrophes signal contractions only, never possessives.

34I

Use apostrophes in forming the plurals of letters, numbers, and words used for their own sake.

35

Problems in Usage
[*usage*]

The alphabetical list that follows is made up of stylistic pitfalls—pairs of words that are confusing, nonstandard forms, spelling traps, and obligatory choices—that frequently give writers trouble. Read through the whole list, but take special note of explanations that seem new or strange to you. It is likely that the distinctions in usage that will give you most trouble are those you have never perceived as problems. Focusing on the entries that seem unfamiliar is one way to single out the discussions that will be most helpful to you.

a, an   Use the determiner *a* before words that start with a consonant sound, even if the word is spelled with a vowel (*a* university, *a* maple tree). Use *an* before words that start with a vowel sound or a silent *h* (*an* owl, *an* hour).

accept, except   *Accept* is a verb meaning "to take." *Except* can be a verb meaning "to exclude," as in "He *excepted* his stamp collection from the bequest," but it is more often a preposition, as in "Everyone was invited *except* me."

access, excess   *Access* always involves the idea of approaching or entering, as in "I have *access* to all the files." *Excess,* is related to *excessive:* "A hurdler can't afford *excess* weight."

adapt, adopt   *Adapting* something means changing it to fit your needs: "Glen helped *adapt* the play for television." But to *adopt* something means to take it up or take it over: "We *adopted* a little girl"; "The school *adopted* my plan."

advise, advice   *Advise* is a verb that means to give counsel to someone. *Advice* is a noun that means the recommendation itself: "She *advised* me to take your *advice.*"

affect, effect   Most often, *affect* is a verb: "This decision *affects* my future." *Effect* is most often a noun: "The *effect* of his decision was to limit my earnings." But this is a slippery pair. *Affect* can also be a noun, meaning a particular emotion, or a verb meaning to pretend: "She *affects* indifference

292

to her father." On rare occasions *effect* can be a verb too. As a verb, *effect* always means "to cause": "The physician *effected* a complete remission."

ahold   This word is inappropriate in formal writing. Correct its misuse by dropping the *a:* "The captain took *hold* [not *ahold*] of the tiller."

ain't   Use *aren't* or *isn't*, not *ain't*.

all ready, already   *All ready* is a pronoun and its adjective modifier: "We were *all ready* to begin." *Already* is an adverb of time: "The loaves had *already* risen."

all right, alright   *All right* is the correct way to spell this combination no matter how it is used: "By then we were *all right*"; "*All right*, I'll do it your way."

all together, altogether   *All together* means gathered in a group: "The boys were *all together* in a corner." *Altogether* is an adverb of degree, meaning *completely:* "Sheila has *altogether* too much confidence in herself."

allude, elude   To *allude* to something is to make a quick reference to it: "The prosecuting attorney *alluded* to her violent temper." To *elude* is to evade: "We've *eluded* your brother."

allusion, illusion, delusion   An *allusion* is a reference to something: "*Allusions* to the Bible came thick and fast." An *illusion* is a false appearance: "Lowering a car gives the *illusion* of greater length." And a *delusion* is a loss of contact with reality: "It was Jane's *delusion* that her sorority sisters hated her."

alot   Not a word. Always spell this as two words: *a lot*.

already   See *all ready*.

alright   See *all right*.

altogether   See *all together*.

also   Not a conjunction: "He washed the dishes *and* (not *also*) the pots." Use only as an adverb in sentences that would be complete without it: "He washed the dishes and the pots *also*."

altar, alter   *Altar* is a noun signifying a table or platform for sacrifice: "The bull was slaughtered before a low *altar*." *Alter* is a verb meaning "to change": "We *altered* our plans."

alternately, alternatively   *Alternately* is an adverb of time meaning "by turns": "Add flour and water *alternately*." *Alternatively* is an adverb of manner meaning "by way of alternative": "She could keep quiet and pay, or, *alternatively*, she could go to the police."

among, between   Both these words are prepositions, but *among* is generally used with objects consisting of three or more things, while *between* is used with objects that consist of only two: "We wandered *among* the booths"; "Gail stood *between* Tony and his brother." *Between* can, however, apply to more numerous objects in sentences dealing with agreements: "A contract was drawn up *between* the three heirs."

amoral, immoral   An *amoral* person, action, or thing is one to which the whole idea of morality is foreign or irrelevant: a tornado is *amoral*, and so are the actions of the criminally insane. An *immoral* person or action is one that should measure up to moral standards but does not: arson is *immoral*.

amount, number   *Amount* is a word used of a commodity that cannot be counted: "The *amount* of sediment in the bottom of the glass was amazing." *Number* applies to things that come in countable units: "The *number* of bison in Poland has recently increased."

analyzation   A pompous way of saying *analysis*.

and etc.   A needless doubling. *Etc.* means "and other things"; therefore, *and etc.* can only mean "and and other things." Drop the *and*.

angry with, angry at   *Angry with* goes with people: "I am *angry with* my parole officer." *Angry at* applies to situations: "I am *angry at* the way I've been treated."

ante-, anti-   *Ante-* is a prefix meaning "before," as in *antechamber,* or *antecedent. Anti-* means "against," as in *antibiotic,* or *antifreeze.*

any   Colloquial and unnecessary when used as an intensifier to modify another modifier, as in "He wasn't *any* better." The solution to this problem is to drop the *any.*

anymore   Should always be spelled as two words: *any more.*

anyone, everyone, someone   Spelled as they are here, each of these is a one-word indefinite pronoun: "*Everyone* needs *someone* but not just *anyone.*" But each is also capable of being spelled as two words when the emphasis is on the *one:* "Every *one* of his friends attended"; "Some *one* answer must apply to them all."

anyplace   This is another combination best spelled as two words: *any place.*

anyway, any way, anyways   As one word, *anyway* is an adverb: "Ted decided to come *anyway.*" As two words, it indicates a noun plus its modifier: "Is there *any way* to relieve the pressure?" *Anyways* is a nonstandard form of *anyway.*

anywheres   Nonstandard for *anywhere.*

as   Used between clauses, this word can lead to confusion. The conjunction *as* has a number of meanings, and the one intended may not always be clear: "*As* he washed the windows, I scrubbed the sink" (the *As* here can mean either *while* or *because*). *As* causes further problems when used incorrectly in place of the conjunctions *whether* or *that:* "I don't know *as* she'll agree with you." It is usually better to pick a more precise conjunction.

As can also be a preposition and creates yet another sort of problem when used unnecessarily before objective complements: "We considered Disco Dancer *as* a sure thing." There should be no *as* in this kind of construction.

ascent, assent   An *ascent* is a climb: "Gail slipped dangerously at the top of her *ascent.*" *Assent* can be a noun or verb, but it always has to do with agreement: "She nodded in *assent*"; "She will *assent* to our proposal."

as good as   This phrase should not be used in the sense of *almost:* "Mother is *almost* (not *as good as*) elected already."

aspects, respects   Used as nouns, these words should be avoided because they rarely mean anything definite. *Respects* often appears in the phrase "in many respects," which can always be omitted; and *aspects* is usually inferior to "points" or "topics."

assure, ensure, insure   To *assure* means to confirm something: "He *assured* me that the gun was unloaded." *Ensure* and *insure* used to mean approximately the same things, but most writers now limit *insure* to matters dealing with insurance policies: "My life is *insured* for fifteen thousand dollars." *Ensure* is left with the general meaning of "make sure": "The net below *ensured* his safety."

as to, as regards   Awkward ways of saying *concerning.*

at this point in time   A politician's way of saying *now.*

awhile, a while   *Awhile* is an adverb of time: "Sit with me *awhile.*" *A while* is a noun plus an article; it is the form you want as the object of a preposition (for *a while,* after *a while*) or in such constructions as "*a while* back" or "*a while* ago."

being that, being as, because of the fact that   Awkward ways of saying *because* or *since.*

beside, besides   *Beside* means "next to": "Hank stood *beside* the steps." *Besides* means "in addition": "I don't like him; *besides,* he squints."

between   See *among, between.*

between you and I   Common, but incorrect. The pronouns are objects of the preposition, so the phrase has to be "between you and *me.*"

born, borne   A thing is *born* when it comes into the world: "The lamb was *born* at midnight." A thing is *borne* when it is carried: "This burden must be *borne.*" But remember that a child that is *born* must first have been *borne* (carried) by its mother.

breath, breathe   The first word is a noun, the second a verb: "You *breathe* every time you take a *breath.*"

bust, busted, bursted   Only the first of these is a word in standard usage, and it is a noun meaning a woman's chest or a statue of someone's head and shoulders. If you need a verb meaning "break," the word is *burst.*

calculate, figure, reckon   Very informal when used to mean "to suppose": "I *think* (not *calculate, figure,* or *reckon*) I'll go."

can, may   Strictly speaking, *can* means "is able to," and *may* means "is allowed to." It is acceptable, then, to ask, "*Can* she run a mile?" But *may* is the right choice when permission is involved: "*May* I have the last piece?"

capital, capitol   The second of these means the seat of government, generally the Capitol Building in Washington or a statehouse: "They repaired the roof of the Capitol." *Capital* is the form for other uses, from *capital* letters to *capital* gains.

center around, center about   Neither phrase makes sense. *Center upon* is the appropriate combination.

cite, site, sight   The first of these is a verb meaning "to refer to": "The senator *cited* our tradition of free enterprise." The second word indicates a place: "The *site* was attractive and well drained." And the last has to do with vision: "You are a *sight* for sore eyes!" "She finally *sighted* the falcon."

climactic, climatic   Something is *climactic* when it provides a climax: "Eruption is the *climactic* phase of volcanic activity." *Climatic* is related to climate: "Siberia is a land of harsh *climatic* extremes."

clothes, cloths   *Clothes* are what you wear, and what you wear is made of various *cloths. Cloths* can also refer to pieces of cloth: "We'll need some *cloths* for cleaning the oven."

complected   A dialect word for *complexioned,* the term you should use in writing: "The man was light-*complexioned.*"

complement, compliment   A *complement* is something that makes a thing complete, as a *complement* of sailors makes up a ship's crew, a grammatical *complement* completes a verb, or a *complementary* angle, when added to another one, makes up a full ninety degrees. A *compliment,* on the other hand, is an expression of praise or admiration, as is a *complimentary* remark.

continual, continuous   Something is *continual* if it keeps coming back: "She was unnerved by the *continual* errors in her play." Something is *continuous* if it never goes away in the first place: "The air conditioner set up a *continuous* roar."

couldn't care less   An informal way of saying someone was indifferent. If you use this expression, be sure to phrase it in the negative; expressions like "He could care less" say the opposite of what they are supposed to mean.

could of, may of, might of, should of, would of, and so on   All these are misspellings for *could have, may have, might have,* and so on.

council, counsel   A *council* is some form of executive or advisory committee: "Jan appealed to the ruling *council.*" *Counsel* is either advice or (in court) the lawyer who gives it: "I ignored their *counsel*"; "Who is *counsel* for the defense?"

criteria, data, media, phenomena   All these are plural nouns. The singulars are *criterion, datum, medium,* and *phenomenon.* Be especially alert concerning *media,* which should always be treated as plural: "The *media* have made their point well."

cute, fantastic, great, lovely, nice, pretty, wonderful   The problem with these and similar expressions of enthusiasm is that they are overused and lack precise meanings. Try to find a word that says exactly what you mean.

data   See *criteria.*

delusion   See *allusion.*

descent, dissent   A *descent* is a coming down in one sense or another: "The *descent* was more hazardous than the climb up"; "She was proud of her aristocratic *descent." Dissent* means disagreement: "Progress will not bow to the forces of *dissent!"*

device, devise   *Devise* is the verb form; it means "to invent." *Device* is a noun: "A *device* is something someone has *devised."*

differ from, differ with   To *differ from* means "to be different from": "Apples *differ from* oranges." To *differ with* is to disagree: "Pete always *differs with* his father."

disinterested, uninterested   *Disinterested* means *impartial:* "His decision was wholly *disinterested." Uninterested* means "indifferent": "I am completely *uninterested* in your vacuum cleaners."

effect   See *affect.*

elude   See *allude.*

ensure   See *assure.*

etc.   Short for *et cetera,* "and others." Do not overuse. Two other points to keep in mind are that *etc.* already has a built-in *and* (See *and etc.*) and that the "others" the word indicates must be clear to the reader. Use *etc.* only to avoid listing the obvious; never use it when you yourself cannot think of anything else to say.

every, ever   *Every* is an adjective meaning "each": *"Every* man must do his duty." *Ever* is an adverb meaning "at any time" or "always": "Have you *ever* been to Boston?" "A girl scout is *ever* willing."

everyday, every day   *Everyday* is an adjective meaning "commonplace": "I wore my *everyday* clothes." *Every day* is a noun plus its modifier. This second form is the one you want after a verb: "She practices with her rifle *every day."*

everyone, every one   See *anyone.*

except   See *accept.*

excess   See *access.*

expect   Use only in cases of real anticipation: "I *expect* to hear from her shortly." It is informal in the sense of "think" or "suppose": "I *suppose* (not *expect*) you're satisfied."

extra   An adjective meaning "additional": "Don't forget the *extra* silverware." This word should not be used as an adverb to mean "unusually": "Clyde is *unusually* (not *extra*) sensitive."

facet, factor, feature, function   These words tend to be overused and misused. A *facet* is one of many plane surfaces, as in a cut diamond. A *factor* is a contributing cause. A *feature* is an especially conspicuous portion of something. And a *function* is a characteristic activity. These meanings are precise and limited, so none of these words should be used when you mean something as vague as "part."

factor   See *facet.*

fantastic   See *cute.*

farther, further   Use *farther* when real physical space is involved: "Port-land is *farther* than Seattle." Use *further* for other kinds of distance: "Noth-ing could be *further* from her mind."

feature   See *facet.*

fewer, less   *Fewer* is for things that can be counted: "Pickles have *fewer* calories than pancakes." *Less* applies to quantities that must be measured some other way: "Lawn mowers use *less* fuel than jetliners."

firstly   *First* is always a better choice than *firstly.*

figure   See *calculate.*

fine   This word should always be used as an adjective: "a *fine* painting"; "I feel *fine.*" *Fine* is too informal for written use as an adverb of manner: "That one will do *perfectly* (not *fine*)."

flunk   Informal for *fail.*

folks   Informal in the sense of "relatives."

former, latter   The *former* is the first of two things you have previously mentioned; the *latter* is the second. When more than two things are involved, use "the first" and "the last."

forth, fourth   The first of these indicates a direction (go *forth*), while the second is an ordinal number or a fraction: "This is my *fourth* cup"; "She inherits a *fourth* of the estate."

function   See *facet.*

funny   Informal in the sense of "strange": "It may be a coincidence, but it gives me a *strange* (not *funny*) feeling."

further   See *farther.*

good and   Informal as an intensifier: "She'll come when she's *good and* ready." Omit the *good and.*

great   See *cute.*

guy   Informal when used to refer to a person.

had ought   A dialect version of *ought.*

hisself   There is no such form; use *himself.*

idea, ideal   An *idea* is a notion or concept, *any* notion or concept. As a noun, an *ideal* is a thought too, but a special kind of thought—one concern-ing perfection: "I have an *idea* she's his *ideal.*" *Ideal* can be an adjective, too, in which case it means "perfect": "Becky has landed the *ideal* job."

illusion   See *allusion.*

immoral   See *amoral.*

imply, infer   To *imply* is to hint: "Manning *implied* something odd was going on at the mayor's office." To *infer* is to guess or conclude, usually on the basis of a previous implication: "We may *infer* that the ship was already sinking, since the lifeboats had been lowered before she was sighted."

infer   See *imply.*

ingenious, ingenuous   *Ingenious* means "inventive" or "clever"; it is usually the word you want: "The float valve was an *ingenious* device." *Ingenuous* means "innocent": "The boy convinced everyone by his *ingenu-ous* expression."

in regards to   Should be *in regard to* or, better yet, *regarding.*

irregardless   Nonstandard form of *regardless.*

insure   See *assure.*

is because   Often misused in explanations. Specifically, constructions such as "The reason *is because* it is durable" should be rephrased to say "The reason *is that* it is durable" or, better, "The reason is its durability."

is when, is where   Misused in definitions such as "A strike *is when* all the pins are knocked down" or "A cafeteria *is where* people eat." Try to be precise in your definitions: "A strike is scored by knocking over all the pins with one's first roll in a frame of bowling"; "A cafeteria is an eating place in which the customers serve themselves, usually from a line of steam tables."

its, it's The *its* without the apostrophe is the possessive form of *it:* "My canary has been neglecting *its* water." *It's* is the contraction for "it is" or "it has." "*It's* well known that *it's* been getting colder each year."

kind of, sort of Informal when used to mean "more or less": "She was *more or less* (not *sort of*) excited."

latter See *former.*

lay, lie See Chapter 11E.

learn, teach To *teach* is to impart information or skills to someone else. To *learn* is to master information or skills on your own or with help. "I would like to *learn* first aid so I can *teach* others."

leave, let Avoid using *leave* when you mean *let:* "Bobby won't *let* (not *leave*) me alone; he keeps bothering me."

less See *fewer.*

let See *leave.*

liable This word is informal as an adjective in the sense of "likely": "You are *likely* (not *liable*) to see her there."

lie See *lay.*

like This word produces many problems. Do not use *like* as a filler-word in writing, the way people sometimes do in speech: "He was *like* fifteen years old." (Omit the *like*).

Remember, too, that when it is not a verb *like* is a preposition, not a conjunction. Its proper role is to introduce nouns ("I collect all sorts of things, *like* old license plates"). It should not be used in place of *as, as if,* or *that* to introduce clauses:

You look *as if* (not *like*) you could use some Gatorade.

She feels *that* (not *like*) the season will be a success.

loose, lose *Loose,* for most practical purposes, is an adjective meaning the opposite of *tight. Lose* is a verb meaning to misplace or suffer the loss of something: "These pants are so *loose,* I'm afraid I'll *lose* them."

lovely See *cute.*

may See *can.*

may of See *could of.*

maybe, may be The single word *maybe* means *perhaps:* "*Maybe* he didn't hear you." As two words, *may be* is always a verb: "He *may be* out of earshot."

media See *criteria.*

might of See *could of.*

must of See *could of.*

myself Use only as an intensive/reflexive pronoun to add emphasis or to show that the actor of a clause also receives the action: "I *myself* prefer chocolate"; "I blame only *myself.*" *Myself* is unacceptable as a grammatically timid substitute for *I* or *me.* Do not write "Donna and *myself* are looking forward to seeing you" or "This has been a great day for Rex and *myself.*" The word is part of the subject of the first sentence; the phrase should be "Donna and *I.*" In the second sentence, the object of the preposition should be "Rex and *me.*"

nice See *cute.*

nowheres A dialect word for *nowhere.*

number See *amount.*

off of, off from   These phrases can always be reduced to the more standard *off:* "Roger got *off* (not *off of* or *off from*) the train."

OK, O.K., okay   These spellings are all acceptable, but it is usually better to pick a more formal word in the first place.

outloud   *Aloud* is preferable.

passed, past   *Passed,* with the *-ed,* is a verb form, the past tense of *pass:* "Hooray! I *passed* calculus!" "Later we *passed* through Little Rock." *Past* is a noun or an adjective having to do with former times: "The *past* is the key to the future"; "He should not be judged for his *past* mistakes."

personal, personnel   The word with one *n, personal,* means "private" or "individual": "She took off three days for *personal* business." With two *n*'s, *personnel* means "employees." But it can sound pompous to talk about "personnel" when you mean employees in a general sense. The word works best when you are talking about people in the military.

phenomena   See *criteria.*

plus   *Plus* is usually a preposition, not a conjunction: it can be used before nouns but not before clauses. Avoid expressions such as "I don't feel well, *plus* I am tired." Replace the *plus* with *and* or *besides:* "I don't feel well; *besides,* I am tired."

pretty   See *cute.*

principal, principle   The second of these, *principle,* is a noun meaning "a basic truth or doctrine": "Martin is devoted to the *principle* of fair play." All the other uses of the word—including such meanings as "leader," "sum of money," or "foremost"—require the spelling *principal:* "Ed was sent to the *principal*'s office"; "Add the interest to the *principal*"; "Greed is his *principal* motive."

raise, rise   These words are rather like *lie* and *lay. Rise* is something a subject does by itself: bread, the sun, sleepers, and hot air *rise. Raise* is something a subject does to something else: you *raise* crops, children, the flag, or Cain.

real, really   *Real* is an adjective meaning "genuine": "This is *real* gold." *Really* is an intensifier (an adverb that modifies other modifiers): "Kenneth is *really* frightened." Be on guard against using *real* where *really* is required: "The night was *really* (not *real*) dark."

reason why   The *why* is rarely necessary: "Haste was the *reason* (not the *reason why*) he made those errors."

reckon   See *calculate.*

respectfully, respectively   Both words are adverbs, but *respectfully* means "with respect," and *respectively* means "each in its own way." "I must *respectfully* disagree"; "Beans fill the stomach and hyacinths the soul, *respectively.*"

respects   See *aspects.*

rise   See *raise.*

set, sit   Another confusing pair of verbs. *Set* usually takes an object and means "put," as in "He *set* the toaster on the counter." But *set* can also appear without an object in various constructions: "How long will it take for the concrete to *set*"; "That hen will not *set*"; "The sun will *set* at 6:45." *Sit* is simpler: it always means "assume a sitting position" and rarely takes an object: "I like to *sit* in the sun."

shall, will, should, would   There is a fading tradition that *shall* and *should* (its past tense) ordinarily go with first person subjects (*I* or *we*), while *will* and *would* are the forms to use with all others: "I *shall* be delighted," but "They *will* be delighted." If you wish to be forceful, however, you may reverse this relationship: "I *will* prevail!" "You *shall* listen to me!" Check with your instructor about whether you are supposed to observe this distinction in your writing. The chances are that you won't have to except in questions. Most writers still prefer *"Shall* we (or *I)* invite her?" to *"Will* we invite her?"

should of See *could of.*

sight See *cite.*

sit See *set.*

site See *cite.*

so One problem with this word concerns its use as a conjunction. Used to connect clauses, *so* should mean "therefore": "I am faster than she is, *so* I got home first." But when there is a sense of intention (that is, when a subject does something in one clause in order to make possible the action in another) the two-word subordinating conjunction *so that* is called for: "She mowed the lawn *so that* (not just *so)* her brother would be free to practice for his recital."

So can also cause trouble when used as an intensifier to modify other modifiers: "Barbara is *so* polite." The *so* in a sentence like this one demands a *that* clause to complete the thought: "Barbara is *so* polite *that* she makes me feel like a lout." Another solution is to replace the *so* with *very* or *extremely,* intensifiers that do not demand a *that* clause.

someone, some one See *anyone.*

sometime, some time As one word, *sometime* is an adverb: "She wanted to visit him *sometime.*" As two words, it is a noun plus its modifier: "She wanted *some time* to herself."

somewheres A dialect word for *somewhere.*

sort of See *kind of.*

such Used before an adjective, *such* works the way *so* does as an intensifier. It demands a *that* clause to complete the thought it starts: not "They are *such* good friends," but "They are *such* good friends *that* they even dress alike."

sure Should not be used as an adverb: "Queenie *really* (not *sure*) likes her Milkbones!"

teach See *learn.*

than, then *Than* is used in comparisons: "Your toes are longer *than* mine." *Then* is the word you want when you mean "next" or "afterwards": "He cleared his throat; *then* he began to sing."

that, which, who *Who* refers to people, *which* refers to things that are not people, and *that* can refer to anything at all. It follows that it is as much a mistake to talk about "the girl *which* you saw" as it is to say "the building *whom* I entered." Some writers even distinguish between *that* and *which,* using the first for restrictive clauses and the second for nonrestrictive ones:

> Judd is a man *who* works hard. (personal antecedent)
>
> Hair *that* is naturally curly can never be completely straightened. (nonpersonal antecedent, restrictive)
>
> Helium balloons, *which* are lighter than air, can lift considerable weights. (nonpersonal antecedent, nonrestrictive)

theirselves A mistake for *themselves.*

them Should not be used in place of *these* or *those* as a demonstrative adjective: "I also want a few of *those* (not *them*) six-inch bolts."

then See *than.*

there, their, they're *There* works either as an expletive or to indicate a place: *"There* are no carrots in my stew"; "You should start to dig over *there." Their* is the possessive form of *they:* "They found a bomb in *their* car." And *they're* is a contraction of "they are": "I think *they're* on the wrong track."

thusly   Not a word. Use *thus.*

to, too, two   *To* is either a preposition meaning "toward" or the sign of an infinitive: "Wanda went *to* the dog show"; "I want *to* live." *Too* is an adverb that can be used as an intensifier or in the sense of "also": "She was *too* weary to care"; "We, *too,* have a say in the matter." And *two* is always a number: "I'll have *two* orders of fries."

uninterested   See *disinterested.*

used to   Be sure you spell this out completely: "Joy *used to* (not *use to*) work on transmissions."

utilize   *Use* is generally more direct and preferable.

ways   Very informal when used in the sense of *distance:* "John has a long *way* (not *ways*) to go tonight."

when   See *is when.*

where   Not a substitute for *that* in sentences such as "I see in the paper *that* (not *where*) the circus is coming to town." For the use of *is where* in definitions, see *is when, is where.*

who   See *that.*

whose, who's   *Whose* is a possessive pronoun: *"Whose* truck were you driving?" *Who's* is a contraction for "who is" or "who has": *"Who's* qualified so far?"

which   See *that.*

will   See *shall.*

wonderful   See *cute.*

would   See *shall.*

would of   See *could of.*

you all, y'all   Dialect pronouns for the second person plural. In writing, use *you* no matter how many people you are addressing.

your, you're   *Your* is a possessive pronoun: "I don't know how *your* notes got in my locker." *You're* is a contraction for "you are": "Dennis still thinks *you're* interested in him."

Four

The Research Paper and Special Forms of Writing

36

The Research Paper I: Selecting a Topic and Using a Library

A research paper can be a big project—an extended essay in which much of the material is drawn from sources other than the writer's personal experience. But it is still an essay: it supports a thesis and follows the principles that govern good essays of any type.

Some Things a Research Paper Is Not.   Students sometimes think of a research paper as nothing more than a collection of published material about a given topic. They shovel in as many references as possible to books, magazines, and newspapers, regardless of whether these sources agree, disagree, or are irrelevant to each other. The result of this process is not a research paper (a documented essay with a central thesis and clear, intelligent organization) but the raw material of a research paper yet to be written.

A research paper is not a grab bag. Neither is it a glorified book report. On the other hand, a research paper (at least at the undergraduate level) is rarely expected to be a major breakthrough in human knowledge. Undergraduate research projects are assigned primarily to introduce students to research methods. Therefore, the thesis, the paper's main assertion, need not be original. If you carefully evaluate and organize the information you gather, you will have created a unique presentation of your subject even if there is not a single new idea in the paper.

Actually writing a research paper, then, has much in common with writing any other sort of essay. You must think through what you want to say, get it down on paper, and carefully revise and check it over. The major difference is that at every step in the process you must take into account the ideas, facts, and opinions you have gained from sources you have consulted.

36A
Selecting a topic

If you are allowed to pick a research topic, pick a subject you would genuinely like to know more about. Make the assignment an opportunity to explore a topic that already interests you. Of course, not every topic you find interesting is suitable for researching. You would have trouble finding material for a research paper on "My Favorite Mechanics in Flagstaff," or "Some Tricks My Dog Learned." Choose a topic about which published information is readily available.

Also, because most freshman research papers in composition courses are relatively short, restrict your topic. "The Civil War" is obviously too large a topic. Even "The Role of the Cavalry in the Civil War" would be too complex to cover in a short paper. On the other hand, "Confederate Cavalry Raids in Southern Kentucky" might be a topic narrow enough to be treated in a short paper.

If you don't already know something about your topic, do some preliminary reading to see what the possibilities are. Get a quick overview of a topic by reading about it in one of the reference books listed later in this chapter. A good encyclopedia article, for example, should suggest many ways in which a broad topic can be restricted for further investigation.

Finally, in choosing and restricting your topic, remember you will have to construct a thesis—an interesting or controversial point to make. Try not to choose cut and dried topics such as the biography of a person ("The Life of Samuel Gompers"), a simple narrative ("The Sinking of the *Titanic*"), or a description of a process ("Darkroom Technique") unless you can think of a way of treating them that is *not* cut and dried. A thesis like "Samuel Gompers was president of the AFL almost continuously between 1886 and 1924" would pretty certainly be a dead end. Your essay will be much more interesting and enjoyable to write if you plunge into a debatable matter with an informed opinion of your own to support: "The sinking of the *Titanic* could and should have been avoided"; "The rise of color photography has brought an end to many creative darkroom techniques."

36B
Doing exploratory research

Once you have a topic, go to the library to see what materials are available. There are several ways of discovering what a library has and where to find it, but most people start with the card catalog.

36B.1. The Card Catalog. The card catalog is an index to all the books in the library, listed alphabetically according to author, title, and (usually) subject. In order to find a specific book, you must know the author's name *or* the exact title. If you have no particular book in mind, you can look under the subject heading to find a work that looks useful.

Most card catalogs are still sets of 3″ × 5″ cards in drawers, but some libraries have transposed their catalogs to microfilm or microfiche form.

306

Regardless of how the card is reproduced, though, it will look something like this:

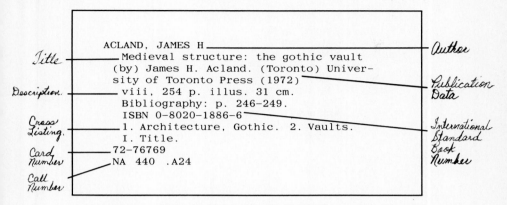

The *call number*, which appears at the bottom of the entry or in the top lefthand corner of the card, indicates the book's location in the library. In addition to providing the *author's name, title,* and *publication data* (place, publisher, and date), the entry describes the book. This sample card describes a book with eight front-matter pages (Roman numerals), 254 text pages (Arabic numerals), and illustrations. The book is thirty-one centimeters in height and contains a bibliography or list of further sources on the same subject. Such a bibliography is often useful for a research project.

The *cross-listed headings* show where else in the catalog the book can be found. The book in the sample card is also listed under the subject headings *Architecture, Gothic* and *Vaults* and under its title. Such cross-listings guide you to headings under which you can find more books related to your topic.

The title and subject entries contain the same information as the author entry; they simply have the title or subject displayed at the top of the card and are alphabetized accordingly:

TITLE ENTRY

```
    Medieval structure: the gothic vault
ACLAND, JAMES H
    Medieval structure: the gothic vault (by
James H. Acland, (Toronto) University of
Toronto Press (1972)
    viii, 254 p. illus. 31 cm.
    Bibliography: p. 246-249.
    ISBN 0-8020-1886-6
    1. Architecture, Gothic. 2. Vaults.
    I. Title.
    72-76769
    NA  440  .A24
```

SUBJECT ENTRY

```
ARCHITECTURE, GOTHIC.

ACLAND, JAMES H
  Medieval structure: the gothic vault
  (by) James H. Acland. (Toronto) Univer-
  sity of Toronto Press (1972)
  viii, 254 p. illus. 31 cm.
  Bibliography: p. 246-249.
  ISBN 0-8020-1886-6
  1. Architecture, Gothic. 2. Vaults.
  I. Title.
  72-76769
  NA 440 .A24
```

36B.2. Classification Systems. A book's call number reflects the library's classification system, an orderly method of identifying and arranging books and other materials in the collection. Most American libraries follow either the Dewey Decimal or the Library of Congress system, classifying and locating materials according to general subject areas. Here are brief summaries of the two systems for comparison:

DEWEY DECIMAL CLASSIFICATION

First Summary

000	General Works
100	Philosophy
200	Religion
300	Social sciences
400	Language
500	Pure Sciences
600	Technology (Applied sciences)
700	The Arts
800	Literature and Rhetoric
900	Geography, History, etc.

LIBRARY OF CONGRESS CLASSIFICATION

A	General Works
B	Philosophy—Religion
C	History—Auxiliary sciences
D	History and topography (except America)
E–F	America
G	Geography—Anthropology
H	Social sciences—Economics—Sociology
J	Political science
K	Law
L	Education
M	Music
N	Fine Arts
P	Language and Literature
Q	Science
R	Medicine
S	Agriculture—Plant and Animal Industry
T	Technology
U	Military science
V	Naval science
Z	Bibliography and Library Science

The Dewey Decimal classification is based on a system of numbers carried to several decimal places: for example, books about the geography of France would be numbered 914.4.

The Library of Congress System uses letters as headings for its twenty-one main classes and subdivides them by adding more letters. For example,

    P = Language and Literature

    PR = English Literature

Additional subdivisions are made by adding numbers to the letters, as in the sample catalog cards above. The books in your library will be shelved alphabetically and numerically according to one of these cataloging systems.

36B.3. Periodical Indexes.   Your research should include not only books but also *periodicals*—magazines, journals, and other publications issued at regular intervals. The most useful index to periodicals is the *Readers' Guide to Periodical Literature,* which lists articles in about 160 general-interest magazines. The *Readers' Guide* is a cumulative publication: an issue is published every two weeks throughout the year; another appears at the end of every month; these are gathered into quarterly issues; and a hardbound index is published at the end of the year. Here are some typical entries:

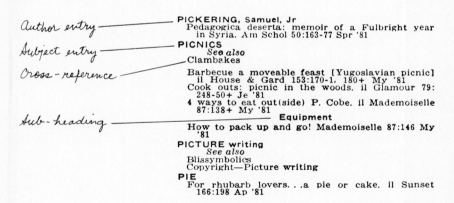

These entries are alphabetized by author or subject. The abbreviations, explained at the beginning of each issue of the index, are simple: the first entry, for instance, refers to an article written by Samuel Pickering, Jr. and entitled "Pedagogica Deserta: Memoir of a Fulbright Year in Syria," which appeared in the *American Scholar,* Volume 50, pages 163–77, Spring 1981.

To find material on more specialized topics, you may have to consult specialized indexes. The following are some well-known examples:

Applied Science and Technology Index (1958–[present])
Art Index (1929–)
Bibliographic Index (1937–)
Biography Index (1946–)

Biological and Agricultural Index (1964–)
Business Periodicals Index (1958–)
Education Index (1929–)
Engineering Index (1884–)
Humanities Index (1974–)
> One successor to *Social Sciences and Humanities Index* (1965–73; before 1965 consult *International Index to Periodicals* [1907–65]).

New York Times Index (1913–)
Public Affairs Information Service Bulletin (1915–)
Social Sciences Index (1974–)
> Another successor to *Social Sciences and Humanities Index* (1965–73; before 1965 consult *International Index to Periodicals* [1907–65]).

36B.4. Reference Works.

Reference works generally give overviews or detailed factual information about a particular field, and they are usually found in a special section of the library. The following books will help you find basic reference works in your field of interest:

> Barton, Mary Neill, and Marion V. Bell. *Reference Books: A Brief Guide.* 7th ed. Baltimore: Enoch Pratt Free Library, 1970.
> Winchell, Constance M. *Guide to Reference Books.* 9th ed. Chicago: American Library Association, 1976.

General encyclopedias offer introductions to a broad range of subjects and often list sources for further reading. These encyclopedias are the most reliable for preliminary readings:

> *Chambers's Encyclopaedia,* 15 vols.
> *Collier's Encyclopedia,* 24 vols.
> *Columbia Encyclopedia,* 1 vol.
> *Encyclopedia Americana,* 30 vols.
> *Encyclopaedia Britannica,* 30 vols.

Special encyclopedias and reference books provide information about restricted areas of knowledge. The following list includes some of the standard reference works within specific subject areas:

ART

Dictionary of Contemporary Photography (1974)
Encyclopedia of World Art (1959–68), 15 vols.
Oxford Companion to Art. Harold Osborne, ed. (1970)
Phaidon Dictionary of Twentieth-Century Art (1973)
Praeger Encyclopedia of Art (1971), 5 vols.

BIOGRAPHY

Chambers's Biographical Dictionary. rev. ed. (1970)
Current Biography. (1940–) Monthly except August; accumulated annually under title *Current Biography Yearbook.*
Dictionary of American Biography (1928–37), 20 vols.; supplements published through 1973.
Dictionary of National Biography (1885–1901), 63 vols.; supplements published through 1971.

FILM, THEATRE, AND TELEVISION

Aaronson, C. S., ed. *International Television Almanac* (1956–)
Baker, Blanch. *Theatre and Allied Arts: A Guide to Books Dealing with the History, Criticism, and Technic of the Drama and Theatre, and Related Arts and Crafts* (1952)
Bawden, Liz-Anne, ed. *The Oxford Companion to Film* (1976)
The Focal Encyclopedia of Film and Television Techniques (1969)
Hartnoll, Phyllis. *The Oxford Companion to the Theatre.* 3rd ed. (1967)
International Encyclopedia of the Film (1972)
New York Times Film Reviews, 1913–1968 (1970–71)

EDUCATION

Encyclopedia of Education (1971), 10 vols.
Encyclopedia of Educational Research, 4th ed. (1969)
Good, Carter V., ed. *Dictionary of Education,* 3rd ed. (1973)

HISTORY—AMERICAN

Adams, James Truslow, ed. *Dictionary of American History,* rev. ed. (1976), 7 vols.
Johnson, Thomas Herbert, and Harvey Wish. *The Oxford Companion to American History* (1969)
Morris, Richard B., ed. *Encyclopedia of American History* (1976)

HISTORY—OTHER

The Cambridge Ancient History (1970–71), 17 vols.
The Cambridge Medieval History (1911–36), 8 vols.
The Cambridge Modern History (1902–26), 14 vols.
Langer, William L. *An Encyclopedia of World History* (1972)
The New Cambridge Modern History (1957–1975), 14 vols.
Steinberg's Dictionary of British History (1971)

LITERATURE

Altick, Richard D., and Andrew Wright. *Selective Bibliography for the Study of English and American Literature,* 6th ed. (1978)
Baugh, A. C. *A Literary History of England.* 2nd ed. (1967), 4 vols.
Cassell's Encyclopedia of World Literature, new rev. ed. (1973), 3 vols.
Dictionary of World Literature, rev. ed. (1968)
A Handbook to Literature. William F. Thrall and others, eds. 4th ed. (1980)
Literary History of the United States. Robert E. Spiller and others, eds. 4th ed. (1974), 2 vols.
The New Cambridge Bibliography of English Literature (1969–76), 5 vols.
The Oxford Companion to American Literature. James D. Hart, ed. 4th ed. (1965)
The Oxford Companion to Classical Literature. Sir Paul Harvey, ed. 2nd ed. (1937)
The Oxford Companion to English Literature. Sir Paul Harvey and Dorothy Eagle, eds. 4th ed. (1967)
The Reader's Companion to World Literature. Lillian H. Hornstein, rev. ed. (1973)

MUSIC

Grove's Dictionary of Music and Musicians. Eric Blom, ed. 5th ed. (1955), 10 vols.

Harvard Dictionary of Music. Willi Apel, ed. 2nd ed. (1969)
The International Cyclopedia of Music and Musicians, 9th ed. (1964)
Scholes, Percy A. *The Oxford Companion to Music,* 10th ed. (1970)
Stambler, Eric. *Encyclopedia of Pop, Rock, and Soul* (1975)

PHILOSOPHY

Copleston, Frederick C. *A History of Philosophy (1947–1966), 8 vols.*
Encyclopedia of Philosophy (1967), 8 vols.
Urmson, J. O., ed. *The Concise Encyclopedia of Western Philosophy and Philosophers* (1960)

PSYCHOLOGY

Encyclopedia of Psychology. H. J. Eysenck and others, eds. (1972), 3 vols.
English, H. B., and A. C. English. *A Comprehensive Dictionary of Psychological and Psychoanalytical Terms* (1958)
Goldenson, Robert M. *The Encyclopedia of Human Behavior: Psychology, Psychiatry and Mental Health* (1970), 2 vols.

RELIGION

The Catholic Encyclopedia (1913), 16 vols.
A Dictionary of Comparative Religion, S. G. F. Brandon, ed. (1970)
Encyclopaedia Judaica (1972), 16 vols.
Encyclopaedia of Religion and Ethics. James Hastings, ed. (1908–27), 12 vols. (reissued 1973, 13 vols.)

SCIENCE AND TECHNOLOGY

The Dictionary of Biological Sciences. Peter Gray, ed. (1968)
The Encyclopedia of Biochemistry. Roger J. Williams and E. M. Landsford, Jr., eds. (1967)
The Encyclopedia of the Biological Sciences. Peter Gray, ed. 2nd ed. (1970)
Encyclopedia of Chemistry. Clifford A. Hampel and Gessner G. Hawley, eds. 3rd ed. (1973)
Encyclopedia of Earth Sciences (1966–)
The Encyclopedia of Physics. Robert Martin Besançon, ed. 2nd ed. (1974)
Encyclopaedic Dictionary of Physics. James Thewlis, ed. (1961–71), 9 vols. and four supplements
The Harper Encyclopedia of Science. James R. Harper, ed. Rev. ed. (1967)
International Dictionary of Applied Mathematics. W. F. Freiberger, ed. (1960)
McGraw-Hill Encyclopedia of Science and Technology. 3rd ed. (1971), 15 vols.
New Space Encyclopedia. 4th rev. ed. (1974)
Satterthwaite, Gilbert E. *Encyclopedia of Astronomy* (1971)
The Universal Encyclopedia of Mathematics (1964)
Van Nostrand's Scientific Encyclopedia. 4th ed. (1968)
The World of Mathematics. James R. Newman, ed. (1960), 4 vols.

SOCIAL SCIENCE

A Dictionary of Politics. Walter Z. Laqueur and others, eds. (1971)
Encyclopaedia of the Social Sciences. E. B. A. Seligman, ed. (1930–35), 15 vols.
Gould, Julius, and W. L. Kolb. *Dictionary of the Social Sciences* (1964)

International Encyclopedia of the Social Sciences. David L. Sills, ed. (1968), 17 vols.

McGraw-Hill Dictionary of Modern Economics. Douglas Greenwald, ed. (1973)

Theodorson, George A., and Achilles G. Theodorson. *A Modern Dictionary of Sociology* (1969)

White, Carl M., and others. *Sources of Information in the Social Sciences.* 2nd rev. ed. (1973)

Worldmark Encyclopedia of the Nations. Moshe Y. Sachs and Louis Barron, eds. 4th rev. ed. (1970), 5 vols.

YEARBOOKS AND ALMANACS

The Americana Annual (1923–)
The Annual Register of World Events (1890–)
Britannica Book of the Year (1938–)
Facts on File (1940–)
Information Please Almanac (1947–)
New York Times Encyclopedic Almanac (1970–)
Statistical Abstract of the United States (1878–)
The World Almanac and Book of Facts (1868–)

Exercise 36–1.

1. How would you begin research on the following topics? Cite specific sources you might consult and explain what sort of information you would expect from each of them.
   a. The development of the laser
   b. The style of Bach's music
   c. The basic tenets of existentialism
   d. The beheading of Charles I of England
   e. The Catholic Church's teaching on purgatory
   f. Information about the first test tube baby
   g. A discussion of the term "elegy"
   h. The verse form of Chaucer's *Canterbury Tales*
   i. Meteors
   j. A definition of Keynesian economic theory
   k. The Great Plague of the Middle Ages
   l. Theories about humor
   m. Justin Morgan

2. Find references to at least five periodical articles on energy conservation. Your references should be detailed enough for you to locate the articles in the library.

3. Compile a list of at least ten books *and* articles on one of the topics in Item 1.

36C
Preliminary reading

Once you have a topic and your exploratory research shows there is plenty of material on that topic in your library, narrow and focus your subject through preliminary reading. Skim through some sources you can depend on: up-to-date articles in standard encyclopedias and reference works, recent books, and the latest articles. If you had decided to write on Abraham Lincoln, for example, reading an encyclopedia article or two and skimming a recent biography might suggest a focus on Lincoln's law career. Additional reading and consideration should make it possible to further narrow this still fairly broad topic.

Toward the end of this preliminary phase, write out a tentative thesis and outline. You might change both later, but they will serve to guide your further reading and help you take useful notes. The outline can be very informal—merely indicating the general direction the paper is likely to take.

Imagine, for instance, that having restricted your topic to Lincoln's law career, you found yourself wondering what effect these law experiences had on his character and style. Thinking about your preliminary reading, you might decide to concentrate on his humor, his thoroughness, and his shrewdness. You would then be ready to write a tentative thesis and outline:

> *Tentative Thesis:* During his early law career, Lincoln learned and practiced qualities that did much to define his later personality.
>   **I.** His humor, early and late
> **II.** His thoroughness, early and late
> **III.** His shrewdness, early and late

This outline, a mere sketch, would be helpful in deciding which details from Lincoln's life would be useful and which you could safely overlook. You would know that it was not just anything about Lincoln's law and later careers you needed, but details that could be used to support your special thesis in your own way.

> *Exercise 36–2.* Do enough preliminary reading on one of the topics listed in Item 1 of Exercise 36–1 to develop a thesis and informal outline.

37

The Research Paper II: Gathering Information

Taking notes is exacting and detailed work, but cutting corners at this stage is a bad idea. Good notes are essential to make your material available in accurate and usable form when you need it. Inadequate notes are worse than useless: they risk a failing grade for plagiarism (see 37C) or inaccurate documentation.

37A
Evaluating sources

Inexperienced researchers often have trouble evaluating sources and identifying the most reliable ones. Not every source is to be trusted: some are outdated, biased, or wrong.

Sources are often classified as *primary* or *secondary*. Primary sources are those written by persons who have direct, firsthand knowledge of the subject. If you were writing on Henry David Thoreau, his own book *Walden* would be a primary source and so would comments about him in the letters of his friend, Emerson. Secondary sources are usually written at a later date and by someone who knows about the subject only indirectly. An eyewitness account of the Battle of Gettysburg would be a primary source for an historian, who then might write a book about the battle that would become a secondary source. In general, the more advanced your research, the more primary sources you should consult. But for research papers in the freshman year, good secondary sources may suffice. When you are writing on a literary topic, however, you must know the primary sources, the novels, poems, or plays you are writing about.

Another way to think of sources is as *scholarly* or *popular*. Scholarly works are produced by writers who have studied a topic in depth and whose work is usually based on primary sources. The historian who draws on eyewitness accounts to write a study of the Battle of Gettysburg might produce a scholarly work published by a university press and aimed at other specialists in the field, who will expect that the source of each fact or piece of evidence will be cited fully and accurately. On the other hand, another writer might draw on the historian's work for a book or an article aimed at the general reader, who may have little knowledge of the subject and who will not want elaborate documentation of sources. For advanced research you will be expected to work mainly with scholarly sources; for a freshman project you will probably be permitted to use high-quality popular sources as well.

What is a low-quality popular source? You probably already know quite well. Simplified accounts of things written for children, sensational books and articles designed mainly to make money, and uncritical discussions written by enthusiasts for some cause are typical examples. Stay away from books like *Suzy Studies Jet Propulsion* or articles like "What the Martians Told Me About God" unless it is the writers rather than their subjects that you want to study.

Another important clue to the usefulness of a source is its date of publication. Recent books and articles usually include the latest information about a topic, and they often cite the most important earlier studies or sources, thus giving you some real help with your own research. But just because a book looks new does not mean that it is. Check the first copyright date on the reverse of the title page before you decide how up–to–date a book is (see 39E).

Exercise 37–1. Classify the following sources as primary or secondary and as scholarly or popular, and evaluate the probable dependability of each according to its date of publication and apparent quality:

a. Helen Gardner, *The Business of Criticism* (London: Oxford University Press, 1959).

b. Harry Snider, "Life After Death: An Astounding, True Story of a Motorcycle Mishap," *Cycle World*, 5 July 1979, pp. 16–17.

c. J. J. Callahan, "The Curvature of Space in a Finite Universe," *Scientific American*, August 1976, pp. 90–100.

d. Lance Morrow, "The Weakness That Starts at Home," *Time*, 4 June 1979, pp. 81–82.

e. Frank Steele, "Two Kinds of Commitment: Some Directions in Current Appalachian Poetry," *Appalachian Journal*, 6 (Spring 1979), 228–39.

f. Theodore Gauss, *Speculations Concerning Space Travel* (New York: Hinton, 1885).

g. Jane Litton, *Thomas Edison: Boy Genius*, The Great American Heroes Series (Boston: Achievement Press, 1936).

h. Mark Twain, *The Adventures of Huckleberry Finn* (New York, Toronto, and London: Bantam, 1965).

37B
Preparing the preliminary bibliography

37B.1. Bibliography Cards.   By the end of your preliminary reading, you will probably have an idea of which sources are going to be most useful. Prepare a working bibliography on 3" × 5" note cards to provide a clear record of the sources you will use in your finished paper (see 39I).

Each bibliography card should contain this information:

1. The library call number and any other location code.
2. Author or editor's name (last name first; *ed.* after editor's name).
3. The title of the book (underlined) or article (in quotation marks).
4. Publication data:
   a. Book: city (and state when the name of the city would not be immediately recognizable), name of publisher, date.
   b. Article: name of magazine (underlined), volume number (if any) and date of issue, page numbers on which article appears.
   c. Newspaper: name of paper (underlined), date, section (optional), page number, column number (optional).
5. (Optional) A note about the usefulness of the source.

Here are sample bibliography cards for a book and a magazine article:

1. Bibliography Card for a Book

call number	PR 2976 .F42
author	Fergusson, Francis
title	*Trope and Allegory: Themes common to Dante and Shakespeare*
publication data	Athens, Georgia: The University of Georgia Press, 1977
usefulness note	*Romeo and Juliet* treated in Chapter II. *Looks good.*

2. Bibliography Card for an Article

<table>
<tr><td>location</td><td>periodicals – 6th floor</td></tr>
<tr><td>author</td><td>Alexander, Charles P.</td></tr>
<tr><td>title</td><td>"Energy: Fuels of the Future"</td></tr>
<tr><td>magazine
and
publication
data</td><td>Time, 11 June 1979, pp. 72-73, 75-76</td></tr>
<tr><td>usefulness
note</td><td>Excellent Survey</td></tr>
</table>

Alphabetize the bibliography cards for the sources you are most likely to use, and put them in a safe place. They are your permanent record of publication data, and you will not need them again until you actually draft your paper. As further research leads to new sources, be sure to make a bibliography card for each one and file it with the rest.

37B.2. Unlocatable Sources. You may hear of an important book on your subject that your library does not have, or one of the periodical indexes may list an intriguing article in a magazine to which your library does not subscribe. You can overcome such problems, if you find out about them in time, by consulting the *National Union Catalog* for books you cannot locate or the *Union List of Serials in Libraries of the United States and Canada* for unavailable periodicals. The first of these reference works will give you all the publication data your librarian needs to get your book through an interlibrary loan. The second not only lists any periodical you are likely to want but also tells which libraries have it. With this information and your librarian's help, you can get a photocopy of almost any article.

37C
Taking notes

37C.1. Content Notes. Now is the time to start digging in earnest. Carefully read the most useful sources you have found and any others they lead you to, taking down helpful information from them on 4" × 6" cards. Cards are better than sheets of paper because they can be stacked in any order, allowing you to treat each item of information as a separate unit and arrange the material any way you please. Using large cards for your content notes gives you space for quotations or summaries and also keeps the content notes from getting mixed up with the bibliography cards.

37C.2. The Format for Content Notes. Each content note card should carry two kinds of information, the note itself and some identification. The identification should include the source of the note in abbreviated form (all you need is enough to lead you to the right bibliography card for the complete data) and the exact numbers of the page or pages where the material appeared. Another useful piece of identification is a subject label, or slug, to show what the note is about. This will be a help when you come to arranging the notes.

The note itself may be a paraphrase or summary in your own words of anything from a single idea to several paragraphs from the source. It may also be a direct quotation or some combination of quotation and paraphrase. Be sure you enclose direct quotations in quotation marks. When you write the paper you will need to know just which words are the source's and which are your own. Finally, if your material comes from more than one page, indicate where a new page begins by putting the new page number in the note enclosed in virgules (e.g. /p. 36/). This way you may decide to use only part of what the note includes and still know just where it appeared.

Here is how a typical content note card might look:

```
1        Fussell, pp. 27-28          War as sport        3

         Sporting spirit in WWI shown by British        4
         soldiers kicking footballs toward enemy
         lines to begin attack. "It soon achieved
         the status of a conventional act of bra-        5
         vado. . . ." Poem in Imperial War Museum
         celebrates a Surrey regiment which kicked
         4 footballs for 1 1/4 miles into enemy
         trenches:

                        The Game

              On through the hail of slaughter,
              Where gallant comrades fall,
2        /28/ Where blood is poured like water,
              They drive the trickling ball.
```

1. Source   4. Paraphrase
2. New page number   5. Direct quotation
3. Subject label

37C.3. Note-taking Techniques. Here are several positive steps you can take toward better notes.

a. Be selective. Everyone takes more notes than appear in the finished paper, and it is better to have too much information than not enough. But you can save a lot of effort by keeping your thesis and provisional outline in mind as you go through your sources. If you are doing Lincoln's law career, there is nothing to be gained by taking notes on his mother's favorite color or the hobbies of his Secretary of State. Limit your notes to things you can actually use in your paper.

b. Skim each source. Knowing how the article or book you are using is organized will help you find the material best suited to your purposes. Knowing what the author's purpose was—the thesis *he* was trying to support—can help you evaluate what he says.

c. Limit each note to one point or idea. A single note card may contain several details and facts, but they should all center on one main idea. To put more than one main point on a card defeats the whole purpose of using cards in the first place: you lose flexibility.

d. Abbreviate words and ideas on your cards, but remember that you must know what you meant when you come to use the note.

e. Get an exact page reference for each piece of information. Whether you quote or paraphrase a source, you will have to provide a footnote in your paper. Save yourself trouble by getting the page references right the first time.

f. Distinguish between facts and an author's opinions. As a researcher trying to arrive at your own conclusions, you will usually be more interested in a source's facts than in his opinions. But if you do record opinions, label them as such ("Smith believes that . . . ") so you will remember not to present them as facts. And remember that those opinions will have to be footnoted in your paper, even if you paraphrase rather than quote them.

g. In general, do not quote your sources without a definite reason. (Reasons for quoting are discussed in 37E.) Most information will fit your own purposes best if you paraphrase it. If you *do* quote, though, quote accurately (see 37D).

37D
Plagiarism

Problems in documentation usually come to a head in the finished paper, but they are almost always rooted in careless note-taking. If your notes do not record precisely what comes from which source, you will have forgotten yourself by the time you compose the paper. And uncertainty on this point can lead to real trouble.

A source offers you two basic things—words and ideas. You are welcome to both if, and *only* if, you acknowledge the extent and the nature of your debt. Problems arise when you use a source's words without indicating they are quoted, when you misquote a source or attribute a quotation to a source in which the quotation does not exist, when you borrow ideas (even putting them in your own words) without noting the source, or when you paraphrase incompletely or inaccurately. Any blurring, whether intentional or accidental, of the true relationship between you and your source is deemed *plagiarism,* and at most schools automatically earns a failing grade.

37E
Quotations in notes

In general, you should quote in your notes only those phrases or passages whose complexity makes paraphrase impossible or whose eloquence seems exactly right for the point you want to make. Here is a passage a note-taker might quote to be sure of getting everything exactly right and to get the benefit of the writer's clear illustrations:

> In a telephone system the meaning of a message received depends on the sender; in a sensory system the meaning depends on the receiver. When nerve impulses travel from a sense organ it is their destination on the cortex which determines, in the first place, the character of the sensation, not the sense organ from which they come. If, when you get a number on the telephone, you give a message, the message remains the same, even if you give it to a wrong number. The result of such an error in the brain is very different. Supposing some vinegar comes in contact with one of the sensitive end organs of taste in the tip of your tongue and "gets a wrong number"—that is, say, supposing the nerve fiber conducting the impulse provoked by the vinegar, instead of connecting with its proper reception area, becomes in some way cut and grafted onto a nerve fiber leading from the ear to the brain—what do you think you would taste? You would taste nothing. You would hear a very loud and startling noise.

> W. Grey Walter, *The Living Brain*

But most quotations are of the eloquent rather than the technical variety. They are chosen because they express a critical idea in a remarkably graceful or forceful way. Imagine you were writing on Thoreau and came across this passage by E. B. White. What sentences or phrases seem particularly quotable?

> There has been much guessing as to why he went to the pond. To set it down to escapism is, of course, to misconstrue what happened. Henry went forth to battle when he took to the woods, and "Walden" is the report of a man torn by two powerful and opposing drives—the desire to enjoy the world (and not be derailed by a mosquito wing) and the urge to set the world straight. One cannot join these two successfully, but sometimes, in rare cases, something good or even great results from the attempt of the tormented spirit to reconcile them. Henry went forth to battle, and if he set the stage himself, if he fought on his own terms and with his own weapons, it was because it was his nature to do things differently from most men, and to act in a cocky fashion. If the pond and the woods seemed a more plausible site for a house than an in-town location, it was because a cowbell made for him a sweeter sound than a churchbell.

Of course, your thesis would determine whether or not a given passage would fit your paper, but in White's paragraph the sentence " 'Walden' is the report of a man torn by two powerful and opposing drives—the desire to enjoy the world (and not be derailed by a mosquito wing) and the urge to set the world straight" is certainly an eloquent summary of Thoreau's psychology; and "a cowbell made for him a sweeter sound than a churchbell," even though it would require some explaining in your paper, is another quotable statement.

A note card for the paragraph about the brain would be easy to write. You would just note the source and page number and then copy down the whole passage, because it is the whole passage that you would plan to use in the paper. The Thoreau note might be a little harder. You would include the source, the page number, and the isolated parts of the total passage that you planned to use, but there might be some more operations involved as well. If you decided to alter the quotations in any way, you should do so only in keeping with the rules explained in Chapter 27. For example, you might decide that the comment about the mosquito wing is less useful to you than it was to White. You could leave it out, but only if you replaced it with ellipses (see 27H): " 'Walden' is the report of a man torn by two powerful and opposing drives—the desire to enjoy the world . . . and the urge to set the world straight." It is important to mark *on your note card* any changes you make in a quotation. Later, you are likely to have forgotten just what you changed.

In dealing with shorter quotations, it is a good idea to include on the note card a reminder of what the quotation concerns or how it may be used. If you picked the cowbell quotation, for instance, it would be best to include a memo to yourself that this is one of the ways White illustrates Thoreau's "cocky" individuality. Without a reminder, you might forget what cowbells and churchbells have to do with anything.

37F
Paraphrases in notes

The majority of your notes should contain paraphrases, or restatements in your own words of material from your sources. Paraphrasing often gives students more trouble than anything else in research projects. Your paraphrases must be usable in form, original in wording, and accurate in content. Paraphrases that fall short in any of these areas almost guarantee trouble later.

37F.1. A Paraphrase Should Be in Usable Form.   By the time you get to the note-taking stage, you should already have a clear idea of what your topic is and how you are going to approach it. Accordingly, good paraphrase notes should include only as much material as you reasonably expect to use. Consider this passage from Jaques Barzun:

> To define pedantry is not an easy thing to do. The meaning assigned should be neutral and fixed. But pedantry is relative to occasion. When it was forbidden as pedantic to quote Greek in the House of Commons, it was not forbidden to quote Latin. Today Latin would be as pedantic as Greek, though in a classics seminar both languages must be quoted, and can be, without taint of pedantry. The idea by which to test pedantry, then, is fitness—and fitness not only as regards time and place, but also as regards degree, quality, amount, or kind. Aristotle was warding off one sort of pedantry when he said that no subject should be treated with more precision than the purpose required. Should one want to know the average number of children in each American family, it would be pedantry to carry the count to five decimal places. The teller of an anecdote who interrupts himself to ascertain whether the event took place on the Tuesday or the Wednesday is a pedant—unless the day matters for an understanding of the point. In other words, it is intellectually right not to try to know or to tell more than a subject contains of significance; or in still other words, knowledge is not an absolute homogeneous good, of which

there cannot be enough. Beyond the last flutter of actual or possible significance, pedantry begins. Now think of the huge yearly mass of scholarly research
and apply the tests of fitness and significance: clearly pedantry predominates;
it is the sea around us.

Jaques Barzun, *The House of Intellect*

It is hard to imagine any reason for doing a complete, line-by-line
paraphrase of this passage. Instead, you should think about how you would
use Barzun in your paper and shape your note to fit that purpose. If you
were comparing definitions of *pedantry,* for example, your whole paraphrase
might be something like "Barzun keys everything to appropriateness: no
one should try to appear more learned than the subject and the situation
demands." On the other hand, if you were writing on contemporary scholarship, you might paraphrase the passage this way: "After defining *pedantry*
as a display of useless or inappropriate knowledge, Barzun goes on to imply
that most current scholarship is clearly pedantic." Either way, your note
would focus on those things in Barzun's passage most useful to *your* essay.

37F.2. A Paraphrase Should Be Original in Wording.   If you think
a quotation is justified, quote exactly and directly (see Chapter 27) at every
step from note card to final draft. But if you decide to paraphrase, recast
your source's ideas in language that is unmistakably your own. Some people
plagiarize deliberately, but a lot more get into trouble by not paraphrasing
properly.

Consider the case of a writer who "paraphrased" the Barzun passage
this way:

```
Barzun, pp. 217-18        Current Scholarship
    If we think of the mass of scholarly re-
search and apply the test of fitness
(whether the subject is treated with more
precision than the purpose requires), it
is clear that we live in a sea of ped-
antry.
```

All the writer of this note has done is to string together a series of short
quotations—"mass of scholarly research," "test[s] of fitness," "more precision than the purpose require[d]." If the note goes into the paper in its
present form, the writer will have plagiarized.

When is a paraphrase plagiarism? In general any two or more significant
words copied directly from your source must be placed in quotation marks.
But it is silly even to flirt with danger. Take the trouble to digest the material
and to record what you have found out in language that comes naturally

to you: "After defining *pedantry* as a display of useless or inappropriate knowledge, Barzun goes on to imply that most current scholarship is clearly pedantic."

37F.3. A Paraphrase Should Be Accurate in Content.

Some writers are so eager to find an authority to help them make a point or so careless in their reading that they distort what their sources said. Any paraphrase of Barzun that said he thought Greek quotations were pedantic or that he had contempt for current scholarship, for example, would be inaccurate. Read carefully before you paraphrase, and make sure your notes reflect what your sources said, not just what you wish they said.

Exercise 37–2. Suppose you came across this passage in the course of your research:

The first and most obvious result of the technological revolution has been to increase the amount of wealth in the form of material things which can be produced in a given time by a given population. For example, in 1913 there was produced in Great Britain seven billion yards of cotton cloth for export alone. In 1750 the total population of Great Britain, working with the mechanical appliances then available, could have produced only a small fraction of that amount. The second result of the technological revolution is that, as machines are perfected and become more automatic, man power plays a relatively less important part in the production of a given amount of wealth in a given time. Fifty years ago, when all type was set by hand, the labor of several men was required to print, fold and arrange in piles the signatures of a book. Today machines can do it all, and far more rapidly; little man power is required, except that a mechanic, who may pass the time sitting in a chair, must be present in case anything goes wrong with the machine. And finally, a third result of the technological revolution is that, under the system of private property in the means of production and the price system as a method of distributing wealth, the greater part of the wealth produced, since it is produced by the machines, goes to those who own or control the machines, while those who work the machines receive that part only which can be exacted by selling their services in a market where wages are impersonally adjusted to the necessities of the machine process.

Carl Becker, *Modern Democracy*

1. For a paper whose thesis was that wealth is unfairly distributed in the modern developed world,
   a. Copy the one sentence you would be most likely to quote in support of your thesis.
   b. Write a summary of that sentence as it might appear on a paraphrase note.

2. For a paper whose thesis was that technology is responsible for a vast growth in production,
   a. Copy the one sentence you would be most likely to quote in support of your thesis.
   b. Write a summary of that sentence as it might appear on a paraphrase note.

3. Evaluate the merits of these paraphrases of the passage:
   a. Becker /p. 25/ thinks modern workmen are lazy.

b. /p. 25/ Shows how production has grown since 1913.

c. /p. 25/ Under private ownership in the means of production and the price system, most wealth, because it is produced by machines, goes to the owners of the machines, while those who work the machines must take what they can get.

d. The author /p. 25/ bitterly attacks technology as a destroyer of the dignity of work and a tool of the rich.

e. Becker /25/ sees technology as a mixed blessing. On the one hand, it has spurred production and reduced the need for human labor; on the other, it has favored the owners of machines at the expense of the workers.

38 The Research Paper III: Organizing and Composing

Suppose you have a thesis for your research paper, a general idea of how you will support it, and sets of bibliography and note cards. Your only problem now is to turn all this material into a readable, convincing, and well-organized essay.

To do this job well, you will have to be more essayist than researcher. It is time to take control of the resources you have gathered and make them serve *your* purposes and support *your* thesis. *You* are the one who makes the decisions about the final outline and thesis; *you* control the paper's stance and persuasiveness; *you* keep the needs of the audience in mind; and *you* integrate the material from your reading into a general writing style that comes naturally to you. Your paper may draw on the efforts of many people, but *you* must be the boss.

38A
Fine-tuning the thesis and outline

When you began your research you had a tentative thesis and a preliminary outline to guide your search for material, but these may need considerable revision once all the results are in. Do not be afraid to scrap your original plans if the material suggests some other focus or organization: such restructuring almost always leads to a tighter, more effective presentation than you could have made before you started serious reading.

Imagine you had decided to write on the atom bomb and had restricted yourself to the bombing of Hiroshima at the end of World War II. During your preliminary research, you might have restricted the topic further, to focus on the aftereffects of the bombing. Your tentative thesis and outline could have looked like this:

Thesis: The physical, psychological, and social aftereffects of the bombing of Hiroshima were devastating.
   I. Physical aftereffects

II. Psychological aftereffects
III. Social aftereffects

Taking notes, though, you might have found that most of your material was about the physical aftereffects, especially the long-range medical complications stemming from the bombing. You seem to have a great deal of data about the medical results of Hiroshima and much less information on the other points you had meant to cover. Don't worry; it is time for an executive decision on your part: limit your essay to the medical consequences of the bombing, and revise your outline accordingly.

38A.1. The Final Thesis.   Reviewing your plans gives you an opportunity to tighten your thesis. You know more now than when you started and maybe you can find a more interesting and effective conclusion. Why should your readers care about the material you plan to present? Your answer will guide you to a workable thesis with a built-in appeal to readers. A thesis such as, "As Americans make decisions about the future of atomic power, they should be aware of the devastating aftereffects of the Hiroshima bombing," would be much more interesting than the general and obvious proposition that the effects of the bombing were "devastating."

38A.2. The Final Outline.   Your paper will need a structure that effectively supports your thesis and effectively presents your data. Think about the thesis first. The sample thesis on Hiroshima, for example, requires two kinds of support: the bombing and its aftereffects must be shown to have been devastating, and this material must be shown to be relevant to current decisions. The structure, then, would seem to have two major divisions: one on the data about the bombing and its effects and one on present-day atomic policies.

It is a good idea to do some arranging of your content notes at this point. Most of the notes will concern the bombing and its effects, and these can be stacked together as one major group of cards. A natural division within this group might be between notes on the bombing itself and those on its effects. Because the research was focused from the first on the results of the bombing, there should be a large number of aftereffect cards. A typical way to divide these further might be into two piles—one concerned with immediate and the other with long-range effects. Of these groups, the larger stack of cards should be those dealing with long-range effects (remember how the research came to focus more and more on medical problems), so a final division might be to separate the long-range effect cards into piles having to do with specific medical problems.

Sooner or later most of your note cards will be assigned to separate piles, and eventually all the piles will be roughly equal. The research and sorting could produce groups of cards concerning the bombing itself; its immediate effects, casualties, and destruction; cancer; leukemia; birth defects; other long-range problems.

Probably there would also be some cards left over, and now would be the time to look at these to see whether any other promising categories emerge. For instance, your leftover cards might produce a new pile on agencies that have investigated the effects of the bombing, and another on the dangers of current nuclear disasters. Any cards that cannot now be classified should be disregarded.

Now you are ready to outline. Each stack of cards represents a subtopic that may be developed to support the paper's thesis. Each pile will become the basis for a paragraph or a block of paragraphs. Now you must decide the best way of arranging these units.

38A.3. Constructing the Formal Outline.   The conventional formal outline generally looks like this:

    I. (Major ideas)
       A. (Subdivision)
          1. (Further subdivisions)
          2. (Further subdivisions)
             a. (Subsubdivisions)
             b. (Subsubdivisions)

Outline headings may be either *topics* (words or phrases) or *sentences.* Generally, sentence outlines are more useful than topical ones. Your teacher will tell you whether a sentence or topical outline is required. If a sentence outline were required for the Hiroshima paper, here is what it might look like:

Thesis: As Americans make decisions about the future of atomic power, they should be aware of the devastating medical aftereffects of the Hiroshima bombing.

    I. The atomic bomb dropped on Hiroshima on August 6, 1945, caused immediate and short-term devastation.
       A. The bomb's explosion caused immediate devastation.
          1. The population of the city suffered thousands of casualties.
          2. The buildings in the city were mostly destroyed or damaged.
       B. The bomb's fallout continued to devastate the population for weeks and even months.
   II. Numerous investigations have been carried out to determine the medical aftereffects of the bomb.
       A. Preliminary investigations were carried out by Japanese doctors and by American doctors and scientists immediately after the war.
       B. Long-term investigations have been carried out by various groups.
          1. An investigation was sponsored by the Atomic Bomb Casualty Commission.
          2. An investigation was sponsored by the Japanese Government.
          3. An investigation was sponsored by the U.S. Armed Forces Institute of Pathology.
          4. Other specialized investigations have been sponsored by several different agencies.
   III. The investigations show what main medical aftereffects of the bombing have been found thus far.
       A. Increased incidences of cancer have been found in Hiroshima survivors.
          1. Stomach, breast, and thyroid cancers have been especially prevalent.

    2. Because of the long latency periods possible with cancer, incidences of the disease are still increasing.

  B. Increased incidences of leukemia have been found in Hiroshima survivors.

    1. A definite link between leukemia and exposure to radiation has been established.

    2. Increases in leukemia have been found among persons who visited Hiroshima within a week of the bombing.

  C. Increased incidences of birth defects have been found in Hiroshima survivors.

    1. Exposure to radiation has been shown to damage chromosome development.

    2. Pregnancies in progress at the time of the bombing yielded a high rate of infants with small-head syndrome.

    3. The long-term genetic consequences of the bombing are not yet fully known.

  D. Increased incidences of other medical problems have been found in Hiroshima survivors.

    1. An increase in cataracts has been found.

    2. An increase in heart disease has been found.

    3. An increase in nervous disorders has been found.

IV. Knowledge of the medical consequences of the Hiroshima bombing should inform current discussion about nuclear power.

  A. There is increasing concern about the spread of nuclear power, especially for military use.

  B. The potential for nuclear destruction is much greater now than it was in 1945.

  C. The Hiroshima studies show that the destructiveness of an atomic bomb is not limited to its immediate effects but must be understood as a serious, long-term medical threat.

The main ideas, identified by Roman numerals, are the major subtopics that underlie the structure of the essay and would appear even in a scratch outline. But notice how much additional detail this formal outline provides. The major subdivisions under each Roman numeral define the particular facets of the main headings that will be discussed. Under Heading I, for instance, Subdivisions A and B specify two causes of the bomb's devastation— the explosion and the fallout; and the further subdivisions of the heading go on to specify two areas devastated by the explosion.

Notice, too, that the discussion of the actual bombing and its immediate effects is put first, where it can be presented most dramatically, and the warning about present policies comes last because there it will have a lasting impact on the reader. Official agencies created to investigate the effects of the bombing are discussed before the results of the investigations so that the material on specific medical problems can be presented in the context of scientific authority. Other arrangements are, of course, possible.

Two additional points should be made about formal outlines. The first is that entries at the same level should be of equal importance and, if possible, in similar form. Repeating key words and concepts helps ensure that items at the same level of the outline are of equivalent importance and that the outline stays on the subject. Notice the close interweaving of ideas in the sample outline; it would be hard for a paper written to this pattern to stray far from its path.

I. The atomic *bomb* dropped on Hiroshima on August 6, 1945, caused imme-
diate and short-term *devastation.*
  A. The *bomb*'s explosion caused immediate *devastation.*
    1. The population of the city suffered thousands of casualties.
    2. The buildings in the city were mostly destroyed or damaged.
  B. The *bomb*'s fallout continued to *devastate* the population for weeks
  and even months.
II. Numerous *investigations* have been carried out to determine the medical
aftereffects of the bomb.
  A. Preliminary *investigations* were carried out by Japanese doctors and
  by American doctors and scientists immediately after the war.
  B. Long-term *investigations* have been carried out by various groups.
    1. An *investigation* was sponsored by the Atomic Bomb Casualty Com-
    mission.
    2. An *investigation* was sponsored by the Japanese government.
    3. An *investigation* was sponsored by the U.S. Armed Forces Institute
    of Pathology.
    4. Other specialized *investigations* have been sponsored by several
    different agencies.

The consistent form of these entries also makes it easy to check the logic
of the argument, to ensure that all the subheadings really do support the
paper's conclusions.

A final point about formal outlines is that no heading or subheading
can stand alone. If you have a I, you must follow it with at least a II. An
A must have at least a B. Each entry represents a division of some larger
concept, and it is impossible to divide anything into one. If you find yourself
with only one subheading, you probably have no division at all:

I. The bomb's fallout caused devastation.
  A. It devastated the population.

In this case, simply include the single "subheading" in the main heading:

I. The bomb's fallout devastated the population.

In topic outlines each heading and subheading is a word or phrase,
rather than a complete statement:

I. Description of the bombing and its short-term effects
  A. The explosion
  B. Fallout
    1. Casualties
    2. Destruction to city
II. Investigations of medical aftereffects
  A. Immediate investigations
  B. Long-term investigations
    1. Atomic Bomb Casualty Commission
    2. Japanese government project
    3. U.S. Armed Forces Institute of Pathology
    4. Other research

III. Medical consequences
  A. Cancer
    1. Incidence rates
    2. Latency period
    3. Mortality rate
  B. Leukemia
    1. Incidence rates
    2. Discovery
    3. Mortality rate
  C. Birth defects
    1. Chromosome damage
    2. Small-head syndrome
      a. Discovery
      b. Retardation
    3. Long-term genetic consequences
  D. Other medical problems
    1. Cataracts
    2. Heart disease
    3. Nervous disorders
IV. Significance of these effects today
  A. Timeliness of issue
  B. Increased power for destruction
  C. Danger in ignoring proven medical consequences of atomic power

Topic outlines take less time and space, but sentence outlines have greater clarity and precision.

38A.4. Additional Research.   It often happens that a final outline reveals a need for more information and research. For instance, the Hiroshima writer might have had nothing on the destructive capacity of present atomic power. The only solution would be to return to the library for more information.

38B
Composing the research paper

In writing a research paper, keep the realities of your situation in mind. You are a student, probably a nonspecialist, writing a reasonable and helpful treatment of a topic you have investigated. The audience to keep in mind is a general one—your classmates will do—and you must convince them of your thesis. If you use pompous diction, your readers will probably think you silly; if you launch heart-wrenching emotional appeals, they will simply be amused. The best way to approach them is to adopt a level-headed tone and to keep their needs in mind by stopping to explain things they might find difficult, by providing concrete details, by being careful about logic and coherence, and by using transitions to make the structure of your essay unmistakably clear. In short, write the kind of paper that you might enjoy reading yourself.

Keep your cards and outline before you as you compose. With notes and outline to help you, it should be easy to decide where each paragraph should begin and end. Stop at the end of each paragraph and reread what you have written to see that it flows smoothly and coherently.

It can be difficult to incorporate research material in your own writing. These suggestions may help:

38B.1. *Spacing Quotations.* Keep quotations to a minimum. If your writing becomes a series of quotations strung together by transitional sentences, it will seem you have not really digested your material.

38B.2. *Quantity of Notes.* Do not feel you must have an authority for every point you make. Use the sources you have found, but be ready to draw your own conclusions. A footnote to someone else's opinion will not *prove* your point. If the support in the paper is unconvincing, readers are free to doubt the conclusion no matter whom you cite.

38B.3. *Consistent Style.* As you work quotations and paraphrases into your paper, avoid sudden shifts in style or grammar. You can alter quotations (see Chapter 27) to fit them to your context, but your sentences and paragraphs must read as if they had all been written by one person.

Notice some of the ways in which the following quotation from Thoreau could be adapted to different purposes and contexts:

> "In short, I am convinced, both by faith and experience, that to maintain one's self on this earth is not a hardship but a pastime, if we live simply and wisely."

a. The beginning or end of the quotation could be dropped without comment:

> Thoreau points out "that to maintain one's self on this earth is not a hardship but a pastime."

b. Words within the quotation could be dropped and replaced by ellipsis (27H):

> Thoreau is "convinced . . . that to maintain one's self . . . is not a hardship but a pastime, if we live simply and wisely."

c. Necessary explanations could be added in square brackets (27G):

> "In short, I [Thoreau] am convinced, both by faith and experience, that to maintain one's self on this earth is not a hardship."

38B.4. *Introducing Quotations and Paraphrases.* Quotations and paraphrases should be clearly introduced, usually with the source identified in the text. This point applies especially to paraphrased material because it may not be clear to your reader just where a paraphrase begins if you fail to introduce it clearly. Here is a paraphrase with no definite starting place:

> We have to adjust our ordinary thinking when we are trying to understand the brain. It can work in surprising ways. For instance, the nature of communications coming into the brain from the rest of the body is determined by the area of the brain where they are received, not by the area of the body from which they are sent. If a person's taste buds, for example, sent a message about encountering the sharp taste of vinegar and the message were somehow

received in the part of the brain that has to do with hearing, the person would not taste anything at all. Instead, he would hear a loud sound.[4]

The paraphrase here is several sentences long, but the footnote seems to apply only to the last sentence. The beginning of the paraphrase must be clearly established:

> We have to adjust our ordinary thinking when we are trying to understand the brain. It can work in surprising ways. For instance, as *W. Grey Walter points out*, the nature of communications . . .

38B.5. *Controlling Your Sources.* Avoid letting sources drown out your voice, imposing their style and structure on your writing. Here is a passage from a paper on *Walden* in which the writer allowed her sources to take over entirely:

> Thoreau shows in *Walden* that "the mass of men lead lives of quiet desperation."[4] According to Leo Marx, Thoreau "uses technological imagery to represent more than industrialization in the narrow, economic sense."[5] Actually, Thoreau is complaining against a mechanistic culture.[6] The working man, in Thoreau's view, becomes nothing but a machine.[7] Thoreau depicts the machine as "an instrument of oppression."[8]

> [4] Thoreau, p. 111.
> [5] *The Machine in the Garden: Technology and the Pastoral Ideal* (New York: Oxford University Press, 1964), p. 247.
> [6] Marx, p. 248.
> [7] Marx, p. 248.
> [8] Marx, p. 249.

This writer simply goes where her sources lead. For contrast, here is a passage from a paper in which the writer makes her sources serve *her* purpose:

> Thoreau finds that man's mistaken notions about economy come from prejudice. He does not mean this in the racial sense, but rather in the sense that man possesses narrow-minded ideas about how life should be lived. As E. B. White points out, Thoreau hated this "self-imposed bondage of men who hung chains about their necks simply because it was the traditional way to live" even more than he hated Negro slavery.[4] Thoreau saw this bondage everywhere around him, especially in his neighbors' dreary lives spent working for goals they had not set for themselves but which had been imposed on them by the market economy.[5] It is this prejudice that Thoreau argues against. He makes a point of rejecting the values of those around him: "The greater part of what my neighbors call good I believe in my soul to be bad, and if I repent anything, it is very likely to be my good behavior. What demon possessed me that I behaved so well?"[6]

> [4] "Henry Thoreau," *The New Yorker*, 7 May 1949, p. 23.
> [5] Marx, p. 247.
> [6] Thoreau, p. 113.

This writer subordinates her research to the point *she* wants to make, and she builds toward her conclusion, bringing her sources together in a smooth, coherent discussion.

38C
Special problems of the longer paper

38C.1. Writing Introductions. In writing long papers, you must be particularly careful to control the unfolding of your argument and consciously help your reader to follow it. One place this battle can be won or lost is at the beginning of your essay. Because of the length and complexity of most research papers, it is usually wise to announce your thesis early and to give an overview of your approach to it. Notice how the following introduction blueprints the essay to follow, declaring the thesis (underlined) and specifying the areas to be covered in the development of that thesis:

THE MEANING OF ECONOMY ACCORDING TO THOREAU

Although the first chapter of *Walden* is entitled "Economy," Henry David Thoreau does not provide a convenient definition of what he means by that term. By "economy" does he mean "ordering one's financial affairs"? In order to live economically must one live in a shanty by a pond as Thoreau did for two years? As is often the case in *Walden*, the reader may at first be confused about exactly what Thoreau means. But a close inspection of the first chapter of *Walden* will show that by "economy" Thoreau means the establishment of basic human and spiritual priorities in life. These priorities can be seen in Thoreau's treatment of the four necessities: food, shelter, clothing, and fuel.

Here the writer arouses the reader's curiosity about Thoreau's definition of "economy" through a series of questions. Then the thesis statement is announced, and the four areas to be discussed in support of the thesis are enumerated. By this point, both the reader and the writer have a clear idea of where the paper is headed and how its elements will be related to each other.

38C.2. Controlling the Middle of the Paper. Good writers tend to see short papers as a succession of paragraphs. The introduction sets the stage, the development paragraphs discuss separate areas of support for the thesis, and the conclusion rounds out the whole. Longer papers are similar, except that their middle can be divided into paragraph groups rather than single paragraphs. Usually these paragraph groups coincide with the main headings in the paper's outline, and the paragraphs within them explore the items in the subheadings.

In the Hiroshima outline, for example, you can see there are four main headings, or four major paragraph groups or blocks of development behind the thesis. After the introduction, which should give the thesis and an overview of the paper's plan, there will be separate sections on the bombing itself, its investigation, its medical effects, and the present significance of all this material. That arrangement might be diagrammed this way:

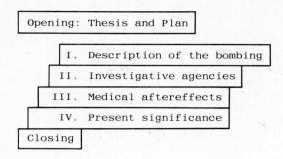

Opening: Thesis and Plan

I.   Description of the bombing

II.   Investigative agencies

III.   Medical aftereffects

IV.   Present significance

Closing

Each of the numbered boxes will contain, in effect, a separate essay, allowing the writer to develop the paper's overall thesis in a series of discrete steps. For example, the first development block will be a description, possibly in two paragraphs, of the impressions the bombing created and the immediate damage it caused.

Thinking of the middle of your research paper as a series of steps or paragraph groups or boxes can help you cut the job down to size and control the structure of your paper. It also provides guidance for your readers. If the audience is going to lose the drift of your argument at all, it will probably be when you move from one development block to another. In the Hiroshima paper, for instance, they might not see immediately why the writer bothers to discuss the agencies that have looked into the bombing's aftereffects. Thinking in terms of blocks, the writer should note that a clear transition will be needed here to maintain coherence. He might then point out in his text that the material about scientific investigations of the Hiroshima data is important because it establishes the credibility of the medical effects that follow.

Transitions are crucial in the longer paper, which may make a complicated argument and cover a lot of ground. And it is usually a good idea to scale the transition according to the importance of the material it introduces. In the Hiroshima essay, for example, the discussion of investigating agencies would grow naturally out of the description of the bombing and would be only a couple of paragraphs long. It could be introduced by a sentence or so at the head of the first paragraph:

> One continuing reaction to the devastation caused by the bombing has been an unprecedented scientific investigation of its effects. In the course of this investigation, Hiroshima has become the most studied man-made disaster in history. . . .

The next block in the paper's development—the medical effects—is not only much longer than the others but more important too: it contains the factual basis for the paper's conclusion. Here is where the writer might include a *transitional paragraph,* a short paragraph which shows readers that a new, major area of the topic will be developed. The transitional paragraph guides the audience by summing up what has gone before and letting them know just what to expect:

As a result of these scientific studies, especially the long-range ones, an enormous amount of data on the effects of unleashed atomic power is now available. These data support some frightening conclusions. Not only the population of Hiroshima at the time of the bombing but their descendants are still deeply affected by the event. They are much more likely than other people to experience a range of medical problems from cancer to birth defects, and their life expectancy has been lowered greatly.

First, there is the incidence of cancer among Hiroshima survivors and their descendants. . . .

Use such a transitional paragraph whenever you want to help your readers follow an especially difficult or important step in the development of your paper.

38C.3. Concluding the Research Paper.   Never let your convictions run away with you: avoid any conclusion your argument cannot support. Be sure you review your paper, and especially your thesis, before you draft a conclusion to the essay. The decisions you made as you classified your material and organized and wrote the paper were all governed by your original thesis. Do not go beyond it in the conclusion to your paper.

38D
Revising the research paper

Check over your draft before you recopy it. This is also the best time to make sure that you have made your debts to your sources absolutely clear by providing formal documentation (explained in the next chapter).

39

The Research Paper IV: Documenting Sources

Documenting your sources repays your debt to the authors whose ideas or words you have borrowed, establishes the authority behind what you say, and enables readers to explore your subject further by consulting the same sources themselves. Most college research papers, therefore, must have footnotes or endnotes citing the sources for the specific quotes or paraphrases in the essay and also a bibliography or alphabetical list of the works consulted.

39A
Systems of documentation

The system of documentation explained in this chapter is a modified version of that advocated by the Modern Language Association of America. It is widely useful, but other professions and disciplines have systems of their own. Always consult your teacher about the type of documentation you are expected to supply. You may find the following list of stylesheets helpful; some or all should be available in your college bookstore or in the reference section of your library. Especially useful is the *Publication Manual* of the American Psychological Association: the parenthetical documentary technique it presents is commonly required for work in education and the social sciences.

American Chemical Society. *Handbook for Authors*. Washington, D.C.: American Chemical Society, 1978.
American Institute of Physics. *Style Manual for Guidance in the Preparation of Papers*. 3rd ed. New York: American Institute of Physics, 1978.
American Mathematical Society. *A Manual for Authors of Mathematical Papers*. 4th ed. Providence, R.I.: American Mathematical Society, 1971.
American Psychological Association. *Publication Manual*. 2nd ed. Washington, D.C.: American Psychological Association, 1974.
Associated Press. *The Associated Press Stylebook*. Dayton: Lorenz Press, 1980.

Council of Biology Editors, Committee on Form and Style. *CBE Style Manual.* 3rd ed. Washington, D.C.: American Institute of Biological Sciences, 1972.

Engineers Joint Council, Committee of Engineering Society Editors. *Recommended Practice for Style of References in Engineering Publications.* New York: Engineers Joint Council, 1966.

Irvine, Demar, ed. *Writing About Music: A Style Book for Reports and Theses.* 2nd ed. Seattle: University of Washington, 1968.

Modern Language Association. *MLA Handbook for Writers of Research Papers, Theses, and Dissertations.* By Joseph Gibaldi and Walter S. Achtert. New York: Modern Language Association, 1977.

Turabian, Kate L. *A Manual for Writers of Term Papers, Theses, and Dissertations.* 4th ed. Chicago: University of Chicago, 1973.

Ulman, Joseph N., Jr., and Jay R. Gould. *Technical Reporting.* 3rd ed. New York: Holt, 1972.

Harvard Law Review. *A Uniform System of Citation: Forms of Citations and Abbreviations.* 12th ed. Cambridge, Mass.: Harvard Law Review Association, 1976.

U.S. Geological Survey. *Suggestions to Authors of Reports of the United States Geological Survey.* 5th ed. Washington, D.C.: GPO, 1958.

University of Chicago. *A Manual of Style.* 12th ed. Chicago: University of Chicago, 1969.

39B
What to note

The purpose of most notes in a research paper is to show indebtedness to a specific source of information.* There is no need to supply a reference for common expressions ("There's no business like show business"), widely held opinions ("Oil is a crucial world resource"), or widely available facts ("Shakespeare died in 1616"; "Madrid is the capital of Spain"). You *do* need to document any direct quotation of other than a common expression; any facts, quoted or paraphrased, not readily available elsewhere; and any opinion, insight, interpretation, or analysis, quoted or paraphrased, arising from your source's particular argument or experience.

You must use your judgment in deciding what to note. Unless you document them, all the facts, opinions, words, and phrases in your paper will be deemed your own. If the material in question is common property (widely known and available, even though you yourself may have had to look it up), then you are as entitled to it as anyone. Do not note it. But whenever your material involves the particular language, contribution, or discovery of your source, a note is called for.

39C
Placing note numbers in the text

Footnotes or endnotes should be numbered sequentially through the paper. The note number should be an Arabic superscript placed at the end of a grammatical unit but as close as possible to the material to which it applies. Most such numbers come at the end of a sentence:

---

* Another kind of note, the *explanatory note,* does not cite a source; rather, it adds to or explains some point raised in the text. This, for example, is an explanatory note.

The invention of antibiotics, for example, has been called "the greatest development in the history of medicine."[1]

If two or more sources are used in the same sentence, place the note numbers so that they clearly refer to different sentence elements:

> In recent years writers have called the Dallas Cowboys everything from "heartless machines"[2] to "the most emotional team in all of football."[3]

A note may also apply to a whole paragraph or even a group of paragraphs. In this case, place the number at the end of the first sentence involved in the reference and explain in the note itself how much of the text that follows is drawn from that source (for more on this point see 39H.1).

39D
Footnotes or endnotes?

Footnotes and endnotes differ in their placement. Consult your teacher to make sure which you are expected to use.

Footnotes are placed at the bottom of the page to which they apply. This is convenient for readers, but it can cause problems for the writer, who has to allow enough room for the notes on each page of text. If you are typing a paper, you have to drop down four lines beneath the last line of text, indent five spaces, enter the raised note number, skip another space, and then begin the note. Individual footnotes are single-spaced, with a double space between:

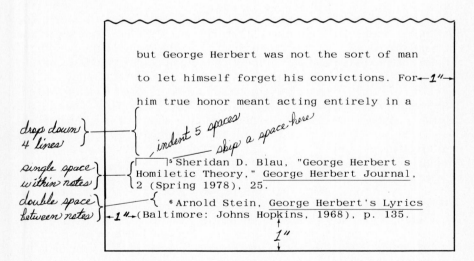

Endnotes, on the other hand, are placed at the end of the text on a separate page or pages. A page of endnotes should have a two-inch margin at the top, the title "Notes" centered, with a four-line space beneath to the numbered notes. Endnotes are typed up just like footnotes, except that everything on the endnote page is double-spaced:

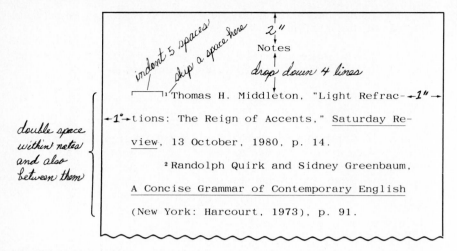

39E
Note content

Whether your paper has footnotes or endnotes, make sure that you give all the information readers need to find your sources for themselves and that you present this information in a standardized way. References to sources are purely functional. Be as creative as you like in your text, but follow the conventions to the letter in your notes.

A citation of a book or part of a book should include the name of the author, the title of the book, the date and place of its publication, the name of its publisher, and the number of the page or pages to which the reference is made. The citation of an article in a periodical should include the name of the author, the title of the article, the name of the periodical, the date of the issue, and the number of the page or pages referred to. In some cases the volume number of the periodical is also required.

The information given in a note should come from the work itself. Never depend on a library catalog or on the cover of a book. Look at the title and copyright pages for the publication facts about a book, the publisher's page (often the one with the table of contents and subscription rates) of a magazine or journal, or the first-page masthead of a newspaper. And doublecheck to be sure you get everything right.

In referring to a book, your goal is to direct readers to the exact page or pages you have in mind. To do this, you will have to indicate which *edition* you are using. Later editions and reprints can have altered contents, and they are generally printed from new plates, so their pagination may be entirely changed. Later *impressions* or *printings*, however, do not need to be specified. These terms mean that the original plates were used for another run through the presses, so content and pagination should remain the same. Consider these copyright entries:

Copyright Michael Grant, 1954, 1958, 1964
First published by the Cambridge University Press 1954
New edition published in Pelican Books 1958
Revised edition 1964

Copyright Kingsley Amis, 1976
Published in 1977 by The Viking Press
Second printing April 1977

Anyone using the Grant book would have to note its complex printing history. It was brought out in hardback by Cambridge in 1954. It was picked up by Pelican, a paperback publisher, in 1958. And this edition, still in paperback, was revised by Grant in 1964. The note would have to refer to the 1964 revised edition, because the other two are likely to be very different.

The Amis book is another story. It was brought out by Viking early in 1977 and sold well enough to justify another run through the presses using the original plates by April of that year. The second printing has the same content and pagination as the first and need not be specified in a note.

39F
Note form

Although the content of notes tends to vary, there are some features of arrangement, punctuation, and spacing that are standard. These sample notes, one to a book and one to a periodical, illustrate those basic features:

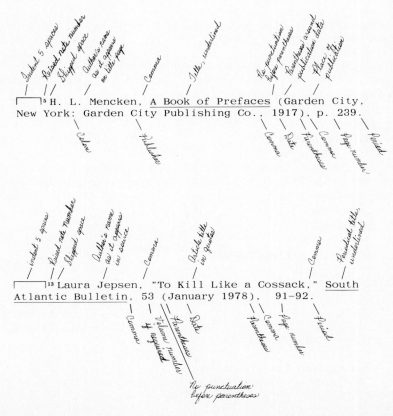

39F.1. Later References. So far we have been talking only about notes for the first reference to a particular source. Later notes to the same source can be abbreviated. The simplest such reference contains just the author's name and a page number:

   [8] Mencken, p. 114.

But if your sources include more than one book or article by the same author, you will also have to include the title (in abbreviated form if it is a long one). By the same token, if you have two authors with the same last name, you will have to give their first names, even in later references.

   [11] Mencken, *Book of Prefaces*, p. 113.

   [16] H. L. Mencken, p. 12.

39F.2. Information Already Included Elsewhere in the Text. If you have indicated in the text itself the author or title or both, you need not repeat these details in the note.

   [20] *A Book of Prefaces* (Garden City, New York: Garden City Publishing Co., 1917), p. 76. [author omitted]

   [32] (Garden City, New York: Garden City Publishing Co., 1917), pp. 43–44. [author and title omitted]

If your paper has a separate bibliography in which the full title of your source, including whatever subtitle it may have, is given, you can leave this subtitle out of the notes.

39G
Sample notes

The following notes are meant to serve as model first references for special situations. The explanations that follow many of them take up matters not previously discussed.

BOOKS

One Author, First Edition:
   [1] Preston Cloud, *Cosmos, Earth, and Man* (New Haven and London: Yale, 1978), p. 335.

   [Here a subtitle, "A Short History of the Universe," is omitted. It will be included in the bibliography. Note also the place of publication. If up to three places of publication are given, mention them all; if more than three are given, use only the first.]

One Author, Later Edition:
   [2] Edgar Johnson, *Charles Dickens: His Tragedy and Triumph*, revised and abridged edition (New York: Viking, 1977), p. 471.

[*Revised* and *edition* are usually abbreviated (*rev. ed.*), but since *abridged* has to be written out, the other terms should be too.]

³ Gilbert Murray, *The Literature of Ancient Greece*, 3rd ed. (Chicago: University of Chicago Press, 1956), p. 18.

Two or Three Authors:
⁴ M. Abercrombie, C. J. Hickman, and M. L. Johnson, *The Penguin Dictionary of Biology*, 6th ed. (New York: Viking, 1977).

[Dealing with multiple authors, be sure to list them in the order in which they appear on the title page, for that order often reflects their respective credit for the book. Note, too, that page numbers can be dispensed with in references to works arranged by alphabetical entries.]

More than Three Authors:
⁵ Paul F. Brandwein, et al., *The Social Sciences: Concepts and Values* (New York: Harcourt, 1970), p. 19.

[This note involved a lot of simplifying. The book it refers to listed eight authors in all. There were also five places of publication, so only the first is given here. Finally, the publishers—Harcourt, Brace, Jovanovich, Inc.—can be recognizably shortened to just *Harcourt.*]

A Book with Corporate Authorship:
⁶ Prentice-Hall, Inc., *1975 Federal Tax Course* (Englewood Cliffs, New Jersey: Prentice-Hall, 1974), p. 5220.

[No author is given for this publisher's compilation of tax regulations, so credit goes to the publishing company itself. Other books without specific authors may appear under the name of government agencies or commissions or private corporations.]

An Anonymous Book:
⁷ *The Story of Burnt Njal*, trans. George Webbe Dasent (London: J. M. Dent, 1911), p. 127.

[The author of this thirteenth-century Icelandic saga is unknown; lead off with the title.]

A Modern Reprint of an Older Edition:
⁸ Cameron Mann, *A Concordance to the English Poems of George Herbert* (1927; rpt. n.p.: Norwood Editions, 1977).

[This concordance first appeared in 1927 and was reprinted without change by Norwood in 1977. Without the reprint notation, readers might think the work was recent. The "n.p." in the publication data shows that the place of publication for the reprint is not given. Use *n.p.* for "no place" and *n.d.* for "no date" when place or date are not given in your source.]

A Book Published in More than One Volume:
⁹ Isaac Disraeli, *Curiosities of Literature*, 4 vols. (New York: Sheldon and Company, 1863).

[This note cites the whole book. A page reference to one of the four volumes would have the volume number in Roman:
⁹ Isaac Disraeli, *Curiosities of Literature*, II (New York: Sheldon and Company, 1863), 305.
Notice that there is no abbreviation *p.* for *page* in references that include specific volume numbers.]

A Book that is Part of a Series:

[10] C. S. Lewis, *English Literature in the Sixteenth Century*, Oxford History of English Literature, No. 3 (New York and London: Oxford University Press, 1954), p. 552.

A Book with a Translator:

[11] Gaius Suetonius Tranquillus, *The Twelve Caesars*, trans. Robert Graves (New York: Penguin, 1957), p. 121.

A Book with an Author and an Editor:

[12] Henry David Thoreau, *Walden and Other Writings*, ed. Brooks Atkinson (New York: Modern Library, 1937), p. 76.

[Here the book consists almost entirely of Thoreau's works, selected and arranged by Atkinson. Thoreau clearly gets major credit.]

Books with Editors but No Single Authors:

[13] Elizabeth A. Livingstone, ed., *The Concise Oxford Dictionary of the Christian Church* (Oxford: Oxford University Press, 1977), p. 521.

[In this book the editor had a number of unnamed people working under her to produce a single, continuous work.]

[14] Marden J. Clark, Soren F. Cox, and Marshall R. Craig, eds., *About Language: Contexts for College Writing* (New York: Scribner's, 1970), p. vi.

[This is a collection of separate essays by various authors. The note, as signified by the lower-case Roman page number, is to the editors' introduction. A note to one of the essays would be like the ones below under "Signed Articles in Collections."]

[15] Geof Hewitt, ed., *Quickly Aging Here: Some Poets of the 1970's* (Garden City, New York: Anchor, 1969), p. xiv.

[An anthology of modern poems by various authors.]

Unpublished Dissertations:

[16] Ralph R. Koening, "Enrollments at Two-Year Colleges, 1977–1981," Diss. University of Arkansas, 1981, p. 211.

PARTS OF BOOKS

A Signed Article in a Collection:

[17] John P. Hughes, "Functional Notions About Language," in *About Language: Contexts for College Writing*, ed. Marden J. Clark, Soren F. Cox, and Marshall R. Craig (New York: Scribner's, 1970), p. 81.

[The name of the article or essay is in quotation marks; the name of the book is italicized, or underlined.]

A Poem or Short Story in a Collection:

[18] Robert Mezey, "Dark Head," in *Contemporary American Poetry*, ed. Donald Hall (Baltimore: Penguin, 1965), p. 190.

[When referring to poems of over thirty to forty lines, it is a good idea to give line as well as page numbers—e.g., p. 190, ll. 138–9.]

344

A Play:
[19] William Cartwright, *The Royal Slave,* in *The Plays and Poems of William Cartwright,* ed. G. Blakemore Evans (Madison: The University of Wisconsin Press, 1951), p. 218 (II, vi, 561–64).

[This reference would lead readers to the right place even in another edition, thanks to the citation of act, scene, and line numbers.]

A Book of the Bible:
[20] 1 Chronicles 15:25–27.
[21] Ezekiel 17:23. (New English Bible)

[The Bible and its books are neither underlined nor put in quotes. Chapter numbers come first, followed by a colon and then the numbers of the verses. Unless specified otherwise, all references are to the King James Version.]

Signed Encyclopedia Articles:
[22] Reginald Crundall Punnett, "Sex," *Encyclopedia of Religion and Ethics,* 1955 ed.

[Publication data, page, and volume numbers need not be given for standard alphabetized reference works such as encyclopedias. The author's name, when given, usually comes at the end of the article, and is often abbreviated.]

Unsigned Encyclopedia Articles:
[23] "Red Deer (*Cervus elephas*)," *Encyclopedia Americana,* 1978 ed.

PAMPHLETS AND GOVERNMENT DOCUMENTS

Pamphlets, short separate publications with soft bindings, are treated as books would be:

[24] W. Nelson Francis, *The History of English* (New York: Norton, 1963), p. 29.

[This work is only forty-one pages long.]

Government documents, on the other hand, pose special problems that can be touched on only briefly here. When in doubt, you should consult your instructor. In general, notes to government publications should start with the name of the agency, followed by the title of the document (underlined). If the author is given, his name, preceded with *by,* comes next. Congressional documents must also be identified according to the house of Congress involved; the number and session of Congress; the identifying number of the document, if any; and the usual information about publisher, place, and date. However, references to the *Congressional Record* may consist only of the title (abbreviated to *Cong. Rec.*) and the date and page number. Most Federal documents are published by the Government Printing Office, which can be abbreviated *GPO.* Here are some example notes:

[25] U.S. Congress, House, Subcommittee of the Committee on Governmental Operations, *Federal Training Programs for Investigative Personnel,* 91st Cong., 2nd sess., H. Rept. 301 (Washington D.C.: GPO, 1970), p. 187.

[26] *Cong. Rec.,* 3 August 1975, pp. 3675–82.

[27] Atomic Energy Commission, *Food Irradiation Contractors' Meeting* (Washington D.C.: GPO, 1968), p. 274.

[28] Western Kentucky University, *Institutional Report to the National Council for Accreditation of Teacher Education* (Bowling Green, Ky.: Western Kentucky University, 1974), III, p. 143.

ARTICLES IN PERIODICAL PUBLICATIONS

Periodicals include what are usually called just *magazines*, but formal documentation requires some further distinctions. There are special procedures for references to *journals*, *magazines*, and *newspapers*. *Journals* are intended for academic or professional readers. Their articles are usually specialized and often contain documentation of their own. Many journals also have continuous pagination: the page numbers in each issue for a given year or volume take up where the previous issue left off. *Magazines* are meant for a general readership; they are the sort of periodicals you might see on a drugstore rack. Reference conventions are slightly different for each kind of periodical publication.

Signed Article in a Journal:
[28] Laura Jepsen, "To Kill Like a Cossack," *South Atlantic Bulletin*, 53 (January 1978), 91.

[The title of the article is in quotation marks, that of the journal is underlined. Because there is a volume number, there is no abbreviation for *page*, and the date is in parentheses.]

Signed Article in a Magazine:
[29] J. Hoberman, "From Ashes to Diamonds: The Comeback of Andrzej Wajda," *American Film*, January-February 1982, p. 58.

[Magazines usually have volume numbers too, but it is more common to identify them by individual issues. Because the date of a magazine issue is important, it is not put in parentheses. *Page* is abbreviated because there is no volume number.]

Unsigned Article in a Journal or Magazine:
[30] "Gaslight and Fallen Souls," *Time*, 15 October 1979, p. 95.

[Except for starting with the title, anonymous articles are handled just as signed ones are. Always give the most precise date available for periodicals, whether it be day, month, season, or simply the year for annual publications.]

Signed Newspaper Article:
[31] Cynthia Gorney, "Boom Time for the Cowboy Artists," *Washington Post*, 7 November 1979, p. B1.

Unsigned Newspaper Article:
[32] "False Missile Alert," *Louisville Courier-Journal*, 11 November 1979, p. A5.

Unsigned, Untitled Newspaper Articles:
[33] Editorial, *Washington Post*, 3 September 1965, p. A11.

Exercise 39-1. Construct acceptable footnotes for the following situations:

1. You want to refer the reader to lines 271–72 of a John Donne poem, "The Second Anniversary." These lines are on page 205 of the edition you are using, the edition prepared by Charles M. Coffin, of Kenyon College. Your book was published by The Modern Library in New York in 1952 and is entitled *The Complete Poetry and Selected Prose of John Donne.*

2. The reference is to page 121 of an article, *"The Jew of Malta* and *Edward II,"* by M. C. Bradbrook as it appears in a collection of articles called *Marlowe: A Collection of Critical Essays.* This book was edited by Clifford Leech and published by Prentice-Hall in Englewood Cliffs, New Jersey. The book came out in 1964.

3. You have quoted from page fifty-two of the May 18, 1978, issue of *Rolling Stone.* There is no volume number for this issue. The quote comes from an unsigned article called "Houston Justice."

4. You have taken two lines, 40–41, from a play, *The Roaring Girl,* by Thomas Dekker and Thomas Middleton. The lines are from Act V, Scene ii, and they are found on page 365 in the second volume of *Drama of the English Renaissance,* published in 1976 by Macmillan in New York. This drama anthology was edited by two people, Russell A. Fraser and Norman Rabkin.

5. You want to refer readers to a whole short story called "Apostle" in the winter 1978 issue of *Kansas Quarterly.* This issue is in the journal's tenth volume, and the author of the story is John Lewter. The story runs from p. 13 to p. 21.

6. You are referring to page 225 of a 1954 reprint of Johan Huizinga's book *The Waning of the Middle Ages.* The reprint was published by Anchor at Garden City, New York, while the original version was published by St. Martin's Press in 1949.

UNCONVENTIONAL OR NON-PRINT SOURCES*

Besides references to books and articles, research papers can require citing other kinds of sources—films, for instance, or performances, personal conversations, or computer materials. The forms for such notes can be a blend of conventional elements and ones designed especially for the occasion. Here are some typical cases:

Films:
[34] James Whale, director, *The Bride of Frankenstein,* with Colin Clive and Boris Karloff, Universal, 1935.

[If the reference were to the work of someone other than the director, the note could be reworked accordingly:
[34] John J. Mescall, cinematographer, *The Bride of Frankenstein,* with Colin Clive and Boris Karloff, Universal, 1935.]

Performances:
[35] Lester Flatt, Earl Scruggs, and The Foggy Mountain Boys, Carnegie Hall, New York, 8 December 1962.

[36] Alec McCowen, *Equus,* with Peter Firth and Nicholas Clay, National Theatre, London, 14 July 1973.

* For ways of citing other nonprint sources, things like maps or charts or filmstrips or microform resources, see Eugene B. Fleischer, *A Style Manual for Citing Microform and Nonprint Media* (Chicago: American Library Association, 1978).

Recordings:

[37] Antol Dorati, conductor, Haydn's Symphony 103 (*Drum Roll*), Philharmonica Hungarica, London Records, STS 15324, 1974.

[38] The Osipov Balalaika Orchestra, *A Program of Classic and Folk Favorites*, cassette, Musical Heritage Society, MHC 6214L, n.d.

[Note the catalog numbers for records and tapes.]

Works of Art:

[39] Annibale Carracci, *Venus and Anchises*, ceiling fresco, Gallery, Palazzo Farnese, Rome.

[40] James Ward, *Captain John Levett Hunting in the Park at Wychnor*, reproduced in *Steeplechasing and Foxhunting*, ed. Michael Seth-Smith (London: New English Library, 1977), pp. 28–29.

[Works of art can be located according to the original or, more helpfully, according to where a reproduction is available.]

Personal Contacts:

[41] Letter from Marie Wright, Administrative Assistant for Fellowships and Grants, American Council of Learned Societies, 28 September 1975.

[42] Telephone interview with John McEnroe, 4 January 1982.

[43] Professor Byno Rhodes, lecture on *Paradise Lost*, Eastern Kentucky University, 21 October, 1982.

Television and Radio:

[Some of the data in these areas can be difficult to find, but the basic idea is to include such information as the name of the particular segment you are noting, the name of the show or series, the originating network, and the date. Names of producers, directors, performers, and writers are helpful too, especially when you are citing the work of one of these professionals.]

[44] Kurt Weill, *Street Scene*, libretto by Elmer Rice and Langston Hughes, with Eileen Schauler, Catherine Malfitano, and William Chapman, PBS, 27 October 1979.

[45] Gene Reynolds, director, "Welcome to Korea," *M*A*S*H*, with Alan Alda and Mike Farrell, CBS, 12 September 1975.

[Notice that the title of the segment is in quotation marks while the name of the series is underlined (or italicized).]

Computer Programs:

[Computer materials take many forms; try to include the name of the program, the originating company or institution, the language, and the machine and configuration for which the program was designed.]

[46] muLISP/muSTAR-80 version 10/06/80, The Soft Warehouse, 8080 or Z80 machine language, for 8080-, 8085-, or Z80-based computer with at least 20K memory, running under a CP/M-compatible operating system.

[47] ADABAS, Software ag of North America, IBM OS, for IBM 370 system with at least 2 megs. main storage.

Exercise 39–2. Construct acceptable footnotes for the following situations:

1. You want to refer your readers to a computer program available from Atari, Incorporated. The program is called Personal Financial Management System

and is suitable for Atari 800 computers with disk drive and at least thirty-two kilo-bytes (32K) of random access memory (RAM). The language is ATARI BASIC.

2. You are referring to the work on the movie *Chinatown* done by Robert Towne, the screenwriter. This film starred Jack Nicholson and Faye Dunaway and was directed by Roman Polanski. It was released in 1974 by Paramount.

3. A reference is needed to a segment of *60 Minutes* written and narrated by Ed Bradley and produced by Joel Bernstein. The segment was called "Homeless" and was broadcast on the tenth of January 1982 by CBS.

4. Cite a letter you received from Mary Tyler Moore, dated June 7, 1983.

5. You are referring to a record released in 1978 by Warner Brothers, catalog number BSK 3239. The record is by Devo and is entitled *Q: Are We Not Men? A: We Are Devo!*

39H
Special kinds of notes

Two special kinds of notes, explanatory and abbreviated ones, have already been discussed. Others that can come in handy are the "covering" note and a hybrid form combining one or more documented sources with some explanation.

39H.1. Covering Notes. There are two kinds of covering notes. One gives the source for a whole paragraph or for a series of paragraphs dependent on a particular authority. The number for such a note is placed at the end of the first sentence of the first paragraph involved, and the note itself is used to explain how far the debt to the source continues. Here is an example to follow in making up such notes:

[48] This and the two paragraphs that follow are drawn from Lin Carter, *Imaginary Worlds: The Art of Fantasy* (New York: Ballantine, 1973), pp. 70–85.

The first part of this note specifies to just how much of the text it applies. The second part is a standard reference to the source.

The other kind of covering note concerns a single source to which you refer repeatedly. Instead of noting the source each time it comes up, you can give the full reference the first time and explain that further references will be handled by giving specific page, line, act, scene, or line numbers in parentheses in your text. Use a form like this:

Robert Graves, *The White Goddess: A Historical Grammar of Poetic Myth*, amended and enlarged edition (New York: Farrar, Straus, and Giroux, 1972), p. 435. All other references to *The White Goddess* are based on this edition. Page numbers are given in parentheses with each reference.

The next time you refer to the book, then, your text might look like this:

As Graves points out on more than one occasion, "woman has of late become virtual head of the household in most parts of the Western world" (p. 482).

To be sure that your notes are clear, you should limit parenthetical references to sources used frequently throughout a paper or a section of a paper.

39H.2. Hybrid Notes. Sometimes a mere reference is not enough. You may want to explain what the readers will find when they get to your source, or lead them to a second opinion, or give two sources for the same idea. In such situations, you can invent combination explanatory and documentary notes to serve your purposes. Here are some examples of such hybrid notes:

[49] Franz Alexander, *Psychosomatic Medicine* (New York: Norton, 1950), pp. 116–17. Alexander's figures differ slightly from the ones given earlier in the text of my paper, probably because he is concerned with gastrointestinal rather than respiratory disfunctions.

[50] Earl Miner, *The Metaphysical Mode from Donne to Cowley* (Princeton: Princeton U.P., 1969), p. 187. For a different interpretation, see Richard E. Hughes, *The Progress of the Soul: The Interior Career of John Donne* (New York: William Morrow and Co., 1968), pp. 81–82.

[51] The authorities seem to agree that this work is of a later period. See, for example, Gower J. Stanton, "A Roman Renaissance," *Smithsonian*, 10 (September 1979), 97; or Richard Brilliant, *Roman Art from the Republic to Constantine* (London: Phaidon, 1974), pp. 212–14.

39I
Kinds of bibliographies

Notes are really part of your text. Each one explains something you have written. A bibliography, on the other hand, is a general, alphabetical list of sources connected with your subject that suggests avenues of further study and research to the readers. The term *bibliography* can describe anything from a whole book of sources to a three- or four-item list. Consult your teacher about the bibliography you are to provide. Here are some of the various kinds:

1. *Bibliography:* a list of every source you can find on a given subject, whether you used all these sources or not.

2. *Annotated bibliography:* a list of sources actually consulted, with a short description of the usefulness and special features of each item.

3. *List of works consulted:* a list of all the relevant works you have seen and at least skimmed.

4. *List of works cited:* a list of sources to which actual references are made in your paper. Unless your teacher specifies otherwise, no descriptions are required.

39J
Bibliographic form and content

Much of the information found in notes and bibliographies is the same, but a typical note identifies a page or so in a book or article, while a typical bibliography entry concerns the whole book or the whole article.

There are only two areas of content difference between bibliographies and notes. In the first place, notes may omit the subtitles of books or articles to be listed in a bibliography, but bibliographies must give the whole title with all its parts. If there is no punctuation between the parts of a title in the original, you can supply a colon (:) between title and subtitle in your bibliography.

Second, although it is usual for notes to refer to a specific page or pages, bibliography entries for books do not contain page numbers. And for books published in more than one volume, it is the *total* number of volumes that is given, not just the number of the volume referred to. For periodical articles, the bibliography entries do end with page numbers— but these indicate the range of pages occupied by the whole article rather than just a specific page or pages from which a note was taken.

Here are two sample bibliographic entries, one for a book and one for a periodical article:

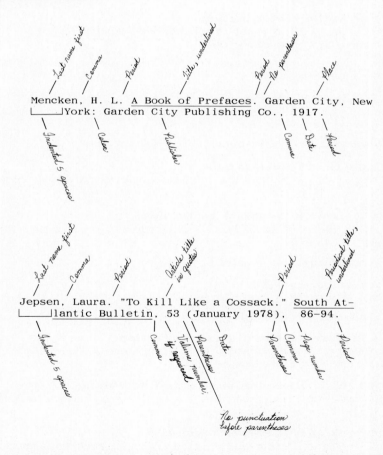

Notice that the authors' first and last names are reversed and the indentation is opposite to that of notes. Both these features are related to the fact that bibliographies are alphabetized. Notice, too, the changes in punctuation, for example, how periods take the place of some of the commas used in notes. Finally, notice that the page numbers at the end of the Jepsen entry do not refer to some specific part of the article, but rather to the fact that the article as a whole begins on page 86 and ends on page 94.

39K
Sample bibliography entries

Use the following entries as models. The explanations that follow some of the entries take up matters not previously discussed.

BOOKS

One Author, First Edition:
Cloud, Preston. *Cosmos, Earth, and Man: A Short History of the Universe.* New Haven and London: Yale, 1978.

One Author, Later Edition:
Johnson, Edgar. *Charles Dickens: His Tragedy and Triumph.* Revised and abridged edition. New York: Viking, 1977.

Murray, Gilbert. *The Literature of Ancient Greece.* 3rd ed. Chicago: University of Chicago Press, 1956.

Two to Three Authors:
Abercrombie, M., C. J. Hickman, and M. L. Johnson. *The Penguin Dictionary of Biology.* 6th ed. New York: Viking, 1977.

[Note that only the first author's name is reversed.]

More than Three Authors:
Brandwein, Paul F., et al. *The Social Sciences: Concepts and Values.* New York: Harcourt, 1970.

A Book with Corporate Authorship:
Prentice-Hall, Inc. *1975 Federal Tax Course.* Englewood Cliffs, New Jersey: Prentice-Hall, 1974.

[Corporate name not reversed.]

An Anonymous Book:
The Story of Burnt Njal. Trans. George Webbe Dasent. London: J. M. Dent, 1911.

[This entry would be alphabetized under *s* for *Story.*]

A Modern Reprint of an Older Edition:
Mann, Cameron. *A Concordance to the English Poems of George Herbert.* 1927; rpt. n.p.: Norwood Editions, 1977.

A Book Published in more than One Volume:
Disraeli, Isaac. *Curiosities of Literature.* 4 vols. New York: Sheldon and Company, 1863.

A Book That Is Part of a Series:
Lewis, C. S. *English Literature in the Sixteenth Century, Excluding Drama.* Oxford History of English Literature, No. 3. New York and London: Oxford University Press, 1954.

A Book with a Translator:
Tranquillus, Gaius Suetonius. *The Twelve Caesars.* Trans. Robert Graves. New York: Penguin, 1957.

A Book with an Author and an Editor:
Thoreau, Henry David. *Walden and Other Writings.* Ed. Brooks Atkinson. New York: Modern Library, 1937.

Books with Editors, but No Single Authors:
Livingstone, Elizabeth A., ed. *The Concise Oxford Dictionary of the Christian Church.* Oxford: Oxford University Press, 1977.

Clark, Marden J., Soren F. Cox, and Marshall R. Craig, eds. *About Language: Contexts for College Writing.* New York: Scribner's, 1970.

Hewitt, Geof, ed. *Quickly Aging Here: Some Poets of the 1970's.* Garden City, New York: Anchor, 1969.

Unpublished Dissertations:
Koening, Ralph R. "Enrollments at Two-Year Colleges, 1977–1981." Diss. University of Arkansas, 1981.

PARTS OF BOOKS

A Signed Article in a Collection:
Hughes, John P. "Fundamental Notions About Language." In *About Language: Contexts for College Writing.* Ed. Marden J. Clark, Soren F. Cox, and Marshall R. Craig. New York: Scribner's, 1970, pp. 77–83.

A Poem or Short Story in a Collection:
Mezey, Robert. "Dark Head." In *Contemporary American Poetry.* Ed. Donald Hall. Baltimore: Penguin, 1965, p. 190.

[This poem is only one page long.]

A Play:
Cartwright, William. *The Royal Slave.* In *The Plays and Poems of William Cartwright.* Ed. G. Blakemore Evans. Madison: The University of Wisconsin Press, 1951, pp. 165–253.

Signed Encyclopedia Articles:
Punnett, Reginald Crundall. "Sex." *Encyclopedia of Religion and Ethics.* 1955 ed.

Unsigned Encyclopedia Articles:
"Red Deer (*Cervus elephas*)." *Encyclopedia Americana.* 1978 ed.

[This entry would be alphabetized under *r* in your bibliography.]

PAMPHLETS AND GOVERNMENT DOCUMENTS

Pamphlets:
Francis, W. Nelson. *The History of English.* New York: Norton, 1963.

Government Documents:
U.S. Congress, House. Subcommittee of the Committee on Governmental Operations. *Federal Training Programs for Investigative Personnel.* 91st Cong., 2nd sess. H. Rept. 301. Washington D.C.: GPO, 1970.

[This report would be alphabetized under *u* for *United.*]

Congressional Record. 3 August 1975, pp. 3675–82.

Atomic Energy Commission. *Food Irradiation Contractors' Meeting.* Washington D.C.: GPO, 1968.

Western Kentucky University. *Institutional Report to the National Council for Accreditation of Teacher Education.* 3 vols. Bowling Green, Ky.: Western Kentucky University, 1974.

ARTICLES IN PERIODICAL PUBLICATIONS

Signed Article in a Journal:
Jepsen, Laura. "To Kill Like a Cossack." *South Atlantic Bulletin,* 53 (January 1978), 86–94.

Signed Article in a Magazine:
Hoberman, J. "From Ashes to Diamonds: The Comeback of Andrzej Wajda." *American Film,* January–February 1982, pp. 58–61.

Unsigned Article in a Journal or Magazine:
"Gaslight and Fallen Souls." *Time,* 15 October 1979, pp. 94–95.

[Would be alphabetized under *g* for *Gaslight.*]

Signed Newspaper Article:
Gorney, Cynthia. "Boom Time for the Cowboy Artists." *Washington Post,* 7 November, 1979, p. B1.

Unsigned Newspaper Article:
"False Missile Alert." *Louisville Courier-Journal,* 11 November 1979, pp. A1, A5.

[The comma, rather than a dash, between the page numbers shows that the article starts on A1 and is *continued* on A5.]

Unsigned, Untitled Newspaper Article:
Editorial. *Washington Post,* 3 September 1965, p. A11.

[Would be alphabetized under *e* for *Editorial.*]

Article Continued on Another Page or Pages:
Bynum, Linda Thorsby. "The Future of Recreation and Parks: A Forecast of Change and Call for Planning." *Parks and Recreation,* August 1979, pp. 22–25, 47.

Exercise 39-3. Construct and alphabetize acceptable bibliography entries for the following sources.

1. An anonymous article on page 3 of the November 13, 1979 issue of *The Wall Street Journal.* The article is called "Reliance Group Agrees to Acquire All UV's Assets."

2. Eoin Young's column, "From the Grid," in the volume 29, November 19, 1979, issue of *Autoweek.* The column starts on page 21 and is continued on pages 37–38.

3. An essay called "Of Tragedy" on pages 804–10 of a two-volume work, *Eighteenth-Century Critical Essays,* edited by Scott Elledge for the Cornell University Press in Ithaca, New York. The year of publication was 1961; the essay is in the second volume; the author of the essay was David Hume.

4. *Eighteenth-Century Critical Essays* (the work mentioned in the last exercise) as a whole.

5. A book published in San Francisco by Freeman, Cooper, and Co. in 1970. The book was written by a Yale professor, Harold G. Cassidy, and is called

Science Restated. It also has a subtitle, *Physics and Chemistry for the Non-Scientist.*

6. A 1960 reprint of Ezra Pound's 1934 book *ABC of Reading.* This reprint was published by New Directions in New York in 1960. Your copy is from the ninth printing.

UNCONVENTIONAL OR NONPRINT SOURCES

Films:
Whale, James, director. *The Bride of Frankenstein.* With Colin Clive and Boris Karloff. Universal, 1935.

Performances:
Flatt, Lester, Earl Scruggs, and The Foggy Mountain Boys. Carnegie Hall, New York, 8 December 1962.

McCowen, Alec. *Equus.* With Peter Firth and Nicholas Clay. National Theatre, London, 14 July 1973.

Recordings:
Dorati, Anatol, conductor. Haydn's Symphony 103 (*Drum Roll*). Philharmonica Hungarica. London Records, STS 15324, 1974.

Osipov Balalaika Orchestra. *A Program of Classic and Folk Favorites.* Cassette. Musical Heritage Society, MHC 6214L, n.d.

Works of Art:
Carracci, Annibale. *Venus and Anchises.* Ceiling fresco. Gallery, Palazzo Farnese, Rome.

Ward, James. *Captain John Levett Hunting in the Park at Wychnor.* Reproduced in *Steeplechasing and Foxhunting.* Ed. Michael Seth-Smith. London: New English Library, 1977, pp. 28–29.

Personal Contacts:
Wright, Marie. Letter to the author. 28 September 1975.

McEnroe, John. Telephone interview. 4 January 1982.

Rhodes, Byno. Lecture on *Paradise Lost.* Eastern Kentucky University, 21 October 1982.

Television and Radio:
Weill, Kurt. *Street Scene.* Libretto by Elmer Rice and Langston Hughes. With Eileen Schauler, Catherine Malfitano, and William Chapman. PBS, 27 October 1979.

Reynolds, Gene, director. "Welcome to Korea." *M*A*S*H.* With Alan Alda and Mike Farrell. CBS, 12 September 1975.

Computer Programs:
muLISP/muSTAR-80 version 10/06/80. The Soft Warehouse. 8080 or Z80 machine language. For 8080-, 8085-, or Z80-based computers with at least 20K memory, running under a CP/M-compatible operating system.

ADABAS. Software ag of North America. IBM OS. For IBM 370 system with at least 2 megs. main storage.

Exercise 39-4. Construct and alphabetize acceptable bibliography entries for the following sources.

1. A lecture you heard delivered by Gerald Ford on the subject of NATO, on March 17, 1980, at the University of Michigan.

2. A July 6, 1956, performance at the American Jazz Festival, Newport, R.I., by the Dave Brubeck Quartet.

3. A painting by John Singer Sargent in the Brooklyn Museum, Brooklyn, New York, called *Paul Helleu Sketching with His Wife.*

4. A painting called *The Eve of Peace,* by George Fredric Watts. This picture is reproduced in a book entitled *The Return to Camelot: Chivalry and the English Gentleman,* which was published by Yale University Press in London and New Haven, Conn., in 1981. The book was written by Mark Girouard and the picture appears as Plate XIX.

5. The motion picture *The Graduate,* which was directed by Mike Nichols and starred Anne Bancroft and Dustin Hoffman. This movie was released in 1967 by Embassy Pictures.

39L
Typing the bibliography

Start the bibliography on a separate page following the text and notes of your paper. Leave margins of two inches at the top and one inch at the bottom and sides. Center your title (you may use "Bibliography," but a more descriptive title such as "List of Works Cited" is often more helpful). Leave a four-line space before starting your first entry on the left margin. Remember to indent by five spaces every line in the entry after the first. Double-space between and within entries, and if you need additional sheets, leave a one-inch margin at the top. (See also the sample bibliography on page 379.)

2"

List of Works Cited

4 lines

Cloud, Preston. Cosmos, Earth, and Man: A

Short History of the Universe. New

Haven and London: Yale, 1978.

1" Johnson, Edgar. Charles Dickens: His Trag-

edy and Triumph. Revised and abridged 1"

edition. New York: Viking, 1977.

Patterson, Carolyn Bennett. "Travels with

a Donkey." National Geographic, 154

(October 1978), pp. 535–60.

Double space within entries and also between them

39M
Abbreviations sometimes used in documentation

We include these abbreviations mainly to help you deal with other people's notes and bibliographies. It is best in your own documentation to limit yourself to the abbreviations already included in the sample notes and bibliography entries.

anon.	anonymous
b.	born
©	copyright
c., ca.	*circa,* or "around" (used with dates)
cf.	compare
ch., chs.	chapter, chapters
col., cols.	column, columns
d.	died
diss.	dissertation
ed., edn.	edition
ed., eds.	editor, editors
e.g.	*exempli gratia* ("for example")
et al.	*et alii,* "and others"
fig., figs.	figure, figures (of illustrations)
f., ff.	and the following page, pages
ibid.	*ibidim* ("in the same place")
i.e.	*id est* ("that is")
introd.	introduction
l., ll.	line, lines
loc. cit.	*loco citato* ("in the place cited"; i.e. in the place referred to by another note)
MS., MSS.	manuscript, manuscripts
n.	note
N.B.	*nota bene* ("note well")
n.d.	no date given
no., nos.	number, numbers
n.p.	no place given
op. cit.	*opere citato* ("in the work cited"; i.e. the work referred to by another note)
p., pp.	page, pages
passim	"throughout the work"
pl., pls.	plate, plates (of illustrations)
q.v.	*quod vide* ("which see")
rpt.	reprint
rev.	revised
sc., scs.	scene, scenes
st., sts.	stanza, stanzas
trans., tr.	translated by or translation
v.	*vide* ("see")
viz.	*videlicet* ("namely")
vol., vols.	volume, volumes

40

The Sample Research Paper

The paper that follows illustrates the formal characteristics of a research paper and should give you an idea of what the finished product looks like. The notes in the margins point out features of special interest.

"Socialized Medicine" Versus "The Voluntary Way":

The National Education Campaign of the

American Medical Association

*The title
is neither
underlined
nor placed
in quotation
marks.*

Raymond T. Tatum
History 161
Professor C. A. Trout
December 6, 1982

Outline

Thesis: The AMA mounted a well-financed and well-organized
        public relations campaign, which occasionally
        included ethically questionable tactics, to defeat
        President Truman's national health insurance
        proposal.

*Sentence
outline*

I. President Truman announced his proposal for national
   health insurance in his 1949 State of the Union
   Address.

II. The AMA immediately hired the California Public
    relations firm, Whitaker and Baxter, to run the
    National Education Campaign to combat the proposal.

III. The campaign was financed through a voluntary
     assessment of AMA members.

IV. The campaign was organized into a four-pronged
    attack.

   A. Campaign literature was produced and distributed.

      1. One poster was the "theme-piece" of the
         campaign.

      2. Pamphlets were produced to appeal to different
         audiences.

         a. Pamphlets were aimed at patients.

         b. Pamphlets were provided for the use of
            doctors and selected laymen.

         c. One pamphlet was addressed to doctors' wives.

   B. Pro-AMA publicity was generated in newspapers and
      magazines.

   C. Speakers' bureaus sponsored by local and state medical societies presented the AMA position before various organizations.

   D. Various groups were encouraged to endorse the AMA position.

      1. Local and state medical societies adopted strong resolutions denouncing the health insurance plan.

      2. Prominent non-AMA organizations were encouraged to endorse the AMA position.

         a. Members of state medical societies attempted to gain pro-AMA endorsements from groups having conventions in their states.

         b. Professional organizers and lobbyists were sent to key states to gain endorsements.

      3. Endorsements by individuals were also encouraged.

V. In some ways, the campaign employed ethically questionable tactics.

   A. Although extremely well-organized and centrally controlled, the campaign was presented as a "grass-roots revolt."

   B. The campaign played on the doctor-patient relationship to generate support.

   C. Some of the campaign literature was pure propaganda based on emotional appeals.

"Socialized Medicine" Versus "The Voluntary Way":

The National Education Campaign of the   *Title
repeated*

American Medical Association

*Opening
attempts
to show
current
importance
of topic.*

During every recent presidential campaign, the issue

of a federally-funded national health care plan has been

raised and debated. In fact, George Silver, professor of   *Identifying
title of
author
establishes
his
credibility
as a
source.*

public health at the Yale School of Medicine, pointed out

in 1980 that the debate "over the value and scope of a

national health program" has been in progress for sixty

years and that the Democratic party has adopted it as a

plank in its campaign platform for the past twenty years.[1]

The most powerful and consistent opponent of the various

national health care plans which have been proposed, all

of which in some way would involve the federal government

in underwriting the medical expenses of some or all of the

nation's citizens, is the American Medical Association. An

examination of one particular campaign of the AMA to block

national health care shows how effective it has been in

defeating such proposals and provides an historical

perspective on this continuing controversy. Specifically,

1

Thesis announced

a close look at how the AMA defeated President Truman's
national health insurance proposal in 1949 shows that the
AMA waged a well-financed and well-organized public
relations campaign, which included some ethically
questionable tactics.

After his amazing election in 1949, President Truman
proposed in his State of the Union message in January 1949
the establishment of national health insurance. His plan,
as summarized by Stanley Kelley, Jr., in his book,
Professional Public Relations and Political Power,[2]
called for complete medical, dental, hospital, and
nursing care for all except the destitute, who would

The writer indicates that the entire summary comes from this source. Additional notes are not needed.

remain charity cases. A national health insurance board
would be created within the Federal Security Administration
and would head a national, state, and local administrative
organization. The program would be financed by a three
percent payroll tax, divided equally between employer and
employee. Doctors and hospitals would be allowed to join
or not to join the program. Patients would still be free
to choose their own doctors, while doctors would be free
to refuse unwanted patients. Physicians would be paid on a
stated fee, per capita, or salary basis by the national

2

health insurance board, with the method of payment being
decided by the doctors under agreement in each health
service area.

Alarmed by the prospect of national health insurance,
the AMA laid plans for the most ambitious public-relations
campaign up to that time. The association hired a
California public-relations firm, Whitaker and Baxter, to
run what became known as the National Education Campaign.
Clem Whitaker and his wife, Leone Baxter, already had a
good deal of experience fighting government health
insurance plans. They had been hired by the California
Medical Association to fight Governor Earl Warren's health
insurance proposal in 1946. Successful in their California
effort, they came highly recommended.[3] —— *A note is needed here even though the material is only paraphrased, not quoted.*

To finance the National Education Campaign, the AMA's
House of Delegates voted to levy a $25 voluntary
assessment on the 145,000 members of the association.
Although some physicians objected to the kind of public-
relations campaign that their money would be used for, the
collection of the levy went well. By the end of 1949,
eighty percent of the doctors had paid their money, and
$2,350,000 had been collected.[4]

3

Once hired, Whitaker and Baxter moved quickly. On February 10, 1949, they opened their campaign headquarters in Chicago. With a staff of thirty-seven, the campaign directors soon developed the basic outline for the campaign.[5] What they came up with was an extremely well-organized public relations campaign divided into four areas: the distribution of campaign materials, a publicity campaign using the mass media, a speakers' committee operation, and a drive for endorsements from national, state, and local organizations.

Identifies four areas to be covered in the paper.

Transition to first area.

The production and distribution of campaign literature was the heart of the AMA campaign. There were several kinds of literature distributed to the public. The "theme-piece" of the campaign was a poster containing a color reproduction of a 19th century painting by Sir Luke Fildes, called "The Doctor." It showed a sick little girl in bed, being attended by an old, gray-bearded, wise-looking doctor. In the background stood the anxious father, while the distraught mother sat at a desk with her head resting on her folded arms. Under the picture appeared this message:

4

KEEP POLITICS OUT OF THIS PICTURE!

When the life or health of a loved one is at stake, hope lies in the devoted service of your Doctor. Would you change this picture?

Compulsory health insurance is political medicine.

It would bring a third party--a politician--between you and your Doctor. It would bind up your family's health in red tape. It would result in heavy payroll taxes--and inferior medical care for you and your family. Don't let that happen here!

You have a right to prepaid medical care--of your own choice. Ask your Doctor, or your insurance man, about budget-basis health protection.[6]

Besides the Fildes poster, the main propaganda weapons used by Whitaker and Baxter were pamphlets. The public relations team created a large number of publications suitable for different audiences. A minimum of ten million copies of each pamphlet was printed, so that both doctors and interested organizations had enough material to

5

distribute. Because a printing job of this magnitude was quite expensive, each pamphlet had to be effective. A *Quote worked into writer's sentence.* pamphlet had to be "brief enough to read--dramatic enough to create sentiment and sound enough to produce action from the thinking people" of America.[7]

One pamphlet written by Whitaker and Baxter was a small "human interest" booklet designed for general use. It was placed in waiting rooms, distributed to patients, and given to cooperating organizations. Illustrated, it explained in simple terms the AMA's position on national health insurance. Another publication was a question-and-answer pamphlet that served as the doctors' campaign handbook. It provided answers for patients' questions, along with handy suggestions for practicing "on the body politic." This booklet was also given to selected laymen important to the campaign. A third booklet, called *Parenthetical references to this key source.* "Calling Every Doctor--This Is An Emergency," was also written for doctors. It briefly presented the AMA's campaign objectives and the procedure to be used to obtain those objectives (Cong. Rec., p. A3175). There was even a publication for doctors' wives, called "It's Your Crusade Too!" It urged wives to keep plenty of campaign literature

6

in their husbands' waiting rooms and to include campaign
pamphlets in their personal mail, "even invitations to
dinner parties."[8]

*Transition to
next subtopic*

Another major part of the campaign was the effort to
generate pro--AMA publicity in newspapers and magazines.
Each county medical society was to establish a press
committee that would encourage local newspaper editors
to take editorial stands in favor of the AMA position
(Cong. Rec., p. A3176). The firm of Hofer and Sons of
Portland, Oregon, was paid by Whitaker and Baxter to
supply country newspapers with "canned" editorials
supporting the AMA. "Hard hitting" statements by medical
leaders to the mass media were encouraged, while the
campaign staff worked with newspapers and magazines by
providing ideas and information for favorable stories.
Once these stories were published, reprints would be used
to reinforce the campaign.[9]

Every county and state medical society was encouraged
to have a speakers' bureau, composed of physicians and
laymen. These speakers would be trained to speak before
organizations on the evils of "socialized medicine." Form
speeches were provided by campaign headquarters, but

7

speakers were encouraged to change these speeches to fit their needs (Cong. Rec., p. A3176).

A very important part of the National Education Campaign was the drive to obtain endorsements by organizations of the AMA stand on national health insurance. Every county medical society in the United States was encouraged to adopt a strong resolution opposing national health insurance. These resolutions emphasized "the danger to the public health" that compulsory health insurance represented and praised the growth of voluntary health plans over the preceding years. Once passed, these resolutions were sent to the congressman (or congressmen) representing the county and to the two senators representing the state. The congressmen were asked to reply, and copies of all replies were sent to the campaign headquarters in Chicago and to the AMA Washington office (Cong. Rec., p. A3176).

Every state medical society received a list of conventions scheduled in its state during 1949. The list contained the name of each organization having a convention, the convention town, the estimated attendance, the right person to contact, and whether the convention

8

was national, state, or local. Each convention would be
encouraged to invite a speaker from one of the speakers'
bureaus. Each speaker would be equipped with a speech
suitable for the audience, additional information in the
form of the question-and-answer pamphlet, and a form
resolution for the convention to adopt. Once an
organization passed a resolution, it was to be widely
publicized as soon as possible. Copies were to be sent to
legislators at the national and state levels and were to
be released to the media (Cong. Rec., pp. A3176–77).

Whitaker and Baxter did not depend completely on
doctors in the endorsement drive. As a test, professional
organizers were sent to eight key states; the results were
worth the effort. During a two-month period, these
organizers obtained 817 endorsements, compared to only 337
endorsements obtained in the other forty states.[10] By the
end of 1949, 1829 organizations had passed resolutions
opposing national health insurance.[11]

Individual endorsements of the AMA campaign were
encouraged by Whitaker and Baxter. By early June, ten
million envelopes and enclosed statements stating the
AMA's objectives were printed and distributed to patients

9

by doctors. Each letter argued that national health

insurance would provide high-priced, inferior medical

care, medical privacy would be diminished, and both

doctors and patients would be under political control.

Recipients were urged to write their congressman and tell

him of their opposition to national health insurance.[12]

Transition to next major section of paper. Although the National Education Program was in many

ways a sincere and honest attempt to persuade the public

and the legislators to accept the AMA position about

President Truman's health proposal, it was also sometimes

misleading and ethically questionable. For example,

although the program was extremely well-organized and

centrally controlled, Whitaker and Baxter, according to an

article entitled "The Anatomy of a Lobby" written by   *Source included in text*

Nathan Robertson, attempted to portray it as a "grass-

roots revolt."[13] As already explained, campaign

literature, including form speeches, were developed by the

national headquarters and distributed to individual

doctors through their state and local medical societies.

Doctors then passed it to their patients, local

newspapers, organizations, and congressmen. Whitaker and

Baxter wanted Congress to believe that the pressure being

10

placed on it was a widespread "grass-roots" pressure not
directed from above.[14]

Another questionable part of the campaign was the way
it used doctors to spread information and to convince
people that national health insurance was a threat to
their well-being. Stanley Kelley points out that Whitaker
and Baxter based much of their campaign literature and *Writer tailors quotation to his needs.*
operation on the close, trusting relationship patients
have with their doctors. Kelley notes, for instance, that
Fildes' painting of the kindly, caring doctor at the *Word inserted in quotation.*
bedside of a sick child shows "the peculiar emotional
force [that] can bind the patient to his doctor."[15] Kelley
concludes that this picture, along with the emotionally
packed message under it, posted in a doctor's waiting room
"could suggest the destruction of the relationship on
which the patient even then might be placing all his
hope."[16] At the very least, most patients would be
extremely hesitant to support a health program which their
doctors opposed.

Finally, some of the literature produced as part of
the National Education Campaign used emotional appeals and
scare tactics to gain support for the AMA position.

11

Whitaker and Baxter from the beginning announced their
intention to produce campaign literature written in
"emotional, fighting prose" (<u>Cong. Rec.</u>, p. A3176). David
B. Truman points out that the main emotional appeal they
used was to label Truman's plan "socialized medicine" and
to claim that it was "alien" and "un-American."[17]
According to Truman, the campaign pamphlet, "The Voluntary
Way is the American Way," attempted to scare readers by
asserting that national health insurance was
"socialization" which would lead to a socialized state.
This passage from the pamphlet illustrates its hysterical
tone: "If the doctors lose their freedom today--if their
patients are regimented tomorrow, who will be next? YOU
WILL BE NEXT!"[18]

The title of the pamphlet, "The Voluntary Way is the
American Way," indicates how the AMA position was
identified with American principles and the President's
health insurance plan with un-Americanism. Ed Cray notes
that the pamphlet goes out of its way to associate the
health insurance plan with the Communist Party, which in
1949 was widely perceived as an immediate threat to the
American government. At one point the pamphlet asked, "Who

12

is for Compulsory Health Insurance?" It answered, "The *Quotation introduced smoothly.*

Federal Security Administration. The President. All who

seriously believe in a Socialistic State. Every left-wing

organization in America. . . . The Communist Party."[19] *Ellipsis and period.*

The National Education Campaign had its desired

effect. President Truman's national health insurance bill

never reached either floor of Congress.[20] The AMA had

waged a very effective, expensive, organized, and *Quick summary of thesis.*

sometimes shady lobbying campaign. In all, 54,233,915

pieces of campaign literature had been distributed at a

cost of $1,045,614.52,[21] while organizational and *Two different sources of information noted.*

operational expenses had added $139,415.27 and

$209,122.90, respectively.[22] But the AMA considered its

money well spent; the spectre of national health insurance

would not haunt doctors for years to come.

13

Notes —— *Endnotes are used but the heading is simply "Notes."*

[1] "The Health-Care Merry-Go-Round," Saturday —— *Author's name is included in the text.*

Review, 16 February 1980, p. 15.

[2] (Baltimore: Johns Hopkins Press, 1956), p. 71.—— *Both author and title included in the text.*

[3] "AMA: The Doctors Gird for Battle," Newsweek, 20

June 1949, p. 51.

[4] Ed Cray, In Failing Health (Indianapolis: Bobbs-

Merrill, 1970), pp. 76-78. *Abbreviated second reference.*

[5] Kelley, p. 73. ————————————

[6] Quoted in Kelley, p. 77. ——————— *The quotation is taken from Kelley, not the original pamphlet.*

[7] Cong. Rec., Appendix, 20 May 1949, p. A3175. The *Covering note explains importance of this source and indicates that future references to it will be parenthetical*

entire lobbying program of the National Education

Campaign as presented by Whitaker and Baxter to the

conference of medical societies, Chicago, February 12,

1949, is included in the Appendix to the Congressional

Record of the 81st Congress. All future references to

this invaluable source will be noted in parenthesis.

[8] Cray, p. 78.

[9] Kelley, pp. 81-82.

[10] Kelley, p. 79.

14 —— *Consecutive page numbering continues.*

[11] James Gordon Burrow, <u>AMA: Voice of American Medicine</u> (Baltimore: Johns Hopkins Press, 1963), p. 364. *"Hybrid" note* For lists of organizations which passed resolutions see Kelley, p. 81; and Donald C. Blaisdell, <u>American Democracy Under Pressure</u> (New York: Ronald Press, 1957), pp. 243–44.

[12] Burrow, p. 363.

[13] Robertson's article, which appeared in the May *Indirect source of the article is cited.* issue of the <u>Progressive</u>, was included in the <u>Congressional Record</u> on June 9, 1949, by Congressman John R. Walsh. See pp. A3603–04. *Explanatory note*

[14] In their plan of action, Whitaker and Baxter point out the importance of "division of work" and "fixed responsibility . . . so that a vigorous grass-roots campaign can be developed" (<u>Cong. Rec.</u>, p. A3176). Kelley also makes this point (p. 73).

[15] Kelley, p. 78.

[16] Kelley, p. 78.

[17] <u>The Governmental Process</u> (New York: Knopf, 1951), p. 231.

[18] Quoted in Truman, p. 231. *Indirect source of quotation.*

[19] Cray, p. 80.

[20] Harold Aaron, "The Doctor in Politics," <u>Consumer Reports</u>, February 1950, p. 75.

15

[21] Kelley, p. 82.

[22] William L. Laurence, "Leaders Rally Doctors of the Country to All-Out Fight on Socialized Medicine," New York Times, 7 December 1949, p. 34.

*Alphabetized
and
double spaced.*

List of Works Cited ———————— *Descriptive
title*

Aaron, Harold. "The Doctor in Politics." Consumer Reports,

   February 1950, pp. 75-78.

"AMA: The Doctors Gird for Battle." Newsweek, 20 June

   1949, pp. 50-51.

Blaisdell, Donald C. American Democracy Under Pressure.

   New York: Ronald Press, 1957.

Burrow, James Gordon. AMA: Voice of American Medicine.

   Baltimore: The Johns Hopkins Press, 1963.

Congressional Record. Appendix. 20 May 1949, pp. A3175-77;

   9 June 1949, pp. A3603-04.   *Subtitle
                                                  included*

Cray, Ed. In Failing Health: The Medical Crisis and the

   A.M.A. Indianapolis: Bobbs-Merrill, 1970.

Kelley, Stanley, Jr. Professional Public Relations and

   Political Power. Baltimore: The Johns Hopkins Press,

   1956.

Laurence, William L. "Leaders Rally Doctors of the Country

   to All-Out Fight on Socialized Medicine." New York

   Times, 7 December 1949, pp. 33-34.

Silver, George. "The Health-Care Merry-Go-Round." Saturday

   Review, 16 February 1980, pp. 15-17.   *Subtitle
                                                  included.*

Truman, David B. The Governmental Process: Political

   Interests and Public Opinion. New York: Knopf, 1951.

41

In-Class Themes and Essay Examinations

In-class themes and essay examinations must be written within a limited period, but their other requirements are the same as for more leisurely writing, with this exception: writing out of class you may have time to correct wide-ranging problems of organization or style, but in-class writing has to be right the first time.

The key to in-class writing is to know exactly what you want to say. You have to construct and focus a thesis that answers the assignment, and you have to know just how you will develop this thesis so as to persuade your instructor.

41A
Understanding the assignment

Assignments for in-class writing range from general topics ("What I did last summer") to specific ones ("Discuss the major materials of Roman architecture and their specific applications"). Your first job is to be sure you understand just what you are supposed to do. For instance, it would be wrong to answer an assignment about what you *did* last summer with an essay about your depression after a period of religious doubt. Such an essay would describe how you *felt* last summer, and your teacher might object that you had not answered the assignment at all.

It would be just as wide of the mark to answer the question about Roman architecture with a discussion of the decline of wood buildings as Mediterranean forests were depleted or with an essay on the Romans' fondness for marble. The question asks for major building materials, not minor ones; and it stipulates that all major materials, not just one, be included. Any good answer to the question would have to list major Roman building materials, discuss such things as the availability of these materials or their association with different periods of Roman history, and describe how each material was used.

It is especially important to note any key terms assignments contain. Questions asking you to *compare* or *compare and contrast* two or more things require an account of the similarities as well as the differences between them. Other questions may limit you to *similarities* or ask for *differences*, or *contrasts*, only. Assignments that call on you to *discuss* or *consider* a subject leave it up to you to decide what form the discussion will take and what conclusions it will reach. Questions that ask you to *analyze* or *explain* demand careful attention to logic, usually the logic of cause and effect. Finally, assignments that ask you to *trace* or present the *history* or *evolution* of something require chronological treatment with a close attention to major changes and developments through time.

You should also consider the source of writing topics. Teachers often have a definite response in mind, and remembering that can help you complete the assignment successfully. You may not be willing to say what your teacher expects, but you should consider his expectations, if only so you can convince him that your ideas are good ones too.

Exercise 41–1.

1. Consider the following topics for in-class writing. What kinds of information does each ask for? What sorts of mistakes might students make in writing on each topic? Which assignments contain key terms, and what do they call for?

    a. Describe the Federal Reserve System's basic tools for regulating the economy and discuss the limitations of each.

    b. The most important things to check before buying a used car.

    c. Compare and contrast two good teachers you had in high school.

    d. Analyze the major weaknesses of the Treaty of Versailles and trace the consequences of each.

    e. Consider the ethical arguments for and against using animals in painful scientific experiments.

2. If you have a copy of some essay examination or other in-class writing topics from another class, bring it in for discussion. Evaluate each question and compare your ideas with those of your classmates and teacher.

41B
Constructing a thesis for in-class writing

Once you thoroughly understand what an in-class writing assignment asks for, constructing a thesis should not be difficult. The thesis will be a one-sentence response to the assignment that you can go on to develop in the rest of your essay: *"Last summer I spent every spare moment working in a variety of jobs on a series of productions by our civic theater group"*; *"At various periods in Roman history major building materials included wood, cut stone, brick, and "Roman concrete"* (*a mixture of water, lime, clay, and stone rubble*), *and the architectural applications of these materials were determined by their availability, the nature of the material, and the demands of the building project."*

A good in-class thesis is not very different from an out-of-class one, except that it should be easier to construct. Your instructor has already restricted and focused the topic, and class experiences will have prepared you to respond. Your job, then, amounts to little more than drafting the thesis and making sure it is technically sound, that it will produce a good essay and an adequate response to the assignment.

How do you evaluate such a thesis? First, be sure it contains an *answer* to the problem posed in the assignment. Simply announcing your topic ("I am going to tell what I did last summer") is like repeating the assignment itself; it gets you no further toward completing the essay. The same objection applies to theses that lack *details*. The thesis, "The Federal Reserve System has many tools for regulating the economy, though each is limited in some way," does not answer a question about *which* tools are available and *how* they are limited.

Second, a good thesis must support development. "I didn't do anything last summer" answers its question, but what would come next? Make sure your thesis opens a door, rather than slamming it shut. A writer working with a thesis like, "There are no ethical arguments for or against using animals in painful experiments," would be in deep trouble from the first.

Once you are certain your thesis answers the assignment and leaves room for development, make sure you have included all the points the assignment requires. "The Federal Reserve System can manipulate the economy through its control of credit, the money supply, and banking regulations," would not be an adequate thesis for the question "Describe the Federal Reserve System's tools for regulating the economy and discuss the limitations of each of them," for it plainly ignores the last part of the assignment.

Exercise 41–2. Does each of the theses below offer an answer to its assignment, provide room for adequate development, and cover all the points specified in the assignment?

1. *Assignment:* Describe at least four situations in which a CPA's correct course is to withdraw from an audit engagement.
   Thesis 1: Business being what it is these days, I don't think a CPA should *ever* withdraw from an audit engagement.
   Thesis 2: A CPA has no choice except to withdraw from an audit engagement if he or she feels incompetent to carry out the assignment or if the client refuses to abide by accepted accounting principles.
   Thesis 3: In this essay I will discuss at least four situations in which a CPA's correct course is to withdraw from an audit engagement.
   Thesis 4: Withdrawal from an audit engagement is ethically unavoidable when a CPA and his client cannot agree on accounting principles, when the CPA knows of or strongly suspects illegal actions on the part of the client, when the CPA feels incompetent to carry out the engagement in question, or when the information supplied by the client is materially inconsistent or inaccurate.

2. *Assignment:* Describe some important differences between high school and college math classes.
   Thesis 1: While my high school and college math classes have covered

much of the same ground, the college work is much faster paced, concentrates on harder problems, and offers less individual attention.

Thesis 2: I have had trouble with college math because the pace is too fast, the problems are too hard, and I do not get the individual attention I need.

Thesis 3: I have been disappointed with college math because so far it has been the same old stuff I had in high school.

Thesis 4: The focus of the paper that follows will be upon the important differences that pertain between high school and college instruction in mathematics.

41C
Outlining your answer

Once you have your thesis, invest a few minutes in sketching and arranging your supporting details. Listing some supporting details can suggest still others, and having your subtopics on paper makes it easy to arrange and rearrange them. An outline provides some other important benefits: it gives you a last chance to check your argument for logic and consistency; it guards against your absent-mindedly leaving something out of the finished paper; and it helps you estimate how much time you should spend on each section before moving on to the next.

41D
A sample in-class essay

At the end of a class in ancient philosophy the students were given a two-and-a-half-hour final examination. During the first hour they worked a series of one hundred objective (multiple-choice and true-false) questions. Then the instructor passed out assignment sheets listing four possible essay topics. Each student was to pick one and spend the remaining hour and a half writing a coherent, well-developed essay answer.

A girl in the front row had no trouble deciding to do the one on the Roman philosopher Lucretius. She had been interested in the readings from Lucretius and had paid special attention to the lectures on his philosophy. She thought she understood his system better than those of some of the other philosophers. And besides, Lucretius had been the next-to-last lecture topic, so everything about him was fresh in her mind.

Her first step was to study the question and decide just what she must do to answer it. It seemed clear that the question—"Discuss some of the more unusual features of Lucretius' philosophy and the problems that drove him to adopt them"—had two parts. She would have to describe these unusual features, and she would have to do some analysis to show how each of the ideas she described was rooted in the problems Lucretius faced as a thinker. She knew what her teacher had in mind, for he had spent a great deal of time explaining how some of the oddest opinions in the works of ancient philosophers make sense when they are considered as necessary developments of the philosopher's basic assumptions.

In Lucretius' case, these basic assumptions were those of materialism—that everything that exists is matter or the space between units of matter, that there is no spiritual level of existence, and that everything must be explained in terms of atoms and combinations of atoms. The question required her to show that some of the notions Lucretius concocted stemmed from the difficulties presented by these basic assumptions.

All this took less time for the girl to do than it does to describe. At the end of five minutes she picked up her pen and wrote down her thesis on a spare piece of paper: "Lucretius was a materialist, and his materialism is at the root of many of his odd opinions." But there was something wrong with this statement: other materialists had not come up with the same ideas as Lucretius, and many of the Lucretian ideas she planned to discuss were not really opinions so much as attempts to resolve problems for which Lucretius had no other answer. She hated to take on another task, but she decided that she could not do a good job with the topic unless she started off with a description of Lucretius' special interpretation of materialism, showed how that got him in philosophical difficulty from the first, and *then* presented the "unusual features" of his thought—not as settled opinions but as inventions designed to extract him from his difficulties.

The girl soon had a new thesis: "The unusual ideas Lucretius presented on motion, the shape of the universe, and such things as life and thought are best understood as conclusions to which he was driven in trying to deal with problems created by his special interpretation of materialism." This version answered the question, left room (maybe too much?) for development, and included everything called for in the assignment. It seemed a little awkward, but it was really a guide for her and need not appear in the paper itself.

The girl's next step was to construct a scratch outline. The first thing she had to show was that Lucretius faced some special problems, and here she made a discovery: Parmenides, she remembered, had got by without inventing strange notions because he had denied that anything ever changed; the shape Lucretius assigned to the universe and a number of his other concepts were related to his desire to include change and motion. Motion was Lucretius' basic problem: without it, he could have been consistent; with it he had to deal with all sorts of difficulties other materialists had managed to sidestep. If this problem of motion was the key to Lucretius' difficulties, it could be given a rather full treatment and serve as background to the other points she would consider. The first part of her outline, then, looked like this:

> *Thesis:* The unusual ideas Lucretius presented on motion, the shape of the universe, and such things as life and thought are best understood as conclusions to which he was driven in trying to deal with problems created by his special interpretation of materialism.
> Describe Lucretius' materialism, Being and Nonbeing, and so on
> Problem of motion in general—atomic snowstorm
> Special motions—gentle swerves

The girl was thinking mainly about the structure of her essay and counting on filling out the structure adequately later. All she included were general headings and a few memory-joggers such as "atomic snowstorms" or "gentle swerves." Had she been less confident, she could have included some details under her headings.

By now fifteen minutes of the allotted hour and a half had elapsed, but the girl's troubles were almost over. It took her only three minutes to complete her outline:

> Transition to problems of life and thought.
> Life—"rarefied wind"
> Mind—fine atoms
> Thoughts
> Perception—atomic films
> Imagination—mixed or floating films
> Conclusion—recall thesis

With eighteen minutes gone, the girl was ready to write. But just then, she noticed that the boy next to her was making anguished faces. Though he had started writing immediately, he was only three sentences into his first paragraph and was destined to spend the rest of the period sighing loudly and trying to peek at what everyone around him was finding to put down.

The girl's paper on Lucretius is reproduced below to show how her eighteen minutes of preparation resulted in a clear and intelligent treatment of her subject. Though she decided not to include the thesis, she kept it in mind and tried to refer to it each time she wrote a transition between paragraphs. She included each new idea that came to her in the process of writing if it seemed to work (for example, she expanded "imagination" to include hallucinations), but she never wandered from her outline. And she paced herself: she had intended to give a full paragraph to each of the final groups of topics in her outline, but toward the end of the period she decided to limit each one to a short, enumerated treatment under the heading of "nonphysical things." This change saved her enough time to check her paper and still hand it in five minutes early. The boy she had noticed earlier had already been gone for fifteen minutes when she finished: he had finally scribbled a page and a half of disconnected ideas and was by then already at the student union explaining to everyone that essay examinations penalize bright students by not giving them time to develop their brilliant but complex insights.

> Discuss some of the more unusual features of Lucretius' philosophy and the problems that drove him to adopt them.

> Lucretius was a materialist—part of a philosophical tradition going back to the Greek atomists—and his particular brand of materialism is at the root of the problems that beset his system. For Lucretius, existence is divided into two categories—Being and Nonbeing. Being consists of solid, indivisible atoms, and Nonbeing is the void that surrounds them. The universe of Lucretius, then, is infinite (once a system contains both Being and Nonbeing, what could possibly be outside to give it boundaries?) and its operations are purely mechanical (if only atoms and void exist, no other kinds of interaction are possible). Lucretius' basic problem, as a result, is to make this stripped-down, abstract idea of the universe consistent with the world as we experience it. Thought

of in this way, the problem is a difficult, maybe an insolvable, one. It certainly drove Lucretius to invent some unusual concepts in his attempt to find an answer.

Perhaps the most basic difficulty Lucretius faced was that of accounting for motion (Parmenides, an earlier materialist, had avoided this problem by denying that there was such a thing as motion). If only atoms and void exist, what could there be to set the atoms in motion? Lucretius never really answers this question, but it leads to a refinement of his idea of the universe that most people would consider unusual. His infinite universe takes on absolute upward and downward directions, through which all the atoms fall at the same rate, like a heavy snowstorm on a calm night.

This idea of falling atoms gives Lucretius motion of a sort, but it does not solve his problem entirely. Lacking any further force, his atoms must fall in straight, parallel lines—with respect to each other, they would not be in motion at all. At this point, Lucretius invented another unusual and unexplained notion, the "gentle swerve." At some time one atom must have slightly swerved from its path and collided with another. This second atom was pushed into others, and the process continued. For Lucretius, all that had happened in the past and all that would happen in the future came about as a result of that first, unaccountable "gentle swerve."

Like other physicalists, Lucretius was also hard-put to explain certain apparently nonphysical things such as life, mind, thoughts, experiences, hallucinations, or imagination in purely physical terms. While such special problems are less basic to his philosophy than the problem of motion and change in general, he showed an equal degree of inventiveness in dealing with them:

1. Life, according to Lucretius, is a rarified wind. It is a wind because the difference between a living and a dead person is that the former breathes and the latter does not. It is rarified because it has to move quickly in order to produce motions in the body it inhabits.

2. The mind consists of atoms which are very fine and smooth. These must also move quickly since it is their collisions with the life atoms that cause the body to act.

3. Thoughts are merely the movements or clashing of the mind atoms.

4. Experiences or perceptions are explained in terms of "films" of atoms that emanate from objects and collide with sense receptors such as the eye. Lucretius develops this idea at some length, saying that it accounts for such things as objects becoming worn (constantly losing "atomic films" eventually takes its toll on them); the working of mirrors (the smooth and tightly packed atoms of the mirror can bounce back the films that hit them); and depth perception (the films push air before them as they move, and the thickness of this layer of air correlates with the distance between object and perceiver).

5. Lucretius also explains hallucinations and imaginings on the basis of his "atomic films." Films which are not received by sense receptors (and this includes the majority of them) do not cease to exist—they float around, sometimes combining with others in unpredictable ways, and are occasionally received when the original object is gone or far away. Our ability to imagine things at will is due to the mind's access to the unreceived films that crowd the air. We simply select the one we want from the many available and so can imagine things that are no longer physically present.

Taken out of context, Lucretius' ideas about such things as the structure of the universe, the cause of change, and the workings of minds and senses may seem more than "unusual"; to most people, they would appear totally arbitrary and unconvincing. But they all arise from the gap between materialistic principles and perceived reality, and they all represent one philosopher's attempt to close that gap.

Exercise 41–3. Evaluate some in-class writing you have done in light of the methods suggested in this chapter. Did you understand the assignment? Did you construct an adequate thesis? Is your answer based on a clear and logical outline? (Your instructor may ask that you bring in a sample of your in-class writing for discussion.)

42 Other Special Forms: Summaries, Book Reports, Business Letters, and Résumés

This chapter covers some special kinds of writing that call for special techniques. But you should be careful not to apply these techniques blindly. In all writing situations, the situation itself is the best guide. If you are responding to an assignment in a particular class, be sure you know just what your teacher expects of you. If you are writing a business letter or applying for a job, adapt your technique to the circumstances.

42A
Summaries

A summary (or abstract or précis) is your condensation of what someone else has written. If you are assigned something to summarize, remember that the watchword is accuracy: you are not expected to criticize, endorse, or react in any way to the material, but simply to condense it.

There are several ways to ensure that a summary is accurate. First, make sure that you fully understand what you are summarizing. Look up unfamiliar terms, carefully trace the writer's logic, or even do additional reading to understand the issues the writer is discussing. If the material is complicated, outline it just to make sure you know how everything fits together. Be alert to anything that seems unconnected with the rest of the argument: it is possible you have not grasped the writer's purpose; a little more thought and everything may fall into place.

In composing the summary, you should put the writer's ideas in your own words. That will make it easier for you to keep your summary coherent and readable, and it will also convince your instructor that you really understand what the original says. Put any phrases or sentences from the original in quotation marks and make sure they fit grammatically into the passages written in your own words.

Keep some distance between yourself and the author you are summarizing, and make clear that you are following someone else's lead by using phrases like "according to the article" or "Smith [the author] maintains."

Finally, your summary should reflect the organization of the original. The author's points should be reproduced in the original order and with a roughly proportionate amount of development. Distinguish essential points, and indicate the kinds of evidence the author offers.

42B
Book reports

A book report includes a summary, but generally other elements as well. Summarizing a book is essentially the same as summarizing a shorter piece, but it is a more selective process. Using the title, the table of contents, and any other guides, such as prefaces or author's notes, identify the main purpose of the book and make it the keystone of your summary. You will not have space for a step-by-step consideration of the book's content, so limit the summary to the author's thesis and the major ways in which he supports it.

The other elements in the book report depend on your instructor. You might be asked to include background information on the author, your own estimate of the value of the work, or even a critique of the way it is written. The reference works listed in Chapter 36 can help you find out about the author's background. If you have to evaluate his work, such sources as *Book Review Digest* and the periodical indexes will lead you to other people's ideas on the subject, ideas which may help you focus your own reactions.

Organizing a book report is not difficult. Whatever background information you include should come first, then the summary. After you have explained about the author and what he has to say, begin any evaluating the assignment may call for. The advantage of this organization is that the factual material will be there to refer to and you will have fully grasped it *before* you start making final judgments.

Most college-level book reports call for some evaluation. Make sure you know what you are supposed to evaluate. If the assignment calls on you to consider the author's argument, it would be beside the point to discuss his style. Instead, you would have to test his logic and persuasiveness: Is the evidence sufficient and convincing? Are there any questionable assumptions underlying the argument? Are the conclusions valid? On the other hand, if the assignment asked you to evaluate style, it would be irrelevant to focus on the author's opinions.

Always support your evaluations with specific evidence. Nothing is less convincing than unsupported opinions like "This is the best book I have ever read" or "The author's style is very confusing." Are the author's arguments illogical? Describe them specifically and show where the fault lies. Is the style exceptionally good? Quote a few outstanding passages to illustrate and prove the point. The more evidence you can provide for your opinions, the better.

Exercise 42-1.

1. Write a two-hundred-word summary of the following essay, "The Papaw: a Tropical Fruit Come North," from Euell Gibbons' 1962 book *Stalking the Wild Asparagus:*

The Papaw looks, tastes and smells like a tropical fruit, although it grows wild as far north as Michigan. It ranges from New York to Florida, and west to Nebraska and all the way down to Texas. Local names are False Banana, Michigan Banana and Custard Apple. All its relatives are tropical fruits, for the papaw is the only member of the *Annonaceae,* or Custard Apple Family, found growing outside the tropics.

The papaw is a small, slender tree, usually eight to twelve feet tall, but occasionally reaching twenty-five or thirty feet, but even these tallest ones will have a trunk diameter of less than six inches. It has large leaves, up to a foot long by five inches wide. These leaves are shaped like lance heads with the broadest part out near the point and tapering toward the base, where they are attached to the twigs with short leafstalks. They have entire margins, are dark green above and whitish underneath.

The flowers, which appear with the leaves in late April or May, are peculiar. They have six petals in two sets, the outer three larger and flattened out, and the inner ones standing more erect and forming a cup with three points. These flowers are about an inch and a half in diameter and are at first green, but turn purple before falling off.

The mature fruit is three to five inches long and is slenderly kidney-shaped, with a smooth yellowish-green skin which turns brown a few days after the fruit is picked. Papaws have large, brown seeds which are surrounded by the sweet and highly flavored yellow pulp. In Indiana, I once heard someone ask a Hoosier lad what papaws tasted like. Since flavors are notoriously hard to describe, his answer surprised me by its preciseness. He said, "They taste like mixed bananers and pears, and feel like sweet pertaters in your mouth." I can't improve on that description.

The fruit usually falls from the tree when mature, and the best papaws are often gathered from the ground. Boys, and those first making the acquaintance of this fruit, usually prefer it dead ripe and very soft. When I was a boy I liked it this way, but after years of eating this luscious wild fruit, I have come to prefer it ripe but still somewhat firm. We used to gather papaws by the basketful and bury them among the oats in the bin to let them ripen to our taste.

Ripe papaws have a heavy sweet fragrance that seems pleasant at first, but if one is continuously subjected to this aroma for several days it becomes cloying. For this reason papaws should never be ripened in the house. The sweet odor will permeate every room. I have known people to be turned against the fruit from having to smell it too long.

Nearly all the papaws gathered in this country are eaten out of hand as fresh fruit. One can, however, cook papaws, or combine them with other materials to make some fancy and delicious desserts. The simplest way to cook papaws is to bake them in their skins. It's a method which I don't recommend too highly, but there are people who relish baked papaws. My own favorite papaw preparation is a fluffy mixture that can be used as pie filling or served in parfait glasses.

In a saucepan, mix together ½ cup of brown sugar, 1 envelope unflavored gelatin and ½ teaspoon of salt. Stir into this ⅔ cup of milk and 3 slightly beaten egg yolks. Cook and stir the mixture until it comes to a boil. Remove from the fire and stir in 1 full cup of papaw pulp. Chill until it mounds slightly when spooned. This will take 20 to 30 minutes in the refrigerator. Shortly before the mixture is sufficiently set, beat the 3 egg whites until they form soft peaks, then gradually add ¼ cup of sugar, beating until stiff peaks form. Fold the partly set papaw mixture thoroughly into the egg whites. Pour into a 9-inch graham-cracker crust, or into parfait glasses and chill until firm. Then lock the doors to keep the neighbors out.

2. Imagine that the papaw essay was a whole book and write a book report on it. Include some information about the author, your summary, and a discussion of the effectiveness of Gibbons' style in your report. Support and illustrate what you say about style.

42C
Business letters

42C.1. Business Letter Form.   Much of the writing people do through-out their lives concerns business—placing orders, making complaints, bidding on contracts, applying for jobs. A lot of the world's work is done through the mails, and business correspondence has become highly conventionalized. Whenever you write to an organization or to someone you do not know well on a matter of business, you will improve your chances of success by observing these conventions.

Here is a typical piece of business correspondence with labels to identify the component parts. It is a good example of how a business letter ought to look.

erhead {

SELWYN TRANSFER, INC.
1704 West Dearing Street   Ann Arbor, Michigan 48104   } *The heading*

May 28, 1983

Arthur Tangley
Meller, Pierce, and Globe
456 Weltmont
Ann Arbor, Michigan 48104   } *The inside address*

Mr. Tangley: } *The salutation*

Carstairs, Fennel, and Associates of 67 Fairfax Place, Dearborn, Michigan 48128 are making their usual audit of our accounts, and we will appreciate your providing them full information on the following matters as of June 10, 1983.

First, a statement of all pending or threatened litigation that you are handling for our company, including a description of how each matter now stands and how each case will be managed. If it seems likely   } *The body*

391

in your professional opinion that any of this
litigation will produce an outcome unfavorable to our
firm, please include also an estimate of our potential
losses, including court costs and legal fees.

Second, any explanation or reservations you consider
necessary concerning our statement to Carstairs,
Fennel, and Associates that there are no unasserted
claims against our company that are likely to be
activated or, if activated, are likely to result in an
outcome unfavorable to us.

The audit is scheduled for completion by June 30,
1983, so we will appreciate it if you can get your
reply to Carstairs, Fennel, and Associates on or
before that date.

Complimentary close

Very truly yours,   *Signature*

The signature block   George Herman Selwyn

George Herman Selwyn   *Signature identification*

GHS:jc — *Initials of writer and typist*
cc: Carstairs, Fennel, and Associates } *Notation of carbon copies or enclosures*

The Heading.   The heading of the letter should include your full address
and the date. If you use letterhead stationery, all you need to supply is
the date. Put it over toward the right margin two or three lines below the
letterhead. If you have no letterhead stationery, put all this information
in a block at the top right of the page:

Selwyn Transfer, Inc.
1704 West Dearing Street
Ann Arbor, Michigan 48104
May 28, 1983

The Inside Address.   The inside address, identical with the address on
the outside of the envelope, is placed flush with the left margin of the
letter, usually two lines below the last line of the heading. If the letter is
short, though, the inside address can be placed lower to help balance the
page.

The Salutation.   The salutation is on the left margin, two lines below
the inside address. You may include the conventional *Dear* in the salutation,

but more and more writers use just the name of the person to whom they are writing. If you do not know who will read your letter, start with "Gentlemen:" In personal letters the salutation is often followed by a comma, but a colon is customary in business correspondence.

The Body.   The body of the letter starts two lines below the salutation. It is single-spaced unless the letter is only a few lines long, in which case it can be double-spaced. Do not indent paragraphs; instead, start everything flush with the left margin. Single-space the paragraphs, and double-space between them. If the letter runs more than one page, use another sheet; never write on both sides of the same sheet.

The Signature Block.   Instead of "Very truly yours," you may use "Sincerely yours," "Cordially yours," or just "Yours." Your signature should go above a typed version of your name. Leave about four spaces between the complimentary close and the typed name for the signature.

Initials, Copies, and Enclosures.   At the very bottom of the letter, two lines below the typed signature and flush left, the initials of the author of the letter (in capitals) are followed by a colon and the initials of the typist (in lower case); these initials are unnecessary when the author and typist are one. On the other hand, the person you are addressing should know if you are sending a copy of the letter to someone else. In the example letter, George Selwyn indicates to his attorney that a copy of the letter is going to the auditors, Carstairs, Fennel, and Associates. If Mr. Selwyn had enclosed some additional documents in the envelope with his letter, he would have added the word "enclosure" or "enclosures" on the line just beneath this copy notation so that the people handling the letter would know that something more was to go in the envelope and Mr. Tangley would know that something had been left out if they forgot.

42C.2. Organization and Style.   For the sake of efficiency, the organization of business letters is almost as conventional as their form. The sample letter opens with the reason for writing: an audit is taking place; information is needed. The next two paragraphs explain the precise information the writer is requesting, an account of current or forseeable lawsuits and their probable outcomes, and the attorney's reaction to Selwyn's statement that he has nothing to fear from previous liabilities. The last paragraph is a request for specific action: the audit is to be finished by June 30, so the attorney should get his reply to the auditors by that date.

This letter is a good model: in business correspondence, explain quickly why you are writing; develop one short paragraph for each major point; and close by telling the reader just what you want him to do.

The style of your business letters should be that of good writing in general: precise, economical, and natural to the writer. Some business writers might write things like this:

> Pursuant to our informal conferring on the occasion of the recent meeting of the City Council in regards the issuance of a joint comunique advising

the need for more adequate landfill facilities, I have decided in the negative on the matter of my participation in same.

If you can boil the meaning—"I don't want to sign your letter about the city dump"—out of this sentence, congratulations. Every effort the writer makes to sound "formal" or "businesslike" takes him further from the first goal of good business writing: efficient communication.

Always try to be courteous and tactful. Business dealings can generate ill-will and impatience, but a careful writer will never let such emotions infect the tone of his correspondence. Even serious complaints can be expressed tactfully, and the effort is worth making: a hot-headed or sarcastic letter is likely to bring out the stubbornness in its recipient. One that is calm and careful to assume the best, on the other hand, increases the probability of a favorable response.

Exercise 42-2. Analyze the style and organization of these business letters:

A. Gentlemen:

Here I am sitting in my bathtub and the lights go out. No one else is at home so I have to go dripping down to the basement to change the fuse. And not one of the little fuses, either. The big one on the top. I had a spare; I'm very careful about things like that. But it was an inconvenience.

Besides, none of the little fuses were burnt out. Now how can the big fuse blow when the little ones are okay? What kind of garbage are you selling? I want my $2.56 back and an apology.

Cordially yours,

A. Piedmont Lucas

A. Piedmont Lucas

B. Dear Mr. Piedmont,

I am in receipt of your missive dated 14 November of the present year. I regret to inform you that institutional policy militates against your final request inasmuch as the information you supply is not only incomplete but wholly unsubstantiated. To bring your claim to a favorable termination, my firm will require the part number and order code of the fuse in

question, date of installation, and date of failure.
We will also require the damaged part itself, to be
inspected for evidence of tampering or abuse. Should
your claim be allowed, we will reimburse any
acceptable shipping and packing costs.

If these terms do not meet with your approval, address
all further correspondence in the matter to our legal
department.

Very truly yours,

Fenwicke O. Hardesty

Fenwicke O. Hardesty

C. Miss Holsapple:

They tell me you are the one who makes the final
decision on refunds at your store. I hope you will do
right because, as you know, widows on fixed incomes
cannot afford to waste anything, and I am out $79.86
for a set of everyday dishes that chipped in my
dishwasher.

I would never put my good china in the dishwasher, of
course, but shouldn't ironstone hold up better? Mrs.
Johnston next door puts hers in all the time, and they
never chipped yet. Maybe the dishes were defective.
They didn't say anything about dishwashers on the
back, but what are you supposed to expect? I bought
them in your Hampton Road store.

They tell me I need to know the date. Well it was at
the beginning of February so you can see it didn't
take long for them to start chipping. I threw away the
sales slip but I can find my canceled check. The
pattern was called "Arabella." The dishes were on
sale, but that should not matter because they are
definitely too weak for the dishwasher. If you don't
make this good, none of my friends will ever shop in
your store again.

Sincerely,

(Mrs.) Lyda Melford

Lyda Melford

D. Dear Mrs. Melford:

Of course we will refund the $79.86 you paid for the
dishes you bought from us. I am only sorry it took so
long to put the matter right. You should get a check
for the full amount in the mail by the middle of next
week.

Yours,

Barbara Holsapple

Barbara Holsapple

42D
Résumés and letters of application

Just about everybody applies for a job at some time or another, and
often the application takes the form of a letter accompanied by a résumé.
The résumé is an outline of your educational and professional background,
and of your interests. The letter covers much of the same ground but brings
the résumé to life and points it at a particular reader.

42D.1. The Résumé.   The important points to consider in making up
a résumé are organization, facts, and clarity. Here is a sample to consider:

<u>John Adam Rackham</u>

453 Kenton   Age: 24
Austin, Texas 78705   Ht: 5-11 Wt: 147
Code 512 478-0983   Married, no children

<u>Education</u>:

  M.S. in Chemistry, University of Texas at Austin,
    June 1982; University Fellowship, 1980-82. Special
    study of toxic gases, Fall 1980; results published
    in the graduate honors bulletin, Spring 1981.

  B.S. with double major in Chemistry and Physics,
    University of Missouri at Kansas City, June 1978.
    Four semesters on Dean's List with a science grade-
    point average of 3.80. President, 1977-78, of the
    Physics Honors Society.

  Attended Xavier University, Cincinnati, Ohio, 1974-
    76. Awarded an Archbishop Sylvestris Scarne
    Scholarship, Fall 1974.

Reitz Memorial High School, Evansville, Indiana.
National Honor Society.

Experience:

Lab and research assistant, Chemistry Department,
University of Texas at Austin, January 1979–June
1981.

Desk clerk, Hilton Inn East, 17337 Independence
Ave., Kansas City, Missouri 64112, August 1977–May
1978.

Publications:

"The Effects of Microconcentrations of Toxic Gases
on Conifers," University of Texas Graduate Honors
Bulletin, 7 (Spring 1981), 183–96.

Interests:

Rock climbing, amateur theatricals, Bluegrass music,
Abyssinian cats, photography.

Organizations:

Student member of the American Chemical Society and
the National Society of Federated Physical Sciences.
Member of the National Chemical Honor Society.
Regional secretary of the Abyssinian Cat Breeders'
Association.

References:

Professor Mark Easterling
Department of Chemistry
University of Texas at Austin
Austin, Texas 78705

Professor Myra Halpert
Physics Department
University of Missouri at Kansas City
Kansas City, Missouri 64115

Mr. George Croaker, Manager
Hilton Inn East
17337 Independence Ave.
Kansas City, Missouri 64112

The categories of information that go into a résumé vary. Other things you could include might be military service, sports achievements, or civic awards and recognitions. Notice that "Education" and "Experience," are presented on a last-to-first basis: the writer starts with his most recent school, degree, or job, and works back from there.

This writer also includes three references (people who will vouch for his ability and character) in his résumé. Before he listed them, though, he wrote to each one asking permission. He limited his choices to people who would give him a good evaluation, and who could cover different aspects of his background. The two professors represent different departments at his two most important schools, and he has also included his old boss from the Hilton Inn to show that he could make a good impression in the working world as well as in the academic one.

Exercise 42-3. Write a résumé of your own, including in it all the information that might appeal to an employer.

42D.1. The Letter of Application.   Most people make up one résumé and send copies to every employer they are interested in. But while the résumé may be only a carbon or photocopy, each cover letter should be a typed original. The duplicated résumé tells a prospective employer that you are organized and efficient in your efforts to find a job; the original cover letter suggests you are making an extra effort to get that particular job.

The letter should follow all the conventions of business letters, with special attention to the opening and closing paragraphs, which give you a chance to aim the letter directly at a particular employer. Anything you can do in these paragraphs to show special interest in the position will work in your favor. Here is a letter that might have been sent out with the example résumé given earlier:

453 Kenton
Austin, Texas 78705
June 21, 1982

Aaron B. Benton, President
Benton Polymers
48 Dunster-Kelly Lane
Cambridge, Massachusetts 02138

Dear Mr. Benton:

Dr. Mark Easterling, my major professor here at the University of Texas, suggested I write to you about the current opening for a junior chemist in your expanded research department. Dr. Easterling tells me he has consulted with your firm, and he thinks I would fit in well there. He speaks very highly of the challenging research program you have underway and the close-knit cooperation of your excellent research staff.

With the help of a University Fellowship, I have just completed my M.S. degree and was lucky enough to see my special project with Dr. Easterling, "The Effects of Microconcentrations of Toxic Gases on Conifers," published in the University of Texas Graduate Honors Bulletin. Before that I had studied physics and chemistry at the University of Missouri at Kansas City.

My previous work experience includes two very different kinds of jobs--lab and research assistant here at Texas and night desk clerk at the Hilton Inn East in Kansas City. I think my lab experience will be invaluable to my work as a researcher, and I hope that the sense of responsibility I gained at the Hilton will help out too.

I have been active in several professional societies and look forward to keeping my memberships alive in the future. My other interests are rather wide. My wife and I are especially enthusiastic about rock climbing and exhibiting and breeding our own linebred strain of Abyssinian cats.

Cambridge is a long way from Austin, but the trip takes only about five hours by air. If you think I have the sort of qualifications your firm needs, I can arrange to be present for an interview any day the week of July 5. I look forward to hearing from you by then.

Sincerely yours,

John Adam Rackham

John Adam Rackham

Notice that in the opening paragraph the writer establishes a personal connection with the business he is applying to through his particular mention of Professor Easterling, whose name also appears, of course, in the list of references on the résumé. The conclusion sounds this personal note again, making the letter seem specifically written for Benton Polymers. If Professor Easterling had not offered such a good opening, the writer could have still achieved a personal touch by stressing his interest in the particular work and the outstanding reputation (or even the geographical location) of the company he was applying to.

The tone of the letter is polite and interested without being overly humble or aggressive. The writer offers his achievements and connections as proof of his ability; he neither begs for the job, nor pretends he is the answer to a chemical company's prayers. Instead, he projects a very realistic estimate of his value to the company and a sincere interest in working there.

The conclusion of the letter ends as any good business letter should—by letting Mr. Benton know what he is supposed to do. The writer wants to come to Cambridge and has set aside the week of July 5 for interviews. Now it is up to Mr. Benton to decide if he wants to offer an invitation. He may write back suggesting another time, or he may decide that he does not want to interview the writer at all. Whatever the case, the writer expects to be notified in a reasonable time.

> *Exercise 42-4.* Write two letters of application to go with the résumé you wrote earlier. In one, apply for part-time work in the library of your school. (Find out who on your campus actually handles such applications and address the letter accordingly.) In the second letter, write to a firm in your college town, asking for full-time summer work. Personalize each letter, and be sure to mention the dates and times when you will be available for an interview and when you will be able to work.

43   A Glossary of Grammatical and Rhetorical Terms

This glossary provides brief definitions of grammatical and rhetorical terms frequently used by instructors commenting on student essays. Cross references indicate the section of the text in which the term is discussed. Terms that have their own headings in the glossary are printed in boldface.

absolute phrase. A modifying phrase, usually consisting of a NOUN or other SUBSTANTIVE followed by a PARTICIPLE. An absolute phrase modifies an entire CLAUSE or SENTENCE. Absolute phrases are set off from their clauses by punctuation; they are not joined by CONNECTORS. When used as the participle in an absolute phrase, the word *being* is sometimes omitted:

> *The snow deepening,* we started for home.
>
> She salted the water, *the lobster waiting in its box.*
>
> *Her father ill,* she entertained his cronies herself. (*being* omitted)

abstract and concrete nouns. See NOUN.

acronym. A name formed from the beginning letters of the words in the title of an organization, invention, technique, or similar entity: UNICEF (United Nations International Children's Emergency Fund); COBOL (Common Business Oriented Language).

active voice. See VERB.

adjectival. Words or word groups, other than true ADJECTIVES, used to modify NOUNS or other SUBSTANTIVES:

> Her *ballpoint* pen was leaking. (noun adjectival)
>
> I want the one *in the display case.* (prepositional phrase)

401

We heard laughter *echoing in the hall.* (participial phrase)

The man *we saw* was much fatter. (adjectival clause)

adjectival clause.   See CLAUSE.

adjectival phrase.   See PHRASE.

adjective.   A word whose function is to modify NOUNS or other SUB-STANTIVES. Aside from descriptive adjectives that name qualities (*solid, fast, weak*), adjectives also include such subtypes as ARTICLES, possessives, and PROPER, DEMONSTRATIVE, and INTERROGATIVE ADJECTIVES:

What French painter sold his last work to a man with that name?

Most adjectives are capable of COMPARISON to show differences in DE-GREE: *good, better, best; strong, stronger, strongest; intelligent, less intelligent, least intelligent.*

See 2D.

adverb.   A word that functions to modify a VERB, an ADJECTIVE, another adverb, or a whole CLAUSE or SENTENCE.

Finally, heavily loaded trucks *quickly* destroy even *very well* constructed roads.

Any one-word modifier that does not modify a NOUN or other SUBSTAN-TIVE is an adverb.

See 2E.

adverbial.   Words or word groups, other than true ADVERBS, used to modify VERBS, ADJECTIVES, ADVERBS, or whole CLAUSES or SEN-TENCES.

We started *home.* (noun used adverbially)

She thinks they hiked *up the creek.* (prepositional phrase)

Where was he *when the lights went out?* (adverbial clause)

adverbial clause.   See CLAUSE.

adverbial conjunction.   See CONJUNCTIVE ADVERB.

adverbial phrase.   See PHRASE.

agreement.   The requirement that SUBJECTS and VERBS match each other in NUMBER and that PRONOUNS and their ANTECEDENTS match in number and GENDER.

My *uncle wants his* money now. (*Wants* agrees with *uncle* in number; *his* agrees with *uncle* in number and gender.)

See Chapters 5–6.

antecedent.   The NOUN or other SUBSTANTIVE to which a PRO-NOUN refers.

> The *lawyers* told *Connie they* could get *her* acquitted. (*Lawyers* is the anteced-
> ent of *they*; *Connie* of *her*.)

See Chapters 6–7.

appositive.   A word or word group that follows a NOUN or other SUB-STANTIVE. An appositive defines, identifies, or renames the word it follows. All appositives are grammatically equal to the words they identify:

> Hidalgo, *a seven year old quarter horse*, was her obsession.

> A third man, *Thompson*, was covering the entrance.

appropriateness (diction).   A general term which refers to choosing language best suited to the audience and subject. English offers a broad range of choices in diction:

Formal English has an elevated form of diction appropriate only for special purposes, such as international treaties, manifestoes, or liturgical solemnities. In formal English, writing is "composing"; a lamp is a "lighting fixture"; and a church service is a "liturgical solemnity." *Informal, colloquial English* is diction at the level of everyday speech. Contractions are acceptable ("I'll," "didn't"), as are shortened forms ("TV," "OK," "comp class"); young men are "guys," to miss class is to "cut," and to be fired is to "get axed." At a still more informal level are nonstandard types of diction such as *slang* and *dialect*. *Slang* refers to catchwords that have not been widely accepted into the language. Some examples are "into" (as in "he's into yoga"), "rip off," "cool it," and "hassle." *Dialects* are patterns of language associated with regional, economic, or ethnic groups. "Y'all," for instance, is a well-known feature of Southern dialects.

Between the two extremes of formal and informal English is *standard English*, the language of careful, popular writing, of good newspapers, and of most books. Written *standard English* is carefully edited and, for the most part, should lean toward the standards of usage for *formal English*. When spoken, *standard English* tends toward the *colloquial*.

For most college writing, standard, edited English is appropriate, while informal or colloquial English, dialect, or slang are nonstandard or unacceptable.

article.   The definite article is the word *the*, and the indefinite articles are *a* and *an*. These words, which are also called determiners, are a special class of adjectives used to signal that a NOUN or other SUBSTANTIVE will soon appear in the sentence:

> *The* running faucet was *a* real annoyance.

The is used with a noun that names a particular or definite person, place, or thing ("*the* lady," "*the* neighborhood," "*the* jacket"). *A* and *an* introduce nouns that are less definite ("*a* lady," "*a* neighborhood," "*a* jacket"). *A* is used when the next word in the sentence starts with a consonant sound (*"a* car," *"a* wallet"). *An* is used when the next word begins with a vowel sound (*"an* epic," *"an* orange").

auxiliary verb.   Auxiliaries are helping verbs that precede a MAIN VERB to establish a particular TENSE, MOOD, or VOICE: *"shall* sit," *"has* settled," *"might have been* bamboozled." MODAL AUXILIARIES such as *can, could, may, might, must, ought, shall, should, will,* and *would* indicate obligation, willingness, capability, or other special shades of meaning: "I *should* help pack"; "She *can* hit the bull's eye."

See 2A, and Chapters 11–12.

awkwardness.   A general term to describe faulty sentence structure. One kind of awkwardness results from the mixing of two constructions in one sentence:

> There are many reasons for favoring capital punishment is sensible. (awkward)

> There are many sensible reasons for favoring capital punishment. (revised)

Awkwardness also results when a clear relationship between the subject and verb of a sentence is not maintained:

> The *officers* of the club *enlarged* the membership. (awkward)

> The *officers* of the club *voted* to enlarge the membership. (revised)

See 8E, 15F.

cardinal and ordinal numbers.   *Cardinal* numbers are ones such as *one, two, three* that are used for counting or expressing amounts. *Ordinal* numbers—such as *first, second, third*—indicate the order of things in a sequence.

case.   A grammatical property of NOUNS and other SUBSTANTIVES, based on the function of the word in its sentence. There are three cases in English: the *Nominative* or *Subjective* case, used primarily for SUBJECTS and subject COMPLEMENTS; the *Objective* case, used for OBJECTS of verbs, verbals, or prepositions and for objective complements and subjects of INFINITIVES; and the *Possessive* case, used to show possession and for subjects of GERUNDS. Nouns and many pronouns have a single or *common* form for both the nominative and objective cases; they change form only in the possessive:

Nominative   Possessive   Objective

Louise shared *Louise's* secret only with *Louise.*

The personal pronouns and *who* and *whoever* have separate forms for each case:

Nominative   Possessive   Objective

I want *my* officers to report directly to *me.*

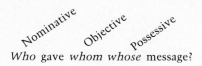

Who gave *whom whose* message?

See Chapter 13.

clause.   A clause is a group of related words that contains a SUBJECT and a PREDICATE. *Independent*, or *main*, clauses can stand alone as complete sentences. *Subordinate*, or *dependent*, clauses refer to or form parts of other clauses: they cannot stand alone. Subordinate clauses may do the work of adjectives, adverbs, or nouns:

Independent clause: Tyrone smelled gas.
Subordinate clauses: That was the day *that Tyrone smelled gas.* (*adjectival* clause)
      When Tyrone smelled gas, he relit the pilot light. (*adverbial* clause)
      She said *that Tyrone smelled gas.* (*noun* clause)

See Chapter 4.

cliché.   Phrases that have become stale through overuse. The dangerous thing about clichés is that they can *pop into your head before you know what's cooking,* and *the next thing you know* your paper is *filled to the brim* with vague, trite phrases.

coherence.   The existence of a clear, logical relationship between each part of an essay. Literally, the term means "sticking together." Essays should "stick together" from one sentence to the next and from paragraph to paragraph. Some common ways of achieving coherence are to limit essays to only one restricted subject, to organize your writing according to a logical pattern, to provide TRANSITIONS between sentences and paragraphs, and to repeat key phrases and words.

collective noun.   See NOUN.

colloquial.   Language appropriate to informal conversation but out of place in formal settings and in most written work. In the following sentence, for example, the verb-form *am gone to* and the IDIOM *what ails her* are colloquial:

I*'m gone to* find out *what ails her.*

Some teachers also consider CONTRACTIONS to be colloquial and unacceptable in written work.

comma fault, comma splice.   Linking two independent clauses with a comma and no conjunction.

I patted his knee right back, he had the grace to blush.

See Chapter 19.

common and proper nouns. See NOUN.

common gender. The practice (which many people find objectionable) of treating all ANTECEDENTS of unknown or mixed GENDER as masculine:

> Everyone raised *his* voice in a universal cry of relief.

Common gender can be avoided by using doubled reference pronouns:

> Everyone raised *his or her* voice in a universal cry of relief.

or by PLURALIZING the antecedent:

> The *people* all raised their voices in a universal cry of relief.

See Chapter 6.

comparative degree. See COMPARISON.

comparison. Changes in the form of adjectives and adverbs to indicate increasing or decreasing DEGREES of the quality named by the positive form of the word:

Positive degree:	ugly	bad	thoughtfully
Comparative degree:	uglier	worse	more thoughtfully
Superlative degree:	ugliest	worst	most thoughtfully

complement. A NOUN or other SUBSTANTIVE or an ADJECTIVE or ADJECTIVAL that follows or completes the meaning of a SUBJECT, OBJECT or VERB.

Subject Complements work through linking verbs to complete the sense of a subject. They may be substantives or adjectivals, and they can range from single words to whole clauses: "She seems *intelligent*"; "I am *the one who called yesterday*"; "The stew smelled *badly burned.*" Adjectival subject complements are also called PREDICATE ADJECTIVES, and substantive subject complements are known as PREDICATE NOUNS or PREDICATE NOMINATIVES.

Objective Complements follow and complete direct OBJECTS. They can also be substantive or adjectival, and they vary in length and construction: "They consider me *insane*"; "She called him her *hero*"; "We found Harvey *very insecure and deeply resentful.*"

Verb Complements are direct or indirect OBJECTS that complete the sense of the action conveyed by the verb: "Don collects *bottlecaps*"; "The nurse guessed *what I was hiding*"; "The mayor presented *Mr. Haspell a trophy.*"

complete predicate. See PREDICATE.

complete subject. See SUBJECT.

complex sentence. See SENTENCE.

compound-complex sentence. See SENTENCE.

compound elements.   Words or phrases made up of two or more equal components. *Compound words* include compound nouns such as *postman* or *cowgirl*, compound adjectives such as *old-fashioned* or *left-handed*, and compound prepositions such as *in pursuit of.* Compound constructions within sentences include compound subjects (*"He and I* are tired"), compound objects ("She hired *Teddy and Aretha*"), and compound PREDI-CATES ("The car *tore around the corner, shot up the street,* and *squealed to a stop"*).

compound sentence.   See SENTENCE.

compound word.   See COMPOUND ELEMENTS.

concrete noun.   See NOUN.

conjugation.   The form-changes a verb undergoes as it moves through the various tenses, persons, numbers, voices, and moods. The following, for example, is the active, indicative, present tense conjugation of "to be":

I am	we are
you are	you are
he, she, it is	they are

For a much more comprehensive listing of forms, see Chapters 11 and 12.

conjunction.   A linking word or CONNECTOR that brings together and relates parts of sentences. *Coordinating conjunctions—and, but, or, nor, for, so,* and *yet*—connect grammatical equals: "She *and* Alex were weary *but* excited"; "The past is important, *for* it determines the future." Correlatives like *neither . . . nor,* or *both . . . and* are coordinating conjunctions that work in pairs: *"Not only* Romans *but also* Greeks contributed to 'Roman Art.' "

Subordinating conjunctions like *because, whether, since, if* or *while* show the subordinate status of dependent clauses: *"Because* it was raining, I put off my usual jog."

See 2G.

conjunctive adverb.   An adverb that connects and relates two main CLAUSES.

Frank was widely known as a weather forecaster; *however,* his forecasts were seldom accurate.

Other common conjunctive adverbs include *consequently, furthermore, likewise, moreover, nevertheless, then, therefore,* and *thus.*

See 2E, 10C 19B, 20C.

connector (connective).   Words or phrases that link words, PHRASES, CLAUSES, or SENTENCES. Common connectors are CONJUNC-TIONS, CONJUNCTIVE ADVERBS, and PREPOSITIONS.

connotation.   The emotional or judgmental meaning associated with some words. "Nature" and "natural" (as advertising writers know) communicate positive connotations; "artificial" is negative. The difference between describing a car as "previously owned" instead of "used," or a dog as a "mixed breed" instead of a "mutt" is attributable to the various connotations of these words. The connotative meaning of a word is another layer of meaning beyond its *denotation*, its literal "dictionary" meaning. Denotatively, a "kitten" is just a "young cat," but connotatively it has all sorts of soft, cuddly, positive associations.

construction.   A general term used to refer to a group of words forming a grammatical unit such as a SENTENCE, CLAUSE, or PHRASE.

contraction.   The omission of sounds or letters from a word or group of words. In writing, the omission is indicated by an apostrophe, as in *I'll didn't, it's.*

See 34G.

coordinating conjunction.   See CONJUNCTION.

coordination.   Linking grammatically equal constructions through words that indicate the relationship between the constructions. For example, COORDINATING CONJUNCTIONS may show coordination between equal words:

Love and *lust* have been confused before.

between PHRASES:

"To be or *not to be.* . . . *"*

or between CLAUSES:

The peace treaty was welcomed by all, but *it was violated within twenty-four hours.*

See Chapter 14.

correlative conjunction.   See CONJUNCTION.

count and mass nouns.   See NOUN.

dangling modifier.   A MODIFIER that is not linked properly to the word or construction it modifies.

Dangling: *Backfiring through the carburetor, I* chugged to a halt.

Revised: *Backfiring through the carburetor, my car* chugged to a halt.

See Chapter 9.

declension.   The INFLECTION of NOUNS and PRONOUNS to show CASE.
Nouns change forms only for the *possessive* case:

Nominative	Objective	Possessive
student	student	student's, students'

Personal pronouns and *who* and *whoever* have different forms for each case:

Nominative	Objective	Possessive
I	me	my, mine
they	them	their, theirs
who	whom	whose

definite article.   See ARTICLE.

degree.   See COMPARISON.

demonstrative adjectives and pronouns.   *This, that, these,* and *those* are pointing words which may function as ADJECTIVES or PRONOUNS.

Demonstrative Adjective: *Those* automobiles have faulty brakes.

Demonstrative Pronoun: *This* is my country.

See 2C, 2D, and 6A.

denotation.   See CONNOTATION.

dependent clause.   See CLAUSE.

determiners.   Words (usually ARTICLES, PRONOUNS, and ADJECTIVES) which signal that a following word is a noun.

The scissors; *her* pocketbook; *fewer* protests.

development.   The specific details, evidence, reasons or explanation provided to support a thesis of an essay or a topic sentence of a paragraph. Some common methods of developing ideas in writing include the following:

1. Illustration—citing specific examples (the most common form of development) to prove or support the thesis or topic sentence. Examples may be either brief or extended (a long example). A story told to illustrate a point is an *anecdote.*
2. Division and Classification—dividing a subject into categories and putting individual units in the categories. For example, students can be divided into the categories of freshman, sophomore, junior, and senior on the basis of academic progress. Note that the basis of a classification system must be consistent—it would be inconsistent to classify students into the groups freshman, serious, left-handed, and wealthy, for then the characteristic on which the classification is based would shift with each new group.
3. Comparison and Contrast—showing how things are alike (comparison) or how they are different (contrast). A comparison can also refer to both similarities and differences. In developing paragraphs and essays, comparison/contrast may be arranged in a *block* pattern or in a *point-by-point* pattern. To develop the thesis that the U.S. and Russian space programs differ in three important ways, a writer

might develop three points about the U.S. program first and then develop the three points in the same order as they relate to the Russian program:

```
U.S. Space Program
Points 1. purpose
       2. support
       3. success
```

```
Russian Space Program
Points 1. purpose
       2. support
       3. success
```

or the writer could discuss both the U.S. program and the Russian at each point of comparison:

```
Point 1, purpose
  —U.S.
  —Russian
```

```
Point 2, support
  —U.S.
  —Russian
```

```
Point 3, success
  —U.S.
  —Russian
```

4. Analysis—explaining how something is done or works (process) or what caused something to happen (cause and effect). Explaining a process (such as baking a cake or getting a blood test) requires that each step be carefully noted in order. The most common pattern of cause and effect development is first to explain the effect (the consequences) and then to explain the cause(s) through citing evidence. Inexperienced writers sometimes oversimplify cause and effect relationships by failing to note multiple causes of complex events.

5. Definition—explaining the meaning of a term. An *extended* definition (as opposed to a formal definition of the sort found in dictionaries) can be developed in several different ways, including comparison and contrast, classification and division, and illustration. Sometimes it is helpful to give the background or *etymology* (history) of the term.

diction. A writer's choice of words. In order to make effective choices, a writer should be familiar with both denotative and connotative meanings of words, as well as the range of language options from the formal to the informal. Although a writer's diction will vary according to the purpose and audience of different pieces of writing, the choice should always be precise and clear. See APPROPRIATENESS, CONNOTATION, CLICHE, DIRECTNESS, JARGON, UNCLEAR EXPRESSIONS, and WORDINESS.

direct address.   A NOUN or PRONOUN, appearing parenthetically in a sentence, that names or refers to the person(s) addressed.

> Waiting for you, *Sylvia*, gives me time to ponder your faults.
>
> *Drivers*, start your engines.

See 24A.

direct and indirect quotation.   Direct quotation contains the exact words of a speaker or writer. Indirect quotation is a summary of those words:

> He said, "I refuse to testify, Senator." (direct)
>
> He told the senator that he would not testify. (indirect)

See 27A.

directness.   Selecting the simplest and most precise words to communicate the meaning intended. Directness is most often violated through vague diction and wordiness. See UNCLEAR EXPRESSIONS and WORDINESS.

direct object.   See OBJECT.

double negative.   Two negative words in the same construction. The pattern is usually nonstandard.

> He *didn't* have *no* paper in class.

ellipsis.   Omission of a word or words from a direct quotation, indicated by three spaced periods (. . .).

See 27H.

elliptical construction.   Omission of a word or words which can be supplied or understood from the context.

> Her car is newer than mine [is].
>
> The coffee was imported from Brazil; the radio [was imported] from Japan.

emphasis.   Constructing sentences, paragraphs, and essays so that important ideas are highlighted or stand out. Within essays, emphasis can be given through allotting more space to important topics. Key ideas can be emphasized by repeating them (in different words) several times in a paragraph or essay. Placing a significant topic last in a sequence or treating it last in an essay also serves to emphasize it. A *periodic sentence*, one in which the most important or dramatic piece of information is withheld until the end, can be used to achieve emphasis at the sentence level:

> After a night of determined and imaginative debauchery, Justin fell to his knees and prayed.

exactness.   See UNCLEAR EXPRESSIONS.

expletive.   *There* and *it* used at the beginning of a sentence, with the actual subject following the verb.

> *There* are always dandelions in my garden.
>
> *It* is scandalous the way some congressmen act.

See 1E.

finite and nonfinite verbs.   Finite verbs can function as the PREDI-CATE of a sentence and have special forms to distinguish person, number, tense, and mood. Finite verbs indicate specific occurrences:

> The bell *rings.*
> The bells *have been ringing* for an hour.

Nonfinite verbs (INFINITIVES, PARTICIPLES, and GERUNDS) indicate general actions and cannot serve as the complete predicate of a sentence. Instead, they function as (1) nouns, (2) adjectives, or (3) adverbs.

> *To run* a mile in four minutes is difficult. (noun)
>
> The swiftly *running* brook disappeared into a cave. (adjective)
>
> We waited *to see* the fireworks. (adverb)

See 2A.

formal English.   See APPROPRIATENESS.

fragment.   See SENTENCE FRAGMENT.

function word.   Words such as ARTICLES, PREPOSITIONS, CON-JUNCTIONS, and AUXILIARIES, which show the functions and grammatical relationships of other words in a sentence.

fused sentence.   Two independent CLAUSES joined without punctuation or a CONJUNCTION between them. Also called a run-on sentence.

> Jerry plays tennis I don't.

See 19C.

future perfect tense.   See TENSE.

future tense.   See TENSE.

gender.   The classification of a NOUN or PRONOUN according to sex—masculine, feminine, and neuter. Only a few nouns and pronouns in English have distinct forms based on gender (these words include such forms as *he, she, it, actor/actress, hero/heroine*).

gerund.   A NONFINITE VERB form ending in *-ing* that functions as a noun.

> *Smoking* is unhealthy. (gerund as subject)

She stopped *smoking*. (gerund as direct object)

See 2A, 3D.

helping verb. See AUXILIARY.

idiom. A conventional expression, the meaning of which is established through usage and which often makes little sense if interpreted word-for-word.

She *caught his eye* just as he entered the room.

Look me up when you're in town.

illogical comparison. An implied comparison between two things that cannot logically be compared.

Helen's attendance was better than last year.

Attendance is illogically compared to *year*. A revision makes the comparison clear:

Helen's attendance was better than it was last year.

See 16D.

imperative. See MOOD.

incomplete comparison. An implied comparison in which the basis for comparison is omitted:

Helen's attendance is much better. (Better than what?)

See 16B.

incomplete construction. A general term referring to careless omissions.

I have everything control now. (careless omission)

Burpsie Cola tastes better. (incomplete comparison)

See Chapter 16.

indefinite adjectives and pronouns. Indefinite adjectives do not specify clear limits (*several* times, *enough* food, *some* money); indefinite pronouns do not refer to specific people or things (*someone, anybody, everything*).

See 2C, 2D, 6C.

indefinite pronoun. See INDEFINITE ADJECTIVE AND PRONOUN.

independent clause. See CLAUSE.

indicative. See MOOD.

indirect object. See OBJECT.

indirect quotation.   See DIRECT AND INDIRECT QUOTATION.

infinitive.   A NONFINITE VERB form most often consisting of *to* followed by the present tense form of the verb. Infinitives function mainly as NOUNS, and sometimes as ADJECTIVES or ADVERBS.

> *To swim* in the Olympics was her dream. (noun)
>
> The time *to start* studying is now. (adjective)
>
> He came *to play.* (adverb)

See 2A, 3B.

inflection.   Changes in the form of words to indicate their various grammatical relationships. Words can modify their form with respect to CASE (*I, me*), GENDER (*he, she, it*), NUMBER (*table, tables*), and TENSE (*look, looked*). The ordered presentation of inflections for nouns and pronouns is called DECLENSION; for verbs, it is CONJUGATION; for adjectives, COMPARISON.

intensifier.   An ADVERB that adds emphasis to the word it modifies: *very* happy, *extremely* successful, *too* close.

See 2E.

intensive pronoun.   A pronoun ending with *-self* which adds emphasis to the noun it refers to.

> I did it *myself.* (emphasizes *I*)
>
> The Governor *himself* attended the ceremony. (emphasizes *Governor*)

interjection.   A part of speech that expresses an exclamation.

> *Wow! Hey! Ugh!*

See 2H.

interrogative adverbs and pronouns.   Words used to introduce questions. Interrogative adverbs include *where, when, why,* and *how;* interrogative pronouns include *who* (*whose, whom*), *which,* and *what.* Interrogative words which modify nouns are sometimes called *interrogative adjectives.*

> *Where* are you going? (interrogative adverb)
>
> *Who* rang the doorbell? (interrogative pronoun)
>
> *Which* python is yours? (interrogative adjective modifying *python*)

See 2C, 2E.

intransitive verb.   See VERB.

inversion.   Changing the normal word order of a phrase or sentence.

> Approaching were ominous, black clouds. (subject follows verb)

irregular verb.   A verb which forms its past TENSE and past PARTICI-
PLE through an internal change in the form of the word, whereas REGULAR
VERBS indicate shifts in tense through the addition of *-d,* or *-ed.* Some
common irregular verbs are *sing, sang, sung; do, did, done; break, broke,
broken; think, thought, thought.* Some regular verbs are *call, called, called;
play, played, played; ask, asked, asked.*

See Chapter 11.

jargon.   A specialized vocabulary used by a trade, profession, or other
identifiable group of people. Jargon is acceptable only in writing aimed at
specialists. An essay filled with references to *treadles, beaters, heddles,*
and *harnesses* might be fine for readers who knew all about weaving, but
it would not be acceptable for general audiences. Some types of jargon (for
example, that which sometimes shows up in government documents and
in reports by educators) are notorious for their inflated diction devoid of
content. These forms should, of course, be avoided.

linking verb.   A VERB that may connect the subject to a PREDICATE
NOMINATIVE or PREDICATE ADJECTIVE. The most common linking verb
is *be;* other linking verbs are *seem, become, remain, appear,* and the verbs
of the senses—*taste, smell, feel, sound,* and *look.*

She *was* jubilant.

He *remained* unmoved by my plea.

The casserole *smells* fishy.

See 1A, 1D.

logic.   Arriving at a valid conclusion through systematic reasoning. The
two main logical systems are *deductive* reasoning and *inductive* reasoning.
   Deductive reasoning is a process of basing a conclusion on a series of
premises or general statements arranged in a conventional pattern called a
syllogism:

All men are mortal. (Major premise)   A = B

Socrates is a man.   (Minor premise)   C = A

Socrates is a mortal. (Conclusion)   C = B

If the major and minor premises are valid, the conclusion should be too.
The following syllogism is based upon everyday reasoning:

All murder mysteries written by Arnault Bradden are gory. (major premise)

Vegematic Murders is a murder mystery by Arnault Bradden. (minor premise)

Vegematic Murders is gory. (conclusion)

   Inductive reasoning is a process of arriving at a conclusion through observing or collecting data. If on several different fishing trips you notice that
you catch the most trout in quiet water just at the edge of rapids, you
may add up these individual instances to a generalization about the feeding
habits of trout.

415

The scientific method is a carefully formulated and controlled version of inductive reasoning.

Good writing depends on sound logic, but not necessarily formal logic. For most writing assignments, sound logic can be achieved through providing sufficient evidence to support the conclusion or THESIS.

main clause.   An independent clause. See CLAUSE.

main verb.   The verb carrying the primary meaning in a verb phrase.

> Diablo had been *barking* ferociously.

mass noun.   See NOUN.

misplaced modifier.   A MODIFIER (usually an ADJECTIVAL or ADVERBIAL) positioned so that it appears to modify the wrong word or phrase.

> He gave Julia a geranium in a pot *that was blooming.* (misplaced)
>
> He gave Julia a geranium that was blooming in a pot. (revised)

See Chapter 8.

mixed construction.   An AWKWARDNESS in sentence structure resulting from joining two (or more) incompatible elements in a sentence.

> By just holding down the shutter release advances the film. (mixed)
>
> Just holding down the shutter release advances the film. (revised)
>
> By just holding down the shutter release, the photographer can advance the film. (revised)

See 15F.

modal auxiliary.   See AUXILIARY.

modifier.   A general term for any word or group of words which specifies, limits, or describes the meaning of another word or group of words. Modifiers function as ADJECTIVES or ADVERBS.

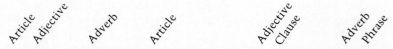

The last man firmly shut the door they had come through behind him.

See Chapters 8, 9, and 10.

mood.   The manner in which or attitude with which a verb is expressed, as indicated by its form. English has three moods: *indicative,* the most common because it expresses ordinary statements of fact ("It *is* raining"); *imperative,* used for expressing commands or requests (*"Fasten* your seatbelt."); and *subjunctive,* used to express a doubt, a desire, a possibility, a condition contrary to fact, or a hypothetical situation ("If I *were* you, I would leave now.").

See 12B, 15D.

nominal.   A word or group of words functioning as a NOUN. See NOUN CLAUSE and NOUN PHRASE.

nominative case.   See CASE.

nonfinite verb.   See FINITE AND NONFINITE VERBS.

nonrestrictive and restrictive modifiers.   A NONRESTRICTIVE MODIFIER provides nonessential information about the word or word-group it modifies. It may be omitted without changing the meaning of what it modifies. Nonrestrictive modifiers are set off by commas.

Jones, *who often camped in the area,* spotted the forest fire.

A RESTRICTIVE MODIFIER provides essential information about the word or word-group it modifies. Its omission changes the meaning of the construction. Restrictive modifiers are not set off by commas.

The camper *who started the fire* is under arrest.

See Chapter 23.

nonstandard english.   Language that does not conform to generally accepted usage. See APPROPRIATENESS.

noun.   A word that names a person, place, thing, event, or idea. Most nouns form plurals by adding *-s*, form possessive case by adding *'s*, and function as SUBJECTS or COMPLEMENTS. Nouns can be classified in the following categories:

Common Nouns: general names of broad classes (such as *book, explosion, idea*)
or
Proper Nouns: specific names (such as *London, Stonewall Jackson, Empire State Building*)

Abstract Nouns: names of ideas or qualities (such as *love, sentimentality, freedom*)
or
Concrete Nouns: names of things that can be sensed (such as *rose, water, pencil*)

Count Nouns: names of things that have both singular and plural forms (an egg, the eggs; a pen, the pens)
or
Mass Nouns: names of things that generally have only singular forms and cannot be modified by *a* or *an* (furniture, salt, courage)

Collective Nouns: names of entire groups of people or things (team, family, committee)

See 2B, 5F, 5G, 30C.

noun clause.   A subordinate CLAUSE that functions as a NOUN.

> *That they arrived at all* amazed us. (subject)
>
> He said *what was on his mind.* (direct object)

See 4B.1.

noun phrase.   A PHRASE consisting of a NOUN or PRONOUN and its modifiers.

> the steadily humming ice cream *freezer* (noun preceded by modifiers)

number.   The INFLECTION of NOUNS, PRONOUNS, VERBS, or DEMONSTRATIVE ADJECTIVES to indicate that they are singular (one) or plural (more than one).

> That boat is hers. (singular)
>
> Those boats are theirs. (plural)

See Chapters 5–6.

object.   A word or group of words that receives the action of a VERB or is governed by a verb or preposition. A *direct object* receives the action of a verb. An *indirect object* tells to whom or for whom the action received by the direct object is done. An *object of a preposition* generally completes the prepositional phrase.

> Glenda ordered a *drink.* (direct object)
>
> Glenda ordered *me* a drink. (indirect object)
>
> Glenda ordered me a drink with a *cherry* in *it.* (objects of prepositions)

See 1D, 3A.

objective case.   See CASE.

objective complement.   See COMPLEMENT.

object of preposition.   See OBJECT.

ordinal numbers.   See CARDINAL AND ORDINAL NUMBERS.

paradigm.   A set of all inflected forms of a word. A paradigm, for example, could show a noun DECLENSION:

> woman, women, woman's, women's

paragraph.   A unit of writing, signaled by the indentation of its first line, which serves to organize the writer's ideas. Paragraphs should be *unified* (treating only one main idea), *coherent* (showing a clear relationship of ideas from sentence to sentence—see COHERENCE), and *developed* (supporting the main idea through sufficient evidence or reasons—see DEVELOPMENT).

A paragraph usually consists of a main idea or generalization, called the

418

TOPIC SENTENCE, and several supporting details or explanations. The topic sentence is often placed first in the paragraph.

parallelism. Placing items of equivalent function and importance in the same kind of grammatical constructions.

> *Foolish* and *headstrong*, Sidney burst through the door.
>
> Alma was blessed *with friends, with health,* and *with contentment.*

Faulty parallelism results from placing items that are not of equivalent function or importance in parallel constructions:

> Sidney is *foolish, headstrong,* and *bursts through doors.*

See Chapter 14.

parenthetical element. A word or group of words inserted into and interrupting the thought of a construction.

> She still lives, *if I am not mistaken,* at the same address.
>
> I called her, but—*imagine this*—she hung up on me.

See Chapter 24.

participles. NONFINITE VERB forms, which may be *present participles*, ending in *-ing,* or *past participles*, ending in *-d, -ed, -t, -n, -en,* or formed by a vowel change (*done, rung*). *Participles* are used in VERB PHRASES and as MODIFIERS.

> Mike *was running* as fast as he could. (verb phrase)
>
> The *running* dogs of imperialism are unleashed. (adjectival modifier)

See 2A, 3C.

parts of speech. The classification of words according to form, function, and meaning. The traditional classifications are NOUN, PRONOUN, VERB, ADJECTIVE, ADVERB, PREPOSITION, CONJUNCTION, and INTERJECTION.

See Chapter 2.

passive voice. See VOICE.

past participle. See PARTICIPLES.

past perfect tense. See TENSE.

past tense. See TENSE.

person. The forms of PRONOUNS and VERBS which indicate whether one (or more) is speaking (first person—*I am, we are*); is spoken to (second person—*you are*); or is spoken about (third person—*he/she/it is, they are*). Verbs other than *to be* are inflected for person only in the third-person singular present indicative ("she reads").

See 2A, 2C, 5A.

personal pronouns.   Pronouns that indicate PERSON. In addition to being inflected for person (first, second, and third), personal pronouns have different forms for NUMBER (singular and plural) and CASE (nominative, objective, and possessive). For example, *we* is a first person, plural pronoun in the nominative case. Its objective case form is *us;* its possessive forms are *our* and *ours.* See 6B for a listing of all personal pronoun forms.

phrase.   A group of words forming a construction or grammatical unit that does not have a SUBJECT and a PREDICATE. See ADJECTIVAL PHRASE, ADVERBIAL PHRASE, PREPOSITION, VERB PHRASE, and Chapter 3.

plain form.   The uninflected form of verbs—such as *cut, run, read*—that appears in infinitives—*to cut, to run, to read*—or in dictionary entries.

positive degree.   See COMPARISON.

possessive case.   See CASE.

predicate.   The part of a sentence containing the MAIN VERB. The *simple predicate* consists of the main verb and its auxiliaries (if any); the *complete predicate* consists of the main verb, its AUXILIARIES, and its COMPLEMENTS and MODIFIERS:

> The students *had been studying all night for their history exam.*

> (*Had been studying* is the simple predicate; the simple predicate and all following words make up the complete predicate).

See 1A.

predicate adjective.   An adjective functioning as a subjective complement. See COMPLEMENT.

> She is *strong.*

predicate nominative or noun.   A noun functioning as a subject complement. See COMPLEMENT.

> She is a *banker.*

prefix.   One or more syllables attached to the beginning of a word. These additions affect the meaning of the word: "*un*aware," "*dis*temper," "*il*legal," "*mis*spell."

preposition.   A part of speech which generally precedes (in a *pre*-position) NOUNS, PRONOUNS, or NOUN PHRASES or CLAUSES which the preposition relates to some other part of the sentence. The preposition and its OBJECT form a *prepositional phrase:*

> He stared *at* the blinking light.
> (The preposition *at* connects its object, *light,* to the verb *stared*).

See 2F and 3A.

prepositional phrase.   See PREPOSITION.

present participle.   See PARTICIPLE.

present perfect tense.   See TENSE.

present tense.   See TENSE.

principal parts.   The three forms of a verb from which all TENSE forms are derived: the present infinitive (*go, jump*), past (*went, jumped*), and past participle (*gone, jumped*).

See Chapter 11.

progressive.   See TENSE.

pronoun.   A part of speech which functions in the place of a noun. See DEMONSTRATIVE ADJECTIVES AND PRONOUNS, INDEFINITE ADJECTIVES AND PRONOUNS, INTENSIVE PRONOUNS, INTERROGATIVE ADVERBS AND PRONOUNS, PERSONAL PRONOUNS, REFLEXIVE PRONOUNS, and RELATIVE PRONOUNS.

See 2C and Chapter 6.

proper adjective.   An adjective derived from a proper noun (*"Irish* tweed," *"Mexican* bean beetle").

See 30D.

proper noun.   See NOUN.

reflexive pronoun.   A pronoun ending in *-self* or *-selves*. It functions as an object, and its ANTECEDENT is the subject of the verb:

She wrapped *herself* in the blanket. (The antecedent of *herself* is *She*)

regular verb.   See IRREGULAR VERB.

relative adjective.   An adjective used to introduce a RELATIVE CLAUSE. The relative adjectives are *what*(*ever*), *which*(*ever*), and *whose*(*ever*):

You can use *whichever* typewriter feels best to you.

relative adverb.   An adverb used to introduce a RELATIVE CLAUSE. The relative adverbs are *where, when, how,* and *why:*

He explained carefully *how* the error had been made.

relative clause.   A subordinate clause introduced by a RELATIVE PRONOUN, RELATIVE ADJECTIVE, or RELATIVE ADVERB. See CLAUSE.

relative pronouns.   Pronouns that introduce subordinate CLAUSES. The relative pronouns are *who, whose, whom, which, what, that, whoever, whomever, whatever:*

The man *who lives next door* is a dentist.

She always does *whatever she wants.*

See 2C and 5D.

repetition.   Although purposeful repetition can help a writer achieve proper EMPHASIS, the technique can be overdone:

> After finishing his work, he looked at the work he had done and decided that his work was the best he could do.

The sentence can be improved by substituting pronouns for needlessly repetitive nouns:

> After finishing his work, he looked at *it* and decided that *it* was the best he could do.

restrictive modifier.   See **nonrestrictive modifier.**

rhetoric.   The study and practice of using language effectively. In relation to writing, *rhetoric* is a general term referring to the process of developing, arranging, supporting, and presenting ideas in prose. Two other areas of study essential for the knowledgeable rhetorician, are *grammar,* the formal analysis of language, and *usage,* the conventions or accepted practices in using language.

rhetorical question.   A question that does not call for an answer. It is usually meant to convey a point.

> What would your mother think if she saw you like this?

run-on sentence.   See FUSED SENTENCE.

sentence.   A construction that contains at least one SUBJECT and PREDICATE and that can stand alone. Sentences can be classified according to purpose as *declarative, imperative, interrogative,* or *exclamatory:*

> We saw a lake. (declarative)
>
> Jump in the lake. (imperative)
>
> Where is the lake? (interrogative)
>
> There is no water in the lake! (exclamatory)

Sentences can also be classified according to structure as *simple* (containing one independent CLAUSE), *compound* (containing two or more independent CLAUSES), *complex* (containing one independent CLAUSE and one or more subordinate ones), and *compound-complex* (containing two or more independent CLAUSES and at least one subordinate CLAUSE):

> Nero fiddled. (simple)
>
> Nero fiddled, and Rome burned. (compound)
>
> Nero fiddled while Rome burned. (complex)

Nero fiddled while Rome burned, and the Christians were blamed for the fire. (compound-complex)

See Chapter 1.

sentence fragment. An incomplete construction capitalized and punctuated as if it were a sentence.

See Chapter 17.

sentence modifier. A word or group of words modifying an entire sentence.

Generally, water runs downhill.

To tell the truth, Jane is not interested.

separable verb. A verb consisting of a main verb and a preposition (*bring about, carry on, talk over*). In a sentence, other elements may come between the parts of such a verb:

Tomorrow we will *talk* the proposal *over*.

simple predicate. See PREDICATE.

simple sentence. A sentence consisting of a single independent CLAUSE.

Jack jogs.

Pat goes scuba diving in the Caribbean every summer.

See 1D.

simple subject. See SUBJECT.

slang. COLLOQUIAL, nonstandard DICTION. Although some slang becomes accepted in standard informal usage, most slang goes out of fashion in a relatively short time (as in "Hey, cool dude, what's coming down?") and should, therefore, be avoided in writing, except for special effects.

See APPROPRIATENESS.

specific and general. Writing consists of a combination of the specific (enumeration of details, individual instances, and examples) and the general (broad statements that may cover a number of instances). General statements, such as the thesis of an essay or topic sentences of paragraphs, enable writers to make one point about several details. Specific details support the general statement and make it clear and alive. For example, the general statement, "Something terrible has happened," can be maddeningly vague until it is tied down to something specific: "My favorite petunia has wilted."

Specific and *general* are relative terms, as shown in this abstraction ladder:

General

creature
animal
domestic animal
pet
dog
Dachshund
my dog named Molly

Specific

Most writing benefits from a high percentage of specific language.

split infinitive.   The insertion of a modifier between *to* and the infinitive of the verb ("to *never* understand," "to *utterly* forget"). In most cases, greater clarity can be achieved by placing the modifier after the infinitive ("to think *creatively,*" instead of "to *creatively* think").

squinting modifier.   A modifier ambiguous in its reference because it can modify either a preceding or a following element.

> The dog she patted *reluctantly* licked her hand. (squinting)
>
> The dog she *reluctantly* patted licked her hand. (revised)
>
> The dog she patted licked her hand *reluctantly*. (revised)

See 8D.

subject.   A NOUN or noun substitute about which the PREDICATE makes an assertion or asks a question. The *simple subject* is the word or group of words with which the predicate agrees. The *complete subject* is the simple subject and all of its modifiers.

> *The bright blue parakeet on the ledge* is mine.

(*Parakeet* is the simple subject; everything from *The* to *ledge* is the complete subject).

See 1B.

subject complement.   See COMPLEMENT.

subjective case.   See CASE.

subjunctive.   See MOOD.

subordinate clause.   See CLAUSE.

subordinating conjunction.   See CONJUNCTION.

subordination.   Making one part of a construction grammatically dependent on another part. Subordination enables a writer to distinguish main ideas from subordinate (less important) ideas:

Although the fire was out, smoke hung over the debris.
    (subordinate idea)   (main idea)

See 4B.

substantive. A NOUN or other part of speech functioning as a noun in a sentence.

    The *coach* is an *expert* on *conditioning.*

suffix. One or more syllables attached to the end of a word to affect its meaning. *Inflectional suffixes* indicate number ("car, car*s*"), case ("boy, boy*'s*"), gender ("hero, hero*ine*"), tense ("laugh, laugh*ed*"), or comparative degree ("sweet, sweet*er*, sweet*est*"). *Derivational suffixes* often change the part of speech of a word: *observe* (verb) becomes *observation* (noun); *royal* (adjective) becomes *royally* (adverb).

superlative degree. See COMPARISON.

syntax. The structure and arrangement of words to form PHRASES, CLAUSES, and SENTENCES.

tense. The form of a VERB which indicates its time or duration. Through the use of INFLECTIONS and AUXILIARIES, verbs show five basic categories of tense:

    eat (present)

    ate (past)

    will eat (future)

    have/has eaten (perfect)

    am/are/is eating (progressive)

The perfect and progressive tenses are *compound tenses* formed with auxiliaries: past perfect (*had eaten*), future perfect (*will have eaten*), progressive perfect (*have/has been eating*), and so on.

See Chapter 11.

thesis. The main idea or central assertion of a piece of writing. A thesis written as a single sentence is called a *thesis statement.* Developing a clear, effective thesis is an essential step in the process of writing. Having a good thesis enables the writer to make purposeful writing decisions (for instance, about selecting supporting details or a pattern of organization). A thesis will also help to ensure that the piece of writing is unified, that it sticks to the main point.

tone. The attitude of the writer toward a subject. A subject may be treated seriously, humorously, ironically, sentimentally, or in any of the unlimited ways humans respond to a topic. Tone is most obviously conveyed through the writer's DICTION. Needless shifts in tone in a single piece of writing should be avoided:

425

Educators should join with representatives of all segments of society to determine the *nitty-gritty* of a good education. (shift from formal diction to slang;
replace *nitty-gritty* with a word such as *essentials* or *basics*.)

topic sentence.   The sentence which contains the main idea or central
assertion of a paragraph. All other sentences in the paragraph explain or
support the central idea stated in the topic sentence. Although the topic
sentence often appears at or near the beginning of the paragraph, the main
idea of a paragraph may occur in more than one sentence or may be implied
(and therefore not stated).

transition.   The bridges between one idea, SENTENCE, or PARAGRAPH
and the next. Transitions are important means of achieving COHERENCE.
Basically, a transition is a directional sign that points the reader to the next
part of the essay. Transitional markers or expressions may be classified according to the relationship they indicate. Here are some common transition
markers.

> *Addition*—and, too, also, furthermore, moreover, additionally, first, second,
>   finally
> *Cause and Effect*—therefore, consequently, thus, as a result, then
> *Comparison*—likewise, similarly
> *Contrast*—but, however, nevertheless, on the other hand, yet, still, in contrast
> *Specification*—for example, for instance, specifically, in fact, indeed, in other
>   words, in particular, that is, to illustrate
> *Summary*—in conclusion, to conclude, in summary
> *Time*—afterwards, then, at that time, before, meanwhile, later, thereafter, later,
>   soon, immediately

transitive verb.   See VERB.

trite expressions.   See CLICHÉ.

unclear expression.   Vagueness in writing, often resulting from
WORDINESS, a lack of SPECIFIC language, or both:

> In the financially straitened circumstances in which the university finds itself
> now, it must continue to maintain a viable and competitive athletic program
> which is desirable because of that program's benefits to the university at this
> time.

With the wordiness and some of the abstract language eliminated, the sentence might read this way:

> In the face of financial cutbacks, the university must now maintain an athletic
> program that makes money.

variety.   Providing sentences of different lengths and structures in order
to avoid monotony and to achieve EMPHASIS.

> My father is standing in the corner. He is wearing a blue suit. He is president
> of the PTA.

These monotonous sentences can be revised into a single sentence using
COORDINATION and SUBORDINATION:

My father, who is standing in the corner and wearing a blue suit, is president of the PTA.

The monotonous repetition of short *simple sentences* is called *primer style:*

Gary went to college. The college was a community college. It was located near Gary's home. Gary commuted to the college each day.

Combine such short sentences into a longer one:

Gary commuted each day to a nearby community college.

verb.   A part of speech that functions as the main element in a PREDICATE and that indicates action or a state of being. Verbs may be *transitive* (if they require a direct object), or *intransitive* (if they do not need an object). Some verbs function in both ways.

He *carried* the load. (transitive)

He *laughed.* (intransitive)

She *won* the prize. (transitive)

She *won.* (intransitive)

See 1A, 2A, and Chapter 11.

verbal.   A NONFINITE verb form used as a NOUN, ADJECTIVE, or AD-VERB. INFINITIVES, PARTICIPLES, and GERUNDS are verbals.

See 2A.

verb complement.   See COMPLEMENT.

verb phrase.   The MAIN VERB along with any MODIFIERS and AUXILI-ARIES.

They *had been living on peanut butter sandwiches for weeks.*

(*Living* is the main verb; every word except *They* is part of the verb phrase.)

voice.   The form of a TRANSITIVE verb that shows whether its subject does the action (*active voice*) or receives the action (*passive voice*).

John *read* the book. (active voice)

The book *was read* by John. (passive voice)

See 12A.

word choice.   See DICTION.

wordiness.   Using more words than necessary to convey a meaning. Wor-diness is an obstacle to DIRECTNESS.

On the subject of taxation, it is perfectly clear and manifest that by the latter part of the present decade a flat tax rate should be utilized and in operation.

Unnecessary words should be deleted:

> A flat tax rate should be used by the end of this decade.

word order. The placement of words in sentences. Because it has relatively few inflectional endings, English depends heavily upon word order to convey meaning.

> Ted hit the ball.
>
> The ball hit Ted.

Index

In the following index the notation (usage) refers to Chapter 35, "Problems in Usage," pages 292–301; and (grammar) refers to Chapter 43, "A Glossary of Grammatical and Rhetorical Terms," pages 401–428.

CORRECTION SYMBOLS

On these pages are some symbols and notations your instructor may use in marking your writing. Each notation is first defined and then referenced to the chapter or section of the book in which the problem it identifies is discussed. "Glossary" means the Glossary of Grammatical and Rhetorical Terms on pages 401–428.

abb.	Faulty abbreviation	32 H–K
adj.	Misused adjective	10
adv.	Misused adverb	10
agr. s/v	Subject/verb agreement	5
agr. p/a	Pronoun/antecedent agreement	6
app.	Inappropriate expression	glossary
awk.	Awkward construction	glossary
block	Block quoting needed	27P
cap.	Missing or misused capital letter	30
case	Mistake in case form	13
cliché	Hackneyed expression	glossary
coh.	Coherence	glossary
comp.	Incomplete or illogical comparison	16
CS, CF	Comma splice or comma fault	19
dev.	Inadequate development	glossary
dic.	Faulty word choice (diction)	glossary
dir.	More direct expression needed	glossary
div.	Faulty word division	33 F–J
doc.	Error in documentation	39
dm	Dangling modifier	9
emph.	Emphasis needed	glossary
exact.	Inexact expression	glossary
frag.	Sentence fragment	17
FS	Fused sentence	19C
gr.	Grammatical error	1–16
idiom	Unnatural expression	glossary
inc.	Incomplete construction	16
ital.	Italics (underlining)	31
jarg.	Jargon	glossary
l.c.	Lower case letters needed	30
log.	Logic faulty	glossary
meaning	Meaning unclear	glossary
mix.	Mixed construction	15F
mm	Misplaced modifier	8
mood	Mood of verb	12 B, 15 D

num.	Numbers mishandled	32 A–G
om.	Omission	16 A
¶	Paragraph	glossary
¶ coh.	Paragraph coherence	glossary
¶ dev.	Paragraph development	glossary
¶ un.	Paragraph unity	glossary
no ¶	No paragraph here	glossary
//	Parallel construction	14
pass.	Unnecessary passive	12A, 15C
p.	Punctuation error	17–27
'	Apostrophe needed	34
[]	Brackets needed	27G
:	Colon needed	20D, 22D
,	Comma needed	20–25
—	Dash needed	
. . .	Ellipses needed	27H
!	Exclamation point needed	18D, 27M
-	Hyphen needed	33
( )	Parentheses needed	
.	Period needed	18A
?	Question mark needed	18B–C, 27M
" "	Quotation marks needed	27
;	Semicolon needed	20B–C, 25B
ref.	Pronoun reference	7
rep.	Needless repetition	glossary
shift	Unnecessary shift in construction	15
sp.	Spelling	28–29
sp. out	Spell out	32
specif.	Specifics, details needed	glossary
sub.	Faulty subordination	glossary
tense	Wrong tense	11A,D, 15B
title	Incorrect handling of title	27B, 31A
tone	Inconsistent tone	glossary
trite	Trite expression	glossary
unclear	Unclear expression	glossary
var.	Sentence structure needs variety	glossary
vb. form	Verb form error	11B,C,E
voice	Voice error	12A, 15C
w	Wordiness	glossary
wc, ww	Word choice, wrong word	glossary
X	Obvious error	

Alphanumeric Key to Contents